CRACKS IN THE CONSTITUTION

BOOKS BY FERDINAND LUNDBERG

Imperial Hearst
America's Sixty Families
Modern Woman: The Lost Sex (in collaboration)
The Treason of the People
The Coming World Transformation
The Rich and the Super-Rich
The Rockefeller Syndrome
Cracks in the Constitution

CRACKS IN THE CONSTITUTION

by

Ferdinand Lundberg

LYLE STUART INC. Secaucus, N. J.

Edited by Carol Bram

Published by Lyle Stuart Inc.

Manufactured in the United States of America

Library of Congress Cataloging in Publication Data
Lundberg, Ferdinand, 1902-
   Cracks in the Constitution.
   Bibliography: p. 326.
   Includes index.
   1. United States—Constitutional law.
2. United States—Constitutional history.
I. Title.
KF4550.L86   342′.73   79-22152
ISBN 0-8184-0279-2

CONTENTS

The idea of a government of laws without men—a sort of transcen-
dental automaton that once wound up will go forever without
human intervention—is one of the vainest illusions that the eighteenth century's enthusiasm for mechanical maxims imposed upon
the spirit of men.

> Morris Raphael Cohen
> *Law and the Social Order*

Whoever has an absolute authority to interpret any law, it is he
who is the lawgiver to all intents and purposes.

> Benjamin Hoadly (1675-1761)
> Bishop of Bangor, Hereford, Salisbury and Winchester

We are under a Constitution, but the Constitution is what the
judges say it is . . .

> Charles Evans Hughes
> Chief Justice of the Supreme Court of the United States, 1930-41
> Speech made while governor of New York State

Ordinarily it is sound policy to adhere to prior decisions but this
practice has quite properly never been a blind, inflexible rule.
Courts are not omniscient.

> Hugo L. Black
> Associate Justice of the Supreme Court of the United States, 1937-71
> Citation from *Green v. U.S.* 165 (1958)

If we don't like any Act of Congress, we don't have much trouble to find grounds for declaring it unconstitutional.
John Marshall Harlan I
Associate Justice of the Supreme Court of the United States, 1877-1911
Citation from James F. Simon, ed., *In His Own Image: The Supreme Court in Richard Nixon's America,* 1973

The American myth is the man who will not be fenced in; the American reality is the man who is drafted to die in far places and for dim purposes.

Clinton Rossiter
Conservatism in America

Though the many are incompetent to draw up a constitution since diversity of opinion will prevent them from discovering how best to do it, yet when they realize it has been done, they will not agree to abandon it.

—Machiavelli
The Discourses, Book I, 9

We elect a king for four years, and give him absolute power within certain limits, which after all he can interpret for himself.

Secretary of State
William Henry Seward

CRACKS IN THE
CONSTITUTION

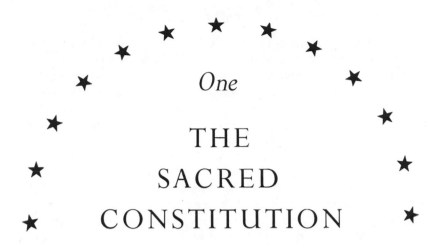

One

THE
SACRED
CONSTITUTION

The Constitution of the United States, at its birth regarded doubtfully by friend and foe alike, feared and roundly denounced by the latter, in the course of time has been transformed into the great totempole of American society. Its general aura is hypnotic to broad sections of the public and even to quite an array of myopic savants. So stunning on such beholders is the entire baroque structure that details of the document tend to become blurred in one great apotheosis of quasi-religious light. It bathes the otherwise discordant political scene in a soft glow of suffused radiance.

The brightness diffused by a putative masterpiece of political architecture meanwhile serves the highly important task of dazzling the vision of a generally confused populace even as that populace decries (as it has done practically from the beginning) the duplicity of politicians who are held firmly in place precisely by the constitutional machinery that is so fulsomely extolled. For the Constitution is peculiarly, and almost exclusively, the special instrument of the politicians and, of course, their close friends, a nuance understood by very few. It is not an "open" constitution like the British but very much a closed labyrinthine affair.

In the meantime, despite its transfiguration over the years for those who view it from a distance, from outside, the Constitution to those who come into close contact with it is still as controversial as when it was first proposed. If anything, it grows more controversial, an unusual phenomenon among governmental systems. And for this there are definite causes. As part of the ever-recurring controversy one hears the questions: What does it really mean? What can it portend? Is it being interpreted properly? Were its framers saints or devils? Are office-holders faithfully guiding themselves by its heaven-sent deliverances?

One hears no such questions about the British or indeed any other operative constitution. It is the simple purpose of these pages to penetrate behind the rhetorical flourishes in the foreground and attempt to get down to the nuts and bolts of the Constitution and especially matters relevant to it. Reality is, strangely, far more interesting than myth, legend and fantasy for the simple reason that the imagination of humankind is no match for the marvels of circumambient existence.

One of the common myths among Americans, most common perhaps among the routinely educated (because they are most successfully indoctrinated), is that the United States government, straining like a shackled bull, is powerfully restrained and fettered by the Constitution, unable to do a great variety of things that other governments may do with impunity and kept tightly within the path of high rectitude. It is very often referred to, and by judges who should know better, as a "limited government" or a "government of limited powers". This, to state at the outset a fundamental conclusion stemming from protracted researches, is simply not so.

For under the Constitution, or despite it, the United States government may do without internal limitation, mainly through the chief executive, whatever it is from time to time minded to do, and has often done so, whatever the Constitution may say or be thought to imply to the contrary. In this respect the United States government is on all fours with any other government, bar none. To this some will say, missing the point, that there are many things other governments do that the United States government does not do. My response to this is that the United States government does not do such things because it does not see them to its advantage. But if it did, it could surely do them, whatever they are.

If this conclusion seems shocking or absurd to any indoctrinated reader, a moment's preliminary reflection will show that it must nevertheless be so.

The Constitution is engrossed on a piece of paper or parchment. While it has induced a certain set of institutional habits, some healthy, others unhealthy, the words thereon have no more coercive operational effect on members of the government than such may from time to time be inclined collectively to accept. There is, in short, no overriding rigor in the document. And it is here precisely the same as with the Ten Commandments, which as everyone knows have long been freely violated in the Judaic and Christian worlds.

Through certain serial and cumulative procedures stipulated in the Constitution a governing personnel is put into place. Once in place this personnel, even in the face of a united hostile populace, cannot lawfully be disassembled except by improbable installments over a long period—too late to prevent many governmental actions whose long train of effects commit the nation for good or ill far into the future. The serial events required to change the composition of the government make it necessary that a hostile and politically active populace maintain its hostility at white heat for such a long period of time as to be beyond human capacity. And no legal political action whatever by the populace can unseat the judiciary. As to all this then, let us say, very good. That is precisely what the framers of the government had in mind.

It is quite different with the British government. In that system, should the electorate be so disposed, the personnel of the entire House of Commons, the Cabinet and the Prime Minister may be retired abruptly to private life in a single election, which can take place at any time. The British electorate, if mightily displeased, has an instant option. That this sort of thing doesn't happen very often is simply because the electorate doesn't will it, not because there is some procedural documentary barrier to it. Comparatively, the British are free, Americans bound.

In effect, then, the United States government is as solidly ensconced at all times—although leaking at many seams—as any government ever was in history, and as proven by nearly two hundred years of uninterrupted operation. There are those moreover who argue that this longish tenure is proof of universal satisfaction with it. Yet long stretches of American history show that this supposed satisfaction is chimerical. It was so shown notably in the full-dress attempt of the South to break away from it by force. American history, as unknown to most of the American public as the history of Tibet, in fact has been studded with fiery denunciations of the system, armed uprisings and low-grade guerrilla and labor warfare, all sooner or later brought under control by the apparatus outlined in the Constitution and, one should not fail to note, by extra-constitutional measures freely, often lavishly, applied.

Again, a full-dress *coup d'état* from outside, which possibility at times grips the imaginations of Hollywood scenario writers, could hardly succeed under any circumstances owing to the complex inner divisions of control and the lines of subordination extending by means of a vast bureaucracy throughout the sprawling country. A *coup de main* at the center, at any rate, would not carry with it dominance over either the bureaucracy or the military, neither of which is subject, once the Constitution is breached from the outside, to a single chain of command.

Extra-constitutional activities to one side, most of what the American government does at most times it is constitutionally fully empowered to do. For the Constitution is couched in such broad interlocking and mutually supporting terms as to amount to a distillation of all conceivable governmental powers. As to the supposed limitations upon it, most of them concern its own inner relationships and etiquette. And as far as formal limitations on external actions are concerned, numerous cases extending almost to the inception show that such can often be disregarded, bypassed or boldly violated, depending upon the mood and perceived exigencies of the moment. A host of instances show this to be true.

The Constitution describes itself as part, and only part, of the supreme law of the land, and so it is. But laws down through history, as is well known, have been repeatedly violated, often with impunity. And whether the supreme law is adhered to or violated, the existing government, with or without popular approval, always proceeds on its majestic way —an undeniably powerful affair.

Since the founding of the republic there has been a ceaseless refrain, mainly carried by politicians, sometimes by lawyers, often by parroting teachers and journalists, that the United States is a government of laws, not men—in which respect it is held to differ from most other governments. This statement, usually reserved for solemn occasions or as a final cruncher in an argument, is usually taken seriously although it is obviously palpable nonsense of the highest order. For all governments are governments of men, who write and interpret the laws and more or less adhere to some, often violate others, trim and shade still others, as the self-serving circumstances of the moment seem to dictate, and often boldly lie about or more or less subtly misrepresent what they are doing.

As musicians say, it is all pretty much an *ad libitum* performance interspersed with many surprising cadenzas, some wildly out of tune. Were the United States a government of laws solely (and I don't assert that stark law is never considered although the law itself is a notorious tangle), with official extemporization playing no role, it could be confined to a computer. Then at least the entire judiciary and much of the bureaucracy could be dismissed, supplanted by computer operators.

As to the supposed beauties of law, and fundamental law at that, it was all strictly legal when President Gerald Ford, at his purely subjective instance, emitted a pardon for former President Richard Nixon, to the consternation and outrage of a vast section of the country. Ford did this in the exercise of one of the constitutionally conferred stupendous powers given to the President. The Constitution does not say who may be pardoned or in what circumstances, only that the President has the power to pardon. And strict adherence to law does not require that beholders be pleased or some great good be obtained. What benefit to the nation was it that Nixon was given a general pardon, and prior to any formal finding of guilt? As it is a tenet of American law, parroted about with sickening frequency, that a man is innocent until proven guilty, Nixon was, legally, a completely innocent man when handed his pardon. Ford therefore handed a pardon to a legally innocent man! And all of it completely constitutional. The pardon, to be sure, had the effect of stopping in their tracks any further proceedings against Nixon, which was its sole objective. For in any further proceedings Nixon, defending himself, would surely have seen fit to bring other political figures into the limelight of unwelcome public attention. The pardon, to be sure a partisan political stroke, stank to high heaven. But it was legal. However, a man who steals a bag of potatoes may spend time in jail—the majesty of the law.

The average person in reading the Constitution, when he notes that the President may pardon, happily assumes that the pardons will be issued to rectify injustices, to free unjustly convicted persons. Such a proceeding all men of good will would approve. But this is not what the Constitution says nor, very probably, what the framers exclusively intended. For, adept politicos, they were well aware of the political uses of pardons and knew that those, by historical precedence, most in need of timely pardons were—politicians and their sponsors. The chief function of the pardon in the federal system and in the states where the governors hold the pardoning power is to free political cronies and loyal party men who have been caught out and usually convicted of a felony. For example, in New York State in 1970 Governor Nelson A. Rockefeller pardoned L. Judson Morhouse, former state Republican chairman and the man who had jockeyed Rockefeller into the governorship. Morhouse, rapacious in his quest for large payoffs from interests doing business with the state, had been convicted of bribery in one case and sentenced to a two-to-three-year prison term. He served only six days of the sentence. As to freeing the innocent via pardons, that function has been one of its most inconspicuously invoked.

Myth and Reality

In examining the Constitution it is necessary, if one wishes to be realistic, to distinguish between the Constitution itself and myths about it. The latter abound and are the source of much public confusion and misunderstanding. What the Constitution sets forth anyone can determine by reading it in less than a half hour, but the *official* meaning, often esoteric to the man in the street (and sometimes even to professors of law!), is always determined by the government itself, on most points by the courts. And this last requires that lawyers play a large assisting role. The courts, too, often disagree, among themselves and within themselves, on just what the sibylline document means.

Whatever anyone outside the President, a majority of Congress and a majority of the Supreme Court may decide about meanings is purely informal; only the meaning set forth by the government is the one that counts. So, it is the government itself that determines what the Constitution permits and does not permit as circumstances arise. As to the lawyers, in every case that goes to the Supreme Court the lawyers on one side, always, are found to be mistaken in their major contention, so that the demonstrated expertise of the legal profession itself about the Constitution is more than a little doubtful. No outstanding so-called constitutional lawyer ever wins all or nearly all his cases. And lawyers who rely literally upon long-received court interpretations may, in the acid test of action, find that they are wrong, that the Court holds against them. The document is therefore definitely sibylline, full of surprises, pleasant or unpleasant to confident litigants.

The situation is even more involved than the foregoing indicates. For the Supreme Court itself often divides 5 to 4, 6 to 3 or 7 to 2 on what the Constitution mandates. If the majority is right in each instance, which the Court itself denies by many later reversals of earlier opinions, how can the minority be so far astray? And the Court itself has in numerous cases not only overruled earlier opinions but even unanimous earlier opinions by new divided opinions. Finding new meanings and applications in the Constitution appears to be an endless task. All this of course is well known but is not even a small fraction of the story.

Something that happens not infrequently is that a trial court and then an appellate court, both federal, basing their findings on a recent prior decision of the Supreme Court, find that their case is reversed as the Supreme Court unaccountably modifies its orientation. An instance of this was supplied in a Supreme Court decision of June 20, 1977, that states may not be required to spend Medicaid funds, jointly supplied by state and national governments, for elective abortions by the indigent. In 1973 the high court, nullifying state statutes of long standing, ruled that abortion was legal, a personal constitutional right available to all women. Now, abortion, properly conducted, is a medical procedure. And according to the Constitution all person are equal under the law. Medicaid, by statute, provides medical care for the indigent. Yet the Supreme Court in 1977 decided that this one particular kind of medical care may be withheld from the poor, if a state so opts, even as more affluent women pay for their abortions. No such court ukase was laid down against plastic surgery or removal of physical blemishes, also elective.

The decision of the Court was 6 to 3. If one contends that the Court was correct in its ruling, one must not only concede that three Justices were mistaken but also that the judges of the trial court and of the appellate court were mistaken in their understanding of the law as previously expounded by the high court.

What had happened was that the majority of the Supreme Court, for reasons not visible on the record, had veered—a frequent phenomenon with the high court. Down through history the Court has frequently pursued a zigzag course, much like a drunken man threading his way down the street.[1] It does this because some of the members from time to time freely inject personal or political notions into the legal equation, may even engage in intramural jockeying for reasons obscure to outsiders. The Court in fact is not as judicially detached as it likes to pretend, and as many persons like to suppose, notwithstanding the black robes of the Justices.

Far from being merely a law-interpreting and law-expounding body, the Court (as astute law professors have observed) is also a policy-generating body—that is, it makes or modifies social and even cultural policy under the guise of applying the Constitution. And there is nothing whatever in the Constitution that confers upon it this authority, which it exercises, most of the time unchallenged, at its own option. When it does this it is in fact legislating, making new law. But the Constitution explicitly gives Congress a monopoly of law-making. Nothing whatever in the document says or implies that the Court appointees may make new law. "The people" nowhere enter into this process.

With a single exception, no myth whatever is incorporated in the Constitution itself, a crisply worded document. The sole myth appears at the very beginning in the words "We the people of the United States . . . do ordain and establish this Constitution for the United States of America."

Now, whatever else may or may not be true of the Constitution, it is a clearly established fact that it was not established by *the* people of the United States either in the sense of the original whole people or even of all or most of those white males, or even a majority of most, who were legally qualified to vote in 1787 and 1788 for members of the state ratifying conventions. Yet it is in these senses that the proposition is propounded in the schools, newspapers and political meetings, without significant exception or qualification.

Were the opening lines to accord with fact, they would read "We, members of divided state ratifying conventions . . . do ordain", etc. This of course, while still requiring much further qualification, would not sound nearly as impressive, as loftily magisterial.

The Constitution, in point of fact, was made operative by extremely turbulent and often quite irregular state ratifying conventions in accordance with a formula presented in the as yet unsanctioned document itself. The Constitution, in point of fact, was rammed through the ratification process by means fair and foul in the face of a largely indifferent and uncomprehending populace. Then, as now, most people didn't know what everything, politically or otherwise, was all about.

But were not these conventions elected by "the people" as countless books and well-meaning teachers tell us—that is, the whole people—in the several states? Not at all. They were elected by those white males eligible to vote *and sufficiently interested in the adoption or rejection of the Constitution.* And these latter were relatively few.

According to Prof. Merrill Jensen, a noted historian who is a specialist in the period, "Far more reasearch is needed before we can know, if ever, how many men actually voted for delegates to the state conventions. An old guess that about 160,000 voted—that is, not more than a fourth or fifth of the total adult [white] male population—is probably as good as any. About 100,000 of these men voted for supporters of the Constitution and about 60,000 for its opponents. But some men at the time asserted that the conventions did not represent popular opinion. Aedanus Burke in South Carolina claimed that four-fifths of the people in that state were opposed. Men agreed that at least a majority of the people in New Hampshire, Massachusetts, and New York were opposed, and even greater numbers in Rhode Island and North Carolina." [2]

These figures were originally put forward by Prof. Charles A. Beard in *An Economic Interpretation of the Constitution of the United States* (1913). And after truly exhaustive research into the varied economic backgrounds of the framers as well as the ratifiers, and a study of all the discoverable voting records in the archives of the thirteen original states and of all votes recorded in the newspapers of 1787 and 1788, Prof. Forrest McDonald, in general a severe critic of Beard, wrote, "It is my conclusion that Beard's estimate of the total vote is remarkably accurate." [3]

"We the people," therefore, comes down to 62.5 per cent of 20 or 25 per cent of eligible voters or from 12.5 to 15.5 per cent of the 624,000 to 800,000 members of the eligible electorate of 1787, consisting entirely of white adult males in a population of approximately three million of which 20 per cent were non-voting blacks. Women, Indians, Negroes and children, naturally, could not vote. The opposition among the actual voters was 37.5 per cent or from 7.5 to 9.87 per cent of the eligible electorate. Those voting favored the Constitution by 5 to 3.

Despite all the hullabaloo, skulduggery and "dirty tricks" by the ratificationists and anti-ratificationists, each side predicting dire consequences if its views did not prevail, most of the eligible voters could not bring themselves to vote for local delegates to the ratification conventions. And this despite the fact that the bedrock form of government was at issue. Although general voting participation has since improved under the stimulus of electronic publicity, it is today rarely exceptional for the total vote of eligibles for President to reach 40 per cent. Only in the election of 1864 did it nearly reach 50 per cent. In the election of 1896 it came to 41 per cent, a proportion it has since invariably fallen short of. It was below 30 per cent in the elections of 1912, 1924, 1948 and 1968. These were the results all along despite the use of extravagant oratory by both sides and assertions that the fate of mankind depended on the outcome. For all other offices in non-presidential election years the voting turnout is almost invariably far less, varying from state to state.

Observers of the political scene usually talk and write as though people in general are intensely interested in government, as philosophical preceptors have long said one should be. But short of a titillating scandal or a roaring dispute, relatively few people are. They don't have the capacity for it. And that, too, in what is often hailed as a stupendous democracy. As many public-opinion polls have shown, most people are unable even to name their Congressmen, Senators and other key officials, nor can they identify vital legislation. Democracy operatively is little more than a fantasy. The fundamental reason for this is that the perceived stakes for most people are too low to justify any great effort.

The fact that few people framed and ratified the Constitution is no decisive point against it, and one must concede, doesn't impugn it. However, it is a decisive point against the myth that they did. Large numbers of people collectively, acting in concert, never directly created nor ever endorsed anything worthy of attention. But large numbers of people have often been roused to oppose, fanatically, valuable ideas and procedures and are still easily induced to do so from time to time.

Government by Consent

With so few voting for pro-constitutional delegates and later for candidates for office, a curious light is thrown on the oft-heard idea that in the United States there is government by popular consent. Elsewhere, according to this idea as bandied about by politicians and public-school teachers, people groan under governments thrust upon them but in the United States there is government by consent only.

The idea, not one of his happier notions, originally came from the philosopher John Locke in his pamphlet entitled *Second Treatise of Government* (1690). This work was very popular with the more literate of rank-and-file American colonists, as much on account of its brevity and simplicity as for its happy tidings about the people's vital role.

What there may be to the idea we may see by referring to Mr. Justice Joseph Story, appointed by President Madison to the Supreme

Court in 1812 where he served until 1845 as the right bower to the redoubtable John Marshall and became one of the major expounders of American constitutional lore. As Story was very much, and for a long time, a governmental "insider," his analysis, which one may look upon at least as semi-official, is to be preferred to one of my own although I agree with him all the way.

The Establishment-esteemed Story, writing as of 1833, the material first used in lectures at Harvard University, said the following: [4]

> Every state, however organized, embraces many persons in it, who have never assented to its form of government; and many, who are deemed incapable of such assent, and yet are held bound by its fundamental institutions and laws. Infants, minors, married women, persons insane, and many others, are deemed subjects of a country, and bound by its laws; although they have never assented thereto, and may by those very laws be disabled from such an act. Even our most solemn instruments of government, framed and adopted as the constitutions of our state governments, are not [sic!] only not founded upon the assent of all the people within the territorial jurisdiction; but that assent is expressly excluded by the very manner, in which the ratification is required to be made. That ratification is restricted to those, who are qualified voters; and who are, or shall be qualified voters, is decided by the majority in the convention [sic!] or other body, which submits the constitution to the people. All of the American constitutions have been formed in this manner. The assent of minors, of women, and of unqualified voters, has never been asked or allowed; yet these embrace a majority of the whole population in every organized society, and are governed by its existing institutions. Nay, more; a majority only of the qualified voters is deemed sufficient to change the fundamental institutions of the state, upon the general principle that the [qualified] majority has at all times a right to govern the minority, and to bind the latter to obedience to the will of the former. And if more than a plurality is, in any case, required, to amend or change the actual constitution of the society, it is a matter of political choice with the majority for the time being, and not of right on the part of the minority.
>
> It is a matter of fact, therefore, in the history of our own forms of government that they have been formed without the consent, express or implied, of the whole people; and that, although firmly established, they owe their existence and authority to the simple will of the majority of the qualified voters. There is not probably a single state in the Union, whose constitution has not been adopted against the opinions and wishes of a large minority, even of qualified voters; and it is notorious, that some of them have been adopted by a small majority of votes. How, then, can we assert with truth, that even in

our free constitutions the government is founded in fact on the assent of the whole people, when many of them have not been permitted to express an opinion, and many have expressed a decided dissent? In what manner are we to prove, that every citizen of the state has contracted with all the other citizens, that such constitution shall be a binding compact between them, with mutual obligations to observe and keep it, against such positive dissent? If it be said, that by entering society an assent is necessarily implied to submit to the majority, how is it proved, that a majority of all the people of all ages and sexes were ever asked to assent, or did assent to such a proposition? And as to persons subsequently born, and subjected by birth to such society, where is the record of such assent in point of law or fact?

Story here refers to essay 12, "Of the Original Contract", in *Essays Moral, Political and Literary* (1752), Vol. 2, by David Hume, Scottish philosopher who was widely read by the British and American educated classes in the eighteenth century and was closely read by many of the more literate early American political leaders. Hume's essay simply demolishes Locke's idea of political consent. Story in fact is guided all the way on the point by Hume. And "David Hume is beyond all question the ablest British philosopher", according to such a recent authority as Prof. John Herman Randall.[5]

In respect to the American revolution itself [Story continued], it is notorious that it was brought about against the wishes and resistance of a formidable minority of the people; and that the declaration of independence never had the universal assent of all inhabitants of the country. So, [it is a fact] that this great and glorious change in the organization of our government owes its whole authority to the efforts of a triumphant majority. And the dissent on the part of the minority was deemed in many cases a crime, carrying along with it the penalty of confiscation, forfeiture and personal, and even capital, punishment; and in its mildest form was deemed an unwarrantable outrage upon the public rights, and a total disregard of the duties of patriotism.

The truth is that the [self-defined qualified] majority of every organized society has always claimed and exercised the right to govern the whole of that society, in the manner pointed out by the fundamental laws, which from time to time have existed in such society. Every revolution, at least when not produced by positive force, has been founded upon the authority of such majority. And the right results from the very necessities of our nature; for universal consent can never be practically required or obtained. The [qualified] minority [and all others] are bound, whether they have assented or not; for the plain reason, that opposite wills in the same society, on the same subjects, cannot prevail at the same time . . . The declaration of independence (which, it is historically known, was not the act of the whole American people) puts the doctrine on its true grounds . . .

As to the numbers favoring the American revolution, which amounted to nothing more than secession from the British Empire, leading latter-day historians appear agreed that about one-third of the colonists favored it (mainly not the upper classes), one-third opposed it (mainly of the upper classes), and one-third were indifferent or neutral, trading during the war with both sides. Those who were in favor had the advantage, as is usually the case, because they were active, in motion toward a visualized goal. Ultimately the activists won mainly because they gained the intervention of France, Britain's long-time enemy which had in 1763 been dislodged by Britain from Canada.

By aiding the revolting colonists France paid Britain back in its own coin. The Americans, in seeking and obtaining this support, perpetrated a bit of the usual historical irony, for France was both autocratic, in fact the leading autocracy then in the world, and Roman Catholic, both of which inclinations were roundly detested almost unanimously by the homespun American colonists. Paradoxically, they all loved Britain far more. But as the admirable Hume remarks, "Any party in a civil war always choose to call in a foreign enemy at any hazard, rather than submit to their fellow-citizens." [6] Later, the Confederate politicians in the Civil War sought assiduously to bring in England or France on their side.

Story mentions neither Indians nor slaves, who obviously also were neither asked for nor gave their consent to be governed. Nor does he touch upon immigrants who might be thought by some to give their consent by asking to be naturalized. While naturalized citizens have indubitably exercised a choice between a native and an adopted government, they are far from registering consent to be governed. For whether they elect to remain under their native government or to be naturalized under another, they are ruled, willy-nilly. As to being governed, they have no choice. Indeed, apart from those who originally plan and install a government, usually becoming governors themselves, nobody anywhere is ever governed according to his consent, all declamations of politicians, editorial writers, schoolteachers and wandering political swamis to the contrary nothwithstanding. So-called free citizens are always in fact subjects, like it or not.

I am not indirectly arguing or suggesting here that had there been broader popular support for or opposition to the American revolution or the ratification of the Constitution the resulting situation would have been preferable. It's simply that the commonly understood and widely disseminated story is false, a fairy tale, and that there was not in fact vast underlying popular support.

Nor is the world appreciably nearer "government by the people" today, whatever this would involve, than it was in the days of autocracies who traced the basis of their authority to God. The autocracies ruled of course by the free application or threat of force; under "the sovereignty of the people" the modern masses are largely ruled through psychological, rhetorical and other forms of manipulation, with naked force discreetly held in reserve, a much more complex and sophisticated process. Ideologically disguised modern autocracies, such as the Soviet Union, still rule by direct force, intimidation and threat while at the same time making supplemental use of psychological manipulation.

Proofs of Excellence

The supposedly long duration of the American government is often put forward by scholars, who should know better, as proof of its superlative excellence in a world that has seen many governmental systems topple, in some countries system after system. In other words, while in the world abroad of less fortunate mortals there is political instability, in the United States, thanks to the constitutional work of men of superhuman insight and a basically superior populace—superior because lowly in origin!—there is a government impervious to the slings and arrows of outrageous fortune. What the Founding Fathers built, it is suggested, was a Rock of Ages, something to be approached by mere mortals with undiluted awe. And here, surely, is the stuff of myth.

The argument of excellence because of long duration involves logical and factual fallacies. The syllogism on which it depends proceeds, first, on the assumption that whatever human institution is long-lasting is *ipso facto* excellent, which in itself begs the question to be proven. Many human institutions—slavery for example—lasted for thousands of years, yet are not therefore considered by the discerning to have been excellent, although slave-owners and their sycophants like it. The government of imperial Rome endured unchanged in form for more than five hundred years, of Byzantium for more than a thousand years (334-1453 A.D.), and of Czarist Russia through the Rurik and Romanoff dynasties for more than a thousand years (862-1917 A.D.). Yet nobody at all argues that any of them were excellent affairs. They are all, on the contrary, freely cited as examples of bad government, of government run amok.

The American form of government may indeed be excellent, might indeed as some claim be the best ever devised (although I don't myself think so), but not because it has endured for nearly two hundred years. Nor are shorter-lived governmental systems necessarily inferior to it. They have foundered in many cases owing to adverse natural and social conditions or because of political pressure by external enemies.

As a corollary to the above argument it is often said that the United States has the oldest extant form of government in the world, but this is also patently false, a typically American form of wild boasting. For the British government, dating it from 1688, is older as an uninterrupted affair, the government of Iceland is more than a thousand years old, and Switzerland traces its federated system back to 1513. One big reason many governmental systems have been interrupted since 1787 is that their home territory was invaded, their capital captured. It was not their form of government that undid them.

The United States came into existence in an era of growing world political instability, rippling out after the rule of Cromwell in Great Britain. And the United States was one of the first of many new types of government, so that, being first, it would continually enjoy chronological precedence in the new wave. To the growing political instability, especially signalized by the French revolution, was added the impact of the industrial revolution. And the United States by its own example of introducing apparent political innovations and trumpeting heady slogans contributed to the growing world political instability. For there can be no question but that the United States, by example alone, was and is a world-destabilizing force in many respects.

The whole period being one of upheaval and repeated upheaval, with old nations scrambling to find new adjustments and new nations rising, such as Germany and Italy, and then Yugoslavia and Czechoslovakia, it is in no way extraordinary that many short-lived governmental systems should appear and disappear. What has protected the United States from similar extreme instability is its geographic isolation, its great vacant spaces and its vast natural resources, none of which is attributable to its political system. The United States might well have succeeded, done as well as anyone may finally decide it has, with any sort of political system whatever. Politics and political leaders did not make the United States pre-eminent, contrary to what is suggested by many historians and journalists; vast natural resources and great distances from dangerous enemies played much more of a role. It might even be said, and well said, that the United States succeeded despite itself, much like the man who fell off a cliff and thereby found a huge virgin deposit of gold.

Nor has the American constitutional system been as tranquilly ascendant during two hundred years as it is claimed. For no fewer than eleven states out of thirty-four, with nearly ten million people out of thirty-two million, seceded for more than four years during the War of the Rebellion (1861-65), keeping the loyal states at bay in one bloody battle after the other. By fiat of the Supreme Court, no state ever left the Union legally, there was no break in the Constitution; in point of fact the sacred Union was sundered during this period. No legal fiction can obscure this occurrence. And the cited principle underlying the war, apart from the material disputes, was a difference in— constitutional interpretation!

In the total of dead the war exceeded American losses in World War II. The death toll of the Union forces in the Civil War was 334,511 and the wounded came to 281,881. American deaths in World War II amounted to 407,316. But when one computes in the number of Confederate dead, in the aggregate of 133,821—and these were still United States citizens according to the dictum of the Supreme Court—the aggregate of American fatalities was 468,332. Property and war material losses were staggering. It was the most destructive civil conflict among modern nations, the worst war of the nineteenth century.

This episode alone hardly supports the idea of a tranquil passage under the Constitution, although the government held together. Was the nation held together by the Constitution despite the divisiveness it failed to quell? Says *The Encyclopedia Americana*, reflecting scores of scholars, "Without subscribing to the great-man theory of history, one may question whether the Union would have been preserved without the exceptional qualities of leadership exhibited during these critical years by Lincoln." [7] In other words, government by one man, who incidentally went far outside the Constitution in order to preserve it. It was the claim of some of the original supporters of the Constitution that it would prevent a civil war. This it manifestly failed to do. Simply as a matter of fact what had been the United States was sundered for more than four years into two nations, two governments, under separate constitutions.

It is even questionable, the Constitution of the Confederate States of America to one side, whether the United States has had only two constitutions—the Articles of Confederation (1781-88) and the document of 1787. A reasonable argument could be made that it has in fact had four: the Articles, the widely lauded document of 1787, the same document plus the first ten amendments, and then these two parts plus the conquest-imposed Thirteenth, Fourteenth and Fifteenth Amendments. If such an argument holds, the actual situation is that there have been Constitutions I, II, III and IV. And additionally there was the Confederate Constitution extending over eleven states.

Merely amending the Constitution certainly does not make it a different instrument. But it seems reasonable to conclude that attaching to it an amendment that significantly changes its thrust amounts, owing to the altered interplay of its parts, to producing a new set of fundamental laws. More especially is this true when the amendments are imposed under duress.

When the document of 1787 was first submitted for public scrutiny, there were many acutely perceptive critical analyses of it published and much outcry against it, with many prominent persons calling for a second revisionary convention which, of all things, was feared by the chief proponents of the newly written Constitution. There were even threats of civil war on the spot. Most impressive to the broad public was the fact that the document included no Bill of Rights, although there were many more substantive arguments against it. In several states ratification took place only with the warning that a Bill of Rights was absolutely necessary.

It was only when the proponents, in greatest fear of the substantive objections, reluctantly acceded to the demand for a Bill of Rights (formally proposed as amendments in Congress in 1789) that most of the populace was appeased. The substantive objections were, in the process, quashed, pushed aside, but time and again later rose unbidden to haunt the arena of American history.

But the first ten amendments, as history has shown, produced a governmental system subtly at variance with the one the framers had proposed, not radically different but different enough to create significant constitutional problems from time to time. They loosened somewhat the tight grip of the original document.

As the Thirteenth, Fourteenth and Fifteenth Amendments swept away the legal basis for slavery, which involved a significant form of property in human beings, their passage also produced a very different fundamental law of the land, a different Constitution. This is not to say that any amendment produces a different Constitution. For many amendments are of slight operational effect.

All of this should go a considerable way toward rectifying the common view of the Constitution. But it is still only a small part of the story.

The General Welfare

The minimal function of a governmental system is to insure that the social system it regulates is in reasonably good order and that the public welfare is being broadly served. In its preamble the Constitution sets forth that one of its aims is to "promote the general welfare", and Section 8 provides that "The Congress shall have power to . . . provide for . . . general welfare of the United States"—the so-called welfare clause. Let me here, in a preliminary way, get some perspective on how this welfare is being provided for now.

I turn here to a book by Prof. Herman Finer (1898-1969), largely because he was so highly esteemed in scholarly circles and also because he wrote incisively about the constitutional problem to which I shall have recourse later. Finer was for many years commonly described as one of our most influential political scientists, author of more than a dozen books and variously professor at the University of London, University of Chicago, and Yale and Harvard Universities. Among the Presidents he thought had "well-considered, well-cogitated ideals of national progress" were McKinley, Taft and Hoover.[8] He was also an admirer of Washington, Jefferson, Lincoln, Wilson and Franklin D. Roosevelt. In other words, a man of catholic tastes in political leaders, no radical, no far-out theorist, no soap-boxer. I say this because the reader is in for something of a shock.

"Let us glance at some of the social and political evils revealed in the last few decades," says Finer.

> The nation's crime rate in every category—murder, manslaughter, assault with deadly weapons, theft, robbery, rape is one of the highest in the world and increases year by year. [It has trebled since he wrote in 1960.] There are far too many districts in American cities where an individual, man, woman or child, cannot venture upon a fairly-lighted street [or in daylight] without fear of attack. A good society should be able to assure its people personal security and the due administration of justice. If they appeal for justice, can they be sure they will get it? Far too frequently, juries are chosen for their prejudices, elected or appointed judges are found to be incompetent, witnesses are suborned or intimidated, prosecutors are corrupted, the police are shown to be dishonest, lawyers prove to be cheats, and justice is not done or is long-delayed.
>
> Fifty years after the publication of Lincoln Steffens' The Shame of the Cities our civic administrations are no less riddled by graft and inefficiency, no less lurid than Steffens described them, hardly diminished in effrontery, as damaging, as audacious, as costly, as disgraceful. Police, civil servants, public contractors connive in fraud and guile. Scores of citizens have exposed malpractice and have sought the reform of the governments of states and cities. But no vigorous conscience insures that their recommendations are fulfilled. There is no center of government to gather up the spontaneous forces of the nation and lift them to effectiveness.
>
> Corrupt and damaging practices have been exposed. Racketeers acting on the flanks of labor unions have found confederates at the heart of our economy, connivers as malign as themselves among businessmen, government officials, and police. In the interest of profit, men have beaten and murdered their competitors. If you kill conscience for profit, why flinch at homicide? If business efficiency and

the wealth of the nation depend on rivalry between individuals and between corporations, who puts a limit to fraud and violence in pursuit of gain?

. . . At once the question of the quality of America's political leadership is raised . . .

Many of our prisons and mental institutions are in a disgraceful condition, some little more than medieval, in a land where the study of criminology and psychology is more intelligent than anywhere else in the world . . . Instances of shocking cruelty, lamentable neglect, brutal inhumanity, are exposed day after day in by far the richest nation in the world, so rich indeed that millions of Americans can be expected to go insane under the ever-increasing burden of their dissatisfactions and their failure to find outlets for their leisure time.

The criminality and misdemeanors of the young threaten to outstrip public control. Our record is by far the worst in the world . . .[9]

And so on, and on and on.

All of this reads like a random sampling of commentary on last week's news reports. But the prospect laid out is nearly twenty years old, has since become progressively more threatening and is sketched by a sober political scientist of the highest stature in a pointedly penetrating book about constitutional flaws.

I refer to this book not for authority on the particular phenomena reported. For that there exists a wealth of detailed studies in depth. I cite it simply because it was written, long before the post-Watergate revelations of government flouting the Constitution right and left over a span of many decades, of corporations engaged in elaborate criminal practices, by a reasonable analytical mind high in the academic hierarchy. Far from having improved, social conditions since Finer wrote have become worse and are slowly and steadily worsening as almost anyone can easily discern. Now the cities are being systematically burned—not merely by pillagers but also to collect insurance, avoid taxes. Instead of the United States one reads about in school history and civics books which are duly echoed in the newspapers, a country progressively moving onward and upward across one peak of incredible achievement after the other, a Banana Republic emerges, the biggest one of all, a land where almost anything untoward is likely to happen any minute, a land with catch-as-catch-can government.

Can such conditions on the fairest continent of all have arisen under the model constitutional system that is celebrated without cessation in the public prints and on public rostrums? Or does the United States harbor a particularly intractable population? Unless the answer to the second question is in the affirmative, the conditions are virtually inevitable, given all factors including the bounty of nature in the equation, under the constitutional system that is so celebrated. Why this should be so it is the intent of this book to explore vigorously.

The number of raging unresolved social problems in the country, many of them politically manipulated with the consequence of yielding substantial financial gains to third parties, is enormous. Sociologists have analyzed these in standard treatises. Granted, most of the human experiences seen in these problems are present in some measure in all societies at all times. The mere fact that such experiences take place involves no problem except to the individuals having the experience. But when the incidence of such experiences becomes massive, they are considered to constitute a roaring problem to society. The only agency there is to deal with such problems is government. And if government does not succeed in holding them within reasonable bounds, it is by that much a failure.

The problems referred to are catalogued by sociologists as stemming most immediately from social disorganization in the United States and in neighboring and affiliated countries; from personal deviations which may be in part genetic and in part environmental in cause; and from sharp conflicts of values within an educationally, economically, ethnically, regionally, religiously and culturally variegated population.

I draw, first, for a survey of such problems, from a book published in 1955, to show that they are not simply current, are in fact of long standing.[10] The roots of most of them go back to the post-Civil War period and some even into the era before that war.

They involve, to begin with, unscrupulous unhindered interest and pressure groups that ceaselessly contend through government for ever-enlarging slices of the national-income pie; next, intensifying crime—lower-class, middle-class and upper-class—and much of it politically protected; then, family collapse under direct and indirect external pressures, mainly economic; heavy population increases traceable to improved medicine, the birthrate, legal immigration and a flood of undeterred politically protected illegal immigration, mainly from Latin America; widespread school and youth problems; racial and religious conflicts; acute mental problems as evidenced in extensive alcoholism, drug addiction, gambling, suicide, wide-open prostitution and a variety of other self-destructive personal deviations; and sub-standard physical health and medical care for millions forced by government-sponsored farm mechanization out of rural environments into cities.

To these may be added as of more recent emergence environmental destruction and pollution stemming from uncontrolled industrialism and speculative development, much of it government-sanctioned or even inspired through the tax laws; sporadic but substantial violations of civil liberties; urban decay and deteriorating housing under politically flashy government "regulations"; and unrestrained exploitation for profit of sexual pathologies under the protection of the hallowed Bill of Rights.

All along, on the economic front, there has been creeping monopoly, more or less winked at by the government and indeed constitutionally protected and politically sponsored.

I focus on the system of government as central to all of this because government is the sole regulator of human affairs in the round. If it isn't the system of government that is at fault, it is the personnel in the government or a combination of the two. Which raises the question of how and why the system fosters this inadequate personnel. And if it is neither the system nor its personnel, it must all stem from a peculiarly intractable population or from surrounding natural pressures.

Now, while something remains to be said about the population, the natural setting in which the United States finds itself is absolutely the most favored in the world. That is a hard fact. It is, or was until it came under pell-mell human attack, a natural paradise surpassing any place on earth with the exception of a few minor areas here and there. Considering the natural setting, and a population that under wartime emergencies has at least measured up to other populations, what else is there left to look for in accounting for the great and destructive disorder in American society other than the prescribed procedures of management and the types of managers that arise under the highly applauded governmental process?

Many readers of course will say to themselves, "This may be all very well, but what is not being said is what is good about the country —more than 90 million people gainfully employed, many of them prosperous and apparently happy, thousands at the beaches, gamboling in parks, filling theaters and stadiums and lazing about in their expensive cars while great technical strides are being reported from every hand in all fields." All this is very true, and deserves to be noted before being swept aside. For the point about the many grinding problems is that they qualify to a considerable degree what is presented as the bright side. It is all more or less like the stately *Titanic* slowly sinking as the band plays for nonchalant dancers.

It is not to be denied that a certain number of people in the United States live in sheltered and favored positions, temporary for some, permanent for others. That is also true in the smaller Banana Republics. But it is safely deniable on the basis of stringent statistical analyses that this number is very large. A great number of the gainfully employed, many temporarily, are subject to one or more of the problems enumerated, assaulted and robbed of their pay on their way home or murdered in their dwellings by thieves. Many of the employed furthermore find their jobs distasteful or unhealthful or their pay too low, accounting for a regular rash of strikes. No matter how delectable one depicts life in the United States as being, one must, in order to achieve true balance, add a very considerable portion of bitters.

To the problems already mentioned might be added government-induced inflation, taxation that consumes more than 40 per cent of national income leading demonstrably to waste of a large percentage of what is taken. Again, there is chronic unemployment. Government, it appears, is going its own way as society steadily goes another.

Under the American political system there is little if anything that anyone can do about all this, and very little from the point of view of individual insight even if one is deep into the government. To get one's hands on any of the carefully guarded controls is practically impossible. True, the Constitution allows one to petition the government. But the document does not stipulate that the government must even consider the petition; it can toss it into the wastebasket.

One may petition, assemble and march in protest to one's heart's content, and many do, fruitlessly. A large section of the American people, and an intelligent section, was daily in vociferous opposition to the undeclared Vietnam War, yet the war ground on for eight years, the longest conflict in American history. The behavior of the government during that war showed that if it wished it could completely ignore all of the people, all of the time.

As concrete disclosures have shown, the opposition to the war was correct, the government itself abysmally wrong in all its major judgements and procedures. Yet most of the errant personnel remained in office for years later, positionally unmoved, many of them taking bows as profound statesmen. In England or France they would all have been quickly cashiered. Especially in the Senate, it will be observed, most of the wartime faces were present long after the war ended, long after their most ardent admirers had fallen into silence.

So, whatever else may be true, it is a fact that all is not well in the constitutional system, although the government, such as it is, still stands and the star-spangled banner still waves defiantly.

Commentary on the Constitution

"No document in the world, outside Holy Writ, has been the occasion of such a mass of annotation and exposition as the Fundamental Law of the American Constitution," wrote a perceptive English scholar, Herbert W. Horwill, more than fifty years ago. "It has been examined as critically and minutely as though believed to be verbally inspired." [11]

The writings on the Constitution indeed are so extensive that nobody in a long lifetime could read half of them. Since this scholar wrote, they have been enormously swollen.

Not only is it true that Biblical commentary alone exceeds in bulk the disquisitional glosses on the American Constitution; it is also true that from 90 to 95 per cent of the mountainous constitutional glossography is either false, misleading or vacuous. A more stodgy, pretentious and dreary set of empty polemics and exegesis, with occasional exceptions, is hard to find the world over.

As a result of the many dubious pronouncements, many canards have been projected into schoolrooms and, later, by the one-time students into the communications media, then into the bedevilled public psyche. In the upshot hardly anybody really knows what the Constitution is all about. Millions are utterly astounded to see dark-skinned people of African vintage suddenly declared full-fledged citizens and the declaration implemented, arrested persons held entitled to consult a lawyer before confessing to serious crimes, large-scale war waged without Congress having declared war, and so on.

There are so many misconceptions imbedded in the American psyche about the Constitution that it is difficult to know where to begin to challenge them point-blank. One such widely shared error, one of literally scores, is that the basic distinguishing mark of the American Constitution compared with the British is that the American is written whereas the British is unwritten.

If it were true that the British Constitution is unwritten, as a long line of impressively certified professors constantly repeat in echo of each other's books, it would follow that the British Constitution could be ascertained only by turning to oral tradition or to unofficial reportage. Long convinced myself of the error of this view, I was at last reassured about my own mental alertness to read the following in Horwill:

> The usual contrasts, then, between the American and the English Constitutions are wholly mistaken. The distinction between them is not that one is written and the other unwritten, or that the one consists of a single document while the other is a composite of many ingredients. The American Constitution has all the ingredients of the English and one more. The supposition that it is more simple and compact and definite is an utter delusion. The one difference between the two Constitutions is that the American possesses, in addition to and antecedently to the various elements of the English, one special section which is prior to all legislative enactments and is not capable of being amended by the legislature.[12]

This is the document of 1787 and its amendments.

But this special section may be interpreted, and very freely, by government agencies, sometimes one way, sometimes another, so even this difference turns out to be less than commonly supposed. For the power to interpret is the power to introduce trills, cadenzas and thematic variations, giving us what is metaphorically called "The Living Constitution." This Living Constitution is whatever the government does and does not do.

Horwill did not claim to be the first to have noticed this. He cited a number of American scholars who had been fully aware that there is a lot more to the Constitution than the document of 1787 as amended, but he noted quite truly that they never thereupon relinquished the misleading terminology. The notion of the American Constitution as written in contrast with the supposedly unwritten British Constitution stems from the period immediately after 1787 when it was in fact all written out in one place, a condition almost immediately altered under the influence of interpretation, formal and informal, legislation and extemporization.

Just what the Constitution of the United States is I shall not venture myself to suggest in view of all the self-appointed experts gyrating on the American scene and ready to pounce on any independent observer who says anything sticky about it. Instead I invoke here the late Prof. Edward S. Corwin of Princeton University, widely recognized by his peers as the outstanding constitutional scholar of our time:

> As it occurs in everyday usage, the term "Constitution of the United States" refers to the document of 1787 plus the amendments which have been added to it. But this, if I may employ an available French distinction, is only the *"formal"* sense of the term. In the *"material"* sense a constitution is a body of rules in accordance with which a government is organized and operates; and in this sense "the Constitution of the United States" comprises a vastly extended system of legislation, customs and adjudications, of which the constitutional document is, as it were, but the nucleus, and into which it tends ever to be absorbed.[13]

The Constitution itself almost fully defines itself as a part of the supreme law of the land in Article VI, Section 2: "This Constitution, *and* [emphasis added] the laws of the United States which shall be made in pursuance thereof; *and* [emphasis added] all treaties made, or which shall be made, under the authority of the United States, shall be the supreme law of the land; and the judges in every State shall be bound thereby, anything in the Constitution or laws of any States to the contrary notwithstanding . . ."

A constitution is the supreme law. And what *supreme law* in the American system is, then, is not only the document of 1787 as amended but also, and equally, the national statutes and the treaties made by the President with the concurrence of the Senate. In other words, any national law is a supreme law—that is, is part of the Constitution. And whether a statute is or is not in harmony with the Constitution the government itself determines—in most cases the Supreme Court but in some cases the President alone and, in reserve and in fact on paper transcending the Supreme Court, the Congress.

So much has been written in dismay about the Supreme Court, nine old men, finding acts of Congress unconstitutional that it is not generally known that if Congress wanted to mobilize itself fully it has the power set forth in the document of 1787 to overrule the Supreme Court. Congress, however, at present consisting of 535 people against nine Supreme Court Justices, would find this very difficult to do in practice owing to its inner conflicts.

The constitutional authority for Congress to act in a way it is in practice never able (except once) to bring itself to act is found in Article III, Section 2. After stating those few instances in which the Supreme Court has original jurisdiction the section reads, "In all the other cases before mentioned [which are all possible cases] the Supreme Court shall have appellate jurisdiction, both as to law and fact, *with such exceptions, and under such regulations as the Congress shall make"* [emphasis added].

In other words, Congress may state exceptions to what is subject to upper-court jurisdiction, a power Congress has only twice sought to exercise, although individual Congressmen have proposed it. One such exception might well be—the unimpeachable validity of acts of Congress! Apart from the difficulty of mobilizing Congress for such action, it should be noted that there are certain advantages, both to Congress and to individual Congressmen, in leaving decision to the Supreme Court. One advantage is that Congress need not shoulder responsibility before the public for editings by the Supreme Court, can have things both ways. It can pass acts that gain public approval but of which many proponents secretly disapprove, and then can commiserate with the public when a "reactionary" Supreme Court nullifies them. After thus playing peek-a-boo and hide-and-seek with constituents, Congressmen can stand for re-election with a clean slate. Justices of the Court, appointed for life, need not seek public approval. The effective regulatory power is obviously left to the Court.

In practice a statute unanimously approved by Congress and signed by the President can be shot down and nullified by five judicial appointees over whom the public has not the remotest control. But all is not lost to the people. For they can now amend the Constitution by a process so complicated that it has seldom succeeded in more than four thousand formal attempts!

The full sweep of the Constitution is shown by the high court interpretations and the United States statutes. The interpretations alone fill 421 closely printed large volumes up to October 1974. More are added each year. As these volumes include the reasonings and rationalizations pro and con of the justices, they cannot all be considered part of the Constitution. But the operative majority opinions very definitely are. If merely such were written down they would fill many large volumes.

The opinions show how the Constitution applies in specific cases that are judiciable, which many government actions are not. Often many intelligent people are very surprised by the decisions, which sometimes bring to light what nobody before ever suspected was in the original document, such as implied powers, inherent power, special privilege. The Court, in other words, finds more Constitution than anyone ever before saw. Some observers accuse it of inventing or legislating, and without any grant of authority to do so.

As to statutes, those of the federal government to 1976 fill 88 large numbered volumes and actually are to be found in 134 volumes because some of the volumes that are numbered extend to two and three extra volumes. To read the Court decisions and the statutes with understanding in a lifetime would be virtually impossible. All of this amplitude of judicial decision and statute law provides a vast terrain for official maneuvering before a baffled public.

For a long time Americans held up their hands in horror that the British Parliament may, under the British Constitution, legislate in any direction it likes. Whatever the Parliament enacts is constitutional. If an enactment is found by the courts to conflict with pre-existing law, it is up to Parliament to repeal one or the other of the conflicting laws, which it does.

In the British case it is an elected body, in effect today one-chambered, of about 625 people, all readily removable by their constituencies, that generates constitutionality. In the American case it is usually five out of nine appointed lifetime Justices, not removable as long as they behave decorously, who perform this office. Which procedure is more democratic and republican, which more autocratic, anyone can tell at a glance.

The decision of Parliament, too, always carries the executive branch along with it. For the executive, consisting of the Prime Minister and Cabinet and always an integral part of Parliament, participates in its proceedings. In the British system, unlike the oft-hymned American, there can be no stalemate between the executive and the legislature, with stultifying effects on the underlying society.

The Constitution, in Article V, provides for the amending process, which it keeps entirely in the hands of officialdom. There is no way "the people", unguided by government, can amend the Constitution.

There are two roads to go toward amendment, one never tried because it is practically impossible. The customary but rarely trod road is for two-thirds of each house of Congress—if they are willing—to vote for an amendment and then refer it for ratification to the legislatures of three-quarters of the states, or thirty-eight states at present. Except for Nebraska each state has a two-chamber legislature and each chamber must approve, another big stumbling-block. The alternative method is for the legislatures of two-thirds of the states to ask Congress to call a national convention to vote on a proposed amendment, after which, the convention approving, the proposal will be sent, upon the instructions of Congress, either for the approval of the legislatures of three-fourths of the states or of a similar number of state conventions. Either way the gauntlet to be run is formidable, with the consequence that there are few amendments.

At no point do "the people" figure in this process, and would not unless Congress set up some method of getting "the people" into cumbersome conventions, which in practice would be pre-empted by the politicians. There is nothing whatever approaching a plebiscite in all this, and in fact the amending process is more remote from "the people"— largely indifferent of course, perhaps made indifferent—than was the original ratification process. I don't mean to suggest out of hand that keeping the people out of it is a bad thing, only that "government of the people, by the people and for the people", even though apostrophized by so worthy a man as Abraham Lincoln, is a nonexistent entity. The people do not govern either directly or through "representatives." The people are governed, but in most cases only dimly realize it. They largely believe, because they have been told so, that they are "free". At least it is a dead certainty that they are not free of government.

Public Opinions re the State of the Nation

While few Americans would dream of questioning the contention that the Constitution is one of the greatest works of man, public-opinion polls long preceding the enlightening post-Watergate disclosures show that most Americans don't have a high opinion of conditions in the country under that very same Constitution. There is here a curious hiatus in the popular mind.

I cite a Harris Survey report of 1971, compressed. By 81 per cent against 11 per cent, grass-roots Americans agreed with the statement that "most elected officials promise one thing at election time and do something different once in office". By 65 per cent against 25 per cent they agreed that "only a few men in politics are dedicated public servants"; in 1965 the same polling agency showed the division at

58–24 per cent. "Most political jobs are not given on merit", thought 63 per cent against 17 per cent. And 63 per cent against 28 per cent agreed that "most politicians are in politics to make money for themselves". Finally, 59 per cent against 20 per cent thought that "most politicians take graft".

As to corruption in general, 49 per cent of the scientifically refined survey sample thought its extent was neither greater nor less than what it had been ten years before, while 35 per cent thought it had increased during the whirligig Kennedy, Johnson and Nixon administrations.

On a softer note, 80 per cent inconsistently believed that "most men go into elected office to help others", 75 per cent believed that "most men in public life have little privacy and are often unfairly criticized", but the number who believed that "men in high office sacrifice money to be in public service" declined from 63 per cent to 49 per cent over the preceding four years.[11]

In 1971, again pre-Watergate, Arthur Miller, political scientist at Ohio State University, presented what he termed "somewhat alarming" findings to the annual meeting of the American Political Science Association. Miller reported that whereas in 1964 only a case-hardened 20 per cent of a polled sample distrusted government completely, by 1970 no less than 39 per cent did so.

The Ohio researcher also uncovered some unexpected factual nuggets that seemed bizarre in the face of cherished common notions. Whereas 38 per cent of the left-leaning or radic-lib distrustful were black, no less than 99.7 per cent of the right-leaning distrustful were white. One-third of what Miller termed "cynics of the left" was under thirty years of age but only 12 per cent of the rightist cynics and disillusioned was in this group of relatively tender years. Miller found more discontent and disillusionment in the time-tempered over-sixty age bracket than in the under-thirty group—the latter commonly supposed to harbor the most discontent by reason of inexperience and half-baked idealistic notions foisted on them by subversive teachers, atheistic authors, soft-headed parents and free-wheeling media impresarios. In brief, Americans of mature and sober years were more disgusted with government than were the inexperienced, starry-eyed young.[15] And the government they were disgusted with was that under the fulsomely lauded Constitution of the United States!

Sociologists Alerted

Sociologists naturally were early alerted by all these reports of public disaffection and put restlessly on the prowl. For, said Prof. Amitai Etzioni of Columbia University in 1968, prior to the reports here cited, "when the leadership of one Administration after another is not trusted by a majority of the public, the country's vital political institutions stand threatened." [16]

This particular observer was especially impressed by the fact that while the leadership in non-governmental enclaves such as science, medicine and business was rightly or wrongly thought at that time by 64 per cent of the citizenry to be better than in the past, the federal government and politics found only a meager 19 and 13 per cent, respectively, believing they had improved. More than 55 per cent in a poll studied by Etzioni felt that "something is deeply wrong with our society"—in itself, for the United States, an extravagantly subversive notion when one considers the historical record of continuous official, corporate, schoolroom and journalistic ballyhoo to the very contrary.

Later Reports More Severe

Pollster Louis Harris in 1973 came forward with findings that the situation was even worse than had up until then been depicted. For, said he, the American people believed that the quality of life in the United States had steadily deteriorated and they were extremely disenchanted with most of their key institutions although they were far from putting their fingers on where the true difficulty lay. Moreover the most respectable and even affluent elements shared fully in these sentiments.

What Harris found was:

That by 52 to 34 per cent a majority thought the quality of American life had worsened in the past decade.

That 64 per cent believed the "tax laws are written to help the rich and not help the average man."

That 68 per cent believed the "rich get richer and the poor get poorer". (In 1966 only 48 per cent thought this.)

That 53 per cent felt "what I think doesn't count much" against 39 per cent who thought this in 1966.

That 43 per cent felt "those in power are out to take advantage of you".[17]

Independent Writers on the Loose

Down through American history, even as the constitutional cult has been extended, every single independent writer who has commented on the American political scene has done so in terms suitable for describing a particularly crooked card game. One of the first was James Fenimore Cooper with *The American Democrat* (1838). The unanimity and ardor with which American writers have lambasted the self-hymned, Constitution-draped American public official and politician is itself impressive, even awe-inspiring.

Added to Cooper we find on the list such Anglo-Saxon public-library, reprint and de luxe edition favorites as Ralph Waldo Emerson, Walt Whitman, Mark Twain, Wendell Phillips, Oliver Wendell Holmes Sr., Henry Adams, Charles Francis Adams, E. W. Howe, Ambrose Bierce, Lincoln Steffens, Samuel Hopkins Adams, David Graham Phillips, Theodore Dreiser, Sinclair Lewis, Ring Lardner, H. L. Mencken, E. E. Cummings and an assortment of others, with not a single foreigner or serious pinko in the lot. It is an American literary tradition to see the creatures of the Constitution more or less as renegades.

As Emerson wrote to Thomas Carlyle in 1835, "Government has come to be a trade, and is managed solely on commercial principles. A man plunges into politics to make his fortune, and only cares that the world shall last his days." Twenty-five years later, in *The Conduct of Life*, Emerson (often sounding the same note in the years between) remarked, "Politics is a deleterious profession, like some poisonous handicrafts. Men in power have no opinions but may be had cheap for any opinion, for any purpose."

Frenchman Alexis de Tocqueville, author of the immoderately praised *Democracy in America* (1835), wrote that "In the United States I never heard anyone accused of spending his wealth in buying votes [that was to come later], but I have often heard the probity of public officers questioned; still more frequently have I heard their success attributed to low intrigues and immoral practices . . . The corruption of men who have casually risen to power has a coarse and vulgar infection in it that renders it dangerous to the multitude." [18]

Viscount James Bryce

More than fifty years later, in 1888, an even friendlier observer swam into view in the person of James Bryce, Regius Professor of History at Oxford University and author of a celebrated work on the Holy Roman Empire. Bryce had more recently produced a massive treatise in two volumes, titled *The American Commonwealth*, intended to portray "the whole political system of the country in its practice as well as its theory". Though a professed admirer of the American system and flattering in the attention he bestowed, Bryce as a high-toned scholar aimed at being even-handed. He therefore felt obliged to deal with "the evils which are now tolerated" but which he optimistically felt—his was the most optimistic century in history—"the reserve force and patriotism of the people would in time eliminate" and make "the country worthy

of its material grandeur and of the private virtues of its inhabitants."
Bryce mapped out, with some caution, terrain later ploughed over with
much more furor by the so-called muckrakers of the early twentieth
century—a muckraker being anyone who concentrated in public writings on the corrupt acts of politicians and corporate manipulators. As
it turned out, in the official view (as shown in the unlovely sobriquet
given them by an irate President Theodore Roosevelt) it was the
muckrakers who were the true public offenders, not the specimens they
wrote about!

As Bryce was later made ambassador to the United States (1907-
1913), very much *persona grata* in Washington after his careful handling
of explosive contemporary materials, his book may be taken as indirectly official or at least quasi-official. For if the United States government did not indirectly endorse his work by accepting him as the
ambassador of His Britannic Majesty, at least it did not repudiate him.
In Britain Bryce was eventually elevated to the peerage, so he was
obviously no Bolshevik or even sideline trouble-maker.

Bryce, astonishingly to most of his middle-class American readership
and to newspaper readers, devoted whole chapters to hitherto largely
unrecognized brass-spittoon politicians, political machines for delivering captive greenhorn voters, boodle rings and bosses, undercover
financial spoils, rigged elections, slush funds, rank corruption and fraud,
exposés of bossism, corporate looting, franchise-grabbing and railroad
land-grabs, well-heeled lobbyists for sinister interests, large-scale grafters
and the like—all strewn like tumbleweeds over the naturally fair American scene.

But in the upshot, and here at variance with the later muckrakers,
Bryce always tended to soft-pedal by way of summary whatever of a
shocking or disgusting nature he had found, thus introducing a sense
of reserve and scholarly balance. As even his pianissimo summaries,
given over to the muted string section of his literary orchestra rather
than to the brass and percussion where they belonged, preserve the
essential fidelity of his more bold thematic account, they can be cited
here as minimally representative of his findings.

> Bribery exists in Congress, but it is confined to a few members,
> say five per cent of the whole number. It is more common in the
> legislatures of a few, but only a few States, practically absent from the
> higher walks of the Federal civil service and among the chief State
> officials, rare among the lower officials, unknown among the Federal
> judges, rare among State judges.
> The taking of other considerations than money, such as a share
> in a lucrative contract, or a railway pass, or a "good thing" to be
> secured for a friend, prevails among legislators to a somewhat larger

extent. Being less coarsely palpable than the receipt of money, it is thought more venial. [Bryce here, probably owing to failure of nerve was self-contradictory as all these involved money, i.e., were "lucrative", lucre-productive. All this was misplaced diminuendo.] One may roughly conjecture that from fifteen to twenty per cent of the members of Congress or of an average State legislature would allow themselves to be influenced by inducements of this kind. [This is enough to swing most decisions.]

Malversation of public funds occurs occasionally in cities, rarely among Federal or State officers. [It was in fact standard procedure in the swarming cities.]

Jobbery of various kinds, i.e., the misuse of a public position for the benefit of individuals, is pretty frequent. It is often disguised as a desire to render some service to the party, and the same excuse is sometimes found for a misappropriation of public money.

Patronage is usually dispensed with a view to party considerations or to win personal support. But this remark is equally true of England and France, the chief difference being that owing to the short terms and frequent removals the quantity of patronage is relatively greater in the United States.[19]

Prior to this summary Bryce had noticed that "A position of some delicacy is occupied by eminent lawyers who sit in Congress and receive retainers from powerful corporations whose interests may be affected by Congressional legislation, retainers for which they are often not expected to render any forensic service." [20] Here the word "retainers" clearly deserves to be set within its own bleak quotation marks.

In his allusions to percentages of the corrupt, Bryce did not bring out that it was really the key or important men, the long-term "swing" people or leaders, always, who were the chief actors in the corruption circus. Novices, newcomers and obscure marginal figures would have been of little use to the seekers after improper privileges. The most corrupt, always, were those like Daniel Webster and James G. Blaine of Maine—Robert Ingersoll's "Plumed Knight"—who stood forth as especially voluble patriots and were regarded as ripe for political promotion to the very top.

In any event, there is very evidently nothing new about the undercover shenanigans of American politicos, especially the big ones, even though members of the lower masses may be latecomers in recognizing what is going on. Anyone halfway informed about the American scene has been aware of all this all along.

Why, then, if it is all a very old and tattered story, much like *The Perils of Pauline* of early film days, bring it up again here and at this time? It is recalled here, sketchily, merely to indicate the continuity of difficulties under the constitutional system, of which there is much more to be said.

It is not to be denied that the Constitution has served many of the purposes visualized by some of its designers and by many of its supporters and admirers down through the decades. At the same time, in the light of the expectancies instilled in the vast majority of the populace, it has been, quite plainly, a huge flop. Once I get deeper into the subject it will be seen why this should be so.

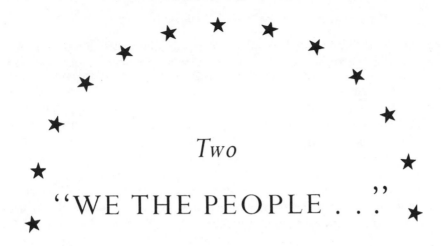

Two

"WE THE PEOPLE . . ."

Ratifiers of the Constitution, as I have just shown, won by 5 to 3, a majority of a 20 or 25 per cent minority of the eligible electorate. There was no general upsurge of enthusiasm or support for the document just as there had been no general upsurge for the revolt against Great Britain, for the establishment of the state constitutions or for the enactment of the Articles of Confederation.

As a matter of fact, none of these events, often celebrated by politicians and magnified in their dimensions by romanticizing historians, had had any electoral sanction at all. They were strictly *coup d'état* affairs, run by small groups of self-styled patriots many of whom bettered their personal economic positions significantly by means of the revolution. Some more critical historians even contend that not only a majority of eligible voters but also a majority of the people as a whole was opposed to the Constitution at the time of ratification. Little, in other words, was as school histories have made it seem.

One such critical historian is Jackson Turner Main.[1] According to Main, who has ploughed over documentary sources as closely as anyone yet has, the anti-Federalists outnumbered the Federalists in Rhode Island and South Carolina by 4 to 1 and in New York and North Carolina by "perhaps" 3 to 1 and had at least a majority in Massachusetts and Virginia. As of June 1788 the two sides were about equal in New Hampshire although the anti-Federalists had earlier been more numerous. Over the entire population, according to Main, the anti-Federalists predominated by 52 per cent.[2]

In this perspective, opinion was about evenly divided, which at least seems plausible, remindful of popular sampling polls about our own impending elections. In any event, there was no hysterical nor even mild popular enthusiasm for the Constitution as implied or flatly stated in many history books.

In the light of the foregoing, the problem arises of explaining why the Constitution was approved by state conventions in the ratio of 5 to 3 of the delegates elected by eligible voters.

The historian Charles Beard, quoting Prof. John W. Burgess of Columbia University, an academic bigwig of pre-World War I days, conveyed the opinion that the writing and adoption of the Constitution amounted to something of a *coup d'état*.[3] For so doing, Beard has been roundly condemned by constitutional cultists although the thought was hardly original with him. In sober truth, the whole process of secession from the British Empire, from the firing of the first shot of revolt onward, was a series of *coups d'état* staged by minorities, the usual political genesis. In the words of Henry Adams, historian great-grandson of John Adams, writing of the constitutional framers, "for the most part they had been traitors themselves." [4]

There was in fact less of an air of *coup d'état* about the framing and adoption of the Constitution than about what had gone before. But it is well within the historical data to say that the pro-Constitution Federalists skillfully finessed all opposition, in the process breaking established fundamental *American* law, by establishing a Constitution that went very much against the grain of a considerable section if not a majority of the population and has proven in action to be quite different from what its boosters claim and have claimed, and less edifying.

Main sees the factors that permitted the Federalist victory as follows: Letters and newspapers addressed to prominent anti-Federalists were delayed intentionally by pro-Federalist postal authorities, thus interfering with communications among the oppositionists (what today would be described as routine political "dirty tricks"). Most of the newspapers were pro-constitutional, dependent then as later upon commercial patrons who were mostly pro-constitutional, and intentionally failed to allow anti-Constitution writers the ample scope given Federalists, flatly misrepresented the true attitude of the electorate and published many demonstrable falsehoods—the usual political bag of dirty tricks. The anti-Federalists were not organized whereas the Federalists were very well organized. The Federalist leaders and spokesmen, largely of the permanent post-revolutionary political establishment, were better known, had greater prestige and therefore carried greater weight with voters. The anti-Federalists themselves voted for men of prestige as convention delegates who were persuaded to switch sides during the state conventions. The Federalists gained early momentum, and never lost it, by forcing through early quick ratification in Delaware and Pennsylvania. And, finally, "there was the promise of amendments without which the Constitution could never have been ratified." [5]

It should never be forgotten that the oft-hymned first ten amendments were not the work of the constitutional convention, but were the progeny of the anti-Federalists. Many of these amendments, those considered most liberal, represented a bitter pill to many of the leading Philadelphia framers although Hamilton at once saw that they made no very great difference, in no way diluted the Constitution.

How Could a Minority Prevail?

The big unanswered question, despite all of the foregoing, is how a vast majority of the people in most of the states could nevertheless passively acquiesce in having a radically different new form of government installed by open vote and why so few of the eligible electorate voted. Distances were great at the time and transportation and communication primitive, roads were few and bad. Yet there were nevertheless elections held in the various local districts; those willing to make the effort could at least vote for local delegates. Universal white male suffrage, in effect, prevailed; property requirements for voting were minimal although not for holding office.

The fact is that there was not a great voting turnout for either side. Most men, it would seem, did not much care either way, and women certainly were not clamoring to vote. Here is a side of the question usually soft-pedalled. By the looks of things the people were in a political stupor.

It has been argued by some historians that had more time been allowed for public analysis the Constitution would surely have been rejected. And this is probably true for the simple reason that the more time one has to analyze any unfamiliar proposition or set of propositions the more likely is one to find them falling short of proponents' claims. It took four years to get the Articles of Confederation ratified by all the state legislatures and yet, despite the cautious delay, the document in action seemed increasingly deficient to more and more informed people.

One of the major reasons the anti-Federalists lost out was that they had no alternative to offer other than the Articles, which everybody admitted needed amending. The anti-Federalists were in the position of having to beat a mettlesome new horse with an obviously lame horse, thereby dampening spirits all around.

The electoral inertia of a large majority of the populace, even though much of it was anti-Federalist, tends to show that its anti-Federalism was at best tepid. Historians and biographers are votaries of documents, necessarily. If they find something written down, they tend to accord it great weight, if only by the attention they lavish on it, and this too in the sphere of opinions. There were indeed many anti-Federalist writings.

What counts, though, with opinion, is the strength, or fanaticism, with which it is held and the amount of time, money and effort the holder is willing to expend to make it prevail. The present national opinion polls illustrate the point. In these people are randomly located, often in obscure places, and asked out of a blue sky for their views on a broad range of subjects. What they respond is duly recorded, sometimes with startling effect. How intensely they feel about what they think however does not appear. When it comes to voting, it often turns out they have not been more languidly interested, for most of them do not vote, many would not walk across the street to register their opinions.

The bulk of anti-Federalists were like this. Although not enchanted by the Constitution, neither were most of them sufficiently enchanted by the Articles of Confederation to bestir themselves for it. The core Federalists, on the other hand, were grimly determined. They, as politically active people who owned a substantial part of the country and saw around them what they considered the politics of naivety, intended to take the government out of the hands of fumblers, mainly in the states, whom they saw as hopelessly childish and politically doctrinaire.

Something we don't know is how many of the voters understood either the Constitution or the Articles of Confederation. Judging by today, when careful surveys show functional illiteracy approaching very close to 50 per cent of the populace despite an immense network of schools, probably not many persons understood either document very well. Both were, from the layman's point of view, highly technical, the Constitution infinitely more technical than the Articles. It has been noticed in voting generally that when issues become very complex more persons than usual tend not to vote or even to read. For which reason politicians like to avoid issues entirely or to keep them simple and primitive, a choice between black and white.

The struggle between Federalist and anti-Federalist has been by some writers represented as one between privilege and democracy, between the rich and the relatively poor, and this is unquestionably wrong. For it has been shown in minute documented detail by Forrest Mc-

Donald, a ranking historian, that the same sort of economic interests from bottom to top were on both sides of the constitutional struggle, at least in the state conventions.[6]

Economics and the Constitution

McDonald got into his researches by investigating the thesis of Charles Beard that personalty interests—holders of stocks, bonds, merchandise, money lent at interest on notes and other such instruments—were the "dynamic element" in putting through the Constitution in opposition to laggard holders of land and real estate and the resistance of subsistence farmers and poor debtors. But McDonald clearly demonstrates, in exhaustive detail, that this was wrong, that the same types of economic interests ranged on both sides and that many earlier proponents of state paper money and laws delaying the collection of debts, devices detested by the framers, were themselves in favor of the new system.

While economic factors played a role, different roles in different states, theirs was not the only role and they were not the class-divisional sort of factors that Beard envisaged. They were in fact often reciprocally competitive interests, of every type. The conflict over the Constitution was a conflict within the same class of people, within an extended group of approximately the same outlook on life.

The differences among the contending parties were far less over the ends, about which there was quite general agreement, than over the means for attaining the ends. The struggle, as a consequence, was not especially bitter and there was a general closing of ranks after the adoption of the Constitution.

The struggle over the Constitution took place really within a like-minded minority consisting of the politicized element of the population. Most of these were property-owners from small to large, their property of every kind, and as such they were naturally interested in the protection of property against political assault as during the revolution. One side was neither more nor less democratic than the other, neither more nor less in favor of the common man or the underdog. In fact, neither side was at all enamored of the underdogs. Certainly very few of the active anti-Federalists, if any, belonged to the pool of very poor whites who had been on the scene since colonial times.[7]

What appears to be the case is that very few if any of "the meaner sort" or "inferiors" (in the language of the day) were involved at all in the struggle. People of this type varied from 25 to 30 per cent of all in rural New England "to well over half in Southern counties," according to sources put forward by Main.[8] In addition the rate of literacy was not very high throughout the populace, especially at the lower levels. Most people probably could not understand the Constitution, any more than they can today.

Just how little of an underdog document the revolutionary Articles of Confederation was can be seen from its Article IV, which read, "The better to secure and perpetuate mutual friendship and intercourse among the people of the different states in this union, the *free* inhabitants of each of these states, *paupers, vagabonds and fugitives from Justice excepted,* shall be entitled to all the privileges and immunities of *free* citizens in the several states . . ." The italicized words are mine.

So, even among the non-slave elements of the population, those whites who were impoverished or vagabonds—the unemployed, unpropertied and possibly disoriented and untended ailing of the day—were constitutionally discriminated against in the happy first Union. The general attitude of the colonists toward the poor, even and especially in New England, was overtly hostile, for such required public assistance at taxpayers' expense.[9] Slaves of course remained slaves, not subject to the glad tidings of liberty for all. For them it was to be the same under the Constitution. Indians were simply fair game at all times and were to continue to be for a long time to come.

Intellectual Sources of the Revolution

The remote intellectual stimulus for the American secession from the British Empire and for the establishment of state governments and the Articles of Confederation came, first, from the Puritan revolution of 1641-60 in England which dethroned Charles I and installed Cromwell as Lord Protector, and the struggle from 1679 to 1710 to exclude the Stuart line from the throne.

These events, including the freeing of the press from licensing in 1695, produced an explosion of writing and publishing on behalf of the Whig Party, especially its radical but never very popular wing, as opposed to the Tory Party which favored the old regime and monarchy over Parliament. The cry of the Whigs was for the supremacy of Parliament over the King and of the radical Whigs for the separation of the executive entirely from Parliament and the abolition of executive prerogative. Separation of the executive was considered by the radical Whigs as the *sine qua non* of political salavation.

As these writings, eagerly read in the American colonies throughout the eighteenth century by such few as had the leisure, the ability and persistence to read, are too voluminous to detail here, the reader is referred to scholarly compilations where they can be found laid out in great profusion. The most complete general treatment is found in *The Eighteenth-Century Commonwealthman* by Caroline Robbins, an extremely valuable guide.[10] There the entire latter-day American political creed can be found sprouting in all its variety. How these ideas were echoed by the more political of the colonists is found in *The Ideological Origins of the American Revolution* by Bernard Bailyn.[11] The upwelling of then radical political ideas during the English revolution is skillfully presented in *The World Turned Upside Down* by Christopher Hill.[12]

While the literature analyzed in these books, especially the one by Robbins, was devoured by interested readers in the colonies, the two most read books, and radical, and very much expressing ideas carried forward during and after the American revolution, were *Cato's Letters*, written between 1720 and 1723 by Thomas Gordon and John Trenchard, and James Burgh's *Political Disquisitions* (1774).

"Where annual elections end, slavery begins", wrote Burgh.[13] If the then popular Burgh is right, slavery has been the rule since the Constitution took effect. Elections, following Burgh, under the new state constitutions of 1776 were made annual and other ideas of *Cato*, Burgh and other radical Whigs were incorporated, particularly the domination of the government of each state by the annually elected legislature, with Georgia, Pennsylvania and Vermont establishing unicameral bodies. In states where an upper house was also installed, its power was little, as was that of the governor (or president as he was known in some states).

State Government under the Confederation

Whatever faction therefore controlled the legislature—and factions often superseded each other by the year—controlled state policy, often sharply altering it on short notice to suit the interests, usually economic, of the ascendant faction. Only in Massachusetts was the governor allowed a veto; in most states he was chosen by the legislature, making him suitably deferential to it. And in most states his term was for a single year while in half the states his re-eligibility to serve was limited. Only Connecticut and Rhode Island preserved their pre-revolutionary governments, which until then were deemed the most popularly accommodating or "democratic" in the colonies.

There were no external checks on the legislatures, either by executive or courts. One result was rapid and frequent shifts of policy in various states, which made for uncertainty which in turn was most bothersome to economic enterprisers large or small. To non-enterprisers it made little perceptible difference.

Voting turnouts however were never heavy and, as I have shown, were not required at all for the establishment of the state governments or the Articles of Confederation. But it had been one of the notions of the radical English Whigs that people wanted to vote for their governors, and frequently, and should do so. This was a notion simply plucked from thin air but it was certainly one method of putting together a government.

Down through history most governors, at least initially, took over by force; in some jurisdictions force continued to be the preferred method. The ancient Greeks apparently introduced voting although it may have predated even them. Kings and emperors in time became hereditary, and appointed underlings. All drew their sanction from God and were appropriately blessed by the established priesthood. The offices of underlings usually in time also became hereditary.

Under this approach the rulers almost from the beginning acquired an exaggerated idea (still often seen in elected office-holders) of what was due to them and an attenuated notion of what was owing to the populace. Whenever the latter became restive it was suppressed by force or intimidation rather than elaborately distracted as today.

The first big modern break with monarchy—already gone in Switzerland and Italian city-states—came in England with the dethroning and then beheading of Charles I in 1649. The country was soon again, almost immediately, under one-man rule in the form of the Lord Protector, Oliver Cromwell. Nominally he was Parliament's man; actually he had more power than the deposed King, who had at least had to face the opposition of Parliament. After Cromwell's death came the Restoration and subsequent governmental changes that gradually reduced the power of the King, increased that of Parliament and finally that of the Cabinet, the Prime Minister and the Civil Service. Meanwhile, on into the nineteenth century, more and more people were being given the right to vote.

But universal white male suffrage was installed much sooner in the United States than in England, undoubtedly encouraging the development in the Old Country and elsewhere, even in countries where today people are as bewildered and nonplussed by the whole idea as they are in many parts of the United States.

No doubt in any country where there is now general suffrage, any proposal to curtail or limit it directly would induce a vast popular commotion. But voting participation in most jurisdictions where it is voluntary—in some countries one is forced by law to vote—is at best languid. One must conclude that where there is free choice, some people like to vote, see some value in it, and others are less convinced or feel disaffected with the methods and prospects offered.

One does not, where voting is general and voluntary, have any great choice of candidates, for nominations are usually manipulated by or restricted to those already deep into the "political game", specialists. The voter never sees before him some authentic detached paragon or savior fresh from the brow of Jove and if he did would probably recoil as from a palpable fraud, too good to be true.

Profiling "The People"

All of which brings us once again to "the people", the basis of legitimacy in modern electoral systems. Invariably extolled by politicians even as they are being manipulated (the praise is itself part of the manipulation), "the people" in their fullness are not very well known even in the presence of elaborate demographic statistics and sample polls. Scientific procedure however, seldom brought to bear in this quarter, can nevertheless supply something of what is left lacking by the process of selective head-counting, individual appraisal and guess-work.

In discussing "the people", I am not, may I remind the reader, staging a digression. For the Constitution opens dramatically with the words "We the people . . ." So any consideration of the Constitution must take into consideration this element, which most constitutional treatises neglect or leave out entirely.

Everybody was not considered "people" by the radical English Whigs from whom the American colonists took their political lines as from a playwright's script. As Robbins says, "The illiterate and underprivileged sections of society were not much considered, though the constantly reiterated appeal to the people sometimes suggests to modern readers, and probably to those of the eighteenth century as well, more of a democratical inclination than in fact may have existed in Cato's mind." [14]

As Cato himself put it, "As by the people I mean not the idle and indigent rabble under which name the people are often understood and traduced, but all who have property without the privilege of nobility; so by the latter I mean such as are possessed of privileges denied to the people." [15] People, otherwise put, were property-owners. The dispute, in short, was between the propertied nobility and the propertied non-nobility. Robbins adds, "Nature, in other words, produced no nobility, but education and property combined to endow certain classes with political rights, privileges and duties."

Everybody, then, was not included among people from a purely political point of view, whatever a biologist or anthropologist might say to the contrary. And this was pretty much the way political elements among the American colonists thought and the writers of the American Constitution as well. Certainly if one does not participate in the political process, voluntarily or involuntarily, one is a political nullity, a political non-person. And if one participates only passively, mechanically, as many do, one is little more than ballast.

The more modern view includes everyone among "the people", even the denizens of Skid Row. In so including them, it becomes more difficult to assess the people, although, thanks again to science, not impossible. But as voting statistics show, even without restrictions half or more of the eligible populace excludes itself from the political process at all times.

The Probability Curves

It is a matter of common observation and experience that people, apart from certain general and absolute characteristics such as each naturally having two arms and two legs and being of either one sex or the other, are very different in detail. They all consist of bundles of characteristics and these characteristics—physical, mental, emotional and moral—are individually present in greater or lesser quantity or intensity. The aptitudes underlying various natural or trained skills also vary from one extreme to the other, from very little to very much.

Science studies such phenomena systematically by means of mathematical procedures, by which it extrapolates from relatively small samples to the population as a whole. For it would be impossible to investigate each member of the population individually for each characteristic and trait except for very superficial data as in a census.

In this procedure what has been learned from observation in a small area or from common experience is reduced, where possible, to numbers, quantities, which in turn are transformed into mathematical equations. In their turn these are rendered graphically in what are known as probability curves. These latter show at a glance the distribution by degrees of some trait or characteristic throughout a whole population, allowing small margins for error.

People, as it turns out, apart from their defining characteristics as a species, are very different from each other, not infrequently as different as the boiling and freezing points of water. Not only are they very different in the quantity or intensity of each characteristic or natural skill but, such characteristics numbering in the hundreds, they are also different in their *combinations,* by varying degrees for each, of characteristics, traits, propensities and skills.

While all this is apparent to limited observation of small numbers of people, it is also true with respect to the whole. It follows that when the politician or statesman refers to "the people" as to a simple, well-understood entity he "represents", he is referring to something of which he knows no more than a theologian does of God.

Graphic curves are either symmetrical or asymmetriacl, according to the way randomly collected data in a sample spread out. In general outline the curves are like the profile of a mountain, peaked or rounded out at the top, leaning to one side or the other (skewed), or one side elongated in a gradual slope on one side and steeped on the other. For renditions of such curves one may consult almost any introductory treatise on mathematical statistics or see Frederick E. Croxton and Dudley J. Cowden's *Applied General Statistics.*

A basic curve, of wide applicability, is absolutely symmetrical and is called the normal curve of probability. It is expressed by a complex mathematical equation that needs no exposition here. Other distribution curves are variants of this one. For the benefit of readers unfamiliar with this mode of approach, let me first show how it works out for a small number—the baseball throws for distance by 303 first-year girls in a middle-western high school.[16]

A record was first made for throws of a ball by the 303 girls, as follows:

Distance in feet	Number of girls
15 but under 25	1
25 but under 35	2
35 but under 45	7
45 but under 55	25
55 but under 65	33
65 but under 75	53
75 but under 85	64
85 but under 95	44
95 but under 105	31
105 but under 115	27
115 but under 125	11
125 but under 135	4
135 but under 145	1
Total	303

Fitting these measurements under the probability curve, which is the Cartesian rendering of the complex algebraic equation, gives the following picture:

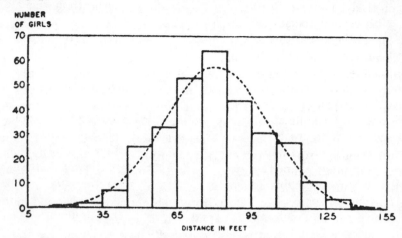

A variant of this same type of curve is given below, showing the kilowatt hours of electricity used per month in 282 medium-size homes in a certain city. It is called the logarithmic normal curve and shows a skewing toward maximum kilowatt usage by a minimum number of homes.

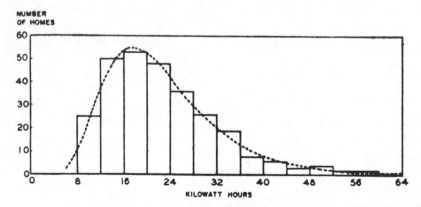

It will be noticed that the upper portion of each vertical rectangle in both diagrams, which in the first diagram represents in height the number of girls throwing each interval of distance, does not exactly fit the curve represented by dots. The failure to coincide represents the margin of error of probability in the sample, which comes about from its smallness. But if the sample were enlarged to take in a whole population, experience shows, it would pretty exactly fit under the curve. If in this case one were to record the throws for *all* high-school girls, they would be accommodated just about exactly under the curve, subject to certain minor reservations. The more cases one obtains, the more precisely does the distribution fit under the curve, from small to great, with certain special exceptions.

We know, then, that this sort of curve or recognizable variant thereof is applicable to definable characteristics of any large population. By keeping these curves in mind and co-relating them with common experience, we have considerable insight into any large population prior to direct investigation.

Relative physical, mental and characterological aspects of people—age, height, weight, shade of skin, color of eyes, intelligence, amiability—distribute in the same way, from a quantified minimum to a maximum, although for some characteristics the curve may be distorted though still definitely recognizable (skewness). In such cases the curve bulges or flattens out at some place but it always envelops the entire population, always has as much area under it and the same amount of area for each person included.

"The people", in short, are all equal in possessing bundles of characteristics, traits and natural dexterities, most of them of the same type, but the intensity or quantity of most of these characteristics and traits vary from person to person just as does the mixture of the ranges of characteristics.

The propensities of people to do certain things, whatever they are, also vary in a similar way. In the mass the range of variation is shown by a statistical curve of probability, which denotes what one would find under each of its points for each *separate* propensity if one could measure the whole population at first hand.

The probability curve tells us nothing about any specific individual. Again, those characteristics that are not quantifiable, such as character traits, can be placed within the whole only impressionistically and therefore non-scientifically. But we know from experience nevertheless that traits are spread in varying strength through the whole population; mathematics shows that their incidence must correspond more or less to one curve or the other. Relatively few bear the trait, whatever it is, at its strongest or weakest, whatever the trait may be.

Each person of course bears each trait in some degree in most cases. While some traits in some people are at a minimum to zero, others may be at a maximum. A brilliant scientist with a deformed body and an acerbic temperament would naturally place near the maximum end of the curve in intellectual powers but near the minimum in physique and amiability. In a test for acuity of vision some persons would be at zero because they are blind. And so on. Very few people, perhaps only a handful, would possess near the maximum a collection of the culturally most esteemed traits. How many? For this we may consult the normal curve again and see that it is a small number.

How exact is all this? When applied to measurable and quantifiable characteristics and natural skills, it is very exact, within certain ascertainable small margins of error. When applied to traits of temperament and character, it is bound to be far less exact in the absence of methods of quantification, but this general way of looking at such phenomena is surely more nearly exact than common assumption or guesswork. If people differ individual to individual as they do in physique and in physical ability, it requires no great stretch to conclude that they also differ among each other in similar degrees mentally, temperamentally and characterologically. And direct observation of individuals confirms this.

The Unpopularity of Voting

All of this applies to voting as well as other political behavior. If one considers the voting history of every person in relation to his opportunities for voting, one can conclude, merely by consulting one of the curves, that it comprehends individuals who have never voted, those who have voted infrequently, voted now and then, voted as the spirit moved them, voted only as some issue seemed important, and on to those who have voted at every opportunity.

Available empirical data support this prospect. In national elections in the United States in recent years only about 40 per cent (or less) of eligibles have voted. In 1896, however, when there was great excitement about William Jennings Bryan and "free silver", the vote of eligibles (only adult males, mainly white) rose to 41 per cent.[17] In congressional elections the voting turnout of smaller constituencies is much less, usually, than for the nation during the presidential elections. In a few states, though, it is higher.

One may safely conclude therefore that where voting is purely voluntary—in some countries legal penalties are imposed on non-voters—far from everybody is interested in voting to the same degree. And the historical data show that at the time the Constitution was adopted there was, as I have illustrated, an extremely small voting turnout. For which reason the grounding of government in the expressed "will of the people" is subject to considerable qualification—that is, if one is considering the whole people.

The fact is that not all people are really interested in government. Many don't understand it at all; some are incapable of understanding it; others, although capable, just don't want to bother themselves with it.

Government, quite spontaneously, is a minority affair from start to finish. Although repugnant to ideologists of democracy, this conclusion is quite evidently true.

The idea of the will of the people moreover is quite ambiguous. For under this idea whatever happens can be interpreted as expressing such a will. If only a small number vote, it can be said that those not voting were content to see the decision go whichever way it went. And if everybody votes and one side wins by a tiny margin, the decision can also be held to reflect the will of the people because they had presumably agreed to abide by any majority vote. Non-voting, as long as somebody votes, is as much acquiescence in the process as voting. For the process of determining government personnel takes place whether all or only a few vote.

Some Major Conclusions

By considering the population under the probability curve whenever there is an absence of precise statistics, one can come to certain other basic political conclusions, most notably with respect to the fundamental principles of political parties. All political parties have what they call a philosophy about the nature of people. Conservative parties, on the whole, look upon "the people" with considerable pessimism, some such parties going so far as to see most of them as depraved and unreliable, hence in need of constant stiff disciplining and supervision. Liberal parties, on the other hand, take an optimistic view, seeing "the people", individually and collectively, as basically good to wonderful and only at times appearing less than good simply because they have been antecedently misguided in an inequitably ordered society. The people, in this view, can be left to their own devices, possibly with some assistance, for the happiest outcome for all.

The permissive liberal, if hard-pressed by opponents of his view, will fall back to the position that all people are at least *potentially* constructive if originated and nurtured under the right conditions, which is irrelevant as well as systematically vague because the multiple conditions of right origination and nurture are so varied, so unknown and so out of control. What people's potentialities are in any endeavor themselves distribute according to the probability curve, from low to high; they differ in a wide spectrum. So the liberal is entirely wishful here.

The conditions of favorable origination and nurture in a widely permissive society are themselves subject to the laws of probability, with a minute fraction of 1 per cent to 25 per cent, more or less, subject to varyingly unfavorable conditions, another fraction of 1 per cent to

25 per cent (again more or less) subject to varyingly improved conditions, another 25 per cent or so to still more improved conditions and a final 25 per cent to varying highly favorable conditions. Pure chance and pure chance alone in every case determines for the individual the intensity of the favorable or unfavorable conditions, barring the direct impact of general calamities such as wars.

Both the liberal and the conservative views, with the probability curve in mind, have to be wrong, and in equal measure. Each however can be looked at alternatively as at least one quarter right. Each is looking only at people filling that portion of space under the curve of probability that suits its own temperamental predilections. Each in short is unconsciously biased, and badly. We see, then, that prevalent party politics, at its very philosophical base, is off to a wrong start, accounting for much more political error along the road.

Bisecting the curve perpendicularly at its midpoint of distribution is a line known statistically as the median. One can divide the space under the curve in many ways, provided one is always sure the area of each division is the same. In this manner the population can be divided into percentages of 1, 5, 10 or 25. If one divides it into percentages of 25, one finds that half of any population is always distributed equally athwart the median line, sort of an area of intermediacy or mediocrity.

As to the general moral orientation of any large populace—its state of goodness or depravity—we may here ponder a brief observation by the sagacious Hume: "Heaven and hell suppose two distinct species of men, the good and the bad; but the greatest part of mankind float betwixt vice and virtue. Were one to go around the world with an intention of giving a good supper to the righteous and a sound drubbing to the wicked, he would frequently be embarrassed in his choice, and would find the merits and demerits of most men and women scarcely amount to the value of either." [18]

For most people would be found in the middle 50 per cent and bordering it, neither notably good nor outstandingly wicked, just drifting along in a catch-as-catch-can way, ready to turn to account anything that might come up. The dispenser of suppers and drubbings would have to search more pertinaciously for those falling at the extreme ends of the probability curve.

But here an interesting observation may be made on the influence of good and evil in the world. If the highly virtuous and the very evil are about evenly balanced under the extreme ends of the curve, the world is at least in balance with respect to these two phenomena. However, evil (as is commonly known) is usually an active force for harm, dynamic, whereas virtue consists to a considerable degree in abstention from evil deeds, passivity at least with respect to proscribed actions. It is not difficult to visualize an aggressively evil person, doing great harm right and left, openly or covertly, but it is difficult to visualize an aggressively virtuous person, forcing his kindness or other good offices upon people right and left. One sees here why evil plays such a large role in history, with virtue continually coming upon the scene very much as an after-thought, wringing its hands in dismay.

At the time the Constitution was written the Federalist leadership believed there was superior public virtue to be found among "the rich, the well born and the able", a phrase that was to be used tauntingly against them with the rise of the Jeffersonian Republican-Democrats. John Adams first gave approving currency to this formulation. He believed when he wrote that nature had impersonally decreed patricians and plebeians, upper and lower classes, superiors and inferiors, gentlemen and simplemen, although he later qualified this view.[19] The first in each coupling, in this view, are socially, culturally and politically most worthy. Adams was basically a conservative, but Hamilton, also conservative, fully embraced the idea of the superiority of the rich and well-born and never gave it up.

Here was a rough and still familiar way of singling out political and social high quality, but it was wholly wrongheaded because character traits as they distribute under the probability curve do not distribute according to social classes, which are denoted by altogether different characteristics. In other words, what is socially "high class" does not place anyone in the maximum range of culturally and morally preferred traits.

Empirically this is made clear by noting hundreds, even thousands, of the rich, well-born and thoroughly schooled who are not able and who in fact fall into the minimum category for the culturally preferred traits. Many, in short, are widely condemned as negative behavioral deviants—scamps and blackguards. High intelligence, talent, genius and outstanding good character are not noticeably associated with the upper socio-economic class, a small and conspicuous group, although such characteristics are by no means entirely absent. But demonstrated avarice and conscientious self-indulgence, conspicuous marks of this class down through history, are not anywhere considered laudable traits. The class as a whole here falls below mediocrity on any systematic scale of moral evaluation.

Also quite wrong is a widespread self-complacent popular view that everybody is a pretty even mixture of good and bad, esteemed and deplored characteristics. While it is true that some people, at least half and a bit more, are pretty evenly so mixed, as the probability curve itself indicates, it is also true according to that same curve that some people, relatively few, are a fairly unalloyed mixture of the most esteemed characteristics—physical, intellectual and characterological—while a balancing few are a varying mixture of the most deplored or condemned characteristics. Some relatively few persons, in other words, are commendable on almost every count (the man who has everything) while a relatively few are condemned through a wide range of characteristics—villains all the way.

The last would be denied by many self-styled liberals, who are really sentimentalists and quite confused in their thinking. That people in general are not so entrancing, actually and potentially, as such liberals claim is shown by their own denunciation of large groups as intolerably bestial: the adherents of Adolf Hitler, the Turks who massacred Armenians, the multitude of racists, the torturers in various dictatorships, the rank-and-file devotees in the United States of the Ku Klux Klan, corporate predators, the stars of organized crime, and so on. That such are wicked through ignorance or insensitivity or because of external influences is a contention that is merely irrelevant. Villainy is villainy for whatever reason. It is something that does demonstrable intentional harm.

The politician who apostrophizes the people is also as far out of focus, is alluding to a very kaleidoscopic quantity. For the people are as varied as their fingerprints. It follows too that the people, in their totality, can really be authority for very little because they see, experience and interpret the world as differently as in the distribution of any other characteristic.

What the politician can do, and does, however, is to depend upon majorities of participants in a process of making choices. There is nothing inherently virtuous about such participants. As to the crude choices made, non-participants have nothing to say, either voluntarily or, where impediments are placed in their way, involuntarily.

In the appeal of the politician to the masses, it is relevant to wonder just how credulous the people are. With the probability curve in mind, we have a pretty good idea that 25 per cent or so must be very credulous in varying degrees, another approximate 25 per cent more inclined to be credulous than not, still another 25 per cent less credulous and inclined to be somewhat skeptical and only something like 25 per cent quite incredulous to skeptical. The skeptics of the world with respect to any prevailing belief are relatively few. We see, then, that the politician, like merchandisers, and purveyors of supernatural doctrines and miraculous cures, always has a large reservoir of potential ready believers available to him. P. T. Barnum understated it when he said there was a sucker born every minute.

That there is no great and general enthusiasm for voting is shown perhaps most dramatically in the United States by the great and expensive lengths to which political parties go in order to "bring out the vote". Millions upon millions of dollars are spent again and again in American elections, sometimes for the purpose of buying votes, sometimes for influencing leaders of large groups to endorse a candidate, and in general for vast advertising ballyhoo via billboards, posters, speech writers and political hustlers, newspaper ads and radio and television programs. To these are added endless exhortations of political mentors to vote and alarmist cries of political partisans that doomsday is at hand, that all must vote. Still, the slightest touch of rain or other weather disturbance is enough to keep large numbers away from the polls. Other large numbers stay away in droves out of habit.

The relevance of all this to the Constitution is:

1. The opening words of the document are distinctly misleading if they are taken to indicate that the entire populace or the white male populace was instrumental in its enactment.

2. Even if all eligibles had participated in the ratification process, there would, in view of the intellectual and characterological disparities in such a large number of people, be no assurance of anything different or better about the situation. The issue was simply one between the Constitution as already written and the Articles of Confederation, the latter no document of deliverance. It was a case of a limited choice.

The phrase "We the people", in other words, neither adds anything to nor detracts anything from the document. It is strictly window-dressing, of no particular significance. It is a politically skillful mythic touch for a document one of whose main functions is to serve both as a screen and a launching pad for practically autonomous, freely improvising politicians—as autonomous as any governmental group in the world. These are the gentry who are sustained in their operations, whatever they are, by the constitutional structure.

In any event, there was no great enthusiasm shown for the Constitution on the part of the active founding populace, and at least 37.5 per cent of that populace was vehemently and pointedly opposed to it— this despite the fact that much later, when propaganda had reached a much higher pitch, it was to be characterized for self-serving reasons to much applause as the greatest document ever struck off by the hand of man. Claims have even been made, and quite seriously, that God guided that hand if he did not do the actual dictating behind the scenes.

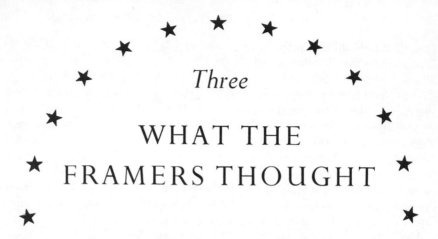

Three

WHAT THE
FRAMERS THOUGHT

The framers of the United States Constitution and leading pro-government contemporaries, contrary to common report, were far from happy about their creation, either at its inception or as it later worked out over the years. They would have been astounded if they had heard anyone predict it would some day be hailed as a masterpiece for the ages. Such a depiction was to originate considerably later with, as it happened, Yankee Doodle boasters emerging after the Civil War. The framers in fact were extremely dubious to negative and in general pretty gloomy about the system they had produced. And with good reason.

All of this, to be sure, is at diametric variance with just about what every commentator, interpreter and historian of the subject sets forth in cold print. And it is just the opposite consequently of what most literate Americans believe to the marrow of their bones and to the tips of their toes.

Even Prof. Corwin, whose extensive writings on the Constitution are among some of the few that may usually be relied upon for contextual justness and nice perception, fell into the error of writing that the framers believed they had produced a superb plan of government. The usually exact Corwin alludes for example to "the view of the Constitution whereby Americans themselves for generations explained their worship of it—*a view which the Framers themselves shared*" (emphasis added).[1]

The framers had no such worshipful attitude whatever; Corwin here is astonishingly wrong. And the simple evidence of their private remarks stands solidly in the way of any warrantable belief that they were votaries of the document. Some framers could barely tolerate it, even though they signed it, perhaps in some cases with a secret shudder.

But in this detail, as in so many others about the American Constitution, evidence is usually sacrificed to cloud-cuckooland wishfulness and afflatus of the most extravagant kind. The common report bears little relation to the reality. A rarity among historians is H. C. Hockett who in his constitutional history acknowledges all too briefly that the leaders of the convention of 1787 who produced the original Constitution were "conscious rather of its defects than its merits . . ." [2] As experienced political managers they knew it was as full of holes as the proverbial sieve although most of them also felt they could live with it for the time being. All, one may well believe, kept their fingers crossed.

The general word bruited about the United States for more than a century now is that the system of 1787 is an extraordinarily superlative affair, a governmental mechanism beyond price and a Rock of Ages in a wicked, wicked world, subject to examination only with bated breath and after one has thoroughly doused oneself with holy water. Consequently, a fairly detailed examination of what the framers themselves thought to the contrary seems very much in point before proceeding, lest the thoroughly indoctrinated American reader's sense of credibility be abruptly over-strained. While people who produce a masterpiece are not always aware of the heights they have attained, it is both very rare, and extremely odd, ever to find any such folk disparaging, especially in private, what they believe to be a reasonably worthy piece of work. It just isn't done, ever.

What the framers privately thought is beyond all else interesting as the simple truth in an area of affairs where the truth is seldom proclaimed, is indeed very much of a luxury. It is the area of political myth. A candid examination of the framers' thoughts furthermore tends to suggest that one is not wholly out of tune with the true American spirit, despite bulldozing politicians and award-seeking professors, if one entertains reservations about the ultra-excellence of various immoderately extolled constitutional features.

If, in other words, one has doubts about various constitutional features, one is in a state of mind similar to that of just about all the framers, including all the most active ones. If, on the other hand, one believes the Constitution to be a marvelous instrumentality, beyond criticism, a pearl beyond price, one is completely out of tune with the sacred progenitors and right in tune with a long procession of thoroughly dubious, often corrupt politicos and their literary flacks and boobish dupes.

The main reason many distinterested inquirers leap to the unwarranted conclusion that the framers were inordinately pleased with their handiwork is that these stalwarts of 1787—except for those who disapproved publicly as well as privately—argued strenuously and eloquently in public for the adoption of the proposed new national system. They so argued because they thought, as they admitted, that what they had managed to put together was the best possible necessary structure the temper of the times allowed, even though privately, off the public record, they thought it defective in all too many ways.

On this point the evidence is crystal clear, startlingly at variance with what one is usually told and what nearly everyone in the United States believes. Privately many of the framers and signers, and important ones to boot, regarded the whole affair as a mess. Some of the leading ones thought this with increasing intensity to their dying days many years later. Each year brought to at least some of them new proof, to their way of thinking, that the Constitution was far from suitable, far from being an excellent mechanism.

There was no belief on the part of anyone of consequence at all in 1787 and 1788, as far as any record shows, that a major masterpiece or even semi-masterpiece of government had been produced. Nor had it been the objective, open or hidden, to produce one. To suggest even by implication that it was is in itself distinctly misleading. All the framers, whatever else one may say about them, were normally sensible men of the world, some of them very intelligent, and not given to baseless enthusiasms or fantasies. Feet pretty much on the ground, they had realistically limited, reasonably attainable aims. Not a single one gave any evidence of a belief that Utopia was being established, could be established, or should be established. Not a single one suggested that a sheltered haven was being prepared for the innumerable heavily laden, bedraggled, scrofulous and oppressed of the earth. All this sort of thing was to come much later in the form of sentimental crowd-titillating campaign oratory.

The Constitutional Struggle

In public the leading elements in the framing had to argue with great pertinacity and care for the new Constitution. They had some very determined and by no means shallow opponents who had weighty objections to make known. And whose American pedigrees extended as far back as, or farther back than, that of many of the framers. It was long the fashion for propagandist-historians to disparage these opponents as featherbrains or worse; as a matter of fact they numbered as many persons of intelligence, good character, standing and substance among them as the proponents.

In the end a good many opponents were more or less doubtfully won over to accepting the new Constitution by the agreement to tack on to it the first ten amendments, the so-called Bill of Rights (which the constitutional convention had pointedly excluded). This late concession had the effect of appeasing agitated elements in many states, especially with the vaguely worded Ninth and Tenth Amendments of doubtful purport.

Later, much later, elements from both sides took to extolling the document as a matter of ritualistic form for the benefit of the hayseed yeomanry, at the same time introducing their own self-serving interpretations, variations, cadenzas and fugues. It was to be more than fifty years, approaching the eve of its total collapse in the Civil War, before the Constitution was to begin being generally vaunted as having about it rare magical qualities of inestimable benefit to all who were lucky enough to be Americans.

The dominant elements in calling together the convention of 1787 and framing the constitutional document were what historians have generally styled nationalists. They were, more precisely, centralizers who were continental and global in their thinking.

What opposition there was at the time and developed later consisted of localists (later called states'-righters) who were more provincial and parochial in their horizons although emotionally they were as nationalistic as anyone. Such claimed to believe in the natural superiority of decentralized government, mainly (as they said) because it was closer to the salt of the earth and supposed object of government, the sweaty tillers of the soil with their on-the-spot natural intuition and supposed innate moral purity. Such claimants, naturally, in time snared the majority of the yeomanry, north and south, on the zigzag road to Appomattox. Until the Civil War most people, north and south, identified themselves with their states. Union regiments of the line in the Civil War were always state regiments, so named.

The chief thrust of governmental power, the centralizers believed (along with most of the world then and later), should come from a single center, a national capital. Such a center, they believed, should be dominated by people who had shown superior capability by being able to attain or retain higher than usual personal stations in life—that is, among other things, they had more money, more potent connections and probably more talent, opportunity and self-discipline. As John Adams put it in the preface to his *Defense of the Constitutions of Government of the United States*, a pre-convention work on the state constitutions, there is a special leading role in government to be played by "the rich, the well born, and the able". This popularly impolitic but partly true remark—especially as to the able—earned him the opprobrium of levellers, democrats and sentimentalists down through the years. The idea, though, was shared by just about every one of the framers and has been pointedly exemplified throughout American history. Skid Row and Tobacco Road have never had, despite the wails of believers in rule from the nether depths, a role to play in American government. Main Street has played a steadily diminishing role.

Government power, the anti-centralists professed to believe (and most strongly after the centralizers took over the new government), should be diffused among the various inherently virtuous states—that is, among the local politicos and padrones. Virtue for them was always to be found near home, evil in distant gilded places—a notion truistic to rustics and backwoodsmen.

Land of Liberty

Libertarian sentiments verging on anarchism flourished naturally on American soil, far from the despots of over-crowded Europe. Americans, both as English colonists and as seceders from the Empire, had long been accustomed to the greatest possible freedom from government restraint short of no government at all. Anyone not a slave anywhere along the Atlantic seaboard who found conditions even slightly irksome at any time enjoyed the local option, widely used to the constant annoyance of employers, of simply moving off to settle elsewhere. Both before and after independence the coastal regions were dismayed about the situation and tried to stop the steady bleeding away to the west of labor supply. Permissiveness consequently reigned to a noticeable degree, especially along the virtually endless frontiers, and the rhetorically fearsome British lion and successor American eagle were seldom more than symbolically present.

White Americans of the day, in point of fact, did not take well to government of any sort, English or on-the-spot American, good or bad. As outlanders, to a considerable extent bush-rangers, and most of them south of New England transported convicts, shanghaied vagrants and indentured servants from overseas, they were politically balky, cranky and touchy. These traits showed in the general preference, north and south, for diffusionist hands-off doctrines up until the Civil War or even afterward. As Tom Paine tersely put it, the least government is the best government.

Many historians portray the convention nationalists or centralizers, adroitly self-styled as Federalists although they were the very opposite, as extreme conservatives, aristocrats and abnormally property-minded. By contrast they see the early states'-righters, with equal adroitness self-styled as Republicans, as more democratic and popularly oriented, more concerned with so-called personal rights than with property rights. Neither party however was the least bit populistic or even unusually libertarian, and certainly not the slave-owning Jeffersonian Republicans. But these managed their rhetoric far more skillfully in harmony with agrarian grass-roots prejudices and expectations even though they were every bit as pro-property and even, in the crunch, as anti-libertarian as the Federalists.

There was no anti-property party on the scene and in fact no discernible anti-property sentiment high or low. The most voluble civil libertarians, such as George Mason and Jefferson, were large slave-owners, a touch of asymmetry for doctrinaires to ponder. The Jeffersonians however became less and less localistic and more partial to centralized government and heavy-handed repressiveness as they snared national office in 1800. But their electoral purely-for-the-occasion states'-rights doctrines of the 1790s lingered on in mothballs, a doubtful curiosity until they were distinterred between 1830 and 1840 by John S. Calhoun and polished up in the service of a now booming slavocracy.

It was these doctrines and their constitutional negations that sharpened into the ferocious Civil War, a bloody blot on the national record and a heavy count against the Constitution as it stood up to that time. But bloody blot though the Civil War was, it has been given highly profitable cosmetic treatment both by historians and Hollywood scenarists so that it is usually presented as an edifying exhibition, a clash between two nobly inspired crusading armies, the Blue and the Gray. As such it fits into what high-royalty historians variously style the tapestry, the procession, the panorama or the mosaic of American History—treacle all the way.

In this approach historical event is viewed as a diverting spectacle rather than as a blundering often stupid process to be distentangled by survivors. The Civil War in fact was the outcome of more than fifty years of intrigue and counter-intrigue among politicians for constitutionally designated offices of honor and profit and lush fringe benefits flowing therefrom. Like all the American wars it was strictly a politicians' war.

The states'-rights notions which had been knocking around since first trotted out in the 1790s by Jefferson and Madison incidentally showed their inherent weakness to full view when put to the test under the Confederate Constitution. As a governmental system they there exposed themselves as automatically self-destructive, pure Jeffersonian moonshine.

The struggle that developed in Washington's second term between Hamiltonian Federalists and Jeffersonian Republicans was strictly one for the reins of office and the monetary benefits of power-holding. No special philosophy or unusual principle was ever at stake, and certainly none on the side of the breast-beating Jeffersonians. As is usual in American politics, most of the formal issues were contrived by the opposition in order to permit the making of glittering debating points, thus bemusing the rustics and snaring their votes. In this game the Jeffersonians were far more adept than the verbally maladroit Federalists.

In order to avoid later confusion in this account about what politicians and professors allude to as American Democracy, it should be noted here that the United States has never had a rank-and-file party other than the pre-Civil War Republican Party of Lincoln and the short-lived Populist Party of the 1880s. And populism never got a genuine foothold in the offices. The major parties, beginning with the Federalists and Jefferson's Republicans and continuing with the Jacksonian Democrats and the Whig Party, and including the post-Civil War Democratic and Republican Parties, have always been Establishment or upper-crust affairs, managed by politicians mainly for sections of the upper crust— business, upper professional, speculative, heavily propertied, corporate and office-holding elements. To suggest anything else even for a split second in view of the readily available facts would be simple nonsense. No undue reflection upon the extant parties is intended by this observation, only a depiction of realities befogged by the ever-present campaign oratory about the marvelous vote-endowed common people.

The rank and file in the United States, for all the professorial vaporing about democracy in echo of the office-holders, has never developed an operative party expressive of its manifold blurred interests, has never indeed even seriously attempted to develop one. No doubt there are many reasons for the mass political ineptitude, but one is certainly that the American rank and file is of such a divergent, essentially lower-class and sub-cultural ethnic, geo-genetic, religious and ideological mixture. In self-estimation this rank and file, mainly composed of easily manipulable elements, as the continuous success of slippery advertisers and up-from-nowhere political juntas show, often still sees itself as a collection of fortunate refugees from European and other world disaster areas. Its members are glad to be ensconced on the lush American plantation, even if excluded from some of its more recondite boons. Continually bamboozled, indeed yearning to be bamboozled, it is always politically demoralized and confused. Despite a profusion of schools and libraries, it is essentially quite gullible.

George Washington and Doubts of the Framers

Everybody high and low who has delved into the question has concluded, and for what seem weighty reasons, that but for the presence
and insistence of George Washington there would have been no constitutional document of 1787. Nor, without his approval, would the country
at the time have accepted any constitutional arrangement whatever to
supersede the Articles of Confederation. As far as the record shows,
Washington had no pet constitutional ideas to contribute, but what he
did want was an end to numerous and growing intolerable situations
that had developed under the Articles, especially the drift toward disunion. As Washington had given a large chunk of his life to leading the
bedraggled Continental Army in the quest for national independence,
he naturally had no desire to see the newly won country fall apart
under the strains of peace, as most of Europe fully expected it to do.

Yet, satisfied up to a point, perhaps more satisfied than most, Washington was by no means carried away by what had been wrought by
the convention. This was clearly shown in a letter dated October 8,
1788, that he wrote to Edmund Randolph, a member of the constitutional
convention and governor of Virginia—an insider. At the time there was
a blizzard of proposals before the country for amendments to the Philadelphia document.

". . . had I entertained a latent hope (at the time you moved to
have the Constitution submitted to a second Convention) that a more
perfect form would be agreed to," Washington wrote, "—in a word that
any [sic!] Constitution would be adopted under the impressions and
Instructions of the members, the publications which have taken place
since would have eradicated every form of it . . ." Washington, in consequence, deplored the movement to attach amendments. "To my
judgment, it is more clear than ever, that an attempt to amend the
Constitution which is submitted, would be productive of more heat &
greater confusion than can well be conceived. There are somethings
in the new form, I will readily acknowledge, wch. never did, and I am
persuaded never will, obtain my *cordial* approbation; but I then did
conceive, and now do most firmly believe, that, in the aggregate, it is
the best Constitution that can be obtained at this Epocha; and that
this, or a dissolution of the Union awaits our choice, & are the only
alternatives before us—Thus believing, I had not, nor have I now any
hesitation in deciding on which to lean." [3]

Here was the very top dog of the Philadelphia accouchement writing
in terms of considerable dubiety to another top dog, one who as a
member of the Philadelphia convention had refused with others to sign
the Constitution although he was finally won over at the Virginia

ratifying convention to give it an eleventh-hour blessing. But Randolph did this, suspicious historians have concluded, not through any sudden intellectual or patriotic conversion but in response to the promise of substantial political preferment under the new government, of which he became the first Attorney General and the second Secretary of State.

Washington in what he wrote to Randolph put his finger on the single reason for accepting the Constitution, *whatever its form*. It would prevent disunion and much confusion. Public discussion prior to the constitutional convention had already visualized at least three central governments in the former colonies: one consisting of the New England states, the other of the middle Atlantic states of New York, New Jersey, Pennsylvania, Delaware and possibly Maryland, and a southern government over Virginia, North Carolina, South Carolina and Georgia.

Not only would these entities, and possibly another on the western frontiers, bicker and war with each other but they would enter into rivalrous unilateral agreements with England, France and Spain, all long-entrenched in extensive North American territories. In this restricted but nevertheless politically vital aim of averting disastrous disunion, of preventing the European foxes from entering the American chicken-coop and adding to troubles, the Constitution was from the start dazzlingly successful, a distinct plus. It produced at a stroke what amounted to an American united front against ever-encroaching Europe, which was even then spreading its tentacles all over the earth for all to see.

But the Constitution was not privately regarded by its own experts at the time, as was later to be widely asserted, as a panacea that would liberate mankind from its follies or even the American people from all the ills, or even the major ills, related to government. The Constitution, in brief, did not solve or come as near as Britain did after 1832 to solving what political philosophers call the problem of government. Nor did any of its signers ever so much as hint they believed it did. They just weren't that idiotic.

For public consumption and to persons not among the constitutional insiders Washington had more reassuring things to say. But whatever the nature of his always reserved endorsement, it was always far from ecstatic, never in the tones of the latter-day constitutional cultists. Washington just wasn't deliriously entranced by the Constitution as a total structure.

Alexander Hamilton

As to Alexander Hamilton, Washington's wartime aide-de-camp, his first Secretary of the Treasury, and in the new government the acknowledged leader of the Federalists, Madison reported that "No man's ideas were more remote from the [constitutional] plan than his own were known to be; but is it possible [Hamilton believed in opting to sign it] to deliberate between anarchy and convulsion on one side, and the chance of good to be expected from the plan on the other [?]" [4]

"General Hamilton had little share in forming the Constitution," wrote Gouverneur Morris, a leading light of the Philadelphia convention who was entrusted with the task of burnishing the document into its final often cryptic literary form. "He disliked it, believing all Republican government to be radically defective . . ." [5]

As early as 1802, after more than a dozen years of government under the Constitution, Hamilton wrote to Morris that the Constitution is "a shilly shally thing of mere milk and water" and "a frail and worthless fabric".[6] Worthless? In saying so this pet of Washington's and high-flying Federalist figure certainly went much further in constitutional disparagement than anyone at all of official eminence has ever since ventured. Even Bolsheviks and socialists say nothing so depreciatory.

Yet Hamilton, free-wheeling politician and itchily ambitious lawyer that he was, despite his feelings of deep discontent about the Constitution from the beginning and despite his later petulance, was in high historical irony to stand forth as its most articulate and passionate champion in the ratification process and the sole—and unauthorized—signer for New York. Hamilton, more extreme than other signers in the contrast between his public approval and his private doubts, certainly signed with his fingers tightly crossed.

What he wrote on behalf of the Constitution in *The Federalist*, later palmed off by imaginative professors on the gullible as high political philosophy, was largely on the order of sedate campaign oratory or a series of lawyer's briefs. He could have written just as well, or better, to opposite effect, and with far more relish. Moreover, what he opportunistically wrote as off-the-cuff early constitutional interpretation by way of reassuring reluctant states'-righters laid an authoritative doctrinal foundation for later squabbles and blood-baths about the standing of the states under the Constitution. And, what is rarely noted, especially by American commentators, he was often wrong in his analyses of how the new system would work. Anyone who reads *The Federalist*, as students are often instructed to do, with a view to learning how the American governmental system operates is being led so far astray as to be lost forever to reality. Yet this is one of the main sources of some of the more literate Americans on the way their government operates today or, more precisely, on the inner spirit of that government.

Benjamin Franklin

Writing to a French friend in April 1788, Franklin, the second-most prominent signer of the Constitution, said, "I am of Opinion with You, that the *two* Chambers [of Congress] were not necessary, and I disliked some other Articles that are in, and wish'd for some that are not in the propos'd Plan:—I nevertheless hope it may be adopted, though I shall have nothing to do with the execution of it . . ." [7]

More on Franklin's constitutional position will appear later although his objection to two houses of Congress was certainly a fundamental one.

James Madison

Madison, often fantastically miscalled "The Father of the Constitution" (a designation he himself pointedly repudiated), more than a year after its signing wrote to one correspondent: "I am not of the number if there be any such, who think the Constitution lately adopted a fault-less work. On the contrary there are amendments wch I wisht to have received before it issued from the place in which it was formed . . . Having witnessed the difficulties and dangers experienced by the first Convention, which assembled under every propitious circumstance, I should tremble for the result of a Second, meeting in the present temper of America and under all the disadvantages I have mentioned." [8]

A few weeks earlier Madison wrote apologetically to another corre-spondent that the Constitution is "the best that could be obtained from the jarring interests of the States, and the miscellaneous opinions of Politicians; and because experience has proved the real danger to America & liberty lies in the defect of *energy & stability* in the present establishment of the United States." [9] In brief, something, anything, was better than nothing.

So it was not merely the feeble general government under Constitu-tion I, the Articles of Confederation, that gave offense to the framers of Constitution II, but also the governments of the states, "the present establishments". It was in the states, collectively and singly, that the worst troubles lay. And almost anything, even the most fastidious framers felt, was better than a continuance in full authority of the diverging, provincial catch-as-catch-can regimes. However, much of what was being perpetrated in the states was much later to be repeated on a larger scale in the national government.

Madison, indeed, the putative constitutional sire, writing in con-fidence to Thomas Jefferson in distant Paris on September 6, 1787, the Philadelphia convention now nearing an end after more than four months of wrangling, was even more negative than any of this about the completed project. And even though not the father, the very young Madison was unquestionably one of the leading constitutional obstetricians, adept in the already long-standing ways of American government. After briefly sketching the structure of the proposed new government, he wrote pessimistically (and realistically) to Jefferson in distant Paris:

"These are the *outlines.* The extent of them may perhaps surprise you. I hazard an opinion nevertheless that the *plan, should* it *be adopted,* will neither effectually *answer* its *national object,* not [nor?] prevent the local *mischiefs* which everywhere *excite disgusts* agst. the *State Governments.* The grounds of this opinion will be the subject of a future letter . . ." [10]

As this is Madison talking, agreed upon by all hands as at least one of the big technical wheels in the formulation of the Constitution, one may be pardoned for quoting him at some length. For what he has to say comes straight from the feed-box, with no oratorical flourishes for the booboisie. What I have just quoted were indeed prophetic words, both with respect to the national government and the states, and does much to establish Madison as a clairvoyant political seer.

Madison made his fuller report to Jefferson on October 24, 1787. Describing the new system of government, he centered his forebodings in the following passages:

> In the American Constitution the general authority will be derived entirely from the subordinate authorities. The Senate will represent the States in their political capacity; the other House will represent the people of the States in their individual capacity. The former will be accountable to their constituents at moderate, the latter at short periods. The President also derives his appointment from the States, and is periodically accountable to them. This dependence of the General on the local authorities, seems effectually to guard the latter against any dangerous encroachments of the former; whilst the latter, within their respective limits, will be continually sensible of the abridgement of their power, *and be stimulated by ambition to resume the surrendered portion of it* [emphasis added]. We find the representatives of Counties and Corporations in the Legislatures of the States, much more disposed to sacrifice the aggregate interest, and even authority, to the local views of their constituents, than the latter to the former. I mean not by these remarks to insinuate that an esprit de corps will not exist in the National Government or that opportunities may not occur of extending its jurisdiction in some points. I mean only that the danger of encroachments is much greater from the other side [sic], and that the impossibility of dividing powers of legislation, in such a manner, as to be free from different constructions by different interests,

or even from ambiguity in the judgment of the impartial, requires some such expedient as I contend for . . . [judicial concurrence in legislation to avoid having it later declared invalid]. It may be said that the Judicial authority, under our new system will keep the States within their proper limits, and supply the place of a negative on their laws. The answer is, that it is more convenient to prevent the passage of a law than to declare it void after it is passed; that this will be particularly the case, where the law aggrieves individuals, who may be unable to support an appeal agst. a State to the supreme Judiciary; that a State which would violate the Legislative rights of the Union, would not be very ready to obey a Judicial decree in support of them, and that a recurrence to force, which, in the event of disobedience would be necessary, is an evil which the new Constitution meant [but failed] to exclude as far as possible . . . [sic!].

The remaining object created more embarrassment, and a greater alarm for the issue of the Convention than all the rest put together. The little States insisted on retaining their equality in both branches, unless a compleat abolition of the State Governments should take place; and made an equality in the Senate a sine qua non. The large States on the other hand urged that as the new Government was to be drawn principally from the people immediately and was to operate directly on them, not on the States; and consequently as the States wd. lose that importance which is now proportioned to the importance of their voluntary compliances with the requisitions of Congress, it was necessary that the representation in both Houses should be in proportion to their size. It ended in the compromise which you will see, but very much to the dissatisfaction [sic] of several members from the large States.[11]

So much, here, for Madison's justly skeptical views.

But Madison was to go much further than this in disaffection. For in a short time he completely repudiated the position he had taken at the constitutional convention and joined himself, with Jefferson, to the views of the states'-righters and anti-Federalists. Madison at the convention had been an ardent centralizer, but in the ten years following the convention, heeding his constituents, he reversed himself by 180 degrees, linked himself with those who sought to recapture the surrendered state power.

In 1798 the Virginia legislature passed what became known as the Virginia Resolutions. They were written by Madison. Kentucky in the same year passed the Kentucky Resolutions, followed by another set in 1799. Both were drafted by Jefferson. Each state in its resolutions held that the Constitution was a compact of the states, which was vociferously denied by the Federalists, who held that it came directly from "the people" as a whole. The resolutions were aimed specifically at the repressive Alien and Sedition Acts. And if it was only a compact among the states, it was terminable at state option, a notion the Confederacy was later to act upon.

The Kentucky Resolutions held that when the national government exercised powers not expressly delegated to it, each state "has an equal right to judge for itself, as well of infractions as of the mode and measure of redress". The Virginia Resolutions held that in cases where undelegated powers were exercised the states "have the right and are in duty bound to interpose for arresting the progress of the evil". Here was the potent and authoritative seed of the later Calhoun doctrine of state "interposition", dredged up most recently by Governor George Wallace of Alabama.

Down through the years furthermore Madison was to express himself against the way the Supreme Court functioned to limit the actions of the states. He did not, as I have shown, at all like the role assigned to the Supreme Court in general by the Constitution.

Madison, in brief, most of his life found himself in disagreement with the way the document he had helped write was used and in fact reversed himself on the way he thought the central government should function. If he was right later, he was wrong at the convention. And if he was right at the convention, he was wrong later. In any event, he did not concur with the application of the Constitution he had helped write, and had signed, and was presumably dissatisfied with it. Madison was very far from being a constitutional cultist.

Nicholas Gilman

Nicholas Gilman, one of two signers for New Hampshire, writing to Joseph Gilman under date of September 18, 1787, referred to the finished plan as "the best that could meet the unanimous concurrence of the States in Convention; it was done by bargain and Compromise, yet notwithstanding its imperfections [sic], on the adoption of it depends (in my feeble judgment) whether we shall become a respectable nation, or a people torn to pieces by intestine commotions, and rendered contemptible for ages." [12] Here was another qualified approval.

William Pierce

A non-signing delegate from Georgia, William Pierce, in a letter to St. George Tucker late in September 1787 said:

> You will probably be surprised at not finding my name affixed to
> it [the Constitution], and will, no doubt, be desirous of having a
> reason for it. Know then, Sir, that I was absent in New York on a piece

of business so necessary that it became unavoidable. I approve of its principles, and would have signed it with all my heart, had I been present. To say, however, that I consider it perfect, would be to make an acknowledgement immediately opposed to my judgment [sic]. Perhaps it is the only one that will suit our present situation. The wisdom of the Convention was equal to something greater [sic]; but a variety of local circumstances, the inequality of states, and the dissonant interests of the different parts of the Union, made it impossible to give it any other shape or form.[13]

Pierce Butler

Pierce Butler, a signer from South Carolina, in October 1787 wrote: [14]

We, in many instances took the Constitution of Britain, when in its purity, for a model, and surely We cou'd not have a better. We tried to avoid what appeared to Us the weak parts of Antient as well as Modern Republicks. How well We have succeeded is left for You and other Letterd Men to determine . . . In passing judgment on it you must call to mind we had Clashing Interests to reconcile—some strong prejudices to encounter, for the same spirit that brought settlers to a certain Quarter of this Country is still alive in it. View the system then as resulting from a spirit of Accomodation to different Interests [sic], and not the most perfect one that the Deputies cou'd devise for a Country better adapted for the reception of it than America is at this day, or perhaps ever will be [sic]. It is a great Extent of Territory to be under One free Government; the manners and modes of thinking of the Inhabitants, differing nearly as much as in different Nations of Europe. If we can secure tranquillity at Home, and respect from abroad, they will be great points gain'd.

Butler, in other words, asked but little.

Robert Morris

Robert Morris, signer from Pennsylvania and wartime Superintendent of Finance under the Articles of Confederation, writing to a friend about the just completed Constitution, said,[15]

This paper has been the subject of infinite investigation, disputation, and declamation. While some have boasted it as a work from Heaven, others have given it a less righteous origin. I have many reasons to believe that it is the work of plain, honest men, and such, I think it will appear. Faulty it must be, for what is perfect? But if adopted, experience will, I believe, show that its faults are just the reverse of what they are supposed to be . . .

Gouverneur Morris

"Those, who formed our Constitution, were not blind to its defects," said Gouverneur Morris in 1811 over a perspective of more than two decades; a New Yorker, he sat and signed with the Pennsylvania delegation and was one of the very influential convention characters.

> They believed a monarchial form to be neither solid nor durable. They conceived it to be vigorous or feeble, active or slothful, wise or foolish, mild or cruel, just or unjust, according to the personal character of the Prince . . .
>
> Fond, however, as the framers of our national Constitution were of Republican government, they were not so much blinded by their attachment, as not to discern the difficulty, perhaps impracticability, of raising a durable edifice from crumbling materials. History, the parent of political science, had told them, that it was almost as vain to expect permanency from democracy, as to construct a palace on the surface of the sea.
>
> But it would have been foolish to fold their arms, and sink into despondency, because they could neither form nor establish the best of all possible systems [sic]. They tell us in their President's letter of the seventeenth of September, 1787; 'The Constitution, which we now present, is the result of a spirit of amity, and of that mutual deference and concession, which the peculiarity of our political situation rendered indispensable.' It is not easy to be wise for all times; not even for the present, much less for the future; and those, who judge of the past, must recollect that when it was present, the present was the future . . .[16]

Writing to W. H. Wells in 1815, Morris said: [17]

> Shortly after the Convention met, there was a serious discussion on the importance of arranging a national system of sufficient strength to operate, in despite of State opposition, and yet not strong enough to break down State authority. I delivered on that occasion this short speech. "Mr. President; if the rod of Aaron do not swallow the rods of the Magicians, the rods of the Magicians will swallow the rod of Aaron."

Morris, in other words, believed in tighter centralization, less emphasis on state autonomy.

> You will ask, perhaps, how, under such impressions, I could be an advocate of the Federal Constitution. To this I answer, first, that I was warmly pressed by Hamilton to assist in writing the Federalist, which I declined. Secondly, that nothing human can be perfect. Thirdly, that the obstacles to a less imperfect system [sic] were insurmountable. Fourthly, that the Old Confederation was worse.

And, fifthly, that there was no reason, at that time, to suppose our public morals would be so soon and so entirely corrupted . . . Surrounded by difficulties, we did the best we could; leaving it with those who should come after us to take counsel from experience, and exercise prudently the power of amendment, which we had provided.

Gouverneur Morris, one of the four principal activists at the convention of 1787, at this later period was loudly calling for the scrapping of the Constitution and the secession of New York and New England from the sacred Union! His sentiment appears to have been shared by non-signing part-time delegate Caleb Strong, who was now governor of Massachusetts. Hamilton, had he still been alive, would probably have been in agreement, and possibly others now long dead.

In a letter of 1814 to Timothy Pickering, Secretary of State under Washington and John Adams, Morris said he would be "glad to meet with someone who could tell . . . what has become of the union, in what it consists, and to what useful purpose it endures." [18] It was now twenty-five years since the Constitution had been declared operative.

William Few

In his unpublished autobiography, written about 1816, William Few, signer from Georgia and later in life a New York banker, wrote that

It was believed to be of the utmost importance to concede to different opinions so far as to endeavor to meet opposition on middle ground, and to form a Constitution that might preserve the union of the States. On that principle of accomodation [sic] the business progressed, and after about three months' arduous labor, a plan of Constitution was formed on principles which did not altogether please anybody [sic], but it was agreed to be the most expedient [sic] that could be devised and agreed to.[19]

Charles Pinckney

Signer Charles Pinckney of South Carolina wrote on January 26, 1789, to Rufus King, signer from Massachusetts, as follows:

You know I always preferred the election [of members of the House of Representatives] by the [state] legislature, to that of the people, & I will now venture to pronounce that the mode which you & Madison & some others so thoroughly contended for & ultimately carried is the great blot [!] on the constitution—on this however more hereafter.[20]

To Madison, Pinckney wrote on March 28, 1789:

> Are you not, to use a full expression, abundantly convinced that
> the Theoretical nonsense of an election of the members of Congress
> by the people in the first instance, is clearly and practically wrong.—
> that it will in the end be the means of bringing our councils into
> contempt & that the legislature [of the states] are the only proper
> judges of who ought to be elected—
> Are you not fully convinced that the Senate ought at least to be
> double their number to make them of consequence & to prevent their
> falling into the same comparative state of insignificance that the state
> Senates have, merely from their smallness?—[21]

Whether one agrees or not with Pinckneys' specific rightist objections,
he was a signer and privately at least in part discontented with what
he had endorsed publicly.

James Wilson

James Wilson, signer from Pennsylvania, a future Associate Justice
of the Supreme Court and perhaps as much as Madison the central
theoretician and technician at the convention (some rank him in legal
lore above all others at the convention), also confessed to reservations
about various features of the Constitution although he was voluble in
his public support for ratification. He and Madison had been repeatedly
voted down on various proposals at the convention. Wilson, in fact,
in his zeal for ratification—shared by all the signers—made many contrafactual statements about the document and its making.

Although the Constitution was, as many delegates admitted privately,
written out of "bargain and compromise", Wilson at the rough-house
Pennsylvania ratifying convention denied this: "I know of no bargains
that were made there." [22]

"In its principles, Sir, it is purely democratical," he also asserted for
the benefit of rank-and-filers (something no signer really believed), and
"the new States which are to be formed will be under the control of
Congress in this particular, and slaves will never be introduced among
them." [23] As the event was to show, this was wholly misleading—but in
what Wilson saw to be a good cause, the usual political story.

Wilson gave the Pennsylvania ratifying convention a completely
misleading account of how the Constitution came to contain no Bill of
Rights. He said:

> Mr. President, we are repeatedly called upon to give some reason
> why a bill of rights has not been annexed to the proposed plan . . .
> But the truth is, Sir, that this circumstance, which has since oc-

casioned so much clamor and debate, never struck the mind of any member in the late convention till, I believe, within three days of the dissolution of that body, and even then of so little account was the idea that it passed off in a short conversation, without introducing a formal debate or assuming the shape of a motion . . .[24]

Wilson spoke thus on November 28, 1787.

On December 4 he declared that in the interval "I have spoken with a gentleman, who has not only his memory, but full notes, that he had taken in that body; and he assures me, that upon this subject no direct motion was ever made at all; and certainly, before we heard this so violently supported out of doors, some pains ought to have been taken to have tried its fate within; but the truth is, a bill of rights would, as I have mentioned already, have been not only unnecessary, but improper . . . Enumerate all the rights of men! I am sure, Sir, that no gentleman in the late convention would have attempted such a thing . . ."[25]

Leaving aside the red-herring notion of *all* the rights of men, a plain step toward a Bill of Rights was as a simple matter of fact proposed, moved for, seconded and thunderously voted down 10 to nothing, with one abstention, on September 12, 1787, at the Philadelphia constitutional convention.[26]

Madison's detailed and almost blow-by-blow account of the convention reports the event:

> Col: Mason perceived the difficulty mentioned by Mr. Gorham. The jury cases cannot be specified. A general principle laid down on this and some other points would be sufficient. He wished the plan had been prefaced with a Bill of Rights, & would second a Motion if made for the purpose—It would give great quiet to the people; and with the aid of the State declarations, a bill might be prepared in a few hours.
>
> Mr. Gerry concurred in the idea & moved for a Committee to prepare a Bill of Rights. Col: Mason 2ded the motion.
>
> Mr. Sherman. was for securing the rights of the people where requisite. The State Declarations of Rights are not repealed by this Constitution; and being in force are sufficient—There are many cases where juries are proper which cannot be discriminated. The Legislature may be safely trusted.
>
> Col: Mason. The Laws of the U.S. are to be paramount to State Bill of Rights. On the question for a Come to prepare a Bill of Rights
>
> N.H. no. Mas. abst. Ct no. N—J—no. Pa. no. Del—no. Md no. Va no. N—C—no. S—C—no—Geo—no (Ayes—0; noes—10; absent—1).

And that was that, Wilson to the contrary later on.

The motion, it is true, was for a *committee* to prepare a Bill of Rights.

So Wilson was trivially correct in saying that no "direct motion" was ever made on a Bill of Rights *per se*. This sort of talk, though, was just familiar lawyerly weaseling.

Actually, as early as August 20 various ingredients of a Bill of Rights were before the convention for inclusion in a Constitution—the writ of habeas corpus, liberty of the press, no peacetime quartering of troops without owner's consent and no religious test for the holding of office.

It was not even true, therefore, as Wilson informed the Pennsylvania ratifying convention, that the "circumstance" of a Bill of Rights had never struck the mind of any member of the convention until within three days of the dissolution of that body.

Contrary to what is freely suggested in the public schools, the convention was not composed of red-hot libertarians or democrats although there were some such in the assemblage. They were not however among the leading lights, who had fish of an entirely different color, size and weight to fry.

Jonathan Dayton

A signer from New Jersey was Jonathan Dayton, who later became a member of the House of Representatives and a wealthy land speculator after whom Dayton, Ohio, is named. A regular member of the Philadelphia convention, Dayton was also a feet-on-the-ground political analyst, successfully staking money to back his judgements. In a letter to John Cleve Symmes, a business associate, dated October 22, 1788, or just as the new Constitution was coming into effect, he wrote: [27]

> The people in their rage for the new constitution, seem to act as if the whole business of the union, nay every thing besides should give way to, or stand still until, it's operation, and they many of them really think, that with a kind of *magic process* it will, at the instant of it's commencement rid us of all our embarrassments, & make our circumstances flourishing—Altho' strongly prepossessed & very partial in favor of that system, (especially when compared with the present) I cannot nevertheless go all lengths with such enthusiasts— *Time* & a variety & succession of political indiscretions have brought upon us the calamities we are experiencing, and nothing but *time* & a series of wise, prudential management and political economy will extricate us from them—
>
> In order to counterbalance the evil predictions of its enemies, the favourers of the new government have been lead to utter prophecies with regard to it as extravagant on the other hand; *the many* have given into the belief & suffered their expectations to be unreasonably raised, expectations not to be gratified, & which in the event of their

disappointment will probably furnish the first ground of discontent & give a new opening for antifederalism under more favorable auspices than heretofore to revive it's attacks [he was clairvoyant here]. Sincerely do I pray, my friend, that my apprehensions may prove to be ill founded seriously do I wish that the hopes of the most sanguine may be answered but well I know that the success of an experiment like this is too apt to depend upon the impressions which it makes at its outset & neither you nor I can undertake to say that this is not one of the last tryals to be afforded to this or any other country, whether the people have ability to govern themselves or not must in all cases submit to receive a master of their own or others chusing—

Whatever else one makes of this, one can hardly consider it to have been written by someone in delirious transports over what had been wrought at Philadelphia.

James McHenry

As for James McHenry, a signer from Maryland, a physician and an aide to Washington in the War for Independence, he stated: [28]

Being opposed to many parts of the system [sic], I make a remark why I signed it and mean to support it.
1stly I distrust my own judgement . . .
2dly Alterations may be obtained . . .
3dly Comparing the inconveniences and the evils which we labor under and may experience from the present confederation and the little good we can expect from it—with the possible evils [sic] and probable benefits and advantages promised us by the new system, I am clear that I ought to give it all the support in my power.

The new system, in McHenry's view, was at least better than the pre-existing system, even though he was opposed to many parts of the new.

In all this commentary, Madison alone seemed to be fully aware, disclosing his awareness only briefly, that the Constitution, despite any virtues it contained, also carried locked within its chaste language several time-bombs. And he was the sole convention participant to live long enough to see some of these bombs approach the point of explosion.

No Private Laudations

Significantly, historians have not been able to dredge up any private communications of the thirty-nine signers or sixteen non-signing convention delegates to colleagues or intimates in which they expatiated on the Constitution as perfect, nearly perfect, the greatest scheme of government ever devised, or even as a fairly good working arrangment. There were of course many strong claims on the controversial *public* record. Here the sky, as in the case of James Wilson, was often the limit. But privately it was otherwise.

Washington perhaps went further than anyone in putting in a good word to some correspondents about the Constitution, to none of whom he wrote in the somber strain of his communication to Randolph.

To David Humphreys on October 10, 1787, he wrote: [29]

> The Constitution that is submitted, is not free from imperfections.— but there are as few radical defects in it as could well be expected, considering the heterogenious mass of which the Convention was composed and the diversity of interests that are to be attended to, As a Constitutional door is opened for future amendments and alterations, I think it would be wise in the People to accept what is offered them and I wish it may be by a great majority of them as it was by that of the Convention; but this is hardly to be expected because the importance and sinister views of too many characters, will be affected by the change. Much will depend however upon literary abilities, and the recommendation of it by good pens should be *openly*, I mean publickly afforded in the Gazetees.

Washington, in other words, saw the need for plenty of persuasion in the "Gazetees", which persuasion was to be supplied by the high-riding Federalists in ample measure. They practically blanketed the country with their hard-sell sales talk, which is what is usually misrepresented as private opinion and belief. The Constitution, in the then state of the public mind, could not be relied upon to carry with it its own recommendation. It had to be argued for strenuously and given many an informal push and pull with political forceps.

To Sir Edward Newenham, Washington wrote as follows on July 20, 1788: [30]

> Although there were some few things in the Constitution recommended by the foederal Convention to the determination of the People, which did not fully accord with my wishes; yet, having taken every circumstance seriously into consideration, I was convinced it approached nearer to perfection than any government hitherto instituted among men. [Here indeed were strong words in favor, but he was now writing to an Englishman, an outsider.] I was also convinced, that nothing but a genuine spirit of amity and accomodation could have induced the members to make those mutual concessions and to sacrifice (at the shrine of enlightened Liberty) those local prejudices, which seemed to oppose an insurmountable barrier, to prevent them from harmonizing in any System whatsoever.

Leading Non-framers Cool to Critical

One of the leading spirits in the American revolution from the first rocket's red glare was John Adams, first Vice President and second President of the United States. During the Philadelphia convention Adams was the American Minister to London and therefore could not be present. As Adams was at the time practically the leading constitutional theorist in the United States, virtually single-handed author of the Massachusetts Constitution of 1780 and of the influential two-volume pre-convention book *Defense of the Constitutions of Government of the United States,* in itself a luxuriant source of many convention notions that were bandied about, what he thought of the document of 1787 is very much in point here.

Adams, the fact is, until very near the end of his long life in 1826 was a consistent detailed knocker of the document of 1787 in private correspondence with various leading figures of the time. In his inaugural address of 1797 however, as a matter of form, he had some innocuously pleasant things to say about it which however were always lacking in his private correspondence. "The operation" of the Constitution, he said upon assuming the Presidency, "has equalled the most sanguine expectations of its friends, and from an habitual attention to it, satisfaction in its administration, and delight in its effects upon the peace, order, prosperity, and happiness of the nation I have acquired an habitual attachment to it and veneration for it." In this last, he was fibbing outrageously.

Writing to John Jay from London on December 16, 1787, Adams sounded quite enthusiastic about the new document, which he said "appears to be admirably calculated to cement all Americans in affection and interest, as one great nation . . . I confess I hope to hear of its adoption by all the States." [31]

Yet only ten days earlier he had confided serious doubts about the new Constitution to Jefferson in Paris. Adams wrote:

> You are apprehensive of monarchy, I, of aristocracy. I would, therefore, have given more power to the president, and less to the senate. [By aristocracy, as his remarks showed, Adams meant what today would be termed oligarchy.] The nomination and appointment of all offices, I would have given to the president, assisted only by a privy council of his own creation; but not a vote or voice would I have given to the senate or any senator unless he were of the privy council. Faction and distraction are the sure and certain consequence of giving to a senate, a vote in the distribution of offices. You are apprehensive that the president, when once chosen, will be chosen again and again as long as he lives. [This finally happened only at

long last in the case of Franklin D. Roosevelt.] So much the better,
as it appears to me. You are apprehensive of foreign interference,
intrigue, and influence. So am I. But as often as elections happen,
the danger of foreign influence renews. The less frequently they happen, the less danger . . . Elections, my dear sir, to offices which are a
great object of ambition, I look at with terror. Experiments of this
kind have been so often tried, and so universally found productive of
horrors, that there is great reason to dread them.[32]

As Adams saw it, correctly in the light of much later history, the
President's lack of direct power over Congress and the ultimacy of congressional reserve power vis-a-vis the President, would tend to foster
unnecessary and disabling intrigues, unsettling to the country. What
Adams did not anticipate however was the difficulty Congress would
usually have of mobilizing its divergent individualities along a single
line of policy and action. Adams saw Congress as shaping into a much
more cohesive body than it has actually been, so that the President
under the Constitution has in fact wielded or had available to him much
of the power that Adams wanted him to have.[33] Adams, the fact is,
was a Gaullist long before the advent of De Gaulle, a devotee of El
Presidente. He was definitely not a monarchist in the traditional sense,
as his enemies freely charged.

This is not the place to go into the whole of Adams's objections to
the Constitution, maintained over more than three decades in a rain of
long letters to Roger Sherman of Connecticut, a framer, and to John
Taylor of Caroline (County), Virginia, a leading theorist of the southern
agrarian faction. And Adams had many objections, most of them technical, to lay on the record. The only reason for citing Adams here is that
he was a big, almost indispensable wheel of the American revolution
and early government under the document of 1787, and he had much
of a decidedly negative nature to say about the Constitution. And this is
one of the reasons American Establishment writers have consistently
given Adams strong downplay in the recounting of American history.

"Our government", he wrote in 1805, "will be a game of leap-frog,
of factions leaping over one another's backs about once in twelve years,
according to my computations." [34] In 1808 he recalled, "I have called
our Constitution a game at leap-frog." [35] He alluded here to the practice
of two parties taking alternate mindless control—no political point to it.

But in 1824, two years and nearly three months before his death at
90, Adams wrote in valedictory surrender to Taylor: "Of the present
Constitution I can only say, with father Paul, 'Esto Perpetua.' I sincerely wish it . . ." [36] His son, who at the very beginning had also
expressed constitutional doubts, was to become the sixth President of
the United States before the father expired.

Thomas Jefferson of Monticello

Jefferson commented at length, pro and con, on the new Constitution in a letter to James Madison from Paris dated December 20, 1787.[37] He had no hesitancy in setting forth what he didn't like: the omission of a Bill of Rights; the lack of any requirements for rotation in office, especially in the case of the President; the binding of all officials by oath to maintain the Constitution, etc.

The fact is that Jefferson was never enchanted with the Constitution as written and did more than anyone else to begin the process of interpreting it—misinterpreting it, if words have meanings—as he wanted it to be. This isn't to say that Jefferson was invariably or even ever right-minded in what he wanted to bring about. It is only to say that he, a conceded bigwig, was not entranced by what the convention had produced. This is all I intend to emphasize.

He showed this, too, in 1801, when he was very probably involved with close political friends in proposing extensive changes in the Constitution along lines laid out already in letters. These friends were John Taylor and Edmund Pendleton, a relative of Taylor by marriage who became his foster father at age three. Pendleton on October 20, 1801, in the *Richmond Examiner* published a list of proposed changes in the Constitution which were probably the product of the joint thought of Taylor, Jefferson and Pendleton.[38]

Under these proposals

1. The President would be ineligible for a succeeding term.

2. Congress would appoint judges and stationed foreign ministers; the pay of these latter would no longer be set by the President.

3. The Senate would be deprived of all executive power—that is, of power over appointments. Senate terms of office would be shortened or the members subjected to removal by constituents.

4. Members of Congress and judges while in office and for a stipulated time thereafter would be ineligible to take any office whatever except President or Vice President, and Judges would be removable by concurring vote of both houses of Congress.

5. The alleged abuse of public credit, or national debt creation, as under the Hamiltonian policies, would be checked by amendment.

6. A fair method of impanelling juries would be prescribed.

7. Powers prohibited in the Constitution would be more explicitly defined so as to prevent fine-spun judicial constructions of such powers.

8. There should be more precision developed in the Constitution about distinguishing the separate powers of the general and the state governments.

Concluding his Jeffersonian proposals, Pendleton observed: "Men advanced to power are more inclined to destroy liberty than to defend it; if there is a continual effort for its destruction, it should be met by corresponding efforts for its preservation." [39] As Lord Acton was to say later in the century, "Power tends to corrupt; absolute power corrupts absolutely."

Later Jefferson addressed himself negatively to what he discerned as an emerging constitutional cult, which he abhorred. He had now served one term as revolutionary governor of Virginia, as a member of the Continental Congress, as Minister to France, as the first Secretary of State, as Vice President and two terms as President of the United States. He wrote:

> Some men look at constitutions with sanctimonious reverence and deem them like the ark of the convenant, too sacred to be touched. They ascribe to the men of the preceding age a wisdom more than human, and suppose what they did to be beyond amendment. I knew that age well; I belonged to it, and labored with it. It deserved well of its country. It was very like the present, but without the experience of the present; and forty years of experience in government is worth a century of book-reading; and this they would say themselves, were they to rise from the dead. I am certainly not an advocate for frequent and untried changes in laws and constitutions. I think moderate imperfections had better be borne with; because, when once known, we accomodate ourselves to them, and find practical means of correcting their ill effects. But I know also, that laws and institutions must go hand in hand with the progress of the human mind. As that becomes more developed, more enlightened, as new discoveries are made, new truths disclosed, and manners and opinions change with the change of circumstances, institutions must advance also, and keep pace with the times. We might as well require a man to wear still the coat which fitted him when a boy, as civilized society to remain ever under the regimen of their barbarous ancestors. It is this preposterous idea which has lately deluged Europe in blood . . . Let us

follow no such examples, nor weakly believe that one generation is not as capable as another of taking care of itself, and of ordering its own affairs . . . And lastly, let us provide in our Constitution for its revision at stated periods. What these periods should be, nature herself indicates. By the European tables of mortality, of the adults living at any one moment of time, a majority will be dead in about nineteen years. At the end of that period then, a new majority is come into place; or, in other words, a new generation. Each generation is as independent of the one preceding, as that was of all which had gone before. It has then, like them, a right to choose for itself the form of government it believes most promotive of its own happiness; consequently, to accomodate to the circumstances in which it finds itself, that received from its predecessors; and it is for the peace and good of mankind, that a solemn opportunity of doing this every nineteen or twenty year, should be provided by the Constitution; so that it may be handed on, with periodical repairs, from generation to generation, to the end of time, if anything human can so long endure.[40]

Jefferson, it is clear, did not believe any constitution could be devised that would forever meet all legitimate needs. And long after the document of 1787 had been placed in operation Jefferson would from time to time rail against one or the other of its provisions. Such railing of course does not prove or even tend to show that the Constitution was truly deficient. But it does show an authentic bigwig back in the salad days was not convinced it was beyond adverse criticism.

The role of the courts especially under the Constitution came to be regarded by Jefferson as pernicious. As late as 1807, toward the end of his second term as President, Jefferson denounced the "error in our Constitution, which makes any branch independent of the nation." [41] He pretty much saw himself as the apotheosis of that nation.

What Jefferson's fixed opinion of the Constitution was, if he had one at all, is hard to make out from his zigzag writings. When the occasion suited him he could profess great devotion and admiration for it, but only as he interpreted it; various actions that took place under the Constitution, actions clearly allowed by or provided for by the instrument, he railed against and objected to.

Very probably Jefferson's fundamental objection to the Constitution was that he had had no part in writing it; nor, what was worse, had he not been directly consulted about what was to go into it. The same observation might also apply to Adams. The fact is that Jefferson was a very mixed up man, probably more so than any other of his time at high American government levels, a proper subject for psychological study. He was however perhaps the most consummate politician produced by the United States in all its history.

Aaron Burr

A leading and notably astute politician-lawyer of the times was Aaron Burr (1756-1836). United States Senator for a term beginning in 1791, then for two terms in the New York State assembly, he was elected Vice President in 1800. Partisan historians down through the years have depicted Burr as a sinister character, of the order of Benedict Arnold, but in this they are 100 per cent wrong, as numerous more recent specialized studies have shown. Burr's opinion on the Constitution therefore is as worth citing as are the opinions of his two self-appointed and more prominent enemies, Hamilton and Jefferson, who were in no way superior to him in character or intelligence. All three were devious operators.

At the time the Constitution was being framed Burr was politically inactive and "neutral", according to his friend and editor of his papers, Matthew L. Davis.[42] Hamilton, always quick with a disparaging and not especially applicable word wherever Burr was concerned, says of him in relation to the emerging Constitution that his "conduct was equivocal".[43] In view of what Hamilton himself said pro and con for the record on the subject this was hardly very damnable.

As to the Constitution, "In common with most of the leading men of his time," says Burr's first biographer, James Parton, "including the framers of the Constitution, and particularly Hamilton, he had a low opinion of the merits of the new system, as a piece of political machinery. Conversing with a gentleman on the subject, toward the close of his life, he used language like this, 'When the Constitution was first framed,' he said, 'I predicted it would not last fifty years. But I was mistaken. It will evidently last longer than that. But I was mistaken only in point of *time*. The crash will *come*, but not quite so soon as I thought.' "[44]

In predicting the end of the Constitution within fifty years Burr indeed was not far wrong although the news of its collapse even today hasn't reached those historians and political scientists who assert that the Constitution has enjoyed an unbroken reign of nearly two hundred years. Burr missed by only twenty-three years if one dates the collapse of the document of 1787 with the opening bombardment of Fort Sumter, April 12, 1861. From then at least until Appomattox, April 9, 1865, the document of 1787 was in suspension, north and south. In the north Abraham Lincoln acted informally as Regent or Lord Protector, boldly assuming various clearly unconstitutional roles, all under a variety of far-fetched special legal interpretations, and all for the preservation of the sacred Union. And had Lincoln not done as he did, both Constitution and Union would very probably have been gone forever. In the southern states the Confederate Constitution, a very different document on decisive points although in most respects the same, prevailed under the hallowed Stars and Bars.

As politicians', historians' and film directors' tribute-time to the long ranks of silent and glorious dead in blue and gray appears now to be approaching, and as the bugles sound "Taps", we may now withdraw, reverently of course, from this aspect of the subject.

A much later remark by a distinguished descendant of the generation of 1787 is similarly critical. What Henry Adams (1838-1918) had to say provides no ammunition whatever for rampant constitutional cultists. Adams, professor of history at Harvard and author of the nine-volume *A History of the United States during the Administrations of Jefferson and Madison*, was the son of Charles Francis Adams, grandson of President John Quincy Adams and great-grandson of President John Adams. His father had been a Congressman and during the American Civil War was Minister to London, where he labored successfully to dissuade the British from backing the Confederacy. A brother of Henry's was president of the Union Pacific Railroad from 1884 to 1890. All of this is merely by way of what lawyers call "qualifying the witness", showing that he is not contaminated with the dread disease of un-Americanism.

Writing to Perry Belmont, son of the banker August Belmont, and Democratic Party fund-raiser, who had written a magazine article about the Corrupt Practices Act in 1905, Adams said: "I imagine that [Senator Philander] Knox or [former United States Attorney General Richard] Olney, if bribed sufficiently high could frame a bill that might advance the object but a mere student is helpless. *Our main difficulty is that our whole political system is helplessly cumbrous and antiquated and beyond patching. We can perhaps make it run your time, but, at the pace since mine began, it will break down like Russia within a perfectly visible date*" (emphasis added).[45]

Russia at the time was in the throes of the 1905 revolution. Had a similar breakdown in the United States, as Adams predicted, been averted by the New Deal improvisations of the 1930s?

Sober End to Convention

The constitutional convention ended September 17, 1787, in an atmosphere of sober apprehension verging on glumness. Appropriately, there was no hint of jollification or bombast in the air. At Philadelphia the feeling in fact was that there was little to cheer about. And just two days before, George Mason of Virginia, one of the convention activists, had stubbornly announced, at considerable forceful length, that he would not sign and put forth his reasons.

After a reading of the engrossed document on the 17th, the enfeebled 82-year-old Franklin, as Madison reports, rose with a speech in his hand that Wilson took and read. As this musingly apologetic speech, coming from such an eminent personage, was looked upon as emotionally appealing precisely because of its melancholy pro-ing and con-ing, it was "leaked" to the outside even though convention proceedings were supposed to be secret.[46]

> Mr. President [Franklin began], I confess there are several parts of this constitution which I do not at present approve, but I am not sure I shall never approve them . . . In these sentiments, Sir, I agree to this Constitution with all its faults, if they are such; because I think a general government necessary for us, and there is no form of Government but what may be a blessing to the people if well administered . . . I doubt too whether any other Convention we can obtain may be able to make a better Constitution . . . It therefore astonished me, Sir, to find this system approaching so near to perfection as it does . . . Thus I consent, Sir, to this Constitution because I expect no better, and because I am not sure, that it is not the best. The opinions I have of its errors I sacrifice to the public good . . . If every one of us in returning to our Constituents were to report the objections he had to it . . . we might prevent its being generally received, and thereby lose all the salutary effects & great advantages resulting naturally in our favor among foreign Nations as well as among ourselves, from our real or apparent unanimity . . .

In brief, Franklin like Washington favored the Constitution because it promised to insure defensive unification, whatever operational defects anyone might reasonably urge against it.

Franklin then moved that the document be signed by the members after appending the following: "Done in Convention, by the unanimous consent of *the States* present the 17th. of Sepr. &c—In Witness whereof we have hereunto subscribed our names." This motion was seconded and passed 10 to 0 with one state divided.

Madison noted that the ambiguous reference to *"the States* present" (with his own emphasis added) had been drawn up by the nimble-minded Gouverneur Morris "in order to gain the dissenting members, and put into the hands of Docr. Franklin that it might have the better chance of success."[47]

The signers, in brief, signed merely as witnesses to the action of the state delegations, not as individual endorsers, although nearly all publicly approved the document despite inner qualms. Those who signed it merely in witness, such as William Blount of North Carolina and Jared Ingersoll of Pennsylvania, later strove for its ratification. But by signing merely as witnesses uncertain signers protected themselves against possible political backfires in their home states. One could claim, in the event of a strong backfire, that one had merely signed as a witness, had not endorsed the cursed document (should it indeed prove to be publicly unwelcome).

In later ratification propaganda it was often stressed by fast-talking Federalists that the Constitution had been endorsed by the convention *unanimously*. Such was not the case at all if one considers those who deliberately abandoned the convention, those who signed only as witnesses, and the three important men—Mason, Elbridge Gerry and Randolph—who at the last moment refused to sign in any capacity.

But much of the public no doubt believed the document had been unanimously endorsed, as many still do. Many today even believe, because the Constitution begins with "We the people . . ." that the document was approved in a popular plebiscite. The Constitution was indeed signed—as in witness—by the delegations of all the states *present*. But there was ambiguity in this expression too. For New York was not present although Alexander Hamilton of New York signed—purely as an individual (and, oddly, one who was known to all the delegates as heartily but privately disliking much in the Constitution). Hamilton had no authority to sign even as a witness for New York, whose two other members—Yates and Lansing—had long been gone in states'-rights dudgeon.

After a vote to increase at the last minute the number of representatives in the lower house of Congress, "Mr. Randolph . . . rose and with an allusion to the observations of Docr. Franklin, apologized for his refusing to sign the Constitution . . . he did not mean by this refusal to decide that he should oppose the Constitution without doors . . .

> Mr. Govr. Morris said that he too had objections, but considering the present plan as the best that was to be attained, he should take it with all its faults . . . the great question will be, shall there be a national Government or not? and this must take place or a general anarchy will be the alternative . . .
>
> Mr. Williamson . . . did not think a better plan was to be expected and had no scruples against putting his name to it.
>
> Mr. Hamilton expressed his anxiety that every member should sign. A few characters of consequence, by opposing or even refusing to sign the Constitution, might do infinite mischief by kindling the latent sparks which lurk under an enthusiasm in favor of the Convention which may soon subside . . .
>
> Mr. Blount said he had declared that he would not sign, so as to pledge himself in support of the plan, but he was relieved by the form proposed [of signing merely in witness] and would without com-

mitting himself attest the fact that the plan was the unanimous act of the States in Convention.[48]

Franklin, out of touch with the inner currents of the convention, now rose to say he had not known in presenting his resolution that any member would balk at signing. He said he felt obliged to Mr. Randolph for having proposed the original plan and by his convention activity "and hoped that he would yet lay aside his objections, and, by concurring with his brethren, prevent the great mischief which the refusal of his name might produce." [49]

Randolph however "could not but regard the signing in the proposed form, as the same with signing the Constitution. The change of form therefore could make no difference with him . . .

"Mr. Gerry described the painful feelings of his situation, and the embarrassment under which he rose to offer any further observations on the subject wch. had been finally decided . . . He could not therefore by signing the Constitution pledge himself to abide by it at all events. The proposed form made no difference with him. But if it were not otherwise apparent, the refusals to sign should never be known from him." [50]

Following some minor business about the disposition of the convention journals "the members . . . proceeded to sign the instrument . . ."

"The Constitution being signed by all the Members except Mr. Randolph, Mr. Mason, and Mr. Gerry who declined giving it the sanction of their name, the Convention dissolved itself by an Adjournment sine die—"

And on this trebly muted note the convention ended and with it Madison's report.

> "In all our deliberations on this subject [said Washington soberly in his letter of transmittal to Congress], we kept steadily in our view, that which appears to us the greatest interest of every true American, the consolidation of our Union, in which is involved our prosperity, felicity, safety, perhaps our national existence. This important consideration, seriously and deeply impressed on our minds, led each State in the Convention to be less rigid on points of inferior magnitude, than might have been otherwise expected; and thus the Constitution, which we now present, is the result of a spirit of amity, and of that mutual deference and concession which the peculiarity of our political situation rendered indispensable.

The main purpose of the Constitution, then, was a national closing of ranks, unification, if words from the leading man have any meaning. Such consolidation was defensive against aggressive foreigners and was thought, optimistically, to end the possibility of internal conflict among the several states. Furthermore the Constitution upon adoption brought to an end the naive politics of constant changes of the rules in various of the states, which changes had produced instability and uncertainty of assorted dimensions.

In any case, as of 1787-88 nobody at all approved of the Constitution 100 per cent, just as nobody disapproved 100 per cent. The finished Constitution indeed was a tangle of procedural and substantive compromises, unpleasant compromises to most of the participants, and remained such even after the forced tacking-on of the first ten amendments under the goad of an irate section of the populace.

Opponents Accepted

Something to notice in our more furiously ideological age is that nobody who opposed the Constitution or who even fought against its adoption to the bitter end was thereafter politically ostracized or made politically *persona non grata.* James Monroe argued mightily against it in the Virginia ratifying convention and finally voted to reject it; but Monroe later became the fifth President of the United States. He was never charged with the presently grave offense of having tried to scuttle the Constitution, which indeed he tried to do. And both Elbridge Gerry and Gov. George Clinton, the latter the leader of the forces in New York opposed to ratification, were later made Vice Presidents.

So, while many proponents of the Constitution later held high office under it, many opponents, and indifferents like Jefferson and Burr, came to hold equally high office. The one requirement exacted of everybody was that they at least give it lip-service, under whatever interpretation, defects and all, after it had been declared ratified.

Strange Merits in the Constitution

What some signers on the other hand saw as meritorious in the new Constitution must strike most modern readers as not a little incongruous on the constitutional road to Elysium. And what accommodating sacrifice some of the strange merits involved, to dwell on Washington's soothing words in this connection, is obscure.

General Charles Cotesworth Pinckney, a signer for South Carolina, in speaking before the South Carolina house of representatives on January 17, 1788, pointed out forcefully that the scheme of government in process of ratification strengthened the institution of chattel slavery. For it made it legally impossible for the national government ever to emancipate slaves (Congress and Lincoln cut that knot at a stroke) and gave the slave states the right to hunt down fugitive blacks who had escaped to non-slave states. Under the Articles of Confederation a fugitive slave who made it to a non-slave state was legally free.

> By this settlement [General Pinckney declared], we have secured an unlimited importation of negroes for twenty years. Nor is it declared that the importation shall then be stopped; it may be continued. We have a security that the general government can never emancipate them, for no such authority is granted; and it is admitted, on all hands, that the general government has no powers but what are expressedly granted by the Constitution, and that all rights not expressed were reserved by the several states. We have obtained a right to recover our slaves in whatever part of America they may take refuge, which is a right we had not before [sic]. In short, considering all circumstances, we have made the best terms for the security of this species of property it was in our power to make. We would have made better if we could; but, on the whole, I do not think them bad.[51]

Speaking again the next day, General Pinckney said, "Another reason weighted particularly, with the members from this state, against the insertion of a bill of rights [which Wilson misleadingly said was never considered]. Such bills generally begin with declaring that all men are by nature born free. Now, we should make that declaration with a very bad grace, when a large part of our property consists in men who are actually born slaves." [52]

As a further bribe for consenting to join the Union, the southern politicians were given in the Constitution the right to have each of their slaves counted as three-fifths of a person in the matter of representation, giving the South disproportionate clout in the new government (Article I, Section 3). The actual representatives however were to be white exclusively and would not represent the slaves. These latter, although conceded to be persons, were not citizens.

But when the Articles of Confederation had been proposed, the southern states objected, successfully, to the proposal that slaves be counted as three-fifths of a person in the proportionate distribution of taxes among the states. Slaves, in other words, were entitled to be rated as three-fifths of a person when it was a question of giving their owners added power but were not to be taken as existing for purposes of tax assessment. This was merely a version of the old game of heads I win, tails you lose.

Again, soon after the government was installed, fierce controversy arose about what a *direct* tax was, to which alone slaves would be subject if they were to be taxed at all. As defined by the courts it became a very limiting adjective, in effect meaning that very little was subject to *direct* taxation, much to indirect taxation. Slaves, as it turned out, were not federally taxed.

At a late stage of the constitutional convention, according to Madison's Notes, "Mr. King asked what was the precise meaning of *direct* taxation? No one answered." [53]

As of 1790 just about 20 per cent of the population of the thirteen original states consisted of enslaved blacks and a precisely unknown but large percentage of white former indentured servants and transported English convicts, one-time slaves for a contractual term—all low men on the totempole of early American society. More than half the population of Virginia and South Carolina was enslaved, about one-third of North Carolina, and one-quarter of Georgia. Virginia with the largest slave population was in a position to breed for more southerly regions, and was consequently opposed to further slave importation. Out of an American population in 1790 of 3,172,444, no lesss than 697,624 or 22 per cent was enslaved and there were 59,557 free blacks in northern and middle states.[54] The United States, in fact, land of imperishable liberty, was the most important slave center in the world, and so remained for more than seventy-five years.

The South Carolina and Georgia delegations in the constitutional convention insisted on the continuance of slave importation as part of the price of agreeing to the Constitution. Virginia, Maryland and North Carolina delegates did not press for the retention of the import trade but also did not demand the abolition of slavery. On this they simply stood pat. The possibility that importation might be ended after 1808 was put into the Constitution to appease northern anti-slave sentiment.

The following states began phasing out slavery by law: Pennsylvania, 1780; Connecticut and Rhode Island, 1784; New York, 1785; and New Jersey, 1786. By judicial decree Massachusetts abolished it in 1783 on the ground that the Massachusetts constitution of 1780, stating that "all men are born free and equal", had abolished it by implication. Those states that abolished slavery had very few slaves; New York harbored the most, with 21,193, New Hampshire had only 157, and Rhode Island only 958.[55]

The Ordinance of 1787, enacted by the Continental Congress while the constitutional convention wrangled, prohibited slavery forever in the northwest territories extending to the Mississippi River. But forthcoming new states such as Alabama, Mississippi, Tennessee, Texas, Kentucky, Florida, Missouri and Arkansas, despite what James Wilson told the Pennsylvania ratifying convention, were to legalize slavery. As it disappeared in northern sections, where the institution had little functional *raison d'être*, it appeared anew in new southern and border states, always under the aegis of the Constitution. There was, in brief, even at the time of the Civil War, according to competent historians, no clear secular trend in the United States toward abolition, north or south.

Had not the politically dominant elements of the South, as a means of retaining equal regional weight in the government, forced the issue of the *extension* of slavery to new western states, there is no telling how, when or if it would have ended. The slavocracy was not terminated in the United States for moral reasons; it committed suicide for political and economic reasons, blinded by simple greed and vaingloriousness, and long after slavery was abolished in most places elsewhere in the western hemisphere. The fact is that the Constitution was a pro-slavery document at least up to the attachment of the Thirteenth, Fourteenth and Fifteenth Amendments in 1865-70.

An Ambiguous Work

That the new Constitution was far from perfect was to be made more and more evident after its adoption in the as yet unending contentions over its semantical interpretation. Madison himself in his correspondence often entered into this bootless argument, and often differed with crucial decisions of the Supreme Court that are looked upon as constitutional landmarks by latter-day constitutional buffs, notably *McCulloch vs. Maryland* (1819) in which the right of states to tax branches of the nationally chartered Bank of the United States was denied. Nor did the courts Madison differed from have on them any original framers. If we cannot rely on the surviving Madison for bedrock constitutional meaning, up to his ears as he was in the process of creation, to whom can we turn for any certain word?

At the time of the convention Madison was a centralizer. He soon evolved, under the pressure of his constituencies, into a moderate states'-righter; had he held to his centralizing convention views, he would simply have committed political suicide, no government career open to him. Writing in 1824 to Henry Lee, older brother of Robert E. Lee, Madison observed "that the language of our Constitution is already undergoing interpretations unknown to its founders will, I believe, appear to all unbiased inquirers into the history of its origin and adoption." [56]

Any reader should now be in a position to see that the Constitution, whatever merits it is held by anyone at all to have, was not regarded by its chief sponsors or any leading contemporaries as approaching anything like sacrosanct status by their own lights, whatever they were in each individual case. And if they did not regard it as beyond critical examination, either before or after ratification, why should anyone?

If one looks to the framers themselves for a cue, the Constitution is wide open to criticism at all times. Concededly, a latter-day citizen does not possess the historical certification of the framers themselves, to which group of masterbuilders I am coming. But, as lawyers would say, the framers themselves certainly opened the door to criticism fore and aft, ventured from whatever quarter. And in so comporting themselves they certainly showed themselves to be exercising to the full the prerogatives of intellectually free men. With a single possible exception none of them was of a temper to be awed by any shibboleth.

Framers Not Wildly Enthusiastic

The thirteen out of thirty-nine signers who privately expressed written doubts about the new Constitution, from minor to serious, included nearly all the men who were either contemporaneously or historically the most important at the convention. One non-signer, who also expressed doubts, said he would have signed had he been present. Three prominent men, one of them very much a convention activist, refused to sign at the last moment.

One signer found great merit in the Constitution because it strengthened the institution of slavery. Actually, all eleven signatories for Virginia, North Carolina, South Carolina and Georgia signed because, along with other things, the document underwrote slavery; they would not, Madison included, have signed had the document rejected it. It is possible furthermore that some of the eight signers for Delaware and Maryland would have abstained had the position of slavery been impaired instead of being strengthened.

Nevertheless, it will be said, and properly, they signed, which is what counts. While this is true, they signed for reasons other than the belief that they were signing a fully acceptable instrument of government. They signed because they saw the necessity for simple unification and greater uniformity in American government.

Furthermore the instrument they privately commented upon is not the instrument as we know it today. It is only part of that instrument. And what most of them commented upon was not the instrument as it stood after receiving the first ten amendments although the later observations of Hamilton, Gouverneur Morris and Madison certainly applied to the instrument as a whole as it stood down to the Civil War.

I have also cited the views of three politically prominent men who did not attend the convention—John Adams, Thomas Jefferson and Aaron Burr. None of these was impressed by the instrument. Jefferson and Burr were at best indifferent. Adams was quite hostile. Yet each went to work politically under it and attained high office from the very start. The framers, in any event, had no worshipful attitude toward what they had put together. Anyone who can believe that after what has been cited can believe anything, no matter how preposterous. The Constitution, in the eyes of the framers, was anything but remarkable.

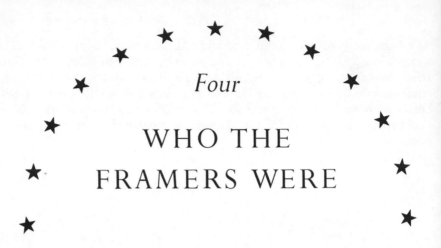

Four

WHO THE
FRAMERS WERE

It has been often written, and more often declaimed to mesmerized audiences, that the United States was very fortunate at its birth in the convocation of a preternaturally superlative group of men able by some miracle to produce such a Protean and beneficent document as the Constitution of the United States. Before looking at the hallowed document itself, with all its wonders, the question arises: Who were these men about whom so many have rhapsodized?

Altogether fifty-five men presented credentials at Philadelphia in the summer of 1787 out of seventy-four authorized by state legislatures at the request of Congress for the meeting, for which there was no grass-roots demand. A quarter of those who checked in stayed only very briefly and another quarter were in and out by fits and starts like restless tourists. No more than five men provided most of the discussion with some seven more playing fitful supporting roles. As the term is understood today it was hardly a convention, more like a political caucus of insiders with a languidly interested small audience.[1]

How could nineteen fail to show up when a new government was to be formed, more especially when the one already in operation was widely claimed as the most excellent ever seen?

It was not in fact the official assignment of the caucus to write a new constitution, which was something strictly illegal it was to do. The congressionally authorized task of the group was merely to propose amendments to the prevailing Articles of Confederation. There could, then, be little sense of urgency except among the few who had some inkling of more extensive plans afoot.

Of the nineteen who failed to keep the fateful rendezvous with history, no fewer than eleven pointedly declined to have anything to do with the affair, were opposed to it, distrusted it, considered it rigged from the start. The remaining eight indicated various excuses—illness (diplomatic or actual), failure of their states to guarantee the heavy expenses of the trip and the long sojourn, the need to attend to urgent personal affairs, a preference for already shouldered official state duties, etc. But would anyone have stayed away, for whatever reason, had he suspected that the convention would produce what a century later under the loftiest political auspices was to be characterized—with no serious dissent then from any quarter—as the greatest work ever struck off by the hand of man since time began?

Analysts have sought various common denominators among the delegates and have, for the most part, found it in the fact that thirty-three were lawyers, a profession easily mastered at the time by bright minds in a matter of weeks (as Hamilton in fact proved). But a far more pervasive common denominator, little noticed by anyone, is that forty-four were present or past members of Congress, forty-six had held political office in their home states including seven who were present or former state governors and five who were high state judges. It was a gathering, almost exclusively, of men who for years, some prior to the revolution, had carried on a counterpoint of effort between the promotion of their own economic interests and parallel activity in the halls of government.

And no fewer than twenty-seven were future members of Congress, two were future Presidents, one a future Vice President, one a Speaker of the House of Representatives, four were future United States district judges and five were future Justices of the Supreme Court. Virtually all those who did not hold office after the Constitution was written simply early gave up the ghost and died.

There is a minor facet to be noticed here. It is often pointed out, sometimes with stalwart American distaste, that the British Constitution is generated piecemeal by act of Parliament. Whatever Parliament decrees becomes part of the British Constitution. But the American Constitution, both the primary document and its later expansion in legislation and judicial decisions, comes from an essentially similar source. The primary document does not stem from the legislature itself but from a special caucus consisting of past, present and future members of the legislature at a particular period in history, persons not authorized (as members of Parliament are) as constitution-makers. While there is nothing historically unusual about this circumstance, it puts a very different light on the proceedings than the one usually cast as a spontaneous mission of selected immortals who formally represented the American people, about 90 per cent of whom were then impecunious farmers, most of whom had little serious grasp of what everything was all about.

The Constitution, in point of fact, was generated along predetermined lines by the government itself, by a small self-selected elite at the center of government affairs all along, the ascendant court-house gang of the day.[2] It was essentially a piece of very general, often vague or ambiguous, legislation, a primary statute. And this fact, although very different from popular myth, is precisely what anyone versed in history should expect to find. It was very much the product of a group of insiders.

Furthermore, all amendments since made to the Constitution, and more than four thousand formally proposed amendments, have since been enacted or rejected by the government, not by "the people" even in the token sense of people acting through delegates elected to a special convention. "The people", most of the time, nearly always, have nothing whatever to do with directing or even influencing the government. Again, all operative interpretations of the Constitution come from the government, without exception. All of which, though strictly true, is directly counter to prevailing and carefully nurtured sentimental myth.

Of the twenty-seven future Congressmen, nineteen made it to the Senate, some after first sojourning on the public payroll in the lower house, at the time referred to in an Orwellian inversion as the "first house". Only in time was the House of Representatives recognized as in fact "the lower house", the lesser house. Until the nineteenth Congress, 1825-27, when twenty-four states including Illinois, Indiana and trans-Mississippi Missouri existed and when Andrew Jackson of Tennessee was a Senator and the immoderately celebrated Sam Houston and Henry Clay of Kentucky were Representatives, there were former constitutional delegates sitting in Congress. The last such delegate to appear, in the eighteenth Congress, thirty-six years after the establishment of the government of Constitution II, was Rufus King of New York. He was paired with Martin Van Buren, soon-to-be President. Political office in the United States is often held on a lifetime basis, even the same office. Finally, in an original presidential Cabinet of five, two were in the first, three in the second and one in the third. Almost all who lived, in short, were headed for political preferment under the new dispensation.

The convention delegates, otherwise put, were for the most part, with few exceptions, routine, active and entirely familiar politicians, doing more or less what they usually did in arranging things, and most of the older ones had plied this metier, either full-time or as a sideline, since prior to the rebellion against Great Britain, mostly as members of the lower houses of the colonial legislatures. They were not a collection of men winnowed out by a broad elecorate (there were property qualifications for voting and holding office) on the basis of perceived technical or general merit for a special task in dedication to the higher verities. Nor were they a group of savants aiming to install basic, universal, timeless principles of government. The unwary reader is drawn by much in the vast almost exclusively propagandist literature to either of these erroneous affirmations. None of this of course reflects invidiously upon them but it does call into question the propagandists who, carried away by their own extravagant fantasies, suggest otherwise.

So, although not written by Congress formally assembled as such, the Constitution was framed in the main with the assent of plain Congressmen, many of whom were sitting at the time, others of whom had sat in the halls of government since before the revolution, and most of whom were to continue sitting for a long time.

Their Political Record

The genial Benjamin Franklin for example—publisher, editor, compiler of homely wisdom, inventor, regarded by some as a topnotch philosopher, dabbler in science and international business factotum and diplomat—was a member of the Second Colonial Congress at Albany, N.Y., as early as 1754. He there proposed a centralized union of the colonies that came to nothing at the time, but the proposal was a precursor, one of many to be suggested, of the later Union. From 1751, with his election to the provincial Pennsylvania assembly, he was ever after a public official in one capacity or other, prior to the revolution representing various colonies abroad as a business agent, after the revolution representing the United States. He was for a time president of the Council of Pennsylvania—in effect the state's chief executive.

Two signers, John Dickinson of Pennsylvania and William S. Johnson of Connecticut, were members of the Stamp Act Congress in 1765. Dickinson, by reason of his writings and his draft of the Articles of Confederation, was a far more important contributor to the orientation of the Constitution than is generally conceded. Six convention members —Thomas Mifflin of Pennsylvania, Gov. Edmund Randolph of Virgina, George Read of Delaware, John Rutledge of South Carolina, Roger Sherman of Connecticut and George Washington of Virginia—were members of the mainly conservative First Continental Congress of 1774.

Eleven men named to the convention, of whom one refused to serve, signed the Declaration of Independence, which was also signed by forty-five others, but five other convention delegates, including Washington, would have signed had they not been called away, Washington to fight the British at Boston. More significantly, several dominant figures at the convention either refused to sign the deathless Declaration or signed reluctantly for reasons that had much to do with their later enthusiasm for the Constitution. Dickinson refused to sign the Declaration. Robert Morris and James Wilson of Pennsylvania, leading figures at the convention, signed it reluctantly, Morris a month late. Many signed with heavy hearts.

Gouverneur Morris of New York, sitting with the Pennsylvania delegation, although not a signer, was opposed to the revolution but, like many other conservatives at the convention, gave it his dubious support. His attitude was shared by William Samuel Johnson. The convention held several other such revolutionary skeptics, who were impelled to support the revolt more by the intransigence and harsh responses of Great Britain to colonial complaints than by the contentions of the radicals, and who now welcomed with the constitutional convention the chance for something of a restoration to a proper traditional—and hierarchical—order.

But six stalwarts who had signed the ineffably holy Declaration, and who were named to the convention, were among those who refused to attend. They were like Patrick Henry of liberty-or-death fame who grounded his refusal to attend on the fact that he "smelt a rat".

Seven of the conventioneers were among the twelve commissioners at the meeting in Annapolis in 1786 that first proposed a general gathering of the states to discuss commercial regulations, out of which meeting eventuated the call of the Virginia legislature to Congress for a conclave to consider amendments to the Articles of Confederation.

Seven were signers of the Articles of Confederation, adopted by Congress in 1777, not finally ratified by all the states until 1781. But the committee that prepared the Articles was entirely constituted of men, with one exception, who were named to the convention. The writer of the draft Articles of Confederation was John Dickinson. His fellow committeemen, save one, who were also named to the Philadelphia convention, were Elbridge Gerry and Francis Dana of Massachusetts; Roger Sherman and Oliver Wolcott (the exception) of Connecticut; Gouverneur Morris; Daniel Carroll of Maryland; and Henry Laurens of South Carolina. Neither Dana nor Laurens came to Philadelphia. The document that Dickinson wrote had a centralizing thrust similar to that of the Constitution that was to emerge but its orientation was radically altered by Congress, then dominated by the radicals as the anti-hierarchical element is styled. But the people who framed the Constitution, now conservatives in the ascendency, had a dominant hand in writing the pre-amended Articles.

With very few exceptions, the persons named and others who showed up at Philadelphia were continually active politically, always at the highest levels, for the most part in national councils. The exceptions however were active in state politics, were office-holders of one sort or the other, usually in the state legislatures. The only persons named to the convention, and present, who had not previously served in Congress were Richard Bassett and Jacob Broom of Delaware, John F. Mercer of Maryland, Caleb Strong of Massachusetts, William Paterson and David Brearley of New Jersey, Alexander Martin and William Richardson Davie of North Carolina, John Blair and George Mason of Virginia, and Robert Yates of New York. And except for Paterson and Mason these were delegates, as the record shows, who were of slight importance in the proceedings other than as voters in their delegations where they were for the most part in irregular attendance. Paterson, Blair, Brearley and Yates were pre-convention state judges.

Five delegates—Langdon of New Hampshire, Livingston of New Jersey, Robert Morris of Pennsylvania, Randolph of Virginia and Rutledge of South Carolina—classify as what today would be called political bosses or power-brokers. They dominated networks of state office-holders.

As to bossism, the case is well put by Prof. Forrest McDonald: "Robert Morris was known as the 'Great Man,' both to his friends and to his enemies. The real financial giant of the period—his brain would have made two of Hamilton's—Morris has rarely been rivaled in economic and political power in the United States. The power he held in the 1780s may be compared to that of the House of Morgan in the early twentieth century, which means that no one knows exactly how great it was. Probably J. P. Morgan would have had to add the secretaryship of the treasury and the control of Tammany Hall to match Morris' power." [3]

For Morris was not only Superintendent of Finance responsible to Congress (1781-83), a virtual financial dictator, and the founder of the Bank of North America (1781) as the first commercial bank in the country, but also the leader of the powerful conservative political faction in Pennsylvania with important business and political associates in nearly all the states. Next to Washington he unquestionably had more personal influence than any other man of his time in the United States.

Langdon was known as "the Robert Morris of New Hampshire".

Most of the older men present had participated in the writing of their state constitutions—Gouverneur Morris in New York, Madison and Mason in Virginia, Franklin in Pennsylvania, George Read in Delaware, and so on.

The convention therefore consisted of men long deep in the political doings of the country, a nuclear group something like an informal politburo. It did not consist, as often implied by starry-eyed writers, of a fortuitous gathering of philosophers, scholars, political scientists, sages, general savants or men uncommonly versed in the lore of the ages. Nor was it by any means the all-star political team the country could have fielded although it included a few stars. Absent were such big names of the day as Jefferson, John and Sam Adams, John Jay, John Hancock, Thomas Paine, Benjamin Rush, Paul Revere, John Paul Jones, "Mad" Anthony Wayne, Henry "Light-Horse Harry" Lee, Patrick Henry (who was named to the convention but disdained serving), Richard Henry Lee (who with Henry was opposed to the proceedings and who would eloquently oppose ratification), and a host of others. But two of fourteen Continental presidents were delegates—Gorham of Massachusetts and Mifflin of Pennsylvania.

According to Melancton Smith, merchant, lawyer and New York political leader for many years, and an active opponent of the new order, "The favorers of this system", in extolling the "character and ability" of its authors, were "not very prudent in bringing this forward. It provokes an investigation of characters, which is an invidious task. I do not wish to detract from their merit, but I will venture to affirm that twenty assemblies of equal number might be collected, equally respectable both in ability, integrity, and patriotism." [4]

Prof. Clinton Rossiter supplies a list of seventy-five names of plausible alternates with several dozen others unmentioned in reserve.[5] The Constitution, for reasons I shall come to, was a document many other assemblies of the day might have written, either along the same lines or with obvious improvements and a different orientation. It was not, in other words, produced by rare virtuosi in the art of writing such documents.

Apart from the two notables, Washington and Franklin, few of the men who later became well known were well known nationally at the time the convention met. Two such virtual unknowns were Madison and Hamilton, protegés of Washington; their political and schoolroom fame began after the convention. At the time the convention met, most of the delegates were probably about as well known to the general public as are those of one's Congressman today, perhaps less so owing to the scarcity of media coverage. That is to say, they were obscure to most of the public, local and national. And for most of them this obscurity, despite the combing of records by historians for shreds of information, has deepened with the years. In any event, few of the framers in their own right interest most people today, either the ignorant or the learned.

Yet in dealing with the delegates most historians take their cue from an obviously politic remark by the master politician, Jefferson. Writing to John Adams in London from Paris under date of August 30, 1787, Jefferson, after complaining that the convention was undemocratically secret, salved his strictures by saying, possibly with tongue in cheek, "It is really an assembly of demigods." [6]

Apart from Franklin and Washington, demigods they were not to the American public, as much controversial political expression of the period shows. Nor did Jefferson really think them such, from Washington down, as many of his later attitudes and pronouncements showed.

Their Economic Status

Aside from being persistent office-holders and lawyers, a third general characteristic of the delegates is that most of them were men of substantial means—inherited, acquired by marriage in many cases (thirteen had married heiresses) or gained by successful commercial, professional and speculative strategies. It was distinctly a gathering of the rich, the well-born and, here and there, the able.

No fewer than twenty-one were rated rich to very rich, with Washington and Robert Morris reputed to be the richest, according to mountains of data excavated from mouldering local and national records by Forrest McDonald.[7] Another thirteen were affluent to very affluent. The four constituting the South Carolina delegation had been very rich but had had their plantations and slaves confiscated by the British during the war. These men however were well on their way back to financial health at the time of the convention. Two others, William Samuel Johnson and Roger Sherman of Connecticut, had suffered reverses during the war but Johnson at least was recovering while Sherman remained in a reduced state. One delegate, William Pierce of Georgia, a merchant, was in serious financial straits, went bankrupt the next year and died in 1789.

While some had suffered diminished fortunes as a result of the war, others made or augmented theirs. Among the latter were Langdon of New Hampshire, Gorham and Gerry of Massachusetts and Robert Morris and Thomas Mifflin of Pennsylvania; with all of these Robert Morris had business dealings as well as with others at the convention. Thirteen, including some of the wealthiest like Robert Morris and Washington, also owed money, but on balance most of them were highly solvent at the time of the convention.

Owners predominently of personal property—merchants and their attorneys and holders of state and continental securities and specie—and owners of land and realty were approximately evenly divided. There were thirty-one in the first group, twenty-four in the second, including Washington. Many of the second group were short of cash in a cash-short society but long on land and slaves—far from indigent.

At least nineteen delegates were slave-owners, sailing before the world under the contrafactual banner that all men are created free and equal, a bit of historical irony for connoisseurs.

Directly or indirectly, as principals or lawyers, the assembly consisted of planters, bankers, merchants, ship-owners, slave-traders and slave-owners, smugglers, privateers, money-lenders, investors and speculators in land and securities. A few, such as Wilson, were early enterprisers in the establishment of factories. It was, with few exceptions, what today would be called a Wall Street crowd; the New York Stock Exchange, significantly, was established three years after the new Constitution took effect.

In brief, all the members of the convention belonged to the upper socio-economic class, had been in it and were struggling to get back, were on its fringes and striving as best they could to get in, or were reluctantly losing their positions in it. In a nation made up almost entirely of unschooled farmers, the group included no working farmers, no yeomen, no artisans, no foremen or overseers, no craftsmen, no fishermen, no seamen, no clerks, no draymen, no laborers for hire although it included one who was a teacher-turned-public-official, and three medical doctors—McHenry of Maryland, McClurg of Virginia and Williamson of North Carolina. The first two were wealthy, the third affluent. Williamson had also been a clergyman.

The nature of property-holdings is an issue because of Prof. Charles Beard's thesis in *An Economic Interpretation of the Constitution of the United States* (1913) that personalty interests were the dynamic element in the framing of the Constitution and that they subtly loaded it so as to favor personalty vis-a-vis land and other interests. The massive evidence as unearthed by McDonald fails to sustain this thesis, in fact refutes it. The gamut of property interests was represented and served. Only four men, McDonald found, worked directly at the convention for the interests represented by their own investments. These were Gerry, King, Sherman and Ellsworth, all public-security holders, and Gerry finally refused to sign.[8]

If it was not one-to-one economic interests that the convention served, what then was the general object of the Constitution?

The clear aim of the Constitution was to launch a system that would protect, and enable to flourish, the *general* interests there represented, not those interests in their particularities. To do this it was necessary to re-establish approximately the hierarchical system that prevailed on the eve of the revolution, before the states proclaimed their individual sovereignty. Until the Declaration of Independence took effect the states were supervised and bound together by Great Britain in a legal and commercial union, which the revolution shattered. With Great Britain removed, there was left with respect to supervision and union a vacuum within which thirteen splinter states struggled to exist, at least nine of them against unfavorable odds. The Constitution, and with it the new government, was created to dispel this vacuum and re-enact, with suitable changes of detail, the overriding role of Great Britain. To accomplish this a Constitution was devised that was in general modeled on the British Constitution but with certain changes of detail to produce the general outcome of the British structure without being an exact copy.

By reason of prevailing ideology and local conditions the United States could not establish an hereditary monarchy, a House of Lords seating a titled nobility, or a House of Commons. But it could, and did, establish elective replicas of each, differently weighted with respect to each other in power. And to put brakes on elected officials who might be too responsive to popular clamor, which brakes were not needed in the predominantly non-elective British system, it established a life-time court system which could act as censor and brake over the states and the legislative and executive branches—the Supreme Court and lower courts. The British did not need such an overriding court system since their King and Lords were born to office for life and had absolute veto power over the Commons, which in any event was itself not then representative of most of the population.

The outcome in both cases was governments that could act as freely as they wished with respect to all matters, as if on ball-bearings, but could not within the bounds of normal probability overrun or seriously discommode established cohesive private economic interests. For what was being restored in full flower by the Constitution was the British commercial and financial system, but now under centralized American auspices.

For a long time American historians, heeding the political charges and counter-charges of the 1780s, claimed that the Constitution was meant to overcome the inadequacies of the Articles of Confederation. But even if the Articles had not contained such alleged inadequacies they would not have been acceptable to the conservatives of the day, who disliked the openness and dispersiveness of the procedures under it. Open covenants openly arrived at was not one of their aspirations.

From the beginning of the quarrel with Great Britain such con-servatives clamored for a centralized government that would be run by a few, what in those days was styled "aristocratic government". The radical element wanted, and initially got in the Articles of Confederation, a government that would at least be accessible to the many, with all their illusions, for which reason they are often referred to as democrats although their conception of democracry did not extend so far as to include Negroes, Indians and other non-whites—or indeed Catholics, women or the always proliferating impoverished.

The movement for independence was initiated and spearheaded by the radicals. But the revolution against Great Britain also contained within itself a domestic revolution, against the domestic gentry whether these were pro-British or anti-British. For the domestic gentry were felt by the lower orders to be as oppressive as were the distant British.

The radicals wanted independence from Britain, right enough, but also freedom from dominance by native gentry. To them this was what liberty meant. The revolution they made they hoped would free them from both, and it was these radicals who established separate state governments and wrote state constitutions that concentrated power in the state legislatures. The radicals were reluctant to surrender plenary powers to any central goverment; hence the limitations in the Articles of Confederation. In the view of the radicals, any man in any political office was a potential tyrant—in effect a tyrant; hence terms of office in the states were short, compensation of officials niggardly, elections frequent. Public officials were regarded by the radicals literally as servants, entitled to little respect.

The conservatives, on the other hand, had favored a central government run by a few from the very beginning of the quarrel with Great Britain. Time and again they had come up with plans for such a government. The first such plan was proposed to the first Continental Congress in 1774 by Joseph Galloway of Pennsylvania, who became a loyalist and left the country. It called for a written imperial constitution that would apply to Great Britain and the colonies. Under it each colony would control its internal affairs. There would however be a central administration consisting of (1) a president-general appointed by the King who would hold office at the King's pleasure and would have a veto over the acts of (2) a grand council the members of which would be chosen for three-year terms by the legislatures of each province. The president and council would constitute an "inferior and distinct branch of the British legislature". Laws applicable to America might originate either in this body or the British Parliament, the consent of the other being necessary for a measure to become law. The plan was defeated by the narrow vote of six colonies to five and later was expunged from the minutes of Congress when the radicals took over. What it amounted to was what later was called dominion government.

The next similar but modified plan, coming now after independence

had been declared against the opposition or with the reluctant acquiescence of most conservatives, was the Dickinson draft of the Articles
of Confederation. Dickinson, as already noted, had refused to sign the
Declaration of Independence to which many others who thought similarly had reluctantly or tardily given their signatures. This coterie of
foot-draggers on independence was prominently represented at the convention of 1787.

It was not that these elements loved Great Britain more than
independence but that they loved centralized and screened government
more than the dispersed and open government favored by the radicals.
While each side, radical and conservative, saw personal interests involved, the dispute was really grounded in philosophic outlook and in
temperament. The radicals saw people in general (excluding Negroes,
women and Indians) as basically constructive and entitled to the greatest
possible freedom, from which only good could flow; the conservatives
saw the people in general as a volatile quantity, all subject to depravity
and the lower social orders inherently more depraved or unreliable
than the higher.

While much in Dickinson's able draft was retained in the Articles of
Confederation and indeed was carried over into the document of 1787,
it was severely modified by the radical elements to remove its centralizing features. After which the conservatives began a rising chorus
of criticism against the Articles and frequently presented new plans
that foreshadowed the document of 1787. The conservatives continually
stressed the desirability of a centralized government and finally succeeded by unfairly blaming all postwar ills on the Articles of Confederation as the radicals had earlier succeeded by unfairly blaming Great
Britain for all ills. It was under the as yet unratified Articles that the
United States had triumphed over Great Britain, then the greatest
power in the world. Yet the system under which a vast empire had been
wrested from the British—the neatest trick of the eighteenth century—was
successfully impugned in the period of after-war weariness and discord,
and was contemptuously discarded.[9]

It was thus the successful aim of the constitutional convention to
freeze the socio-economic situation at the *status quo ante* the Declaration
of Independence and to keep it frozen except for cumbersome and
difficult processes permitting change. In so aiming, the convention
failed to reckon with the dissolvent forces of history, although the
conception of a rigidly fixed, forever certain Constitution still lives on
in perhaps most American minds capable of contemplation. For it is
as impossible to build for all time any predetermined governmental
system, to recall what Gouverneur Morris said about democracy, as to

build a palace on the surface of the ocean. Forces of relentless change in a Heraclitean world modify any system.

And that the delegates to the convention knew what they were attempting is shown in the fact that the general type of economic interest there represented, except for the one in chattel slavery, has indeed flourished and dominates the country politically to this day. The modern large corporation and bank represents the utmost institutional flowering of this system.

It has consequently been the plaint of many critics that the framers of the Constitution were unduly property-minded, stressing property rights at the expense of other personal rights. They were in fact no more property-minded than their radical states'-sovereignty opponents of the day, who forced in additional reinforcements for property in the first ten amendments. All political actives of the day in fact were property-minded. All, without exception, agreed with a favorite Whig writer, James Harrington, author of *The Commonwealth of Oceana* (1656), that "Domestic empire is founded upon dominion. Dominion is property, real or personal; that is to say, in lands or in money and goods." [10] Harrington alluded of course to private property.

To get around the massed political and social power of private property, later socialists postulated a system in which there would be no private property, a system in which all productive property would be nationalized. But such a system, as has been clearly demonstrated, hardly distributes political power. As events have shown in Russia, China and other countries with governments modelled on theirs, a system of nationalized property simply concentrates dominion in fewer hands than ever, in the managers of the party in permanent office. Nationalization of property is a clear and inescapable pre-condition to naked dictatorship.

Those who style themselves *democratic* socialists, in contrast to the authoritarian Russians, visualize a system of multi-party free elections in the presence of nationalized property. Such a system presupposes that men ensconced in government, with full dominion through control of the nationalized economy, will surrender their dominion through an election and resume the status of private citizens. They will quietly go, it is assumed, from the status of having full power to the status of having no power at all—a pipe-dream if ever there was one. It has never happened anywhere, for multi-party elections are not permitted and never will be.

The men in office know they are committed, no less, to the elevation of the human race to chimerical astronomic heights through the imposition of socialism. Why should they, then, make way for another set of office-holders? Contrary to procedures under the system of private property, office-holding under socialism is not a game of leapfrog but a service dedicated (at least in theory) to elevating the populace to undreamed-of heights of cultural and general self-development. Why, then, should already committed socialists step out of office? Obviously it is the duty of the incumbents to remain, forever.

What has actually happened under the banner of socialism is that those once ensconced in power have established one-party police-states, meanwhile exercising intense cultural and political censorship over the populace, all individual political maneuvering confined within the single party. The populace is reduced to the status, at best, of wards. It seems extremely improbable that under a system of nationalized property one can ever avoid a full-dress police-state. It is true that one can have a police-state under the system of private property also, although it is difficult to establish without injuring property relationships. For certain forms of property are made to benefit at the expense of others.

So, whether property is publicly or privately owned, dominion is bound to rest in the hands of those in charge of it, whether as private owners or as nominal public servitors. It is a basic universal fact of government of all types, with never an exception of record. The rank-and-file man of little or no property has little autonomous political power in any system, none whatever under nationalization. On this solid fact he is forever caught like a fish on a hook.

As to the reinforcement of property rights in the first ten amendments, it is seen in the Third Amendment forbidding the quartering of troops in private houses, in the Fourth Amendment prohibiting "unreasonable" searches—that is, arbitrary searches—and seizures of private possessions, in the Fifth Amendment under which no person may be deprived of property without due process of law, in the Seventh Amendment requiring jury trials in civil suits, and in the Eighth Amendment forbidding excessive bail and fines. Either of the latter two could be equivalent to confiscation. In short, many opponents of the Constitution felt the framers had not gone far enough in protecting property against the encroachments of officialdom.

The United States government owns a great deal of property—government buildings, equipment, land, roads. The rank-and-file American citizen has no more to say about the use or disposition of that property, or indeed any special concern about it, than he has to say about the installations of any corporation. True, he may make suggestions to officialdom, which may be accepted or rejected, more probably the latter. He may agitate, demonstrate, join in assemblies, write letters to Congressmen and the newspapers, issue statements. But if through inner processes of government the decision goes against him he is without recourse, as much so as any Soviet citizen in the face of a Kremlin decree.

Their Intellectual Level

As to the intellectual level of the framers, most American historians place it very high. While I would not for a moment dispute the claim that they were generally sensible and practical men, allowing for momentary lapses here and there, nothing on the record sustains any notion that they were, as a group, extraordinarily learned or profound thinkers or even unusually capable.

How the historians come to their position may be illustrated by an example. Says Clinton Rossiter on this theme, "The Convention was just as rich in learning as in property and experience."[11] In short, it was absolutely topflight. How do we know this? As this historian writes, "In an age when few men went to college, even from the most lofty families, the Framers were conspicuous for the number of their degrees, whether learned or honorary." That one is a learned man because one has passed through some college, either today or in any age, is certainly a notion that will uniformly astonish all scholars, who are the ones most familiar with the uneven performance of college students.

Rossiter noted that twenty-five men who attended the convention had been to college. But the one man who held the convention together by the mere force of his presence and was its main guarantor in the public eye, Washington, had not gone to school beyond the fifth grade. The man next in importance in the public eye, Franklin, was also a non-college man, largely self-taught. Hamilton, a big post-convention name but out of tune with the drift of the convention, dropped out of college in his first year. And Robert Morris, silent at the convention but a potent force in assuring its success, was also among the non-collegians. And so was George Mason of Virginia, a heavy contributor to the discussions, a very weighty person of the day although in the end a non-signer; the finished document did not suit him, and he actively opposed it. Non-college people, in short, were every bit as active and as essential to the convention as collegians, perhaps more so.

Of the twenty-five college men on the scene, only three made heavy inputs to the proceedings—Madison and Wilson, who are widely designated the main architects of the Constitution, and Gouverneur Morris, something of a wild card. Two played significant secondary roles— Paterson and King. But both Madison and Wilson were overruled by the body on some of their most cherished suggestions even though they fought doggedly for them.

To continue with Rossiter: "If we add to this list the names of those (like Dickinson and Rutledge) who studied law at one of the Inns of Court in London, attach to names already on the list (like Johnson, Paterson, McClurg, and Williamson) the degrees they won for graduate work at home and abroad, take note of the professorships or tutorships of Baldwin, Houston, Williamson, Wilson, McClurg, and Wyeth, and count up the honorary degrees that had already come to such as Franklin (LL.D., Edinburgh, 1759) and Washington (LL.D., Harvard, 1776—an interesting year to get an honorary degree from Harvard), we arrive at a sum of college experience that was perhaps the most astonishing feature of the Convention." There is, it should be noticed, no "college experience" attested to by an honorary degree. And this of Rossiter's is itself an astonishing statement, in harmony with the inflated commentary on the convention and the Constitution that is fairly standard.

As to "professorships", Houston had indeed been a teacher of mathematics at the College of New Jersey but had long since given it up in favor of public office. In any event, he left the convention after a week on account of illness, soon to die, and never returned. Wyeth was a long-time professor of law at the College of William and Mary, and reputed to be a very good one. But Wyeth too left soon after the convention opened owing to the illness of his wife, who died during the proceedings; he never returned.[12] Neither man had much of a hand in the proceedings.

Baldwin, a lawyer and a former member of Congress, tutored in theology for four years after graduating from Yale; Williamson, also a student of theology, after graduating from the College of Philadelphia briefly taught mathematics, then took up medicine, was North Carolina surgeon general during the war and then entered Congress; Wilson, penniless, first taught Latin on coming to this country, soon gave it up for law and politics and occasionally lectured on law; and McClurg, who graduated from William and Mary and then was awarded an M.D. by the University of Edinburgh, was a part-time professor of medicine at William and Mary. McClurg became Secretary of Foreign Affairs for Virginia in 1783. Anything like a representation of academia at the convention was thus essentially nil. And except for Wilson none of these was of much consequence to the convention.

Again, to associate as a glistening plus factor the collegians at the convention with the latter-day Ivy League of comprehensive universities, as Rossiter does, is distinctly misleading. The colleges of the colonial period were quite rudimentary and, in general, graduated students at a much earlier age than do present-day colleges, often as early as age sixteen. They were palpably below the level of a latter-day first-class secondary school. As of 1800 when conditions were, if anything, improved over pre-revolutionary days, "Education in such institutions of higher learning as there were consisted largely in a study of the classics (Harvard included Hebrew), a little history, some natural science. Harvard, in addition to President Willard, boasted a faculty consisting of professors of divinity, mathematics and Greek, four tutors and a steward.

"Arrangements were simple, how simple is suggested by a letter from Benjamin Waterhouse to President Willard . . . He pointed out to the President that he has kept the carpet clean, turned up the seats and never lectured in rainy weather. He was greatly annoyed at being turned out of his room. During eighteen years of work, he pointed out, he had never been given a lecture room for the Theory and Practice of Physics, and that some of his medical lectures he had even had to give in undergraduates' rooms. As for suggestions that he could give them in the future in the dining room, or the chapel, he wrote, 'Both are totally unfit; besides, I wish to be indulged with a room out of which I cannot be turned by any professor, tutor, librarian, or cook." [13]

"The deficiency of this late eighteenth-century education was chiefly in science. Some strides had been made in the study and use of motion and of force, but the results do not seem to have been considered of sufficiently demonstrated value to be taught to the young.

"Except for this, the system seems to have been good, despite Anne Ritson who, referring to the cultivation of the mind in Virginia in 1800, said,

> A disappointment there you'll find
> No care was taken of the mind." [14]

Nor were English universities in the eighteenth century distinguished educational centers, and this refers especially to Oxford and Cambridge, at a low ebb in their histories. The Scottish universities however were then of higher caliber, both in general sophisticated esteem, in the quality of their instructors and in the demands on their students.

In general, American higher education of the period showed concern mainly over religious instruction, reliance on the classical background "and the purely material ends sought by the mathematical sciences, skill in conjoined proportion, alligation and the casting of interest, and the ability (much in demand today) to understand and use the celestial navigational triangle." [15]

Any suggestion, then, that there was on the scene at the Philadelphia convention a sharply honed, academically fine-tuned intellectual crew is simply at variance with all evidence, more of which could be cited. Delegate Gouverneur Morris at a later date scorchingly denounced the caliber of American college education, of which he had direct experience as a 16-year-old graduate of King's College.

Actually, on the basis of education in schools of a socially prestigious aura the intellectual light of the convention was General Charles Cotesworth Pinckney of South Carolina, an outstanding spokesman for slavery. As a child he was sent to England and ran the course at the Westminster School and Oxford University, then the law courts. Then he attended the Royal Military College at Caen, France, returning to Charleston in 1769 to begin the practice of law at age 23.

None of this is to suggest that the convention was not under disciplined intellectual guidance, which came for the most part from the two Jameses, Madison and Wilson, George Mason and John Dickinson.

The foundation for Madison's orderly, comprehensive and somewhat schematic mentality was laid long before he attended the College of New Jersey where he concentrated on literature, philosophy, theology and the principles of government. His prior schooling had been at home under his clergyman-father, then in the school of Donald Robertson in King and Queen County, Virginia, for five years, and then under the intensive tutorship for two years of the Rev. Thomas Martin, a learned clergyman. The true key to Madison's studiousness was Robertson, a graduate of Aberdeen and Edinburgh Universities and a stickler for precision. Madison, an apt student and diligent reader, became if anything over-studious, so much so that for a time he damaged his health.

The sources of Wilson's mental acuteness were similar although experienced at first hand. Born in Scotland, and of a more restless disposition than Madison, Wilson attended the universities at Glasgow, St. Andrews and Edinburgh although he does not seem to have taken a degree. Nor, for that matter, did the great Hume, who left Edinburgh University after three years with no degree, yet has ever since been the focus of studies by scores of professors with strings of degrees.

These two men, although able, did not have the most far-ranging brains at the convention. For such one must look to Dickinson and tutor-educated Mason. Had it not however been for Washington's aversion to dictatorship or monarchy, proposed in precisely these terms by a number of friends of the convention, the gathering could easily have gone hog-wild to the right. It had enough elements in it sympathetic to such a turn but they lacked a plausible figure to place up front and hide behind. By his attitude Washington showed his better judgement.

A note on education: Everyone who is educated is self-educated, whether he has been to school or not. Schooling is an external process, of aid to education as are the ministrations of a physician in a birth. Education is an internal experiential process, and is stimulated by listening to good discourse, by wide reading, by disciplined research in the field or by well-directed laboratory work. But the emerging educated person is really doing it all himself, always. The best teacher in the world can't lift or inspire an utter oaf. And if one confines one's reading to low-grade material there is little or no aid to education.

Of educated men without degrees the convention also had a few, the outstanding being Washington, Mason, Dickinson and Franklin. On the whole, however, even after noting the presence of formally cultivated men like William Samuel Johnson, it was a gathering of routine politicians, eyes open for the main chance of a purely material nature. They were all, in one way or another, realists, not idealists. What makes them different from latter-day politicians is that in an age of few distractions many—at least twenty—were readers to varying extents in law, government, history and classics. It is this, it seems, that gives them a tone that most later counterparts, dependent on ghost-writers and ghost-researchers, products of slapdash schools to a great extent, seem to lack.

Academia however has commemorated a few of these men in the names of universities and colleges and especially public high schools. The little-schooled Washington has four universities and one college named after him and shares the name of one university and one college. A state and city are also named after him. Colleges are named after Dickinson, Hamilton and Madison, and Franklin has a college and a university named after him and shares the name of another college. But no others of the fifty-five appear to have been so glorified.

A Reunion of Military Veterans

Something kept very much of a secret in most writings about the convention is the military background of most of the delegates. In some ways the gathering took on the complexion of the general staff of the war of the revolution.

There was, first, the commander in chief of the Continental Army in the presiding chair, the redoubtable George Washington. Then there were Generals C. C. Pinckney and Thomas Mifflin, the latter both major general and quartermaster general. There was also James Wilson, brigadier general (briefly) of Pennsylvania militia, James McClurg, surgeon general of Virginia troops, Pierce Butler, adjutant general of South Carolina troops, Gunning Bedford, lieutenant colonel and muster-master general, George Clymer, deputy commissary general of prisoners, William Livingston, brigadier general of New Jersey militia, John Dickinson, brigadier general of Pennsylvania militia, and Hugh Williamson, surgeon general of North Carolina forces. To a considerable extent it was a gathering of revolutionary generals, men used to wielding authority over the rank and file.

Colonels in the group were Alexander Hamilton, who became a major general and inspector general of the United States Army from 1798 to 1800, David Brearley, Alexander Martin, William Richardson Davie (wounded as a member of the Pulaski Legion and North Carolina cavalry), John Langdon, Nicholas Gilman and William Few. Majors and captains were Richard Bassett of Delaware, William Pierce of Georgia and Rufus King. John Francis Mercer of Maryland was a lieutenant with the 3rd Virginia regiment, was wounded at Brandywine and ended as a lieutenant colonel and chief aide-de-camp to General Lee. Edmund Randolph of Virginia was a deputy muster-master and aide-de-camp to Washington. General Pinckney was taken prisoner and exchanged. General Mifflin was the chief aide-de-camp to Washington. Capt. Pierce was aide-de-camp to Generals Sullivan and Greene and was cited for intrepidity in action by Congress and presented with a sword. Daniel of St. Thomas Jenifer of Maryland was listed as a hospital physician and surgeon, what today would be called a medic, the lowest rating on the scene. Dayton was an aide-de-camp to General Sullivan, was taken prisoner and exchanged. General Mifflin was a major aide-de-camp to Washington. Abraham Baldwin of Georgia was a brigade chaplain and William Blount was paymaster of the 3rd North Carolina infantry.

In all, twenty-seven delegates to the convention, mostly men long known to Washington, had been officers of the revolutionary war.[16]

Nor is this all. In 1783 the Society of the Cincinnati was formed, consisting of veteran officers of the Continental Army. Against this society rose a strong grass-roots hue and cry, alleging that its members planned to establish an hereditary aristocracy, a special privileged group, possibly with Washington as king. Although rightists in varying degree, the rightism of only a few extended beyond the parameters of discussion at the Philadelphia convention. On the other hand, they were all far from democrats.

Fifteen delegates were already members of the society at the time the convention met and three joined subsequently. Those already members were Baldwin, Brearley, Dayton, Dickinson, Gilman, Hamilton, Jenifer, Lansing, Livingston, McClurg, Mifflin, Pierce, C. C. Pinckney, Washington and Yates. King, Gouverneur Morris, James Wilson and Benjamin Franklin joined at different times after the convention.[17] Those who had not been officers, like Morris, Lansing, Yates and Franklin, were designated honorary members. Such a substantial infusion of the controversial Cincinnati into the ranks of the convention is rarely, if ever, alluded to by historians. Some, such as Lansing and Yates, fought against adoption of the Constitution.

Washington was probably better acquainted with more convention members than anyone else. All stood in some awe of him, in part owing to the habitual remoteness of his bearing and in part because he was their victorious commander in chief, by now literally the toast of two continents.

The attitude toward Washington is illustrated by an anecdote, possibly apocryphal, that has survived. At a social gathering outside the convention somebody offered to bet a dinner and drinks for a dozen or so people that nobody would dare go up to Washington, tap him on shoulder and say, "My dear General, how happy I am to see you look so well." One-legged, devil-may-care Gouverneur Morris took the bet, and won, but confessed after enduring Washington's cold silent stare, "I have won the bet but dearly paid for it, and nothing could induce me to repeat it." [18]

Religion and Duelling

The genteel tradition of historical writing has largely obscured under layers of edifying varnish the individualities of all except very few of the men of Philadelphia, 1787, who for different reasons have become prominently historicized—Washington, Franklin, Madison and Hamilton. The first two, it should be remarked, as far as the record shows, played only supervisory roles at the convention, anxious mainly that the gathering come to amicable agreement on a predetermined goal.

Only one, Richard Bassett of Maryland, converted by Bishop Asbury in person, stood out as a religious enthusiast, a born-again Christian. Even those like Madison, Williamson and Baldwin, who had early in life studied theology, were not what is called believers. The assemblage was one of deists or rationalists, giving only *pro forma* acknowledgement to religious establishments, thus reassuring religious elements. It was, as their lives and labors showed, a gathering of hard-bitten secularists.

While it would be wholly erroneous to depict the convention as a nest of gunfighters, there were many present who had given and were ready to give "satisfaction" to any other gentleman at the drop of an unseemly word, and there were others who had "assisted" at duels.

One member, Major William Pierce of Georgia, absented himself from the convention to fight a duel in New York with one John Auldjo who had pressed for the payment of a commercial debt; the duel was aborted, with satisfaction to the ruffled Pierce, through the intercession of Alexander Hamilton. The latter was to die at the hands of Vice President Aaron Burr in a duel in 1804. Hamilton's eldest son had by then already been killed in a duel.

Richard Dobbs Spaight, who became governor of North Carolina, was killed in a duel in 1802 at the hands of a rival for office, which was often the sub-surface prize at stake in these duels. For office in the great American democracy for many meant the difference between personal security and an uncertain existence. More generally, a duel was a way of covering over the confused mental state of a challenger or offender, or both.

The *code duello* at the time was solidly established in the United States. "The formal duel had a vogue in America from colonial days to 1883." [19] Many men of the revolutionary period, especially political and military figures, participated in duels either as principals or seconds. The formal duel shaded off historically in the catch-as-catch-can western gunfight celebrated endlessly in popular films in face of the fact that most were simple drunken brawls or cold assassinations. The duel was also long a standard institution in the South until replaced for excitement in a dull milieu by the fairly casual lynching of Negroes—the local grass-roots democrats expressing themselves.

A widely travelled Englishman, Andrew Steinmetz, writing as late as 1868, said, "America is a country where life is cheaper than anywhere else . . ." Whereas in other countries duelling is an "offhand diversion", he wrote, when "men fight in the States they fight in earnest, 'killing is the word.' Revolvers are forever revolving. There is no objection to fowling pieces [shotguns], to rifles, to bowie knives; the last are ever ready. A pretense to scratch the back of the neck whips out the formidable tool into action . . ." [20]

While there was little or no duelling in puritan New England, which long supplied its somewhat self-righteous self-image to the entire United States, in the rest of the country the duel was very much in style. "If one were to paint a duelling map of the country in this early-republic era, all the New England states would be left white; New York, New Jersey, and Pennsylvania would be pink, shading southward in a deeper tone to blood red in South Carolina and Georgia." [21]

Duelling had been standard in the Continental Army, whose officers up to the level of general would apparently just as soon open fire on each other over differences as on the British. [22] Derogatory remarks about General Washington provoked at least two celebrated army duels. The son of Congress president Henry Laurens of Charleston, a member of Washington's staff, severely wounded General Charles Lee in a duel, and General John Cadwallader of Pennsylvania in 1778 shot General Thomas Conway in the mouth. "While Conway lingered between life and death he wrote a full confession [of 'The Conway Cabal'] and apology to Washington." [23]

In post-convention days, for nearly a hundred years, many Congress-men and governors of states were principals in duels, and it was rather common for judges in the South to engage in such affairs and to have loaded pistols with them on the bench to cope with disgruntled litigants. But the only recognized gunfighter to attain the White House was Andrew Jackson, experienced both in the formal and the spur-of-the-moment gunfight. Many American publicists, however, especially with American involvement in World War I, waxed indignant over the custom of uni-versity duelling in Germany, holding it to be a barbaric custom typical of the infinitely militaristic Hun.

When Hamilton was stricken in 1804, General Charles Cotesworth Pinckney, a convention delegate now a presidential aspirant, tried vainly as its president general to get the Society of the Cincinnati, veteran revolutionary officers' association, to interdict duelling. "Duelling is no criterion of bravery," wrote Pinckney. "I have seen cowards fight duels, and I am convinced real courage may be better shown in the refusal than in the acceptance of a challenge." [24] Such words from a South Carolina officer and gentleman were most unusual.

Pierce Butler, himself a duellist, gave refuge on his St. Simon Island estate to Aaron Burr after the killing of Hamilton.[25] Burr, condemned in the effete North, was lionized in the virile South.

So it is evident that the elements at the convention were not all as broadly philosophical as commonly depicted. "And yet Washington never gave nor accepted a challenge, or was party to anyone else's quarrel on the field." [26] Washington, as one usually finds, was something apart, always the nonpareil.

Their Eclipse

As a collection of supposedly highly sagacious men the post-convention careers of the framers raise a big question mark. For ten of the band of fifty-five went broke or into bankruptcy with several of them, patent overreachers, involved in the first of many colossal financial scandals of American history, two died in duels, one became a shattered drunk-ard, two flirted with treason, one was expelled by the Senate, and one went mad. In short, seventeen carried within them the seeds of their own destruction.

Beyond this, six blameless delegates suffered for many years in shat-tered health, one was poisoned by an irate heir-to-be, one disappeared without trace, and another, the austere Washington himself, probably died from mistaken medical practice. To top all this, others fell to quarreling bitterly among themselves about politics (which philosophers would be loath to do) and about interpretations to be placed upon the Constitution they had collaborated in framing.

All in all, as far as the destinies of most of them were concerned it was an ill-starred and vulnerable group. For their misadventures in life far over-stepped the probabilities for fifty-five geographically dispersed men of various ages and origins.

Toward Apotheosis

What most fixes attention in the post-convention history of most of the framers is their generally routine or non-distinctive performances, descending toward drabness or the trivial. In this connection one must always remember that as part of the politically motivated glorification of the Constitution they are nearly always hailed as an exceptionally sagacious galaxy although the sagacity of most showed itself neither before, during nor after the convention. If they were indeed so masterful then, excepting a very few, they manifested it in one shining episode. The available record fails to sustain even this reduced claim.

Equally notable is the readiness with which they switched political coloration in their subsequent quests for office. Many who had been firm centralizers at the convention, including Madison, became more or less ardent states'-righters, and some who had been voluble on behalf of states' sovereignty became impassioned centralists. There were the makings in these shifting positions of the later "loose" and "strict" constructions of the Constitution, which could be turned on and off like hot and cold running water.

A number started dying off right after the convention ended, removing them from further consideration. William C. Houston of New Jersey died at age 42 in 1788 of tuberculosis. William Pierce of Georgia, now bankrupt, died in 1789, aged 49. David Brearley of New Jersey, born in 1745, the famed Benjamin Franklin of Pennsylvania, born in 1706, William Livingston of New Jersey, born in 1723, and Daniel of St. Thomas Jenifer of Maryland, born in 1723, all succumbed in 1790.

The outstanding and generally unsung George Mason of Virginia died in 1792, aged 66. He was followed the next year by Roger Sherman of Connecticut, born in 1721, after having served in the House and Senate. The next to go was Daniel Carroll of Maryland, born in 1730, died 1796, and then George Read of Delaware, born 1733, died 1798. Each sat in the new Congress, and Read ended as chief justice of his state.

Nathaniel Gorham of Massachusetts, aged 58, died in 1796, and

James Wilson, aged 54, died in 1798, both after suffering strokes. Both were involved at the end in crushing financial calamities as land speculators.

Many members of the convention were speculators in public lands (as well as in public securities), what today are called wheeler-dealers, but the group centered in Philadelphia around banker Robert Morris, with connections to others in more distant parts, was the biggest and became the most notorious.

Morris, for a time a Senator in the new government, went bankrupt for untold millions in the 1790s and served three-and-a-half ignominious years in debtors' prison in Philadelphia. There Washington, ever grateful for his financial operations during the war, several times visited him. Morris took with him into ruin several of the framers, notably Fitzsimons, Mifflin and Wilson, and brought losses to many others.

Wilson had been appointed by Washington a Justice of the Supreme Court in keeping with his policy of stacking the Court with Federalists but while sitting came under siege of his creditors. He first went literally on the run to New Jersey, to escape the New York and Pennsylvania laws, and then fled to North Carolina, where he was pursued by Pierce Butler of South Carolina, a convention delegate, who claimed Wilson owed him $197,000. Gorham, also associated with Morris in his schemes, went under in a scheme of his own involving western New York lands.

Involved as investors with Morris were many Philadelphians who lost heavily. His name was anathema in Philadelphia for decades. What happened, briefly, was this: the speculators, scenting a vast immigration from Europe, contracted to buy millions of acres of public and privately owned land up and down the Mississippi Valley west of the Alleghenies. There, huge tracts had become part of the public domain, one of the concrete prizes sought from Great Britain behind all the revolutionary declamations about constitutional violations. Britain had impeded settlement to keep the Indians from combining with French and Spanish, about whom Americans had less reason to be fearful. Payment for these lands was generally to be made in continental and state securities at par. But the securities, in the 1780s and early 1790s, were selling at abysmally depreciated prices, available to all comers with money, at a bargain.

The speculators aimed at a double killing: to pay for the low-priced land with securities at par which had been acquired at a deep discount, and then to sell the land to greenhorn settlers at an appreciated figure for cash and mortgages. Had the scheme succeeded all would have been incalculably rich, beyond the wildest dreams of avarice.

Two unexpected but not unforeseeable events brought the scheme to earth in ruins. First, the funding plan for public securities launched by Hamilton as Secretary of the Treasury in the new government (and

Hamilton himself lost some $30,000 through Morris) drove the price of the securities up toward par as the central government assumed and guaranteed the debt with its new general taxing power to make it good. So the securities, in which another set of speculators, including many other delegates, made large profits, were no longer available at a bargain. Then the developing Napoleonic wars, setting Europe once again aflame and leading to renewed French-British hostilities on the high seas, quenched any hope of an early vast immigration into the New World.

Morris had apparently not foreseen the stunning financial success of the new government and its effect on securities prices, and he was many years off in his anticipation of the vast immigration. Inherently the operation was too grandiose and risky in any case, the brainchild of gamblers scenting huge windfalls at public expense. What the scheme revealed, as do all similar ventures, was the philosophic poverty of its participants.

Meanwhile Washington died in 1799 after serving two successful terms as President. Fallen ill with a sore throat, retrospectively diagnosed by some as a streptococcal infection, he was drained by his physician of a quantity of blood, a procedure contra-indicated in later medical practice. If it wasn't the throat ailment that killed him, the blood-letting surely did.

He was followed the next year by John Rutledge, born in 1739, who had lost his sanity. Rutledge had been appointed a Justice of the Supreme Court, had resigned to become chief justice of South Carolina and had then been appointed Chief Justice of the Supreme Court, which appointment was not confirmed by the Senate because of his over-wrought public opposition in the interval to the Jay Treaty with Britain, a Federalist venture. Rutledge may have been slipping mentally at the time he savagely denounced the treaty. John Blair of Virginia, also a Justice of the Supreme Court, born in 1732, also died in 1800 as did Thomas Mifflin, governor of Pennsylvania from 1790 to 1799, who was born in 1744.

Thomas Blount of North Carolina succumbed to a stroke in 1800 after having fallen into national disgrace. For engaging in a conspiracy of land-grabbers to induce a British and Indian attack on Spain's Florida and Louisiana he was expelled from the Senate by a vote of 25 to 1 on July 8, 1797. The House of Representatives contemplated impeaching him, it not yet having been decided that legislators were not impeachable. Blount thereupon removed to Tennessee, was elected to the state senate and by it elected its presiding officer.

Both Spaight of North Carolina, born in 1758, and Hamilton of New York, born in 1757, went down, as already noted, in duels—in 1802 and

1804 respectively. Hamilton was one of the few convention delegates to make a notable post-convention record. As Washington's first Secretary of the Treasury he put the national finances on a sound conservative footing, after which he became the leader of the Federalist Party. He went into eclipse in 1800 when the country repudiated the high-riding Federalists with the election to the Presidency of Thomas Jefferson of the Republican Party, later named the Republican-Democratic Party. The game of leapfrog for offices had begun.

Robert Yates of New York and William Paterson of New Jersey died in 1801 and 1806 respectively. Yates, a pro-state man who walked out of the convention midway and who vigorously opposed adoption of the Constitution under the pen-name of "Brutus", a long-time New York judge prior to the convention, had become chief justice of New York and had attempted with Hamilton's help to win the governorship in 1789. For Yates in an abrupt about-face had come to ally himself with the new order. He had earned Hamilton's respect by showing in his writings a thorough grasp of how the new Constitution, especially its court system, would actually work. Paterson at his death had put in thirteen routine years as a Justice of the United States Supreme Court.

Wyeth of Virginia, who played little part in the convention, reverted to the teaching of law. He died in 1806, poisoned with arsenic adminstered by a wastrel great-nephew.

Robert Morris died in penury in 1806, a pensioner of Gouverneur Morris. He had been released from prison in 1800 with the passage of the national bankruptcy act, a beneficiary in this way of a provision in the Constitution. He still owed more than $3 million which was never paid, a vast sum for those days.

Ellsworth of Connecticut, Alexander Martin of North Carolina and Baldwin of Georgia died in 1807. All had been almost uninterruptedly on the public payroll since the Constitution took effect. Ellsworth had been a Senator, Chief Justice of the Supreme Court (1796-1800) and special envoy to France. Baldwin served ten years in the House and eight in the Senate. Martin also held seats in both houses.

The survivors now began dropping off more rapidly—Dickinson (virtually retired for twenty years) in 1808, the ultra-obscure Jacob Broom of Delaware in 1810, Fitzsimons in 1811, Bedford in 1812, Clymer and Randolph in 1813, Gilman and Gerry in 1814, Basset in 1815, McHenry and Gouverneur Morris in 1816, Langdon, Williamson, Strong and Johnson in 1819 and Davie in 1820.

All, with the exception of Gouverneur Morris, held or contended for political office all along the way or lived in unproductive retirement on their ample incomes. Fitzsimons of course had fallen into reduced circumstances through association with Robert Morris. McHenry had been an undistinguished Secretary of War under President John Adams. Clymer had lived in indolent retirement since 1796. Randolph, first Attorney General of the United States, later as Secretary of State under Washington came under a cloud, suspected of corrupt dealings with the French, and resigned. He then engaged in private practice, his financial affairs in a tangle, and became a defense counsel for Aaron Burr. William Samuel Johnson had been made president of Columbia University, formerly King's College, but resigned in 1800 to finish the next nineteen years in increasingly bad health, palsied.

Bedford served quietly to the end as a federal district judge. Gilman and Langdon of New Hampshire were indefatigable office-holders, Langdon in the state legislature or governorship, Gilman in the United States Senate.

Strong and Gerry spent what remained of their lives in contending against each other for top office in Massachusetts, Strong trouncing Gerry five times. But Gerry won in 1810. Gerry also put in the years 1789-93 in the House of Representatives, was a United States commissioner abroad in the XYZ Affair of redolent notoriety and became Vice President of the United States in 1812.

Exceptional among these figures was Gouverneur Morris, an unreconstructed rightist to the very end. Morris was an aristocrat by birth, training and temperament, and at times appropriately high-handed. A grandson of Lewis Morris (1671-1746), judge, royal governor of New Jersey and first lord of the manor of Morrisania, N.Y., son of Lewis Morris (1698-1762), judge and second lord of the manor, he was half-brother to Lewis Morris, third and last lord and a signer of the Declaration of Independence.

A graduate of King's College at sixteen, the wealthy Morris was initially opposed for conservative reasons to separation from Great Britain but after the Battle of Lexington threw in his lot with the revolt and in 1775 sat in the revolutionary Provincial Congress of New York for Westchester County. He took a leading part in writing the very conservative New York constitution, was a strong supporter of the Continental Congress and from the very beginning was a proponent of a strong central government. From this position he never wavered.

He sat in the Continental Congress from 1778 to 1779 and was a staunch partisan of Washington's military policies. Upon his defeat for re-election he moved to Philadelphia, resumed the practice of law and became Assistant Superintendent of Finance under Robert Morris, no relative. He was a hand-picked delegate from Pennsylvania to the constitutional convention, in which he played a prominent but at times erratic role. The sort of government he would have preferred would just about have obliterated the states. It would have had a President elected for life, a Senate of men appointed by the President for life, and suffrage in national elections restricted to freeholders—that is, owners or life lessees of real estate. He opposed equal representation of the states in the Senate. Universal suffrage he thought ludicrous, not realizing that most people would not exercise theirs, would not know how to apply it if they did or even be interested in learning.

After the convention Morris purchased Morrisania from his half-brother, went there to live but soon departed for France to act as an agent for Robert Morris. He was gone for ten years, was appointed a commissioner to negotiate with the British about debts, trading posts and commercial rights and in 1792 was appointed Minister to France from which vantage-point he was an eye-witness to the French revolution. Without the authorization or knowledge of his government, Morris engaged in a plot to assist Louis XVI escape from Paris. He was withdrawn in 1794 when the French ambassador was recalled from the United States, and spent some years travelling about Europe and engaging in amorous adventures. He served an appointment as United States Senator from 1800 to 1803 to fill a vacancy, for a while attended to personal affairs and in 1810 became chairman of the commision to build the Erie Canal, a project he had been recommending for nearly twenty-five years.

Always a tight Federalist, the policies of Jefferson continually raised his hackles. He opposed Jefferson's self-wounding embargo and the War of 1812 and endorsed the Hartford convention that considered separating New England from the sacred Union. Delegate Caleb Strong was also a supporter of the Hartford convention. At the end of his life he was completely disillusioned with the course of political events, thought the Union a failure.

Morris, like his outlook or not, was a man of very considerable ability, much of it misdirected, and always an activist. His writings on the French revolution, in the form of a diary published in 1888, were later praised as source material (*Dernier Essais de Critique et d'Histoire,* 1894) by the eminent French critic and historian, Hippolyte Taine (1828-1893), which fact alone, although meaningless to most of the public, puts Morris among the framers in very much of a choice class. He could easily, had he been so inclined, have become a high-level professional writer as he had demonstrated as far back as 1780 in a series of penetrating essays on the nation's finances published in *The Pennsylvania Packet*. It was these essays that brought him to the attention of Robert Morris and led to his becoming Assistant Superintendent of Finance from 1781 to 1785. Morris, no democrat, was nevertheless no mere political time-server or opportunist like so many other convention delegates. He was fluent in both French and English.

The remaining few, hardly any of them distinguished in any way other than by their attendance at the convention, now began dropping off rapidly. John Francis Mercer, who was in Philadelphia no more than ten days, died in 1821. He had served two terms in Congress and was governor of Maryland from 1801 to 1803. Luther Martin, a voluble states'-sovereignty man at the convention, later a vociferous Federalist, died in 1826 a penniless alchoholic who was taken into the home of Aaron Burr in New York. Martin had been one of counsel at Burr's treason trial, was attorney general of Maryland from 1778 to 1805 and from 1818 to 1822.

Pierce Butler died in 1822, Charles Pinckney in 1824 and General C. C. Pinckney in 1825. Butler, although serving twice in the Senate and as a director of Robert Morris's creation, the Bank of the United States, spent most of his later life as a wealthy South Carolina planter and of course gentleman. Charles Pinckney, on the other hand, was a continual office-holder—a multi-term governor of South Carolina in the 1790s, ardent convert to Jeffersonianism who served in the Senate from 1798 to 1801, Minister to Spain from 1801 to 1805, again governor and state legislator on his return, and again in Congress from 1819 to 1821. The Federalists of Charleston referred to him as "Blackguard Charlie" because of his now radical democratic pretensions, which made him an idol of the lower orders, and as "Constitution Charlie" for his pretensions to having been the author of most of the Constitution. Madison made it clear in correspondence that Pinckney, who had falsified his age to make it seem he was the youngest man at the convention, had grossly exaggerated his own convention role. General C. C. Pinckney devoted most of his time after the convention to his law practice and the life of a Carolina gentlemen although he was one of the diplomatic negotiators in the XYZ fiasco and returned to the army in 1798-1800 when war with France seemed likely. He was the Federalist candidate for Vice President in 1800 and for President in 1804 and 1808.

Jared Ingersoll of Pennsylvania, James McClurg of Virginia, Jonathan Dayton of New Jersey, Rufus King of New York (although a delegate from Massachusetts at the convention), and William Few of Georgia, died in 1822, 1823, 1824, 1827 and 1828 respectively, leaving only three other delegates still alive: John Lansing of New York, William Houstoun of Georgia and James Madison of Virginia.

Ingersoll was an off-and-on-again office-holder and successful lawyer, counsel among others for the banker Stephen Girard of Philadelphia and on the losing side in two noted cases before the Supreme Court, *Chisholm v. Georgia* and *Hylton v. United States*. Otherwise he functioned as a Philadelphia judge and alderman and as attorney general of Pennsylvania, 1790-99 and 1811-17.

McClurg simply practiced medicine until his death but served on the Virginia governor's council and, like a number of his colleagues, was a director of the Bank of the United States.

Dayton, while serving as a Federalist in the House, 1791-99, and the Senate, 1799-1805, also engaged in extended land speculations and has Dayton, Ohio, named after him. Illness prevented him from joining Aaron Burr in his escapade down the Mississippi and so led to the quashing of his indictment for treason, which nevertheless put him under a public cloud. Burr, to be sure, was acquitted.

Rufus King was a continual office-holder or office-seeker, welcome equally to Federalists or Republicans. Adept always at landing politically on his feet, he was a Federalist Senator from New York in 1789-96, Minister to Great Britain under Washington, Adams and anti-Federalist Jefferson, 1796-1803, Federalist candidate for Vice President in 1804 and 1808 and for President in 1816, and Senator elected by an anti-Federalist Republican state legislature from 1813 to 1825. On top of which he was reappointed Minister to Great Britain by John Quincy Adams.

William Few of Georgia was first in the Senate and then spent three years as a federal judge, after which he moved to New York where he became an alderman, assemblyman, prison reformer and banker.

Lansing, a states'-sovereignty man at the convention who walked out with Yates midway, departed the earth in 1829 in what were sinister circumstances. He was a New York supreme court justice from 1790 to 1798, chief justice from 1798 to 1801, chancellor from 1801 to 1814 and a regent of the state university. Upon leaving the bench he returned to private practice in Albany. On a trip to New York City to handle some legal business for Columbia University he one evening went to the dock at the foot of Cortlandt Street to post a letter and was never seen again. Whether the victim of foul play or not he certainly came to an end by unknown misadventure. As he was 75 years old he may well have met his death at the hands of predators, for which some evidence existed according to Thurlow Weed, a New York politician of the day.

Next to slip off, in 1833, was William Houstoun of Georgia. A cipher at the convention, Houstoun was also a cipher in life, as far as the record shows, living in quiet retirement on his wealth. Like many of the other conventioneers he never cut much of a public figure.

Alone remaining now was James Madison, down through the years widely and erroneously hailed as the "father" of the Constitution. Who made what input into the Constitution has long been a subject of intense discussion among constitutional scholars, the underlying assumption being that whoever made the largest contribution is entitled to the greatest honor, owing to the presumed superlative character of the document as a whole. If, on the other hand, the document were not immoderately celebrated, there would be little point in claiming auctorial honors for anyone.

Madison in fact was not the father of the document either as the indispensable source or the principal source. He never claimed to be such and indeed denied it, which denial, made late in life, is often attributed to modesty. But why should anyone deny authorship or chief authorship, especially of a putative masterpiece, if he was in fact the author? Madison, in making his denial, pointed out correctly that many men had had a hand in laying out the Constitution. In fact Madison, a topic in the next chapter, had no original or unique thesis to present to the convention. In this he was like everyone else present.

What was original and unique about the Constitution was only its special synthesis of ingredients, none of which except in minor details derived originally from anyone present including Madison, whose function was that of an amanuensis and a powerful advocate on the convention floor of widely discussed views. As such he played a stellar role.

Madison died in 1836, aged 85, the last survivor of the band of 1787. Unlike most of the others he was a man all along without considerable property and without a profession. He was in fact all during his working life a government careerist, a self-made specialist in the details of government. He was not a lawyer although many historians astonishingly say he was. He could easily have become one.

He left the College of New Jersey, the nucleus of what became Princeton University, after six months of further study beyond his graduation in 1771. He continued reading in theology and public law at home although he had no religious affiliation, said later that he had a Unitarian preference. The upheavals of the times turned his thoughts to the colonial struggle and in December 1774, at the age of 23, he was elected to the Orange County, Virginia, revolutionary committee of which his father was chairman. Thereafter he was seldom to be without a political office, elected or appointed.

He was elected a member of the Virginia Convention which in May 1776 requested the Continental Congress to declare independence of Great Britain. Defeated for re-election (because he refused to treat liquor to the voters!), he thereupon served two years on the Virginia Council of State. Recognizing his careful and well-stocked analytical mind, the legislature in 1779 appointed him to Congress where he served the limit of three years. He then entered the Virginia legislature and from there was propelled to the Annapolis Convention of 1786, called to consider commercial regulation of the Confederation, which led to the call for a convention to consider amending the Articles of Confederation.

Where Madison, a careful student, was different from most of his political colleagues was that his mind systematically sought out fundamentals, moved from effects back to causes. This characteristic made him invaluable in committee work and elsewhere. While in Congress he asserted that body had implied power to coerce the states into conformity, although later, in shaping the Constitution, he saw that in actual practice such coercion would lead into undesirable overt conflict.

After the Constitution was ratified he sought a seat in the Senate but was blocked by the opposition of Patrick Henry, at which he ran for the lower house where he came into conflict with many of Hamilton's policies. He served until 1797. By this time he had changed from an extreme centralizer to a supporter of Jefferson and states' rights. As I have shown, he wrote the Virginia Resolutions of 1798 directed against the Alien and Sedition Acts of the Federalist Party. Here he asserted the right of the states to interpose collectively against laws they thought unconstitutional, a doctrine demolished by the Civil War.

In 1801 Madison became Jefferson's Secretary of State and, with Jefferson's support, was elected President in 1808, in which office he served two terms. Upon his retirement he became a strong critic of the nationalistic trend of Supreme Court decisions although he upheld the right of the Court to make final decisions. He served in the Virginia state constitutional convention of 1829-30 and was a proponent of sending Negroes back to Africa as colonists as a way of solving the problem of slavery in the United States. He was himself a slave-holder.

In all this time few persons, except the participants, had known what took place at the constitutional convention, whose secrets were well guarded except for brief reports by some of the delegates on bits of the proceedings here and there. The official journal was practically worthless, merely recording the numerical votes on each question. No doubt this was what the secrecy-minded delegates wanted. But Madison, with a livelier understanding of the implications of the proceedings than perhaps most participants, had written a very detailed day-to-day report, which historians treat pretty much as a stenographic record. It was far from that, however, as Madison had himself been a constant participant on the floor and in committees but, subject to omissions of nuances and other lacunae, it is the best we have.

Comparison of Madison's very full report with the fragmentary reports on particular episodes by Yates, McHenry, Paterson, Pierce, King, Hamilton and Mason shows that the various reporters did not always perceive the scene in the same way. At times the lesser reports are fuller, more informative than Madison's cryptic treatment of the same episodes. Yet, without Madison's gratuitous back-breaking service, one would be absolutely blind about the convention, as the entire country indeed was until his report was made public in 1840 after Congress purchased it from his estate for $40,000, a colossal bargain.

Why had Madison kept his detailed report to himself all these years, showing only parts of it to Jefferson? In many ways Madison was enigmatic. One surmise has been that he did not want the report made public earlier as it showed him playing a role at the convention less popular than the one indicated by his later states'-rights stands. Madison at the convention in fact fought hard, and unsuccessfully, for measures that would have made the government much more authoritarian than the one that actually emerged. Even late in life, he (like John Adams) was opposed to general popular suffrage.

What was initially startling about Madison's report was that it showed the convention as a group of men intent upon securing various special economic interests, not the philosophically detached cogitators they had been held in propaganda to be. Who got what when where and how was a consideration always to the fore at the convention, no gathering of visionaries or messiahs.

Any idea that the convention had been devoted to devising the best possible government out of the many logically possible was shattered in the reading of the report. From the very beginning the convention had known, in general, where it was heading, thus leading to many early departures. And any idea that the convention had addressed itself even superficially to various alternatives was likewise shattered.

Eight Outstanding Characters

As to the men of the convention who stayed to the end, about whom so much has been heard, few in their careers lived up to their portrayal as members of a collection of unusually talented people. There was, first, Washington, always the nonpareil as revolutionary commander in chief and as the first and possibly most successful President. There was, next, Madison, who despite his later political wobbling was on the whole studiously competent. Hamilton played little role at the convention but was nevertheless an outstanding personality although flawed by over-striving pretensions, which led to his downfall. Gouverneur Morris was also an outstanding character although very much biased toward the extreme right. Wilson, a first-class mentality but nevertheless deeply flawed by his get-rich-quick passion, proved to be no man for all seasons. Franklin, little more than a figurehead in the convention, was a man of much-noticed varied prior achievement. Dickinson, though very much of a rightist, was a man who, mainly prior to the convention, had made outstanding contributions. Finally, there was George Mason of Virginia, a non-signer and perhaps more far-seeing and balanced than any of the others, the author of the original Virginia Bill of Rights and long a wise participant in and student of government.

This yields us eight characters weighty on balance in their various ways. As for the remainder, the best one can say is that most were routine or parochial or both. The parochialism of most, although understandable, was astounding in men who participated in the formulation of a reputed deathless document. Anyone who doubts this assertion need merely inquire into their lives and outlooks.

In cross-section, finally, the framers were predominantly a group of the leading men of the day and also, overlapping simultaneously, long-time Congressmen or state politicians, lawyers, military officers (enough present, including combat veterans, to give the meeting at least the flavor of a *coup d'état*), and financial and political wheeler-dealers. Exceptions from any of these categories were fewer than the fingers of one hand.

Five

THE
GORGEOUS
CONVENTION

The constitutional convention of 1787, an historical event of first-class importance, was itself an entirely routine, utterly uninspired political caucus. Contrary to a great deal of word-mongering by professed savants, it produced absolutely no prodigies of statecraft, no wonders of political ratiocination, no vaulting philosophies, no Promethean vistas. No rabbits were pulled from a magician's hat at Philadelphia although most writings about the event, their authors playing the heady roles of oracles, buoyed by simple consequent afflatus and out to flabbergast an over-gullible commonalty with tidings of yet another deliverance from Satanic forces, suggest on various levels and in various ways that the gathering represented the greatest breakthrough in human affairs since the proclamation of light by Jehovah.

Most alumni of the American school system, indoctrinated from ears to toes, believe that to this day, with a fervor at least equal to that of true believers in communism, socialism and the old-time religion. We see here the central source of the irritation displayed by sensitive Americans at recurrent disclosures of uncouth behaviors and grand deceptions by government officials at all levels—one more case of reality intruding on fantasy. The chief fantasy in American life is the popular conception of the Constitution as a document of salvation. And the Constitution is the prime warrant—indeed the magic talisman—of the American politician, in the name of which he performs his tightrope acrobatics.

The central achievement of the convention, a big one, was the tentative union—at least until 1861—of the runaway squabbling states. The simple act of unification in all countries—Italy, Germany, Holland, Ireland, Poland, China—is similarly intramurally celebrated, and similarly gives rise to wondrous tales and produces outsized heroes— Cavour, Bismarck, Paderewski, Mao Tse-tung, Lenin. All these have their counterpart, *mutatis mutandis* always understood, in George Washington. Yet solid American unification was not actually achieved until Appomattox, at bayonet point.

The final document, contrary to widespread supposition, marked out absolutely no new directions in government. It was a case of very old wine in a fancy new bottle all the way, and much of the wine was rancid. The document for example not only underwrote slavery to the hilt but reinforced it. As John Adams said in 1788, "What is the Constitution of the United States but that of Massachusetts, New York and Maryland! There is not a feature in it which cannot be 'found in one or the other."[1] Nor in a welter of earlier charters.

What the document did was to provide the channel for the restoration of the American states to the general course they were on, under the Union Jack, prior to the declaration of independence in 1776 but now under native rather than British rulers. It was the old store but under new management, newly decorated and expanded. Natives had been in charge since 1776, to be sure, but they were not united and were very often at odds. The new document ended most of the churning and backing and filling of contending political groups in the thirteen states that had cut loose their British ties in the revolution, the war and the subsequent peace. Despite all surface change, everything now reverted pretty much to the original position but with an entirely new set of slogans. In keeping with the French saying, everything changed yet everything remained the same.

What was produced was a new synthesis of familiar elements in government, in general within the main parameters of the British Constitution but now in republican rather than monarchical wrappings. Prior to the revolution, says an eminent recent historian, "The Americans were not an oppressed people; they had no crushing imperial shackles to throw off. In fact, the Americans knew they were probably freer and less burdened with cumbersome feudal and hierarchical restraints than any part of mankind in the eighteenth century. To its victims, the Tories, the Revolution was truly incomprehensible. Never in history, said Daniel Leonard, had there been so much rebellion with so 'little real cause.' It was, wrote Peter Oliver, 'the most wanton and unnatural rebellion that ever existed.' The Americans' response was out of all proportion to the stimuli: 'The Annals of no Country can produce an Instance of so virulent a Rebellion, of such implacable madness and Fury, originating from such trivial causes, as those alledged by these unhappy people.' "[2]

Except for a wider and somewhat freer (although largely unin-

terested) electorate in the United States, there was practically no difference in the basic thrust of the British and American Constitutions
after 1787. Whatever the differences of detail, they both pointed to the
same ends: the preservation in each country (after allowing for different
conditions) of the sort of societies already established and the material
elevation of a small section of the people over all others—historically
the outcome under all forms of government, including the Marxist
ones. As for the specific ingredients of the American Constitution, nearly
every one of them could be stamped with the benchmark "Originated
in England" with not the slightest violation of the verities. Only the
mixture was different.

The Immortals Assemble

Delegates began arriving in Philadelphia early in May 1787. The meeting, set by the Confederation Congress after ceaseless agitation and
confabulation by commercial and professional people and leading land-
holders, was definitely not officially called to write a constitution but
merely to amend the unwieldy Articles of Confederation. What it did
was, strictly viewed, illegal. The Congress at this time was practically
moribund and the more settled parts of the country were gripped by
postwar inflation and a commercial depression, phenomena which were
to become familiar and recurrent down through American history.

To a very minute degree almost everything known to be of record
about the convention in the way of reports and eye-witness commentaries is to be found in the four volumes, revised, of *The Records of the
Federal Convention of 1787* (1911, 1937), compiled by Max Farrand
and recopyrighted in 1966 by Yale University Press. From this basic
material (available in cheap editions) or from earlier printings of
Madison's *Journal* has exfoliated a deluge of books (but not nearly as
many as about the Constitution itself), of appeal to almost every variety
of reader mood although most line up on the side of celebratory afflatus, pure hagiology. The cold record is not enough to produce the
desired ecstatic reaction.

Beyond this, everything is interpretative or rearranged narrative, and
most of the interpretation is celebratory, designed to prove how near
to perfection the system is. What flows from such assumed excellence
is not usually what one is told to expect.

To go over the whole story once again, blow by blow, when Farrand
and scores of derivative accounts are readily available, would be only
to embroider what is now commonplace to the informed and easily
accessible to anyone seriously seeking enlightenment. What I intend
to do instead is to distill out of the record basic significances generally
suppressed, unnoticed or lost sight of. One would suppose that by now

everything possible has been said about the convention, but I think not, as what follows will show.

Historians have written much by way of extolling and comparing the "contributions" of various participants in the convention and have singled out James Madison and James Wilson as the two master architects, with George Mason, Gouverneur Morris, Roger Sherman or some other favorite as secondary operators. As the emergent Constitution was in the main a surprisingly faithful selective but hardened and reinforced composite of the Maryland, New York and Massachusetts state constitutions, dating respectively 1776, 1777 and 1780, the authors of these must surely be turned to in any quest for architects. Actually, anyone at all of moderate debating skill, armed with these three documents, would have been the equal of anyone at the convention in constitutional *savoir faire*.

John Adams wrote nearly all of the Massachusetts document of 1780, and in only a few days, with Maryland's and New York's before him, and the chief writers of the New York constitution were Gouverneur Morris, John Jay and Robert R. Livingston. Madison and Wilson were so enamored of the New York constitution that they fought doggedly at the convention to incorporate its council of revision into the national document, losing all the way. While very articulate in the proceedings, neither Madison nor Wilson were as dominant or original as most writers make them out to be. Actually, John Adams, recognized by scholars as the most forceful and penetrating American political theorist of the day, was the invisible theoretical force of the convention. Even many of the convention speeches of Hamilton, Gouverneur Morris, Madison and Wilson were taken almost verbatim from Adams's just published first volume, *Defence of the Constitutions of the United States of America*,[3] itself a compound of quotation.

Adams, in point of fact, had more than this to do with the shaping of the Constitution. For Adams, the spearhead of the movement for independence, who could well be termed the "father" of independence, was the chief individual force behind the writing of most of the state constitutions. He wielded this influence through his book *Thoughts on Government* (1776) and in a blizzard of letters he sent to revolutionary political figures in most of the states. As to *Thoughts on Government*, Adams noted in his diary that "The Gentlemen of New York availed themselves of the Ideas in this Morsell in the formation of the Constitution of that State." [4]

Only in Vermont, Pennsylvania and Georgia, which set up one-chamber legislatures and shadowy executives, was Adams ignored by leaders who were more swayed by the naive but widely popular Tom Paine.

Adams has been given downplay in most historical writing because his writings and deeds do not lend themselves to crowd-titillating propaganda. For Adams had a way of seasoning his observations with unpalatable truths that disturbed the powers in all political camps. From the point of view of manipulative politics Adams was, in the phrase of David Freeman Hawke, "the man who talked too much."

So, what the framers found in the constitutions of New York, Maryland and Massachusetts, was either pure Adams or a reworking of his notions.

"Living in London, he was one of the most vital forces in the Convention at Philadelphia." [5] The absent Adams apart, there was neither a dominating theoretical influence nor the need for one as the distinctive groups present were basically in agreement from the beginning about what was desirable and brought the main though mutually diluted outlines of their Adamite visions to life in the finished document.

Although no individual theorist on the ground dominated, the convention nevertheless sheltered two dominating personalities without whom it would almost surely have foundered. These were George Washington and "Great Man" Robert Morris, both of whom are treated by most historians pretty much as convention appendages, at most as public-relations figures, impressive to the unthinking public but of no consequence in the proceedings. Together, in fact, they constituted the living core and determined unifying force of the convention. They were the magnates, giants among midgets.

As to Morris, historians write with surprise and "disappointment" that he never spoke a word as far as any record shows. Washington, who presided by acclamation (significantly) after being proposed by Morris, spoke only once, briefly, near the very end, and only voted to break ties in the Virginia delegation. Neither man in fact needed to speak as the floor was filled with their subordinate mouthpieces—their political protegés or men to whom they were one-to-one mentors, sponsors, paying clients or dominant business associates.

Washington, who had outfoxed the British in a long and wasting war, had a personal influence over everyone who came near him such as no individual has since ever had in American public life. In the context he stood much in the position Napoleon held in France some ten years later, and could have named himself first consul or emperor. Many, in and out of the convention, were ready to second such a motion. But Washington, personally a retiring man, rejected such florid roles. Not only did he embody the essence of magnetic leadership but the majority of the convention had been among his officers in the revolutionary war, most of them known to him personally, and all of them more or less in awe of him. Morris for his part had intimate financial connections as a banker with at least a quarter of the convention delegates. Significantly, Washington stayed at Morris's home all during the convention.

Franklin, lost in the numerous Morris-oriented Pennsylvania delegation, was the true public-relations figure of the convention, his more indulgent views about the common people seldom prevailing. Widely renowned by reason of his many inventions (he was the Edison of his day), Franklin was an enfeebled octogenarian, had to have his speeches read by others, was carried to the convention each day in a sedan chair.

The leading Morris mouthpiece on the floor was James Wilson, his personal attorney for many years and associate in many land speculations who was to go bankrupt with him late in the next decade. Of equal caliber was Gouverneur Morris, a Robert Morris banking associate and his selection earlier on as Assistant Superintendent of Finance. When either Gouverneur Morris or Wilson spoke—and they were among the most frequent and aggressive speakers at the convention—they projected views that were either shared by Robert Morris or originated with him. A clear majority of the Pennsylvania delegation was under the patronage of Robert Morris.

A majority of the Virginia delegation was a Washington affair. Judge John Blair was a close friend whom Washington in 1790 appointed to the Supreme Court; George Wyeth left early and need not be counted; Dr. McClurg, as already pointed out, had been a Washington military aide during the war, and Madison, then virtually unknown, had attached himself to Washington as a protegé. Without the guaranty of Washington and the Virginia delegation, mousy Madison would have had little standing at the convention. The only two genuine independents in the Virginia delegation were George Mason and Gov. Edmund Randolph, neither of whom finally signed the Constitution, much to Washington's chagrin.

As to Madison, a government careerist all his life, his specific politics is always accounted for by whose protegé he made himself. Under the towering Washington at first, as Washington slipped from the scene Madison put himself under the tutelage of Jefferson, under whom his career was further advanced. His subordination to these two men parallels his shift from an earlier ultra-rightist Federalist position to the later states'-rights stance—almost an about-face.

In addition to Madison, Washington had another young protegé on the convention floor, the redoubtable Alexander Hamilton. Chief aide to Washington during the war, a prominent rightist in New York and at the convention, he would be appointed Washington's first Secretary of the Treasury in the upcoming government and would become the leader of the Federalist Party. But Hamilton was a minority of one in the states'-rights New York delegation, which would walk out early, angry at the course of the proceedings.

The Washington-Morris combination had friends in other delegations— Langdon and Gilman of New Hampshire, Caleb Strong, Nathaniel Gorham and Rufus King of Massachusetts, and for most purposes all of the Connecticut and South Carolina delegations with scatterings of friends elsewhere.

Significantly, the Virginia and Pennsylvania delegations were the most aggressive in pushing for strong centralization and were the first to convene in Philadelphia on May 14. The members of the two delegations had much in common to talk about, with Washington and Morris, old friends and wartime campaigners, binding them together.

The convention, then, as indicated earlier, was not a collection of detached groping individuals coming together for the first time to find out what they each thought and where they should go but was very much a prefabricated group affair with certain internal differences of emphasis, mainly with respect to concentrating authority in President or Congress.

There were, first, the tight nationalizers. Next came those who were in accord with a national government but wanted the states as separate entities to retain a corporate voice. Last, and a distinct minority, came those who opposed the states surrendering any power at all to a central government. These, and the ones who finally refused to sign, were regarded as belonging to the "popular" party. As for flat-out democrats, there were none in sight.

Looking at the convention in this way casts a very different light over the scene than the one usually encountered in most history books, which portray for the most part an assemblage of detached, equivalent individuals, all revolutionists, some possibly political savants or at least personages of extraordinary wisdom, each liable to come forward with almost anything in the spectrum of possibility and get serious consideration for it.

Old Wine in a Fancy New Bottle

What the finished Constitution became, then, was a selective codification of items, first strained through the Maryland, New York and Massachusetts constitutions, that had been on the English and American political scene for a long time. The selection was stepped up, reinforced, to restore American society to the point prior to the break of 1776 with Great Britain and to contain and neutralize the anarchic thrust against *all* governmental authority that was a distinct component of the revolutionary ideology of the time.

The convention was not summoned to *discover* or *invent* a Constitution, as often suggested. For the leading constitutional proponents knew in general what they wanted and had several scenarios ready on which to work.

As the convention managers knew what they wanted, why did they need to go to the trouble of holding the convention and then state ratification conventions? The purpose of the conventions was to get some show of formal approval, and thereby authentication, for each detail in a new document and then to gain such approval for the whole in the state conventions. These latter were not permitted, by convention stipulation, to select or reject details of the proposal submitted. At the state level approval was an all or nothing affair. As to changes, it was widely recognized that certain reforms were absolutely necessary. Conventions were thought by the framers better for the purpose of ratification than the state legislatures because the latter were two-house affairs in all except two extant states, which permitted delay and obstruction (features retained by careful design in the two-house Congress). That the conventions were elected by "the people," although so it was claimed, was not the decisive point. For the legislatures were also elected by "the people."

What the Philadelphia meeting constituted, in addition to an authenticated caucus, was, for some, an instructional seminar on the fine points to be covered and an editorial conference that discussed and accepted, rejected or revised proposed details on grounds of expediency. As far as novelty went, the product was strictly a scissors-and-paste affair, a collage. From beginning to end the convention was run by political sophisticates who knew what they wanted and, in the main, got it.

The ingredients, present for the most part in certain state constitutions, are to be found earlier strewn, word for word, through stacks upon stacks of colonial charters back to the original charters which were in fact the corporate charters of private companies organized for profit.[6] One legalistic cliché follows another in a long procession. The United States in fact began as two private corporations, the London Company and the Plymouth Company (1606).

All the early settlements of British North America were in fact private profit-seeking enterprises launched by stock-issuing companies, were not except incidentally religious or idealistic in nature. Contrary to much propaganda, American settlement was not a religious enterprise, seeking religious freedom or spiritual purification. In time the settlements were transformed into the colonial governments, now becoming public rather than private enterprises.

Nearly every significant turn of phrase in the Constitution already had legal standing at the time of the first settlements and each has been traced back to the original discoverable source by a pertinacious scholar.[7] As a consequence, the language of the Constitution, stately to modern ears, at the time of its composition was already very old and had a familiar ring to anyone versed in legal and governmental documents and charters. None of this language originated at the convention, nor was it there employed for anything other than traditional governmental ends. There was not in fact anything revolutionary about it, either in the form it took or in its objectives. In fact, just the opposite.

Whatever was revolutionary about the American revolution, in other words, ended with the ratification of the Constitution although the rhetoric of the revolution, equivalent to modern political campaign oratory, continued and became part of the inflated rhetoric of American politics, where it remains to this day. Americans therefore can have it both ways: they can have a thoroughly non-revolutionary, basically traditional type of government and at the same time may indulge in a wide range of heady revolutionary slogans, freely brought to bear at all times. In keeping with the slogans they can keep fresh before their eyes ever-receding Utopian vistas, much like desert mirages.

What the American revolution came down to, then, was a simple secession from Great Britain with a new government soon established that had a structure and procedures somewhat different from the British but was devoted to the same general ends as the British government before and after the revolution. And further secession was to have attractions for many Americans for a long time afterward, with many proposed by individual states north and south and eventually tried by a bloc of southern states to the accompaniment of maximum carnage.

Three Phases of Progress

The convention moved through a few simple phases over a time span of 120 days. Called for May 14, 1787, at the State House in Philadelphia, it did not begin until May 28 because delegates were late in arriving and some did not straggle in until as late as August.

The first phase produced the enactment of simple rules of orderly procedure, of which the one that later aroused most critical comment was the rule of secrecy.

With the entirely sensible rule of secrecy (although Jefferson professed not to like it) was demolished, at the origin, one of the shibboleths of democrats of that day as well as this. The United States government, contrary to widespread popular belief, has always had its official secrets and secret proceedings (of which a long list might be made), behind which officials at times conceal their personal deficiencies and self-serving or anti-public actions. In a world that holds governments ready to administer to others the final *coup* at any moment, it would be bizarre if secrecy were ruled out. The lately heard doctrine of "the people's right to know" has no basis at all in the Constitution or anywhere else. It is an assertion out of thin air. The Constitution, in fact (Article I, Section 5), allows for discretionary secrecy in the proceedings of Congress. The Senate in fact kept all its proceedings secret until 1794, when it voluntarily decided to go public. The White House has always had its secrets.

True, there was no question at the convention of keeping foreigners in the dark. But in order to insure uninhibited discussion secrecy was necessary. For otherwise the delegates would have felt forced to play to the popular gallery outside. Instead of their true views they would have spouted blarney.

On May 30 the convention moved on in its first phase and resolved itself into a committee of the whole "to consider the state of the American union". In this committee all discussion and votes were tentative, simply to determine the sense of the meeting, although throughout the convention questions that had once been decided were allowed to be brought forward again and again for more discussion and voting. All the main divergences of the convention emerged at this stage.

The convention as such did not open until June 20, when the second phase began, but the main perspectives were now before the body, with the main objections and suggested variations. From now on, until the very end, it was a program of inserting after-thoughts, chiseling down and sandpapering various items and making deals.

The convention continued until July 27. By this time it had, including the votes in the committee of the whole, taken 231 votes, most of them purely parliamentary—to postpone, to reconsider, to amend, etc. The affirmative results were now turned over to a committee of detail and the convention adjourned until August 6.

This important committee consisted of Rutledge of South Carolina as chairman, Randolph of Virginia, Gorham of Massachusetts, Ellsworth of Connecticut and Wilson of Pennsylvania. Virginia, Pennsylvania and Massachusetts were the largest states at the convention, containing nearly half the American population. All the committee members were lawyers except Gorham, a Robert Morris associate. Rutledge, Ellsworth and Wilson were future Justices of the Supreme Court, Randolph a coming Attorney General and Secretary of State.

Voting in the convention was by states, each state having one vote whatever its size or the size of its delegation. The largest delegation by far was that of Pennsylvania, no doubt because the convention took place on home ground. Of the thirty-nine signers of the document more than half came from the Philadelphia region—eight from Pennsylvania, five from Delaware, four from New Jersey and three from Maryland, a very one-sided concentration.

Various drafts of the committee of detail were preserved by Wilson and the final draft was presented to the convention.[8]

In the third and final phase from August 6 to September 17 the draft was subjected to intense discussion, revision of detail and sandpapering and it was finally turned over for processing by a committee of style. This latter consisted of William Samuel Johnson of Connecticut, Hamilton of New York, Gouverneur Morris of Pennsylvania, formerly of New York and one of the authors of the bellwether New York constitution, Madison of Virginia, and Rufus King, then of Massachusetts, later Senator from New York. The final polishing was entrusted to Morris.

It will be noticed that the large states were prominently represented on this final committee as well, with the addition of New York, which was recognized as a potentially large state. Which is not to say that the small states were considered unimportant, for they in fact were most numerous and had most to gain from the Constitution. Only nine states were required for ratification. It was recognized however that without the large states the new system could hardly be operative.

In the ratification process most of the small states ratified without difficulty. Uproarious trouble came only in the conventions of the large and more populous states—Virginia, Pennsylvania, New York and Massachusetts.

The Washington-Morris, or large-state and strong-executive combination, it will be noticed, was fully and ably represented both on the committee of detail and the committee of style. These bodies, selected by the delegates voting by states, consisted of what were thought to be the most reliable men—that is, the most tradition-oriented. In the case of neither committee were there any visionaries. On the committee of style all were lawyers except Madison and, as noted already, on the committee of detail all except Gorham.

The composition of the committees reflected the fact that the constitutional ingredients agreed upon represented a granting of concessions by the political organizations of the large states to the political organizations of the small states. For the large states were clearly guiding the proceedings.

A Trio of Scenarios

The basic scenario was presented point-blank in fifteen resolutions by Randolph of Virginia on behalf of his delegation before the body transformed itself into the committee of the whole. It was therefore known as the Virginia Plan. In the course of the discussion it was eventually challenged by the New Jersey Plan. Both plans were obviously gambits. Alexander Hamilton presented his own plan, and a generally ignored snippet of a plan was presented by Charles Pinckney, who many years later claimed that the finished Constitution was largely his plan. Careful historians agree with Madison that Pinckney was at the very least self-deluded.

Developed by the Virginia delegation, the Virginia Plan was probably drawn up by Madison and was certainly approved by Washington. The New Jersey Plan was concurred in before presentation by Connecticut, New York, New Jersey, Delaware and at least by Luther Martin of Maryland. Hamilton did not concur with the New York delegation.

The Virginia Plan envisaged a central national government but the small states, thinking this required proportional representation on the basis of state size, feared they would fall under the domination of the larger states, so they balked. The impasse was solved in one of the immoderately celebrated convention compromises by conceding each state equal representation in the upper house and representation by population in the lower house. Thus, whatever the merits of any proposal, the upper house could always block the lower house, and vice versa.

All the plans presented, the dispute between large and small states to one side, were strongly rightist in tone although in the course of discussion, and with eventual electoral approval in mind, the more stringent rightist proposals were, in the main, toned down.

There were two prevailing situations most of the delegations disliked and were determined to get away from: (1) the lack of cohesion among and supervision over the volatile states and (2) the orientation of the governments in most of the states that made them subject to popular majorities.

As to the latter, most of the states had one-year terms for all offices, the result being frequent elections, which in turn entailed the active electorate, or "the people," having a frequent say in matters of state. Whatever annoyed a sufficient bloc of the electorate—shortage of money, inability to pay debts or taxes owing to economic conditions—would often be met by the election of a legislature that would issue paper money, declare moratoria on debt or tax payments, and the like. After all, in the naive view what is a "people's government" for except to accommodate in-group people in any and all difficulties? It was not enough that government concerned itself with general matters or the special welfare of the affluent.

In most of the states, excepting New York and Massachusetts, nearly all power was concentrated in the legislature. The governor had slight power and in some states, such as Pennsylvania (which also had a single-chamber legislature), the governor was merely the president of a governing council. Only in Massachusetts, New York and emerging Vermont was the governor elected by the electorate; elsewhere he owed his office to the grass-rooted legislature. Only New York, Delaware and South Carolina had more than a one-year term for governor, although the latter two forbade re-election.

While four states had property requirements for being governor— South Carolina, Maryland, Massachusetts and New Jersey—eight states did not.

Most states had executive councils appointed by the legislature for one-, two- or four-year terms and the task of these councils was to advise and supervise the governor, always a suspect figure because under royal rule the governor was the King's henchman.

Only in Massachusetts, Maryland, Delaware and New York did the governor possess substantial authority but except in Massachusetts no governor could take independent action. In all states the governor was commander in chief of militia, in half the states he might issue pardons, and in two he was limited to reprieves. Half allowed him to impose embargoes when the legislature was not sitting but they were effective for only thirty days. He could not adjourn the legislature and could appoint a limited number of officials but New York placed the power of appointment in a special council selected by the legislature.

Only New York, Massachusetts and the South Carolina constitution of 1776 gave the executive a veto, which two-thirds of the legislatures could override.

The 1778 constitution of slave-dedicated South Carolina contained the following quaint testimony to a belief in supernatural authority: "That there is one eternal God, and a future state of rewards and punishments. That God is to be publicly worshipped. That the Christian religion is the true religion. That the holy scriptures of the Old and New Testaments are of divine inspiration, and are the rule of faith and practice."

State senators, formerly councilors to the governor, no longer got their power from the royal government but from the larger property-holders in the electorate. Three states had substantial property requirements for the senate—New Jersey, Maryland and South Carolina—but four states had none at all and others had lighter requirements.

Four of the ten bicameral states had annual terms for the senate but Maryland had five years and New York four. About one out of four senators throughout came from what had been the colonial elite. Seven states denied the senate any right to originate bills but the senate was generally allowed to try impeachments and share in appointing.

Pennsylvania, Georgia and emerging Vermont vested almost all authority in unicameral legislatures, detested by all except Franklin at the convention. I designate Vermont as emerging as it was not yet recognized as a state, its area still claimed by New York. It did not participate in the convention, nor did Rhode Island.

From the royal to the independent period there was not much change in popular voting requirements. Property requirements had always excluded most subsistence farmers (a majority), artisans and wage workers. While some states retained these requirements, New Hampshire, Vermont, Pennsylvania and North Carolina extended the franchise to all white males over 21, and Maryland, New York and Georgia reduced the property requirements. But there was, in consequence, not much increase in the actual number of voters.

Five states allowed any voter to become a legislator. North Carolina required the ownership of 100 acres, which meant little as land in the state was plentiful and cheap. Maryland and New York required £500 of property and South Carolina more.

Elections in most of the states took place every year, especially for the lower legislative house, whereas under the royal government they had taken place every three or four years.

Eight states had declarations of at least limited personal rights in their constitutions (four had full declarations) and the rest stipulated a few. These forbade excessive fines, searches and seizures without warrants, and the quartering of troops in private homes—all permitted under the Crown. Only three called for freedom of speech and the press, writs of habeas corpus, and reform of the penal code. Six states guaranteed the right of the eligible people to assemble, petition and instruct their representatives. Vermont and Pennsylvania required the publication of all bills before passage and four states required legislative journals to be published promptly, three required legislative sessions to be open to the public and four the recording of roll-call votes. None provided for complete religious freedom.[9] Voting generally was open, not by secret ballot.

Details of the Scenarios

The Virginia Plan called for a national legislature of two houses, with representation proportioned to free inhabitants or to financial contributions. Members of the lower house were to be elected by the people of each state and of the upper house by the lower house out of nominees of the state legislatures, both to receive "liberal stipends" and to be ineligible for any other office during tenure. Each house would have full legislative powers, including the power "to negative all laws passed by the several states contravening in the opinion of the national legislature the articles of union" and to bring force to bear against any defaulting state. The legislature would elect a one-man national executive who would wield all executive powers vested in Congress under the Confederation.

The executive and a certain number of the national judiciary would constitute a council of revision to examine each act of the legislature before it took effect and each act of a state legislature; the dissent of this council would constitute a rejection unless the law was again passed by the national or state legislature by a certain large percentage of votes. Under this form of veto any law that became operative would be absolutely constitutional, a marked difference from the system that finally emerged.

Also proposed was a national judiciary to be chosen by the national legislature and to hold office during good behavior, with a supreme court at the top which, among other things, would hear cases of impeachment. Provisions were also requested for the admission of new states, for insuring republican governments in all states, for amendments, for oaths of allegiance, and for special assemblies to be chosen by state legislatures to ratify the suggested changes. Terms of office were left blank, to be filled in by the convention.

The New Jersey Plan, put forward by Paterson and backed by several of the small states, was presented on June 15. It called for the continuance of the Congress existing under the Articles of Confederation but would authorize new powers for it: to raise a national revenue independently of the states, to levy import duties and postal charges, to pass acts regulating trade and commerce among the states and with foreign nations, to impose penalties for non-compliance, to conclude treaties binding on all the states, to make requisitions of the states in proportion to the population. As to executive power, it called for a joint executive of several persons, sort of a junta, each member to be removable by Congress on the application of the governors of the states and none to be in command of any troops. Also proposed was a judiciary to be concerned with federal matters. Any states resisting this authority could be proceeded against with the power of the confederated states—in effect, a guarantee of civil war. The same defect was in the Virginia Plan.

This New Jersey Plan amounted at most to an amendment of the Articles of Confederation with a view to giving Congress greater general powers but without altering the centers of power in the states.

On June 18 Hamilton presented his own plan. Historians in general have never taken Hamilton's plan seriously, have felt Hamilton to be out of tune with the convention and with "the people". They have ascribed this to the fact that he was foreign-born although many others at the convention were foreign-born—Robert Morris, Wilson, Fitzsimons, Butler. Actually, Hamilton's proposal was brilliant, in substance, as a maneuver and as a method of showcasing himself as a prospective leader of the dominant rightish elements of the country. His proposal represented the beginning of his climb toward leadership of the Federalist Party, for (1) it showed how much of a rightist he was (very palatable to most of the gathering) and (2) it showed state-oriented people at the convention just how far the larger states might go if pushed too hard.

Hamilton's scheme, much more crisply written than either of the other two, called for the legislative power to be vested in two houses. The lower house would be elected by the eligible citizenry for three years, but the upper house or senate would be elected to serve during good behavior (in effect, life) and would be chosen by special electors who would be elected by the eligible citizenry. Upon death, removal or resignation a senator's place would be filled out of the district whence he came.

The executive power would be vested in a man titled governor who would serve during good behavior (in effect, life). He would be chosen by special electors chosen by the same election districts that supplied the legislature. The governor would be the executor of all laws, have an absolute veto on all bills enacted by the legislature, make treaties with the advice and approval of the senate, be commander in chief in time of war, be the sole appointer of chief departmental officers, nominate all other officers and ambassadors subject to senate approval, and hold the power of pardon except for treason, when he might act only with senate approval. Except for the life term he very much resembled the President that actually emerged.

Upon the death of the executive the president of the senate would serve in his place until a successor was selected.

The senate alone would have the power of declaring war, of advising on treaties, of approving or rejecting all appointments except the heads of executive departments.

There would be a supreme judicial authority of a certain number of men, presidentially appointed, who held office during good behavior and had original jurisdiction in all cases of capture and appellate jurisdiction in all cases in which citizens of foreign countries or the revenues of the general government were involved. The national legislature would institute courts in each state for the "determination of all matters of general concern". The courts however would be subordinate to the executive and the legislature.

The governor, senators and all officers of the government would be liable to impeachment for wrongful conduct and upon conviction would be removed from office and disqualified from holding "any place of trust or profit". Impeachments would be tried by a court composed of the chief judge of the superior court of each state, provided such a judge held office during good behavior and had a permanent salary. Elected or non-salaried judges would not be acceptable.

All laws of particular states contrary to the Constitution or laws of the general government would be "utterly void". To prevent the passage of new obnoxious laws the governor or president of each state would be appointed by the general government and each state governor would have an absolute veto on all laws passed in the state of which he was governor or president.

No state might maintain military forces, and the militia of the states would be under the sole and exclusive direction of the United States, which would appoint and commission all the officers. (Under this arrangement the states would not have been able to mobilize forces against the national government as many of them did in 1860-65).

Many years later John Quincy Adams thought Hamilton's plan a quite good one. It was not, in any event, as bizarre a structure as many historians make it out to be. There was however no way of removing the executive or a senator by a vote of no confidence on the part of anybody—special electors or common voters.

Features of all the plans, themselves derivative, are in the Constitution of the United States. Hamilton's plan however brings out more strongly features that the leaders of the convention really desired— much longer terms, a dominant executive, many fewer elections than the state constitutions allowed for and less direct election and power of removal of government officials by the undependable people. In both the Hamilton and the Virginia plans the people were to elect the lower house only and were to have no further hand in directly electing anyone. Hamilton did not become *persona non grata* to Washington because of his highly authoritarian plan. Washington himself was a believer in a strong independent executive.

As things have evolved, "the people" have increased their electoral power—and Wilson favored direct election by the people all along the line although he was no democrat. Instead of state legislatures electing to the Senate as in the original Constitution, "the people" of the states now do this and the President, although still formally elected by the Electoral College, is in effect elected by direct vote under a party label. Both these arrangements were unacceptable to the framers of the Constitution. The alterations however have produced no substantial change in the basic nature of the government because the nominations are still contrived by small groups of strategically placed professionals.

The Electoral College vote for President, a feature taken from the Maryland scheme of electing senators, was something Hamilton wanted more widely utilized. And Hamilton favored a chief executive and Senators elected for life!

The Electoral College for a long time was not as presently constituted, with the electorate voting at least nominally for electors who in turn vote for Presidents to whom they are already committed via political parties. In New Jersey electors were chosen by the state legislature until 1816, in Connecticut until 1820, in New York, Delaware and Vermont until 1824, in Georgia (excepting one year) until 1824, and in South Carolina until 1868. Massachusetts chose electors by various methods and did not finally settle upon popular election until 1828.[10]

Until the advent of John Quincy Adams the general electorate played a role in only a very few states in the election of presidential electors and until James Earl Carter in 1976 no role whatever in the nominations.

Until Andrew Jackson, presidential candidates were selected by congressional party caucuses and since Jackson by state party leaders acting through rubber-stamp convention delegates.

That the convention favored a long term for the executive is revealed in the fact that early in the sessions and throughout, the term of the executive was set at seven years but at the very end of the convention, without any further discussion on the floor, the term was suddenly reduced to four years, no doubt in fear of public disapproval of the longer term.

The partiality for long terms was also shown in the six-year term for Senators, as compared with five years in the New York constitution. There never was any convention dispute over life terms for judges.

Whereas under most of the state constitutions anyone, by becoming politically active, might get into the government or gain an influence over it, the object of the constitutional convention was to place as much distance as possible between the people and government without excluding the people entirely. A grass-roots party might conceivably get control of the lower house in a single election but it could never simultaneously dictate the composition of the upper house and the person of the executive. Nor could it hold the lower house for more than two years without another election.

Although theoretically a popular party could take control of the lower house and the Presidency in one election and the Senate in two, factors other than the structure of government serve to keep the people divided and sub-divided: differences of region (north, south, east and west); differences of economy (industrial, agricultural, grazing, mining); differences among urban, suburban and rural; differences of religion, temperament, race, national origin, culture, sex, class, aptitude, age, personal experience, educational attainment, wealth, etc. "The people," especially in the United States, are far from being a cohesive, like-minded collection, contrary to common belief and modern political doctrine. Wilson showed some subtlety of thinking when he proposed making all offices electable by the populace direct. He seemed to sense that on a national basis such a provision would produce stalemate at dead center, desirable from his point of view. For the idea of all the delegates was not to permit any wide deviations from established norms. Too much deviation in any direction produced instability, uncertainty, which of all things was most abhorrent to the delegates and their supporters.

A Potpourri of Compromises

For a long time it was the fashion of the schools to teach that three "great" compromises had taken place at the convention: (1) between the large and small states by which population was represented proportionately in the lower house and by which the states were represented equally in the upper house, individually, territorially and politically; (2) between the North and the South according to which each slave in the South was to be reckoned as three-fifths of a person (instead of one or none) in apportioning lower-house representation and undefined direct taxes among the states; and (3) between North and South in giving Congress power to pass navigation acts, which were wanted by the mercantile North, but prohibiting interference with the importation of slaves for a period of at least twenty years.

The so-called three-fifths compromise however was not really a compromise but a carryover from the Articles of Confederation and was also part of the New Jersey Plan. The agreement on representation in Congress did represent a compromise between the large and the small states but the navigation acts and slave-trade provisions represented a bargain, a deal, a *quid pro quo*, rather than a compromise between North and South.

Actually, the Constitution is mostly a tissue of compromises from beginning to end, what Prof. Farrand has called a "bundle of compromises".[11] There was in fact compromise all along the way.[12] Even the most innocuous-sounding items in the document are compromises. Article II, Section 1 reads, "The judicial Power of the United States shall be vested in one Supreme Court, and in such inferior Courts as the Congress may from time to time ordain and establish." The compromise here is represented by the word "may". For some delegates wanted such courts mandated and others were opposed to such courts at all.

Elsewhere the document reads, "The House of Representatives shall be composed of Members chosen every second year . . ." Here too is a compromise, for some delegates wanted one-year terms, others three-year terms. The compromise consisted of two-year terms.

The way the President was to be selected was also a compromise. At the convention it was variously suggested that he be appointed by the national legislature, appointed by the state executives, elected directly by the people, elected by the state legislatures. The compromise worked out, drawing upon the Maryland method of installing Senators, was the Electoral College—a method that really worked only in the case of Washington. "The people" elect electors, who in turn theoretically elect Presidents.

The length of the President's term also represented a compromise among delegates advocating four years to fifteen and even life, with the convention at first determined upon seven years and no re-election and then at the eleventh hour settling upon four years with no limitation upon re-election. As the document stood until recently amended, a President could hold office from four years to life. Franklin D. Roosevelt was elected in 1932 for what turned out to be the remainder of his life—to 1945.

It had been the intention of the convention to leave to the electors' dirt-level discretion the choice of a President but the upthrust of parties brought about the concentration of votes on party candidates, arrangements at first being made by congressional party caucuses and, with the advent of Andrew Jackson, by party conventions.

So many compromises were worked out at the convention that the myth took root among pundits that a distinctive trait in the American character is the spirit of compromise and concession. There is little support to be drawn from the convention for this entirely groundless notion.

In reality most of the delegates were flinty hard-liners, determined to have their way, never to yield on anything substantial. They were willing to make purely political compromises, in minute details of the structure of government, in the *means* of carrying on government, but they were adamantly resistant to any compromise when it came to the *ends* of government. Ends of government are strewn about in economic and social structure, and here the convention held firm, single-minded, intractable. While the tissue of compromises in the Constitution gave rise to innovation in the extraordinary complexity of its structure, much like a Rube Goldberg machine, it left the economic and social situations right where they were when the ties were broken with Great Britain.

In many of the states after the ties were broken, during the war and afterward, there were large discontented groups clamoring for a variety of changes, chief of which were demands for debtor relief, tax relief and the issuance of paper money. Hard-pressed debtors had risen in armed revolt in Massachusetts. The war and its inflation had injured many. But none of these discontented groups was represented at the convention, whose members mostly believed in reverting to the state of affairs that had prevailed under British rule.

Various economic provisions in the new Constitution struck directly at the discontented—Congress was empowered to raise revenue by taxation, one more taxing agency, to appropriate and to borrow money without limit on the credit of the United States and to regulate from a national point of view foreign and interstate commerce; official salaries were made liberal and certain; and "all debts contracted and engagements entered into before the adoption of the Constitution shall be as valid against the United States under this Constitution, as under the Confederation"; the emission of bills of credit, the coinage of money and the impairment of the obligation of contract by the states were prohibited. What many opponents feared, the new government turned out to be a tax-collecting and debt-creating machine without parallel.

The New Jersey Plan was almost as explicit in the same direction.

As there was little disagreement with any of the economic and financial provisions proposed, there was no need for compromise in this quarter. There was indeed little discussion about them.[13]

Whenever anyone at the convention made a suggestion that infringed on someone's special economic domain, he soon learned what was negotiable and what not. Many of the northern delegates for example lustily denounced slavery and the slave trade, wanted them abolished.

Luther Martin of Maryland proposed a prohibition or tax on the importation of slaves and stated, among other reasons, that

> it was inconsistent with the principles of the revolution and dishonorable to the American character to have such a feature in the Constitution.
>
> Mr. Rutledge did not see how the importation of slaves could be encouraged by this section [Madison reported]. He was not apprehensive of insurrections. . . Religion and humanity had nothing to do with this question—Interest alone is the governing principle with Nations—The true question at present is whether the Southern States shall or shall not be parties to the Union. If the Northern States consult their interest, they will not oppose the increase of Slaves which will increase the commodities of which they will become the carriers.
>
> Mr. Ellsworth was for leaving the clause as it stands. Let every State import what it pleases. The morality or wisdom of slavery are considerations belonging to the States themselves—What enriches a part enriches the whole, and the States are the best judges of their particular interest. The old confederation had not meddled with this point, and he did not see any greater necessity for bringing it within the policy of the new one.

Mr. Pinckney. South Carolina can never receive the plan if it prohibits the slave trade. In every proposed extension of the powers of Congress, that State has expressly and watchfully excepted that of meddling with the importation of negroes. If the States be all left at liberty on this subject, South Carolina may perhaps by degrees do of herself what is wished, as Virginia and Maryland have already done.

Adjourned.[14]

And that was the end of that.

On all points of an economic and social nature, any proposals of a change from the pre-revolutionary social past similarly met a stone wall although there were not indeed many such proposals. What each section insisted it had to have it got. Thus the South demanded and received a prohibition against taxes on exports, which in general are as legitimate an object of taxation as anything else. The South did not want its agricultural exports taxed. Other countries tax exports but not the United States. The South also demanded and got the new right to recapture escaped slaves from distant states.

When the committee of detail presented its report, it contained the sentence, "No Navigation Act shall be passed without the Assent of two thirds of the Members present in each House." [15]

The operation of ships in the ocean-carrying trade and fishing was vital to New England and the Middle States and these recognized at once that the requirement of a two-thirds vote would be an almost insuperable barrier to any affirmative action, as it is wherever it appears in the Constitution. Navigation acts, among other things, regulate competitive foreign vessels.

The barrier had been raised by the South, which professed to fear that northern vessels, without free competition from foreigners, would over-charge them. With the necessity of a two-thirds vote in Congress the southern states would be able to control the content of any navigation acts. The *quid pro quo* for permitting navigation acts to be passed by an ordinary majority was permission for importation of new slaves for a period of twenty years, a distinct reinforcement for slavery which already shackled 20 per cent of the population.

In any event, although the Constitution as completed was a tissue of compromises, large and small, none of the compromises touched upon anything fundamental, and none especially did anything but reinforce established ways in economics, law or social structure. The Constitution in fact was the means by which the traditional establishment, with new personnel, was re-establishing itself.

Not that this was a necessarily undesirable outcome. It was just different from what is commonly represented and consequently supposed: that the Constitution represented a historical departure into an era of salvation for the infinitely deserving common man. The common man in point of fact was going to be allowed to remain as common as he wanted to be, but the Constitution, contrary to political blarney, offered him no bonuses for it.

Down with the People

What the delegates thought about various items standard in American campaign oratory is well worth noting, is of pointed instructional value and constitutes the most significant part of the convention. The remarks clearly came from men who stood for no nonsense.

Sherman of Connecticut, who had started life as a shoemaker, commenting on the Virginia proposal that members of the lower house be elected by "the people", said he was opposed. "The people, he said, (immediately) should have as little to do as may be about the Government. They want [i.e. lack] information and are constantly liable to be misled."

Gerry then spoke up.

> The evils we experience flow from the excess of democracy. The people do not want [lack] virtue; but are the dupes of pretended patriots. In Massachusetts it has been fully confirmed by experience that they are daily misled into the most baneful measures and opinions by the false reports circulated by designing men, and which no one on the spot can refute. One principal evil arises from the want of due provision for those employed in the administration of Government. It would seem to be a maxim of democracy to starve the public servants. He mentioned the popular clamour in Massachusetts for the reduction of salaries and the attack made on that of the Governor though secured by the spirit of the Constitution itself. He had he said been too republican heretofore: he was still however republican, but had been taught by experience the danger of the levelling spirit . . .
>
> Mr. Gerry did not like the election by the people . . .
>
> Mr. Butler thought an election by the people an impracticable mode.[16]

So did Mr. Pinckney and others.

Gerry, who turned out to be something of a states'-righter, later again returned to the assault.

> In England [he said], the people will probably lose their liberty from the smallness of the proportion having a right of suffrage. Our danger arises from the opposite extreme: hence in Massachusetts the worst men get into the legislature. Several members of that body had lately been convicted of infamous crimes. Men of indigence, ignorance and baseness, spare no pains however dirty to carry their point

against men who are superior to the artifices practiced. He was not disposed to run into extremes. He was as much principled as ever against aristocracy and monarchy. It was necessary on the one hand that the people should appoint one branch of the government in order to inspire them with the necessary confidence. But he wished the election on the other to be so modified as to secure more effectually a just preference of merit. His idea was that the people should nominate certain persons in certain districts, out of whom the state legislatures should make the appointment.[17]

Gouverneur Morris was fully in accord with this line of thinking as it came out on July 2. "Every man of observation had seen in the democratic branches of the state legislatures, precipitation, in Congress changeableness, in every department excesses against personal liberty, private property and personal safety." For which reason he wanted a lifetime, aristocratic Senate, appointed by the executive, to stand up against a democratic lower house. It was the wealthy Morris's idea to segregate and isolate from each other the democratic and the aristocratic, the non-affluent and the rich. He said:

> The rich will strive to establish their dominion and enslave the rest. They always did. They always will. The proper security against them is to form them into a separate interest. The two forces will then control each other. Let the rich mix with the poor [in the same assembly] and in a commercial country they will establish an oligarchy. Take away commerce, and the democracy will triumph. Thus it has been all the world over. So it will be among us . . . He fears the influence of the rich. They will have the same effect here as elsewhere if we do not by such a government keep them within their proper sphere. We should remember that the people never act from reason alone. The rich will take advantage of their passions and make these the instruments for oppressing them. The result of the contest will be a violent aristocracy, or a more violent despotism. The schemes of the rich will be favored by the extent of the country. The people in such distant parts cannot communicate and act in concert. They will be the dupes of those who have more knowledge and intercourse. The only security against encroachments will be a select and sagacious body of men, instituted to watch against them on all sides. He meant only to hint these observations, without grounding any motion on them.[18]

And what Morris foresaw has happened.

Wilson, Madison and Mason argued in favor of election by the people, the latter two at least of the lower house. Mason "admitted that we had been too democratic but was afraid we should incautiously run into the opposite extreme. We ought to attend to the rights of every class of the people. He had often wondered at the indifference of the superior classes of society to this dictate of humanity and policy, considering that however affluent their circumstances, or elevated their situations might be, the course of a few years, not only might but certainly would, distribute their posterity throughout the lowest classes of society. Every selfish motive therefore, every family attachment, ought to recommend such a system of policy as would provide no less carefully for the rights —and happiness of the lowest than of the highest orders of citizens."

In this view, as expressed, Mason was a minority of one. Wilson grounded his view on expediency, saying that "No government could long subsist without the confidence of the people." [19]

On the question six states voted for election of the lower house by the people, New Jersey and South Carolina voted against, and Connecticut and Delaware were divided. So the motion carried, but barely.

Democracy and "the people" came up for a drubbing from time to time again in the debates. Randolph, arguing for a small upper house, "observed that the general object was to provide a cure for the evils under which the U.S. laboured; that in tracing these evils to their origin every man had found it in the turbulence and follies of democracy; that some check therefore was to be sought for against this tendency of our Government: and that a good Senate seemed most likely to answer the purpose."[20]

At this stage on the question of having Senators chosen by the state legislatures the motion lost, 9 to nothing, with Delaware divided.

Hamilton, in presenting his plan, drove home the point. "The members most tenacious of republicanism, he observed, were as loud as any in declaiming against the vices of democracy . . . Give all power to the many, they will oppress the few. Give all power to the few, they will oppress the many." [21] A gloomy view, but historically true.

> All communities [said Hamilton, according to the report of Yates] divide themselves into the few and the many. The first are the rich and well born, the other the mass of the people. The voice of the people has been said to be the voice of God; and however generally this maxim has been quoted and believed, it is not true in fact. The people are turbulent and changing; they seldom judge or determine right. Give therefore to the first class a distinct, permanent share in the government. They will check the unsteadiness of the second, and as they cannot receive any advantage by a change, they therefore will ever maintain good government. Can a democratic assembly, who annually revolve in the mass of the people, be supposed steadily to pursue the public good? Nothing but a permanent body can check the imprudence of democracy. Their turbulent and uncontrolling disposition requires checks.[22]

Hamilton was certainly naive, and ignorant as well of much European history, in believing that "the rich and well born" "will ever maintain good government." But Hamilton (what those who take his *The Federalist* as profound philosophy overlook) was ever the partisan, as extreme in his way as any street-corner demagogue. He was in fact a demagogue of the rich, whether well-born or not.

This is seen very strikingly for example in his reference to "the amazing violence and turbulence of the democratic spirit",[23] which blandly overlooks the violence and turbulence of the upper ruling classes of Europe for centuries. No democratic movement Hamilton could have known about ever paralled the depredations of the European baronage. People are people of whatever social level. Hamilton was simply a man of limited experience, vicarious and personal.

Hamilton indeed viewed mankind in toto as wholly depraved. "All the passions then we see, of avarice, ambition, interest, which govern most individuals, and all public bodies, fall into the current of the States . . ." [24] Tom Paine saw just the opposite: the people as wholly good but depraved by government. Both, separately projecting the conservative and the liberal-democratic views, were equally extreme, equally prone to faulty generalization—a common failing. Hamilton and Paine were methodologically and temperamentally very similar.

The more discerning Gouverneur Morris, no radical, did not agree with Hamilton on this point. Said Morris, "Wealth tends to corrupt the mind and to nourish its love of power, and to stimulate it to oppression. History proves this to be the spirit of the opulent." [25] True. Morris was far more the philosopher than Hamilton, at least on this point.

Hamilton, who had been a young radical during the revolution and who had roundly denounced the ultra-conservative New York constitution of 1777, did a complete political flip-flop in his ascent from oblivion. After great success in the army, during which he became Washington's private secretary, he married in 1778 Elizabeth Schuyler, a leading heiress, and was soon transformed into the chief spokesman of the wealthy class and for a new national Constitution. Hamilton had as much as anyone to do with bringing about the convention. "Most of Hamilton's life was spent in combatting the ideas he had confidently advanced in 1777." [26] He was ever voluble on the failings of "the people" and termed them "ambitious, vindictive, and rapacious".[27]

The key to Hamilton's character is his impetuosity at all times, in whatever enterprise he was engaged. Far from being a philosopher, of government or anything else (contrary to a large number of putative savants), Hamilton was a partisan politician and a brilliant one. Born on the island of Nevis in the West Indies in 1755, Hamilton was "illegitimate", was abandoned by his father, and at the age of 12, his mother now dead, went to work for merchants at Christiansted. A quick intelligence, he so distinguished himself in a variety of ways that a clergyman went out of his way to raise funds to send him to mainland America to complete his education. He landed in 1773, enrolled in a grammar school in Elizabethtown, New Jersey, and in 1774 entered King's College, later Columbia University. He dropped out in about a year and, devoid of any political grievance, became embroiled in revolutionary politics, joining a band of volunteer troops that raided British installations. He made fiery speeches, wrote inflammatory letters to a newspaper and published two powerful and influential pamphlets—*A Full Vindication of the Measures of Congress from the Calumnies of Their Enemies* (Dec. 15, 1774) and *The Farmer Refuted* (Feb. 15, 1774).

After a distinguished, and impetuous, military career in combat and out, Hamilton in 1782 was admitted to the bar after three months of study in Albany, which testifies at once to the ease of becoming a lawyer in those days and to Hamilton's innate ability. In the same month, backed by the Schuyler family, he was elected to the Continental Congress from New York. The next year he opened a law office at 57 Wall Street, a poetically fitting address, and in 1784, at age 29, became a founder and director of the Bank of New York, which still flourishes as a bastion of vintage wealth.

Hamilton left the constitutional convention on June 30 because the other two New York delegates had walked out in disgust, terminating the New York delegation. On July 19 Washington wrote to him, "I am sorry you went away. I wish you were back." Hamilton's seemingly extreme views, it is clear, did not dismay the general. Hamilton returned on August 13, found some merit in the draft that was emerging (or a future role for himself), participated in the final committee of style, and did more than any other man, especially in New York, to get the Constitution ratified. He was a one-man army. In New York it was uphill work all the way as the state and the entrenched Clinton machine was against the Constitution in every particular.

It seems safe to say this: if Hamilton had opposed the Constitution it would have had a harder time being ratified by the requisite nine states. He could have ripped apart all the arguments for it as easily as he did those against it in *The Federalist* papers.

What was most important in society in the view of the men of the convention was frequently stated. "An accurate view of the matter would nevertheless prove that property was the main object of society," said Gouverneur Morris.[28] Rutledge agreed: "Property was certainly the principal object of society." [29] Nobody disagreed. Yates quotes Gouverneur Morris as saying on July 5, "Men don't unite for liberty or life . . . They unite for protection of property."

Throughout the convention, especially in discussions of property requirements for voting and holding office, the idea of property was kept central. The delegates in this were merely projecting the widely approved Lockean idea that the proper concern of government was the protection of life, liberty and property, although their idea of property was narrower and more concrete than that of Locke.

But to the multitude outside, most of whom were without property except in their own persons or talents, the word was never inspirational. Jefferson in 1776 deliberately avoided it in writing the Declaration of Independence. His well-known substitute was of course "the pursuit of happiness", which he probably derived from Hume, with whom it was a favorite and oft-repeated phrase.[30]

Jefferson was so obsessed in his opposition to the use of the word "property" that even much later when he was ambassador to France, "his friend Lafayette brought around an early draft of the Declaration of Rights of Man for him to look over. Among the inalienable rights listed there was man's right to property. Jefferson suggested that the word be dropped out." [31] It certainly had no mass appeal.

No doubt Jefferson was reminded of the Humean formulation by reading Virginia's Declaration of Rights, published in a Philadelphia newspaper in May 1776. The first of eighteen rights found there, written by Mason, read, "That all men are born equally free and independent and have certain inherent natural rights, of which they can not, by any compact, deprive or divest their posterity; among which are the enjoyment of life and liberty, with the means of acquiring and possessing property, and preserving and obtaining happiness and safety." [32] In the rewriting by Jefferson for the Declaration of Independence, property was dropped out of Mason's reasonable declaration.

A revised version of the Virginia declaration, arriving some days later, contained the phrase "pursuing . . . happiness" but retained the politically indelicate but entirely sensible allusion to property.

Since ancient times philosophers had noticed that happiness was a supreme objective of people and by the time of Hume and fellow Scottish moralists the notion had taken root that the basic quest of all people, at all times, was happiness, *tout court*. In brief, whatever people do, for whatever seemingly mysterious reason, they are engaged in the pursuit of happiness. They can do nothing else. In the Jeffersonian formula, then, which is often injudiciously cited as distinctively and exclusively American, people are to be permitted to do whatever they would in any case do. The Jeffersonian formula concedes nothing, confers nothing, is politically empty but at the same time seems to promise something. One can be deprived of life, liberty or property but one cannot be deprived of the pursuit of happiness although, to be sure, one can be hampered in such pursuit as well as mistaken in the means of attainment, as many people are.

But although Jefferson, appealing to the broad public, found property to be a taboo word, the significant point, the men at the convention thought otherwise. With them it was a favorite word, often brought to the fore as a matter of the deepest concern. The "pursuit of happiness", like all men being created equal and self-evident truths, was just part of the Jeffersonian moonshine, so much crowd-titillating pap, and did not come up at the convention.

Because Madison emerged as the chief spokesman for the Constitution, what he said at the convention has considerable weight. In discussions of the terms for Senators—with suggestions ranging from four to nine years and even to life—Madison (as reported by Yates), replying to Pinckney's contention that six years was too long, remarked that "we are now forming a body on whose wisdom we mean to rely, and their permanency in office secures a proper field in which they may exert their firmness and knowledge.

"Democratic communities may be unsteady, and be led to action by the impulse of the moment. Like individuals they may be sensible of their own weakness, and may desire the counsels and checks of friends to guard them against the turbulency and weakness of unruly passions. Such are the various pursuits of this life, that in all civilized countries, the interest of a community will be divided. There will be debtors and creditors, and an unequal possession of property, and hence arises different views and different objects in government . . . The landed interest, at present, is prevalent; but in process of time . . . the number of land-holders shall be comparatively small . . . If these observations be just, our government ought to secure the permanent interests of the country against innovation. Landholders ought to have a share in the government, to support these invaluable interests and to balance and check the other. They ought to be so constituted as to protect the minority of the opulent against the majority." [33]

The central purpose of the secret convention however was more sharply brought into relief by Madison himself in his own report of the same speech on the same day, June 26. He said:

> In framing a system which we wish to last for ages, we should not lose sight of the changes which ages will produce. An increase of population will of necessity increase the proportion of those who will labour under all the hardships of life, and secretly sigh for a more equal distribution of its blessings. These may in time outnumber those who are placed above the feelings of indigence. According to

the equal laws of suffrage, the power will slide into the hands of the former. No agrarian attempts have yet been made in this country [that is, division and apportionment of lands by law], but symptoms of a levelling spirit, as we have understood, have sufficiently appeared in certain quarters to give notice of the future danger. How is this danger to be guarded against on republican principles? How is the danger in all cases of interested coalitions to oppress the minority to be guarded against? Among other means by the establishment of a body in the government sufficiently respectable for its wisdom and virtue to aid on such emergencies the preponderance of justice by throwing its weight into that scale. Such being the objects of the second branch in the proposed government he thought a considerable duration ought to be given to it. He did not conceive that the term of nine years could threaten any real danger . . .[34]

Sherman of Connecticut could not stomach this last. "Government is instituted for those who live under it. It ought therefore to be so constituted as not to be dangerous to their liberties. The more permanency it has the worse if it be a bad government. Frequently elections are necessary to preserve the good behavior of rulers . . . he thought six or four years would be sufficient. He should be content with either."[35]

Madison at the time of the convention clearly was not far from the thinking of Hamilton, his future collaborator on *The Federalist* papers. The minority to be protected under the emerging Constitution was not any minority or all minorities. It was the minority of the opulent.

This orientation of the Constitution, as well as the detailing of numerous defects in the original document from a hypothetical popular view, was first given intensive analysis by Prof. J. Allen Smith of the University of Washington in *The Spirit of American Government*, first published in 1907. Now something of a classic, it was reprinted by Harvard University Press in 1965.

There is no need to do what has already been done, and adequately done, once again. But rather than report an old analysis, or embark on a new one, what will serve at this point is a quotation from that master of constitutions, John Adams. The quotation will also show why Adams is consistently given downplay among votaries of the Constitution, who largely man the propaganda switchboards.

Said Adams in 1822:

> The merit of effecting the establishment of the Constitution of the United States belongs to the party called Federalists—the party favorable to the concentration of power in the federal head. The purposes for which the exercise of this power was necessary were principally the protection of property, and thereby the Federalist Party became identified with the aristocratic part of the community. The principles

of Federalism and aristocracy were thus blended together in the political system of the Federalists, and gathered to them a great majority of the men of wealth and education throughout the Union.[36]

Would one need anything more than the long-considered testimony of this topflight insider, iron-clad patriot and eagle-eyed analyst?

None of this indicates that the delegates were unduly propertarian, as sometimes suggested, for there were events in their experience that showed the status of property might indeed be precarious. And property, public or private, is important. About one-third of the American population remained loyal to the Crown when another third had plumped for revolution. In all, some 100,000 loyalists fled to Canada, England or the West Indies while others remained to fight with British forces or to spread defeatest notions. "Test acts" were passed by the revolutionary state legislatures, themselves self-constituted, without legal basis, and these acts required open repudiation of loyalty to the King. The acts were implemented by more severe measures: nine states exiled prominent loyalists, stigmatized as Tories, five disfranchised all who declined to repudiate the Crown, and in most of the states loyalists were expelled from all public offices, barred from the professions and obliged to pay double or treble taxes. Late in 1777 Congress recommended that the states expropriate all who had "forfeited the right to protection" by refusing to turn against the legally constituted government. So, expropriation, long before Marxism was heard of, was part of the American *modus operandi*.

Here came one of the first big bonanzas of the revolution for far-sighted patriots. The states passed confiscation acts, put properties up for sale at cut prices which only the affluent could pay, and a new set of owners was installed. There was much attendant graft. The state of Maryland made more than $2 million and New York more than $3,600,-000 from these forced sales. Eventually, in consequences of the British-American peace treaty, the United States government paid £3,292,452 in compensation of 4,118 claims, a very large sum for the times. In the long run, in other words, the American taxpayers paid for these properties. "The people", indeed, always pay.

The other big bonanza of the revolution was the trans-Allegheny domains in which patriot speculators made and lost fortunes.

The men at the convention, in their concern about property, were well aware that thousands of parcels of land and buildings had been wrested from their lawful owners by kangaroo legislatures and they did not wish to see it happen to them even though their supporters had shared in the *al fresco* redistribution. They remembered too how easily the patriotic mobs had been stirred up against the loyalists by the gentry of the patriotic party, who had inspired the mob action in many instances. In all such matters it is always a question of whose ox gets gored, and the convention stalwarts had no intention of seeing theirs similarly gored if they could prevent it by a suitable arrangement of words. Hence the strong property protections in the Constitution, buttressed by a long line of subsequent Supreme Court decisions.

In passing, one sees here why the "patriotic party" and its levelling ideas were at first so triumphant and then with the end of the war seemed to distintegrate. The measures taken in the late 1770s against the loyalists had the effect of exiling at least half and probably more of the pre-independence conservatives from the political scene. After the war many of these returned or came out of hiding and added their voices to those of conservatives of the patriotic party who were the prime movers in supplanting the Articles of Confederation by the Constitution of 1787.

Plain Speaking about Civil Rights

I have pointed out in an earlier section that a bill of rights was pointedly rejected by the convention on two occasions, and was to become an item of serious objection during the ratification process. Some of the delegates during this process were to defend the absence of such a bill.

Roger Sherman of Connecticut was one such. Writing in the New Haven *Gazette and Connecticut Magazine* during November and December, 1787, he said,

> No bill of rights ever yet bound the supreme power longer than the *honey moon* of a new married couple, unless the *rulers were interested* in preserving the rights; and in that case they have always been ready enough to declare the rights, and to preserve them when they were declared . . . the sole question (so far as any apprehension of tyranny and oppression is concerned) ought to be, how are Congress formed? . . . how far have you a control over them? Decide this and then all the questions about their power may be dismissed for the amusement of those politicians whose business it is to catch flies.[37]

Sherman was entirely correct, as the history of the Bill of Rights has shown. Whenever the government saw fit to ignore it and violate its provisions, as notably during the second Wilson administration and the administrations of Presidents Kennedy, Johnson and Nixon, it was as though non-existent. State governments have violated it with impunity, for decades on end, with no objection from the national government.

The Battle for Ratification

As usually set forth in brief accounts for those who read and run, the Constitution was quickly and easily ratified in a succession of state conventions to the jubilant accompaniment of a cheering populace. The reality however was quite different, of the order quite literally of a bar-room brawl accompanied by a storm of spoken and written criticism from men who were the intellectual equivalents, or superiors, of every single delegate to the Philadelphia convention. Neither side in the struggle had a clear preponderance of brains, insight or good intentions.

The order of ratification was as follows:

	Date ratified	Margin of approval/disapproval
1. Delaware	Dec. 7, 1787	30–0
2. Pennsylvania	Dec. 12	46–23
3. New Jersey	Dec. 18	38–0
4. Georgia	Jan. 2, 1788	26–0
5. Connecticut	Jan. 9	128–40
6. Massachusetts	Feb. 6	187–168
7. New Hampshire	Feb. 20 (convention adjourned amid strong opposition)	30–77
8. Rhode Island	Mar. 24 (rejected in a popular plebiscite)	237–2,708
9. Maryland	Apr. 28	63–11
10. South Carolina	May 12	149–73
11. New Hampshire	June 21	57–47
12. Virginia	June 25	89–79
13. New York	July 26	30–27
14. North Carolina	Aug. 4 (rejected)	75–193
15. North Carolina	Nov. 21	194–77
16. Rhode Island	May 29, 1790	34–32

Seemingly off to easy acceptance with unanimous early votes in three states and easy victories in two more, leaving only four more to go for full ratification as prescribed in its own formula, the Constitution had great trouble elsewhere.[38]

The document was in trouble in fact as soon as it got to Congress from the Philadelphia convention. The quorum for the first discussion consisted of thirty-three members, of whom eighteen had rushed up to New York from Philadelphia—a travelling phalanx. They and other convention members would later, for the most part, also appear as delegates in state ratifying conventions, thus doing triple duty in getting the Constitution adopted—in the Convention, in Congress and in the state conventions.

In Congress Richard Henry Lee of Virginia moved that a clutch of amendments should be added before the document was sent to the states, and the states could then choose between the original script and an amended version. Their combined recommendations would then be the subject of a second convention. In this way, as he saw it, everything would be above-board. Such a proceeding however was sharply opposed by the Federalists from Philadelphia, who knew that a second convention would undo much of what they had done.

Had the Federalists wished, they could have forced the issue, but doing this would have entailed a disturbing struggle, focussing unwanted public attention and leading to delay. They preferred expediting the document as quietly as possible on its way and getting it as quickly as possible to Pennsylvania especially, a key state where their political friends were temporarily in the ascendancy.

In consequence the Federalists decided to compromise and send the document on to the states without any recommendations, either of approval or dissent. Although the Congress had not always been of Federalist orientation, it was at this crucial moment predominantly of that cast. Earlier Congresses would undoubtedly have seen eye to eye with Lee and his supporters.

However, it seemingly leaked out to the public that Congress was unanimous in recommending the document. This same tactic was used in alluding to the alleged unanimous approval of the document by the Philadelphia convention. In employing such tactics the Federalists made shrewd use of what was later known as "the bandwagon" technique—everybody is for, nobody is against, get aboard.

All the five easy and early ratifiers, small states, were in serious internal difficulties of one kind or the other and needed unification the way a drowning man needs a raft. Without the Constitution they would have foundered, probably would have been absorbed by larger neighbors.

Delaware, a splinter offshoot of Pennsylvania, was too small (population 1790: 59,096) to succeed as an independent state. Maryland, although larger and stronger, suffered from a variety of internal weaknesses. A hampering lack of deep-water port facilities plagued Delaware, New Jersey and Connecticut, making them dependent on unsympathetic Pennsylvania or New York. Georgia, newly settled, with a small population (1790: 82,548) and vast territory, was under heavy and constant Indian attack with which it was unable to cope alone.

In Pennsylvania, second only to Virginia in size and development, the situation was different. This state, like Virginia, Massachusetts and New York, had prospects of succeeding as an independent nation. It had a radical democratic constitution and since the revolution had spawned two rival parties—the Constitutionalist and the Republican. The former was a staunch partisan of the state constitution and drew much of its strength from rural regions, the rest from the artisans and mechanics of Philadelphia. The upper-class Republican Party, hostile to the state constitution, was dominated by Robert Morris and had its supporters in Philadelphia and the eastern counties.

Control of the legislature had oscillated between these two parties, each leapfrogging the other into office, and at the time the federal Constitution was submitted was in the hands of the Morrisites. The Constitution arrived from Congress by special courier late on September 28, 1787, and the legislature was due to adjourn the next day. A new legislature was to be elected in October and there was no telling what its composition would be.

The nineteen members of the Constitutional Party absented themselves from the assembly, preventing a quorum and thereby any vote. A large gang of Republican stalwarts—goons, in the parlance of today—was thereupon organized to search the city. Two absent members were found, seized and forcibly dragged into the assembly, yielding a *pro forma* quorum.[39]

The assembly, thus extra-legally constituted, voted that a public election be held in early November for delegates to a convention that would meet on November 21. A vociferous campaign was then launched by the Federalist Republicans, drawing in such political writers as James Wilson, Tench Coxe and Noah Webster, already known as an educator. The anti-Federalists responded with their own spokesmen and writers and ran a strong ticket headed, of all people, by Benjamin Franklin. But although the city of Philadelphia was ordinarily about 60 per cent Constitutionalist, the artisans, mechanics and tradesmen, sensing prospective gains for themselves as entrepreneurs, now favored the Federalists and voted heavily for Republican candidates. The Republicans also gained unexpected votes in the three counties around Philadelphia, which gave them a majority of the convention.

But the convention debates extended for nearly a month, with oratorical bombardments from both sides. James Wilson, heading the Federalists, argued from the stance of a theoretical democrat while his opponents argued as theoretical republicans—a reversal of their actual philosophical positions! Any strategy to win, the usual political phenomenon. When the vote was finally taken by the exhausted delegates, the Federalists prevailed by 2 to 1.[40] But they knew they had been in a fight.

The next ratification rough-house came in Massachusetts. Of the 355 convention delegates elected, Forrest McDonald concludes at least 200 were initially opposed to ratification. But the Federalists waged a more skillful propaganda campaign and seduced the dominant figure in the opposition, former Gov. John Hancock, who had it in his power to tilt a decisive batch of convention votes. Hancock, a vain demagogue, was promised the Vice Presidency by the Boston Federalists and, if Virginia did not ratify in time to qualify Washington, even the Presidency. He instantly became a fervent supporter of the Constitution. And with delicious perfidy the Massachusetts Federalists, when it later came time to choosing the Vice President, solemnly put forward John Adams, consigning Hancock to the ash heap. The debates extended for a month before a vote was taken, and the opposition made much of the fact that the Constitution contained no declaration of rights as in the forepart of the Massachusetts constitution, that it tolerated slavery, that it excluded religious tests for office-holders and that it was deficient in a variety of other ways.

When the vote was finally taken, the Federalists won, but just barely, by 19 votes or a shade more than 5 per cent. The lever used by Hancock to tip the balance was the motion recommending amendments on people's rights.

Later in the month New Hampshire, with an ascendant opposition denouncing the Constitution's support of slavery, was ready to reject the document, when the Federalists adroitly moved for an ajournment. New Hampshire did ratify in June, but with a marked lack of enthusiasm as reflected in the 57-47 vote, a margin of less than 10 per cent.

South Carolina seemingly lined up for the Constitution without difficulty, 2 to 1, but there was nevertheless trouble in the legislature about convoking a convention at all. The anti-Federalists failed by only one vote to prevent its being held. After that it was plain sailing, for nearly half of the 149 who voted for ratification were related by blood or marriage to the Rutledge and the two Pinckneys who had graced the Philadelphia convention! [41]

The requisite nine states had now ratified but another resounding brawl faced the document in the Virginia convention. And Virginia as well as New York was vital to the success of the emerging Union.

Virginia had introduced a dangerous ingredient into the struggle: they were howling for a second convention to remedy what critics saw as defects in the document. Federalists however saw such a second convention, with everybody now more and more alert to long-range implications, as threatening to the success of their hitherto successful plans. Virginia could well, despite the assent of nine conventions, send everything back to the starting point, paving the way for new wrangles.

The situation in Virginia had its own unique characteristics. First, the Federalists had won over to their side Gov. Edmund Randolph, who with George Mason had refused to sign the Constitution. Randolph at the time had called for a second convention, which call was taken up enthusiastically by anti-Federalists in Virginia and elsewhere to the consternation of the Federalists. But by the time of the Virginia convention Randolph had made his flip-flop, and historians note that "he was financially embarrassed in 1788 and emerged in 1790 on solid footing and as the holder of more than $10,000 in public securities; that he was politically ambitious and emerged in 1789 as the first attorney general of the United States." [42]

With respect to figures such as Hancock in Massachuetts and Randolph in Virginia, both darlings of dirt-level rank-and-file voters, one should note remarks of Gouverneur Morris at the Philadelphia convention: "Loaves and fishes must bribe the demagogues. They must be made to expect higher offices under the general than the state government." [43]

In Virginia the Federalists at the outset nursed a small majority, a consequence of their greater organizing ability. On the floor they enjoyed the forensic services of George Wyeth, James Madison, Edmund Pendleton, George Nicholas and John Marshall. Against them were pitted George Mason, William Grayson, James Monroe, Benjamin Temple and Theodorick Bland. But the anti-Federalists also had the formidable services of Patrick Henry who for twenty-three days dominated the convention with his arguments and oratory, on one day speaking for seven hours. The spectators' seats were all taken every day. All who attended came only to hear one man—the nonpareil Patrick Henry.

The burden of his speeches was that the Constitution spelled the death of liberty, echoing the prophetic words of George Mason at the close of the Philadelphia convention: "This government will set out [commence] a moderate aristocracy: it is at present impossible to foresee whether it will, in its operation, produce a monarchy, or a corrupt, tyrannical [oppressive] aristocracy; it will most probably vibrate some years between the two, and then terminate in the one or the other." [44] The words in brackets are Madison's own corrections.

Madison, writing to Hamilton toward the close of the Virginia convention, said he feared that Henry, despite the Federalist majority, would succeed in converting the convention to his views.

The New York convention had opened on June 17, while the Virginia convention was taking place. The known anti-Federalists were in a majority by 46 to 19, sure of winning. The proposed Constitution was expounded clause by clause by its outnumbered friends, led by Hamilton, with the anti-Federalists seldom deigning to respond. They were awaiting news from Virginia that the convention there had ratified only on condition that a second convention be held to consider amendments. They were not aware of Randolph's defection. Meanwhile the news came that New Hampshire had ratified unconditionally.

When the news arrived that Virginia had ratified without proposing a second convention, the anti-Federalists were thrown into confusion.

Their ranks now suffered defections of those who were not party stalwarts and did not understand the unseemly clamor for a bill of rights considering the fact that the New York constitution did not have one. Hamilton here stepped forward with argument the waverers found powerful, including the indirect suggestion that New York City might secede. After many caucuses the anti-Federalists under Gov. George Clinton finally decided to ratify "in full confidence" that desired amendments would be obtained. So on July 26 twelve Clintonians flouted the instructions of their constituents, seven abstained and ratification took place, 30 to 27.

Although defeated, the Clintonians still had a majority as shown by the forcing of their opponents to sign a "unanimous" letter requesting a second convention—this before voting for ratification. So New York's ratification was in effect conditional. And with Virginia and New York in the line-up the initial rejection by North Carolina and the sullen delayed action by Rhode Island meant little.

But the cry for amendments, mainly in the form of a bill of rights, intensified as the new government was formed. Virginia sent two anti-Federalists to the first United States Senate, and Patrick Henry even tried to gerrymander Madison out of a seat in the lower house. Madison however campaigned door-to-door as a staunch friend of a bill of rights, won, and led the fight against considerable opposition for the first ten amendments in Congress.

Vast clamor had built up during the ratification campaigns about the absence of a bill of rights. But this clamor, often represented as a cry from the stricken American heart, was only a campaign tactic, linked to the call for a second convention. Contrary to a great deal of later patriotic propaganda, Americans of the time, no more than later, were not red-hot civil libertarians. They never were, astonishing though this statement may seem to many well-schooled persons. Only the conventions of South Carolina and Massachusetts of the first eight ratifiers had recommended the inclusion of a bill of rights. The defeated minorities in Pennsylvania and Maryland however had joined in the clamor, and anti-Federalist propagandists all over had taken up the theme. If remaining conventions made such recommendations, it seemed that a second convention would be necessary to harmonize all proposals with each other.

When Madison in Congress got down to examining suggested ingredients for a bill of rights, North Carolina and Rhode Island had not yet ratified, and neither had its own bill of rights. Five states, two of which had no bill of rights, had formally requested the addition of a bill of rights, and suggested items had come in from nine states in all. Altogether 186 amendments were submitted, which Madison reduced to

80 of a substantial character. But all nine states asked for a prohibition against interference by Congress with the time and place of holding elections, restrictions on the taxing power (!) and a declaration that all powers not delegated to the federal government were reserved to the states.

In McDonald's summary, "Seven states spoke for jury trials, six called for an increase in the number of members of Congress, protection of religious freedom, and a prohibition of standing armies in times of peace. Five wanted prohibitions against quartering troops and against unreasonable searches and seizures, and protection of the right of the states to control the militias, the right of the people to bear arms, and the rights of freedom of speech and of the press. Four states requested guarantees of due process of law, speedy and public trials, the rights of assembly and petition, limits on the federal judicial power, and a ban on monopolies, excessive bail, unconstitutional treaties (!) and the holding of other federal office by members of Congress." [45]

Madison, the House, and then the Senate whittled all these down into twelve amendments although the House made them equally applicable to the states, which the Senate cancelled. Two were not ratified. The remaining ten, affixed to the Constitution and known as the Bill of Rights, were ratified by the requisite states. The object of adding them to the Constituiton was to kill the movement for a second convention, which it did.

The presence of the ten amendments in the Constitution was the offspring not of libertarian fervor but of separate campaign strategies by anti-Federalists and Federalists—in the first instance clamor for them in the hope of forcing a second convention into being and in the second instance conceding them and thus avoiding a destructive second convention. The aim, in any case, was not to guarantee rights already codified by some states, only four of which had bills of rights.

There were, in any event, four states in which more than half of the voting population was opposed to the Constitution—Virginia, New York, North Carolina and Rhode Island.[46] Four states were divided: Pennsylvania, Massachusetts, South Carolina and New Hampshire.[47] Only in the limping states of Delaware, New Jersey, Maryland, Georgia and Connecticut was there great enthusiasm for the document.

The point of all this is merely to show that to the revolutionary generation the Constitution was not the divinely inspired structure it was later converted into by propagandists, the structure within which politicians play a cat-and-mouse game with a broad public and without which they would have very little status.

The literature of the revolutionary generation shows what these people thought, pro and con, and it has been left to historians of recent years to unearth and showcase most of the early literature critical of the Constitution.[48] Much of this literature, particularly the writings of Robert Yates under the pseudonym of "Brutus", make Federalist apologetics seem like feeble stuff. This is particularly true with reference to the highly touted *Federalist Papers,* written under the name of "Publius", by James Madison, Alexander Hamilton and John Jay. It was the powerful analysis of "Brutus" that called forth the response of "Publius", which has come to be hymned, despite its manifest thinness and errors, as a profound analysis of the American Constitution. One gets far more enlightenment by reading "Brutus".

The question remains, however: Why, if there was so much merit in the contentions of the anti-Federalists, was the Constitution such an initial success? For a brief answer to such a cogent question one can do no better than to turn to George Washington.

Writing to the Marquis de Lafayette on June 19, 1788, while waiting for the ratification of one more state to make the Constitution operative, Washington said "and then, I expect, that many blessings will be attributed to our new government, which are now taking their rise from that industry and frugality into the practice of which the people have been forced from necessity. I really believe, that there never was so much labor and economy to be found before in the country as at the present moment. If they persist in the habits they are acquiring, the good effects will soon be distinguishable. When the people shall find themselves secure under an energetic government, when foreign nations shall be disposed to give us equal advantages in commerce from dread of retaliation, when the burdens of war shall be in a manner done away by the sale of western lands, when the seeds of happiness which are sown here shall begin to expand themselves, and when everyone (under his own vine and fig-tree) shall begin to taste the fruits of freedom, then all these blessings (for all these blessings will come) will be referred to the fostering influence of the new government. Whereas many causes will have conspired to produce them." [49]

Six

GOVERNMENT
FREE STYLE

The United States government, widely thought by a propaganda-saturated and myth-ridden populace to be held in severe check by iron-clad constitutional restraints, can in fact do anything in the realm of possibility it deems expedient, with or without the approval of the electorate or a majority thereof, inside or outside the terms of the Constitution. In this it is like every other fully operative government in the world, past or present, although the fact is far from what most Americans, educated or not, believe to be the case.

The government can in fact do most of what it does under the narrowest possible interpretations of the Constitution, which is a very broad-ranging document, although it can operate further afield under broader or fanciful official interpretations—of which history records many. But owing to its divided powers it cannot always develop a coherent policy. As a consequence it sometimes wallows uncertainly.

Beyond all this it can operate surreptitiously far outside the crisp stipulations of the ultra-sacred document and has often done so long before the advent of wild-catters John F. Kennedy, Lyndon B. Johnson and Richard M. Nixon as chief executive officers of the United States. Decades earlier Woodrow Wilson put all of these into the shade in jumping the traces of the Constitution and, prior to Wilson, Theodore Roosevelt carried out a number of known extra-constitutional exercises of significant proportions. At least as far back as the Presidency of Andrew Jackson, perhaps even earlier, one can find clear instances of actions by higher-ups skirting the Constitution. All this is without considering the elasticity of Supreme Court decisions.

There is, as a matter of simple fact, nothing whatever external to the government, least of all the myth-ridden electorate, to keep it on any discernible constitutional track. The government is completely autonomous, detached, in a realm of its own, and relates itself to the society it supervises as it alone thinks advisable from time to time. Any idea it ever acts involuntarily, at the behest of popular elements external to it, will not bear the slightest examination. No government of course governs in the sense of playing an active role in everything that happens in any society. What government does, mainly, is to supervise, and to intervene or not in order to shape or modify what is happening in areas of chief interest to it—except in those few but significant areas where it takes an initiating role. Its area of main interest is economic at all times.

All of the foregoing is axiomatic, bedrock, for anyone who wishes to understand American or any other government operations. The constitutional shackles and barriers that hold back the United States government in the imaginations of many people from an extended roster of widely deplored acts, then, are like a silken thread attached to a free-ranging young bull.

Contrary to the political myth of myths, the United States is not subject to government by a majority of the citizenry, passive or active. Once installed, the government and every single elected official is completely independent of any section whatever of the general populace. Each elected individual, in a very real sense, is a distinct and separate political party. It is this that accounts for the repeated wails of winning electoral majorities when they see elected officials doing the precise opposite of what they had solemnly promised, giving them war instead of peace, as Lyndon B. Johnson promised in 1964, planning war even as he shouted "Peace".

It also accounts for the government ignoring, year after year, decade after decade, the reasonable demands of 70 to 90 per cent of the people as revealed in public opinion polls—for gun control, for stringent limitations on immigration both legal and illegal, for effective actions with respect to high and rising rates of crimes directly against the person, for an end to the persistent traffic in illegal narcotics, for a damper on consumer fraud, for much greater tax equity, for a halt to government-induced inflation that erodes the savings of the prudent, for an end to palpably reckless government borrowing and spending on ill-conceived projects of principal benefit to politically connected contractors, and for effective measures against a bewildering variety of other widely deplored transgressions contrary to popular common sense. Such demands, as the record shows, are judiciously ignored or temporized with, at times through the passage of equivocal laws or regulations. As the man in the street commonly says, "Nothing happens." The government cannot be budged, despite public clamor.

Apocryphal or not, a story about Huey Long is to the point. Elected governor of Louisiana after promising to reduce taxes, in his first message to the legislature he called for a tax increase. To an aide who drew attention to this inconsistency, Long nonchalantly replied, "So I lied." Long was at least frank, which most officials are not. Demonstrated bad faith however did not impede his career, no more than the careers of many counterparts who have acted in the same way. For an office once gained under the American system is held for a fixed term of years—usually four—and when election time rolls around again new questions are to the fore, old faults hidden in the shuffle. If the wayward official stands for re-election, his opponent may, despite all, be deemed more undesirable. Or the wayward official may now have been "kicked upstairs" to a judgeship or the Cabinet, on his way up the political escalator.

The government is equally successful, when it mobilizes itself to the task, of imposing generally unwanted laws and rulings, good or bad. An example from among many is the unanimous decision of the Supreme Court in *Brown v. Board of Education* (1952-55) that ordered an end to the separation of the races in public schools. This decision and its subsequent court-implemented interpretations was completely in harmony with the Constitution as written. It reversed the long-standing decision in *Plessy v. Ferguson* (1896) in which the Court held, with the notable dissent of Justice John Marshall Harlan, that separate public facilities were permissible for Negroes as long as they were "equal". The Constitution however contains no suggestion whatever that any group of law-abiding citizens might be sealed off by law from other citizens. The Court in *Plessy*, as it does from time to time, for good or ill, was simply inventing law, without explicit or implied constitutional warrant.

That the public, or a large section of it, is no greater devotee of constitutional punctilio than the government was shown in the outcry and general public resistance, north, south, east and west, to a long string of court-ordered implementations of the *Brown* decision. Local uprisings in force were many and it was only when it became evident that the government was in dead earnest that the objectors gave way sullenly, reluctantly. Had there been a popular plebiscite on continued segregation of blacks there is no doubt it would have been resoundingly approved.

Why had the Court, and a majority of Congress tacitly, changed its views? To this there were many answers given, including the influence of books reporting the bedraggled condition of the American Negro.

While many influences no doubt went into the changed state of mind of the Court, little attention has been given to Chief Justice Earl Warren's admission that foreign opinion of the United States had played a role, that the Court had not suddenly awakened to what the Constitution required. Foreign opinion was in fact the decisive factor, the overriding factor.

At the time of the decision, the United States had been for some ten years, as a consequence of World War II, the leading power in the world, notably the leader of the bloc that espoused "freedom" against the Soviet bloc which espoused despotic regimentation of people. The United Nations was formed in 1945 under American auspices, and people of all nations, colors and beliefs had joined or were invited to join. The United States in short was now forced to transact business face to face and deal politically in all parts of the world and with all kinds of people. Prior to the war most of these people had been dealt with through white colonial intermediaries.

As most of the people of the world are conspicuously "colored" in some way—yellow, reddish, light brown, dark brown verging toward black—it was embarrassing for American representatives to face constant questioning about the reasons for the evident subjugation and oppression of the Negro in the United States. Added to this the Soviet Union and its fanatical dupes constantly screamed in mock-indignant protest about the shabby way Negroes were treated in the United States, thereby intensifying American embarrassment although few people anywhere were sufficiently informed to understand that most people under Soviet rule are continuously subjugated and mistreated very much as Negroes were in the United States.

With all this, the Cold War at its height, the Court patriotically acted as it did, thereby removing the United States from an untenable world position. Now, instead of having epithets hurled at it, the United States got praise from abroad. The pro-Soviet propagandists suddenly dropped the theme. Instead the clamor shifted to the domestic scene where the government had more control, to the large and unquestionably majority white element that wanted to keep the Negro in his subordinate position.

Although couched in legal and constitutional terms the decisions in *Plessy* and *Brown* did not relate fundamentally to constitutional problems, to intellectual difficulties about the law. They related to practical problems, political in nature. At the time of *Plessy* the problem was to placate morose southerners for their defeat and humiliation in the Civil War, as a result of which the Negro was the prospective gainer and white political and economic dominance in the South was threatened. At the time of *Brown* the larger problem was that of placating excited world opinion, with which the United States now had to reckon in its struggle with the Soviet Union. The Court, in other words, had not suddenly "got religion".

None of the historical advances made by the Negro on the American scene has been attributable, it should be noted, either to the happy workings of democracy or the innate good will of the white majority. Had it been left to the white majority, even in a direct plebiscite in recent times, the Negro would still probably be in a condition bordering on slavery. Free popular voting would have condemned the Negro to be forever unfree. All the legal and constitutional advances made by the Negro have been the consequences of impersonal statecraft exercised with other ends in view. So much for the innate good will of "the people".

The first blow against the shackles that bound the Negro was Lincoln's limited Emancipation Proclamation, which in fact went no further than congressional legislation had gone. It liberated slaves only in areas that in 1863 were not already under federal control. Where there was federal control slaves remained slaves.

Following the Proclamation, with the Civil War ended, the ascendant Radical Republicans in Congress passed and had ratified (the ratification taking place coercively in the South either under military government or as a condition for the re-entry into the Union of the rebellious states) the Thirteenth, Fourteenth and Fifteenth Amendments. The object of these forced amendments, on their face, was to give full civil rights to Negroes, but the political objectives of the Republicans was to break the all-white political power of southern Democrats in their home bailiwicks, at the root. In Alabama, Florida, Louisiana, Mississippi and South Carolina, Negro voters were in a majority, were numerous in Virginia, North Carolina, Georgia, and elsewhere.

But the new amendments were for a long time not enforced with respect to the Negro although the Supreme Court suddenly interpreted the Fourteenth Amendment—surprise! surprise!—as giving new rights to corporations against regulation by state legislatures.

Subsequent to the Reconstruction period, Republican governments, with the concurrence of the Supreme Court, abandoned the project of fully integrating the Negro into society in the interests of reconciling southerners to the new state of affairs and getting support in the South for Republican corporate policies. In so doing, they abandoned Negroes to the will of their former masters, which was to keep the blacks permanently subjugated and humiliated. The southern attitude was tacitly shared by many, perhaps most, northern whites, especially of the lower and middling classes.

It was here that the Negro found himself, always arbitrarily discriminated against, subjugated, segregated, humilated at every turn, when the Warren Court announced its about-face in *Brown v. Board of Education.*

Because most people in the world have darkly pigmented skins, and the United States government must in its own advantage deal with such people, the American Negro today is in what is actually a strong political position. It is this rather than some mysterious change of heart that accounts for the many feverish governmental measures, some of them misguided, to rescue him from some of the effects of his long captivity.

The decision in *Brown v. Board of Education* clearly went against majority opinion and is merely one example, among many, of governmental autonomy, whether exercised by the courts, Congress or executives, severally or jointly. One can, in other words, forget the mirage of government by the people.

A Repository of Unlimited Power

The makers of the American Constitution aimed, as I have stressed, to restore and freeze to the greatest possible extent the *status quo ante* 1776, thereby defying a section of the populace, mainly agricultural, that believed it had a "natural" right to take any political action for which it could gain transitory popular support. Prominent signers were by no means thoroughly pleased with the document, because they did not believe it sufficiently rigid, thought it offered too many placatory loopholes to the popular element. It was however the best they could achieve and it was rigid enough to hold under austere Federalist interpretation for some seventy years, after which the dike gradually crumbled.

Unstabilized by the bloody Civil War, the government, now Republican, increasingly extemporized with the advent of the industrial revolution, from time to time did whatever it thought necessary or whatever most pleased it in defiance of radical democratic shibboleths, and justified what it did by increasingly bizarre semantic variations on the Constitution, delivered in the main via the Supreme Court. In short, it stretched the straitjacket fashioned by the framers, sometimes necessarily (as Lincoln did during the Civil War under self-construed war powers of the President), sometimes wishfully and class-servingly as by the later Supreme Court—at all times proving again and again, contrary to the maxim laid down by James Harrington, that one is governed by men, not by impersonal laws.

Even when interpreted as narrowly as possible the Constitution confers virtually illimitable powers on the government. It could almost be said that no matter what the government does, even the narrowest of interpretations gives it just about all the powers any government could desire although it may not locate and concentrate those powers where imperious officials prefer them. For the bottom-most line of the Constitution consists of broad-ranging Article I, Section 8, Sub-section 18, which allots to Congress power "To make all laws which shall be necessary and proper for carrying into execution the foregoing powers, and all other powers [sic] vested by this Constitution in the Government of the United States, or any department or officer thereof." What is "necessary" and what is "proper" is of course determined by the government itself. A vast chasm of possibility opens here when one considers what many Presidents and Congressmen have thought necessary and proper.

The "foregoing powers" alluded to are set forth in seventeen subsections and relate to virtually everything subsumed under the concept of sovereignty. The broadest of these is to provide for the "general welfare of the United States", which makes only the sky the limit because what arguably constitutes welfare is extremely broad and diverse. One man's welfare is another man's poison, so what promotes welfare must depend from time to time on the decision of some limited number of persons. It isn't something self-evident.

Another very broad category is "To raise and support armies", which most laymen assume refers to *domestic* armies that will be pitted against hostile foreigners. But the provision neither says nor implies this although perhaps the framers in their haste and under the limited horizons of their age thought it did. In fact, however, the United States raises and supports with funds and materials foreign armies (South Vietnam, South Korea and others) and could, if the government thought "the general welfare" required it, import them for use against a recalcitrant section of the citizenry as Francisco Franco used Moroccan troops to topple a duly elected Spanish government. The British cousins of the framers used thousands of German troops in the attempt to subdue the revolting colonists. True statecraft is impersonal, unsentimental.

Beyond this, without explicit limitation, the government can according to the document of 1787 lay and collect taxes without limit, borrow money as it see fit without limit (thereby obligating the populace to repay and to pay interest), regulate any and all commerce to make it vanish or flourish (subsidizing whatever it sees fit), set rules for naturalization of foreigners (allowing them in without stint to depress wage levels) and for bankruptcies, coin and set the value of money (steadily depressing its value, if so minded, and thus penalizing the prudent), punish counterfeiting and a variety of other statutory crimes, establish post offices and roads, underwrite science and useful arts (however these may be construed), establish courts inferior to the Supreme Court and make or alter all court jurisdictions including that of the Supreme Court, punish piracies and high-seas felonies, declare war (by word or tacit deed), maintain a navy, organize a militia, and establish a city.

These are powers originating in Congress and are not by any means exhaustive of governmental powers, which are limited only by the boundaries of possibility. Other powers originate with the President— the power to make treaties that are law all over the United States (with the assent of two-thirds of the Senate), grant pardons and re- prieves, execute the laws made by Congress (or not execute some or only lightly execute them), appoint civil officers and all judges, make war without any congressional declaration of it under his authority as Commander in Chief of the armed forces and in general do a great variety of things prescribed and unprescribed. As to the last, he can and does issue "executive orders"—in effect, decrees—and make non- treaty agreements with foreign governments and do a great many other unstipulated things.

Nor is this all. The Supreme Court by its power of judicial construc- tion—that is, by making inferences from the Constitution and developing general rules such as those of implied powers and inherent powers— has greatly extended both its own and the power of the general govern- ment so as to fill completely the field of power.

It is nevertheless often said that the United States has a limited government. It is, first, not limited against any action external to it but is internally restricted vis-a-vis its various divisions. The Supreme Court for example cannot openly make a law although it can find in a law or a combination of laws what hitherto nobody suspected was ever there—in effect enacting a law. The Congress cannot execute one of its own laws but it can bring various inconvenient pressures to bear against the President to see that he executes, or does not, certain laws. The President cannot make a law although in foreign affairs he is practically a law unto himself and does in fact make domestic law in wholesale fashion. On the domestic scene he can bring various emphases to bear, or not bear, in executing the statutory laws. He can, in other words, see that they are executed selectively, which is a necessity anyhow in view of the excess of laws. Operatively this amounts to altering the spectrum of laws as examined by a naive reader. Beyond this, quite apart from any law, the President can—and often has done so—issue executive orders that amount to novel decrees. In other words, laws.

The excess of laws arises from the desire of legislatures, federal and state, to placate vociferous and naive elements of the public who seem to think that placing some law on the books solves a problem. Such window-dressing laws are freely passed simply as exercises in legislative public relations. For unless a law is implemented by appropriate enforcement machinery it is merely something that clutters the law books and is brought forward only occasionally for token enforcement or selectively to intimidate someone—inequality before the law!

British Experience Refutes Framers

The three divisions of the American government operate under the immoderately celebrated system of checks and balances. The framers of the Constitution believed that if any one person or group of persons controlled all the major government functions, or more than one, the basis for oppressive tyranny had been established. That this theory is false is shown in the case of Great Britain, where the legislature and the executive are inextricably joined and the courts have no more to do with the government than to apply the law as handed to them by the legislature. The courts cannot nullify or decline to enforce a law although they may find contradictions in laws which the legislature must untangle.

Great Britain, in its constitutional development, has exploded most of the political notions of the framers, who fervently believed, among other things, that a two-house legislature was necessary to prevent unwise and precipitate action at the behest of an often misguided electorate. Here, too, British development has found otherwise. For Great Britain has reduced the House of Lords to little more than a ceremonial chamber. The monarch has been similarly reduced.

Why advert to Great Britain, which figures in the consciousness of most Americans very little? The reason is that the British Constitution was a many-splendored thing to the American framers and, as a matter of fact, is a prime model of reasonable government to most students of government all over the world. Governmentally the British self-adjusting system stands to the American as a new Rolls-Royce to an old tractor. And as lobbyists know, the old tractor requires much grease.

One of the features of the British government that many of the framers most feelingly admired, with no dissenters, was the House of Lords, which in 1787 held a veto power over the House of Commons. Many also admired the King's prerogative or absolute veto power over anything Parliament proposed, although Franklin pointed out that it had not been used since the revolution of 1688, when the modern British Constitution was launched. The American presidential veto is a modification of the old British royal prerogative, almost as effective. In other respects, too, the presidential prerogative is very broad.

In the course of remodelling their Constitution the British have ridden roughshod over all those features of it that the American framers uniformly most admired.

Today any bill passed by the House of Commons other than a bill to extend the maximum duration of Parliament, which is five years, can be passed against the veto of the House of Lords after a delay of one year or, if it is a money bill, a delay of only one month.[1] If it wishes, the House of Lords may polemize against a bill, hoping thus to stir up adverse public opinion, but this is rarely successful. In the end the House of Commons prevails although cogent criticism from Lords may bring about modifications. So the role today of the House of Lords is almost entirely advisory. It cannot block anything.

The House of Lords today numbers more than a thousand members, "most of whom attend rarely or not at all".[2] Seldom are more than eighty peers in attendance, rarely more than two hundred.[3] No bill proposed by a Conservative government has been rejected by the House of Lords since 1832, and for more than ninety years no Conservative bill has been amended against Cabinet opposition. In the meantime the British Constitution has been altered so that the House of Lords cannot insist upon anything at all against any kind of government.

The British government consists of a committee of the House of Commons called the Cabinet, which is presided over by the Prime Minister. The members of the Cabinet are, except in certain extraordinary circumstances, all elected members of Commons and, if not, a "safe" seat is found for the outsider. The members are called ministers and are in most individual cases made head of the various key government departments although there are some ministerial department heads that do not join the Cabinet.

The Cabinet, called "The Government", exists because the Prime Minister has been elected out of its own membership by a majority of Commons which is ordinarily of a single party, Conservative, Liberal or Labour. The Prime Minister selects the members of the Cabinet, with the advice and consent of his party in Commons. At times there are party coalitions that form a government, but always by a majority vote.

The members of the Commons are elected from districts by citizen voters. All adults have the suffrage. While these individual voters will have no more to say about what the government does in particular instances than American voters, or how the government elected by the majority party implements its policies, they do have far, far more than the American voter to say about which line of policy the goverment constituted by the winning party follows. And they are sure of a definite line of policy which the American voter never is.

For British voters, unlike American voters, do not vote for random

unpredictable and often bizarre individuals but for people committed
to a certain fixed party policy that has been publicized, criticized and
debated in newspapers, over radio and television, in magazines and at
political rallies. Each party guarantees that the people elected under
its label will vote according to party policy in Commons. For a party
to fudge on its policy would be for it to court political extinction unless
it could come up with compelling excuses.

There is little or no chance that any candidate for the Commons
will promise one thing and then vote in Commons some other way. The
reason for this is that he does not stand for election as an individual
but as one committed to a policy hammered out by committees of
permanent parties, which are continually active through local organizations in each district. Unlike in the United States where party headquarters are set up just before elections, after which they fold up their
tents like the Arabs and as silently steal away, the headquarters of all
the major parties, in London and in the election districts, are always in
existence and in communication with their members in the Commons.

The reason there is slight chance of any member of the Commons
defying the orders of his party to vote a certain way is what the
British call "party discipline". In exchange for giving a candidate the
use of the party label and the party endorsement, each party in return
demands, and usually gets, political obedience. This doesn't mean that
members aren't free to vote according to their own judgement. But they
may not do so when "the whips" are applied, when the government in
power or the party in opposition calls for obedience, as they regularly
do. If however members defy party orders, they may be deprived of
party endorsement, and British voters will not vote for anyone without
the endorsement of some party that lays out clear party principles. If
nevertheless a district returned such a recalcitrant member, he would
have no choice but to join the opposition, which members sometimes
do even while Commons is in session.

It is right here, through party discipline, that the British parties,
and government, exercise control over what steps a government wants
to take. Commons does not get members, as the United States Congress
does, who put forward their own policies and make deals with other
members in order to forward measures clamored for in their home
districts or by hidden patrons.

The control-points in the American system—and all governments
have such control-points, their incidence out of reach of the electorate—
are, first, the Senate, which can kill, modify or ignore any measure that
comes to it from the lower house, and vice versa; second, the President,
who can veto it—and most presidential vetoes are final—and, finally,
the Supreme Court, which can find many measures unconstitutional or

can modify them in some way so as to make them more or less effective.

In the American system a fire that invisible political managers do not want is allowed to build, sometimes to vast proportions, before it is put out. And some never are. In the British system such fires are kept from getting any sort of start, are largely confined to inter- and intra-party struggles. In the United States the process may go as far as to enact an absurd constitutional amendment such as the Eighteenth, decreeing the abolition of alcoholic beverages. It took fifteen years of joint governmental sabotage of enforcement and the lawless resistance of a minority segment of the public to nullify this amendment by the passage of another, the Twenty-first.

The greater freedom of members of both houses of Congress however makes possible in the American system much dealing or horse-trading among the members, and between the two houses, with the result that much muck is tracked into the government and much dubious legislation enacted—or good legislation defeated—and expense incurred, against the will of a majority of the country or of party leaders. The congressional "pork barrel" is an illustration of this. In this the members reciprocally vote special benefits, often absurd, for their home districts at the general taxpayers' expense and require presidential approval in return for enacting some presidentially desired bit of legislation. The process amounts to blackmail, bribery and extortion all around.

A President, with a majority of his own party in Congress, is not even nearly in control of Congress the way a British Prime Minister is usually in control of the House of Commons. Congress, if a key bloc wishes, can set at naught the dearest wishes of any President for some action by that body. Nor need this opposition consist of a majority but simply of a key group that refuses to co-operate with a near majority. All the "special interests" of the country have such key groups in Congress, many of the members of which from Daniel Webster of Massachusetts to Eugene Talmadge of Georgia have been disclosed to be in receipt of a flood of ever-running secret funds from their supporters, necessarily relatively wealthy people. Any realistic account of Congress, and even of the Presidency, must note the influence of outside money. Presidents Lyndon Johnson and Richard Nixon, and Vice President Agnew, were all shown to be in receipt of such secret payments while in high office. A large section of Congress is always secretly funded from outside, mainly by corporations. Yet most accounts of the American constitutional system virginally make no mention of this highly significant factor.

While outside money and influence once played a commanding role in the British government, a fact that was fulsomely and reprehendingly alluded to at the American constitutional convention, successive parliamentary reforms have reduced it to a minimum, although what may still go on secretly or indirectly can only be mentioned as a possibility. The British method of operation makes it very unlikely that the American scale of operation outside the publicly understood rules exists.

What serves to keep the British government relatively free of corruption, which is always prevalent in the United States on the state and federal levels, is the way the system is structured.

The party that won the most parliamentary seats at the most recent general election forms the British government, the Cabinet. Its members sit on benches in the Commons facing all other members—Labour, Conservative, Liberal, and small minority parties, if any. The party that won the second-largest number of seats forms what is known as the Opposition and its chief figures sit on the front benches, facing the chief ministers of the government across a wide aisle. Speakers from each side, upon being recognized by the Speaker, rise to address the assembly.

When bills are discharged from committee and come before the Commons they are closely debated and, finally, amended or passed as presented, then get further editorial attention in the House of Lords. These debates, sometimes turgid, are also often quite sharp and the interested part of the public gets an opportunity to learn from newspaper reports precisely what is going on, everything—or nearly everything—in the open.

Once a week there is a question period during which the chief ministers, and ministers not in the Cabinet, may be questioned by the Opposition. The questions are often searching and must be answered truthfully. For deliberately misinforming the Commons under questioning, any member, including a minister, faces almost certain expulsion if the untruth is made evident. In the United States, on the other hand, a long line of Presidents, beginning with Jefferson, has deliberately lied to and misled Congress on vital matters.

In its questioning the Opposition is not endeavoring to topple the government at all times although it may be gunning for the removal of some minister whose department has come under adverse scrutiny. It is usually endeavoring at least to cast doubt on the wisdom of the government in power. Each minister is responsible for his department and for the official acts of his subordinates, and if the departmental affairs are found to be in bad order, he is almost certain to be replaced. There is nothing like this in the American government where departmental heads are responsible only to the President, and he, short of offenses that theoretically merit impeachment, is responsible to nobody. He cannot be dislodged even if the bulk of the country has completely lost confidence in him, as in the case of Herbert Hoover from 1930 to 1932.

Under the British system, on the contrary, not only a minister but the entire Cabinet including the Prime Minister can be removed at any time by a majority of Commons on a vote of simple confidence. Such a vote is not often taken, but when it is it is a serious matter, with the factors involved transcending party loyalty for some members. For there must be defections from the ranks of the government party or bloc for such a vote to succeed.

If it succeeds, the government resigns and is reconstituted by the majority party with new men, at times even a new Prime Minister, or the issue is placed before the electorate in a new general election. The voters then decide and if they elect again a majority of the party that was in power before, this same party establishes a new Cabinet, with perhaps some or even all of the former members in it. If the Opposition gains a majority in the election, it takes over the government.

Having said all this, it is necessary to say that there is informed opinion to the effect that the central force in the British government is not in Commons or the Cabinet but in the upper civil service of the departments. It is for example the higher civil servants, specialists, long experienced in their jobs, permanently installed, on whom the ministers of the succeeding governments depend for guidance. Problems of the modern world are so complex that they only yield, if at all, to trained minds. Politicians, so the argument runs, could not do anything so difficult as to run any government. At best they are adept at manipulating the public. They stand in the forefront and take the bows and blame, but permanent civil servants must work out solutions to problems for which the politicians take the credit, at least in most instances. It is somewhat similar in the United States government, where permanent government employees guide the presidentially appointed department heads, supplying the facts with which to join not infrequently incoherent policy.

Ivor Jennings remarks that "members of Parliament have usually to be drawn from people with rather superficial minds." [4] If this is true, what would one say about Congress?

The advent of war brings a change in the British system. The two major parties then form a coalition, with a coalition Cabinet. This wartime Cabinet rules by orders in council—that is, by decrees. In World War II the Cabinet was reduced in size, to about seventeen, with ministers who were not in the Cabinet members of the Privy Council.

The Lord President of the Privy Council, in charge of domestic affairs for the time being, was himself a member of the Cabinet, whose other members devoted themselves to prosecuting the war. What this amounts to is flat-out dictatorship, but collective dictatorship.

The United States similarly constitutes itself as a dictatorship, one-man presidential dictatorship, in time of war, with Congress voting anything the President requests. An exception exists in the case of war carried on by executive order, as in the case of the Korean and Vietnamese wars. The widespread public resistance to the Vietnamese adventure was made possible only because of the absence of the wide range of control measures automatically brought into operation with the formal declaration of war by Congress. Although Congress did not declare war with respect to Vietnam, it in effect supported the President throughout with the exception of a very small number of opponents of the war, who were disregarded.

A difference between the British and the American wartime systems is that Britain in war is under the direction of a group of the highest political leaders of the two leading parties while the United States is under the direction of a single man all of whose advisers are subordinates and subject to his pleasure. In war the United States is not only under a dictatorship but under a one-man dictatorship.

In any event, the British, compared with the Americans, get a far better estimate of the qualities of their leaders through the way Commons is organized. With the chief members of the government on the front benches of one side, they are faced by the front-benchers of the Opposition. These latter are made up of the persons who are bound to compose the Cabinet of any succeeding government. Their leader, presumably the next Prime Minister, is paid by the government as leader of the Opposition.

Out of the open interplay and repartee between these two groups the public can make its own judgements about the qualities of the various men at the top. Unlike the case very often of an American President, there is simply no chance of a person coming up from nowhere, given a bath in instant publicity and propaganda, elected to head the government, and thereafter carefully controlling his public appearances. In Britain nobody in recent times gets high up in government without first serving a long apprenticeship in the open rough and tumble of the House of Commons. For the British to install an enigmatic "dark horse" in the highest office or even an intermediate one would be unthinkable. The British consequently are rarely stung as Americans often are by confected personalities never much exposed in a public forum.

Divided and Ruled

In forming the American government the central idea of the framers was to implement the Roman maxim "Divide and rule." Not knowing that the populace, by reason of its future heterogeneous composition (as distinct from the homogeneous British population), was going to divide and sub-divide itself into many particular bickering groups, the framers set about dividing them structurally with great rigidity.

They conceded the House of Representatives as the "popular" branch and stipulated that the members be elected by the eligible (male white) populace every two years from districts with a minimal population of 30,000, reduced at the last minute from 40,000. Some districts today actually take in a half million or more people. The Senate they looked upon as the "aristocratic" branch, allowed each state two Senators to serve six years each and to be appointed by the state legislatures. The electorate had no vote at all here. The Senate was constituted by staggered voting, one-third being elected every two years. In this way a rejection even by the state legislatures of all or most of the Senate in a single election was guarded against.

The President was elected for a term of four years, and would be re-electable indefinitely, but he would be elected not by "the people" but by an Electoral College composed of persons elected according to ways decided in each state, for a long time in many states by the legislature. By amendments to the Constitution after much popular clamor Senators were in 1913 made electable by direct popular state all-male vote, and the President was limited to two terms in 1951. Women didn't get the right to vote until 1920. The Electoral College, as earlier noted, broke down after Washington's terms, and its members were made into rubber stamps first for congressional party caucuses and then for candidates selected by juntas of state political leaders in party conventions, which were frankly clownish affairs, as though in self-parody, until the advent of television let the public in and brought about fairly sedate gatherings. The real work of candidate selection goes on off-camera behind closed doors.

The lower house today receives 435 members from districts scattered over the country, and the Senate 100 from the states. Every two years a third of the Senate must stand for re-election. But the system guarantees that the electorate in any single election, should it be so minded, cannot reconstitute both houses. Two-thirds of the Senate is going to remain no matter what the public mood is during any election.

Although the members stand for election mainly as Republicans or Democrats, no tight party organization has been developed as in

Britain and throughout Europe. In Britain, as Ivor Jennings remarks, "The parties are not mere electioneering organizations, as they tend to be in Canada and the United States, but are truly based upon competing political principles." [5] Nobody has yet been able on the basis of their actions to show any clear difference between the Republican and Democratic parties, mere labels for candidates of disparate—and not fully known—outlook.

The oft-hymned wisdom of the framers has been obviously over-ridden by the country in the constitutional amendment making Senators electable by the citizens, and in effect the President as well, but the electorate is nevertheless politically divided into separate jurisdictions—by districts for Representatives, by states for Senators and by the country as a whole for President. The only official the entire country votes for is the President. In Britain no official is voted for by the entire country although voters of the winning party know that men suitable to them will be not only Prime Minister but members of his Cabinet and the heads of the government departments as well. Americans in voting for a President rarely know who department heads will be and it is often the case that complete unknowns are named by the President. Newspapers carrying long biographies first acquaint the public with the backgrounds of the presidential choices but the country knows less about their characters and principles than about those of the almost unknown incoming President.

Many members elected to Congress who are of the same party as the winning candidate for President do not adhere to views he has enunciated and do not hesitate so to inform their constituencies.

While British voters have a firm idea of what direction their prospective Prime Minister will take in power, Americans have no such firm idea about the President. For whatever a presidential candidate promises, and whatever the always ambiguous party platform states, it does not commit Congress. Far into his first term many who voted for a President are surprised, pleasantly or unpleasantly. They may be just as surprised by the performance of their Representatives and Senators. On top of this, they may be surprised by rulings of the Supreme Court. It is usually a series of surprise parties. Many of President Nixon's staunchest supporters were unpleasantly surprised and shocked by his sudden diplomatic overtures to Communist China, which he had spent years in denouncing as the scum of creation. Nixon-haters were equally surprised, but pleased.

The American electorate—left, right and center—is probably the most bamboozled and surprised in the world, unless it is the Italian. In the meantime, Constitution-boasters mindlessly cheer without cessation.

As each state is constitutionally entitled to two Senators, the Senate is not proportioned to population. For this reason a bloc of fifteen to twenty states in the Senate, with a population of less than 10 per cent in the 1970 census, can prevent any legislation or other measure proposed either by the House or the President or both of these jointly and clamored for by a vast majority of the populace. The reason for this is that under a Senate rule—and under the Constitution each house of Congress may make its own rules—each Senator is entitled to "unlimited debate" unless voted down by a large majority of the Senate—for many years by 66 per cent, now by 60 per cent. What is politely called unlimited debate is also known as the filibuster, a Spanish word for pirates. In the filibuster a group of Senators takes the floor one after the other and talks for hours on end, halting all other Senate business. Most Senators are reluctant to vote an end to "debate" as the filibuster is looked upon as a prerogative of every Senator. What the filibuster amounts to is sabotage of the majority will, which is what is generally regarded as undemocratic.

It was by means of the filibuster that the southern bloc in the Senate for decades blocked the passage of legislation that would have eased arbitrary restrictions directed against Negroes. Individual voters in the small states therefore cast a "heavier" vote for Senators than voters in the larger states, and thus have a greater role in blocking the House.

Owing to the special composition of the Senate, everything else apart, one cannot say that the United States operates under the rule of the majority, either of the populace or of Congress. One sees here a very great difference between the American and the British government. Whether majority rule is necessarily a great boon has never been proven, but the frequent claim, at any rate, is that the United States has it. This claim is precisely not so, and one is doubly sure of it when one notices that the Supreme Court is conceded the power in justiciable cases to nullify the joint acts of both houses of Congress that have additionally been approved by the President.

The Justices of the Supreme Court are appointed by successive Presidents as vacancies occur in a court quota that is set by act of Congress. The appointments, mostly of politicians or strong political partisans, usually anything but profound legal scholars, are subject to approval by a majority of the Senate unless held up by a filibuster, in which case as of now 60 per cent of the Senators present must vote closure or the appointment will fail. Some appointments are bottled up a long time in committee. If an appointee fails to get Senate approval, the appointment simply fails and another appointee must be named. Many concededly excellent men have been blocked by Congress from the Court.

The Supreme Court presently consists of nine members, of whom only five are usually necessary to make a decision. There is nothing whatever in the Constitution that says a majority decision of the Court should prevail. The Constitution is silent on the point—one of its numerous silences. Nor has Congress prescribed that a majority decision should prevail. Majority decisions prevail simply through autonomous usage and convention, as in the case of many procedures on which the Constitution is silent. Furthermore, there is no explicit direction in the Constitution nor any statute that the Court may veto national legislation or turn it in directions not set forth by Congress.

For such a large power to depend on deductions from detached phrases in the Constitution is indeed strange, a topic to be touched on later.

Majority decisions came to prevail because in appellate courts, with several judges sitting, it had long been the custom in Britain and America for the decision to be made by a majority. But the Supreme Court, as top legal scholars recognize, is more than an appellate court, more than a body that simply applies the law. It is a policy-making body, empowered not only to state the law but taking upon itself with no explicit warrant the right to interpret the Constitution finally and absolutely and to impose its views of public policy. More than this, it can nullify or modify a law, and has often done so, merely because it deems it on vague principles to be unwise or otherwise objectionable.[6] It determines the ultimate legality or illegality of governmental actions.

The framers professed to be seeking to avoid tyranny of any kind, and this included especially "the tyranny of the majority" or majority rule. By this criterion the British people today are always under a tyranny, for in the matter of policy they are always under the rule of a majority in the House of Commons that has been elected by a majority of the electorate. In Britain the average poll in parliamentary elections is 75 per cent and in local elections around 50 per cent.[7] In the United States the poll in presidential elections is seldom above 40 percent, and at rare times up to 50 per cent, and in congressional elections, varying from state to state, it is usually far below 50 per cent. In 1978 two thirds of the electorate failed to vote in congressional elections.

Constant alarm is expressed in many quarters, with earnest meetings held to study the problem, about the low participation in the United States of the eligible electorate in voting. Much of this low participation however stems from the fact that people see that their votes so often "don't count", produce no result. And one reason for this is that the votes are distributed to various bodies that can successfully nullify each other—the vote for congressional Representative, for Senator, for President and, in the same way, for state assembly, state senate and governor. What the voter is giving with one vote he very often is taking away or cancelling with another instead of, as in Great Britain, voting for a single representative committed under discipline to a single pre-announced point of view.

After the Constitution was adopted, so enchanted were the political actives of the time with its operation, that they gradually replicated most of it in the states. In most states the governments are set up on the same model. One therefore sees much the same procedure on every level of government in the United States.

A voter for example may vote for his Representative who promises to vote for lower taxes. He votes for a Senator of the same party who, representing a larger population, may not be so clear on the subject and who in fact does not favor lower taxes. The same party may put forward a President who says nothing on the subject but will, when the time of decision comes, favor higher taxes. The same sort of merry-go-round often takes place on the state and local levels. The voter is reduced to the condition of one of Pavlov's experimental dogs—apathetic, inert, disinterested.

For the parties represent no fixed principles, no special philosophy. They are both "pragmatic"—that is, willing to see their candidates do and say whatever is necessary to get elected. And furthermore, even if they do all act in unison in showdown votes, the unelected courts may nullify what they have enacted—and almost surely will if it represents any unusual departure from past custom.

It is commonly said by pundits that the United States has a representative democracy. If this is true, it is surely a *monitored* or *guided* representative democracy, monitored and guided by appointed lifetime judges. "The people" theoretically name their freelance random repre-senatives but these same representatives are all subject to veto or rescript by men the people have had no hand in selecting and who may in fact be abhorred by a majority of the people.

There is however no concerted outcry by Congress or the President against this seeming Court dominance except at rare crucial intervals, when the nine gentlemen of the Court find, as in the 1930s, that they must yield to the President. As nearly everybody who is politically active is generally satisfied with the unparelleled role of the Court, why advert to the subject at all? Most people active in politics in fact are quite content with the role of the Court, which seems strange as the Court certainly very often has interfered with the exercise of power by Congress and the President.

Why should imperious political elements take so kindly to being thwarted? Have they attained levels of reasonableness unusual in politicians?

One explanation for the acceptability of the Court, and of intercession by the court system in general in public policy questions, is that the courts in general, life-tenured, so often rescue the legislatures and executives from their own reluctant acts. Legislatures, including Congress, are often driven in their need for votes to enact some measure simply because of widespread popular clamor or because of the clamor of a militant minority group that promises to be vindictive at the polls unless it gets what it wants. And what it wants may be unconstitutional as well as unwise.

An illustration may be found throughout the thirty years after World War II in the way certain religious groups prevailed upon cowed state legislatures and governors to pass laws giving support with public tax money to religious schools in defiance of the First Amendment. A great variety of such laws were passed, one after the other in many states. For an elected public official to oppose them in many jurisdictions was to commit political suicide, which few politicians like to do. The elected officials simply gave way, depending upon the courts to halt the contagion, which they did by invoking the First Amendment (separating church and state) and Fourteenth Amendment (no abridgement of citizens' immunities) to the Constitution. In so doing they rescued the legislators, who could only say, "That's the Constitution as the Supreme Court sees it. We must all bow to the law."

The fact of judicial review enables legislature and executive in many instances to escape responsibility for making final decisions, especially unpopular final decisions. Here the mythology about the Constitution and the Founding Fathers comes into strong play. Who in his right mind could call them into question?

Yet it should be noted, and noted well, that a very broad spectrum of the citizenry does call them into question indirectly. For there is a widespread distrust and detestation of the politician in the United States as shown in ratings given by many public polls. Politicians are the holders of and contenders for public office, past and present. They are the mechanics and chauffeurs of the Constitution and the subordinate state constitutions, the ones who make the semi-system operative.

Now, if the Constitution were the marvelous mechanism that every school, every newspaper and every public figure asserts it to be, with few dissents, it is strange that the chief acolytes of the document, those put in place under its terms, should be in such bad odor. Some of the public revulsion against the American politician of course is based upon misunderstanding and typical American over-expectancy of what government in general can accomplish. But far from all. For what brings the politician most of the time into such bad odor in the United States is his demonstrated ability more or less surreptitiously in the constitutional system to sell the favors of the government to the highest bidder and to weasel around his proper duties in general. A very wide public in the United States believes it is being systematically bilked by the politician although it does not see that he is facilitated by the nature of the constitutional system.

In Great Britain, on the contrary, politicians are accorded a great deal of respect.

> Jokes are made about politicians in England as elsewhere; but the note of contempt and distrust which is evident in some countries is noticeably absent. It is something to be Prime Minister, it is also something to be a member of Parliament. There is prestige attached to the House of Commons. It has a dignity which it rarely forgets . . . Political ambition not only is a virtue; it is commonly regarded as a virtue. A person does not soil his reputation by standing for election. It is not uncommon for individuals to choose a political career, not because money can be made out of it, but because "it is something to have been Prime Minister," or even to have been a plain member of Parliament.[8]

The repute of the British politician therefore does not cast a dark shadow over the British Constitution.

After the decision in *Brown v. Board of Education*, there was a big outcry against the Supreme Court, particularly in the South, and from many quarters in the hinterland came the demand to impeach Chief Justice Earl Warren. Such outbursts have been seen after other decisions, with respect to other Justices. There was even an attempt in Congress, led by Congressman Gerald Ford, to impeach Justice Douglas on flimsy grounds. His true offense was that he was a stalwart of what many hinterland voters called "the liberals" on the bench.

Such popular movements against the Justices, of which there have been many in history, get nowhere because they are not sufficiently concentrated. But Congressmen of the disaffected regions could not survive the same ire. The Court, in short, often "takes the heat" off elected officials.

This sketch of the American system of government under the Constitution is not complete, however, without returning to Congress. Added to the delay and circumlocution deliberately built into the system, the Congress through its own rules has added to the labyrinth constructed by the framers. They have devised the committee system and the rule of seniority for its members.

No legislative body of any considerable country can function without committees to prepare the details of bills. The British Parliament has such committees and so does the American Congress. A difference between the two bodies however is that in the British system the Cabinet, "The Government", determines when a committee of its own disciplined supporters shall discharge its findings. In the American system in the usual case the committee chairman makes this determination.

The chairmen of the key standing committees in both houses of Congress, on which members of both parties serve simultaneously, occupy their positions by reason of length of service in the assembly, by the rule of seniority. In general, these are the men who have been most often re-elected and who hold "safe" seats, often for a lifetime, which are located mainly in politically non-competitive rural districts of low educational level and absence of general sophistication. "Safe" scats in metropolitan areas are located in districts of a single ethnic or religious composition but similar to the rural safe districts in that they are usually of low cultural level. In other words, the very bottom of the barrel holds the determining voice in this key aspect of government.

No bill can be voted out of a committee without the consent of the chairman who can, and often does, simply pocket it and forget about it. This procedure is more effective in the Senate than in the House but it has long been standard in both bodies, with some signs of relaxation now, probably temporary, in the House. A committee can, by majority vote, override the decision of its chairman but the committee members, most of them insecure in the respective establishments, very rarely do so. For the chairman has many boons to distribute, such as positions on sub-committees and chairmanships thereof as well as other desirable assignments. There is, too, always the support to be sought of the chairman and his long-established friends for special legislation wanted by a member for his home region. The good-will of the favor-dipensing majority and minority leaders may also be at stake.

Says James Bryce in his celebrated *The American Commonwealth:*

> The deliberations of committees [in Congress] are usually secret. Evidence is frequently taken with open doors, but newspapers do not report it, unless the matter excites public interest; and even the decisions arrived at are often noticed in the briefest way. It is out of order to canvass the proceedings of a committee in the House until they have been formally reported to it; and the report submitted does not usually state how the members have voted, or contain more than a very curt outline of what has passed. No member speaking in the House is entitled to reveal anything further.

This system, Bryce remarks,

> gives facilities for the exercise of underhand and even corrupt in-
> fluence. In a small committee the voice of each member is well worth
> securing, and may be secured with little danger of a public scandal.
> The press can not, even when the doors of committee rooms stand
> open, report the proceedings of fifty bodies; the eye of the nation
> can not follow and mark what goes on within them; while the subse-
> quent proceedings in the House are too hurried to permit a ripping up
> there of suspicious bargains struck in the purlieus of the Capital, and
> fulfilled by votes given in a committee.[9]

As Prof. J. Allen Smith remarks, "A system better adapted to the purpose of the lobbyist could not be devised." [10] Washington consequently
swarms with the very highly paid lobbyists of the major economic interests and many of the minor ones, all zeroed in on Congress and especially
on key committee chairmen.

Congressional committees usually contain members of both parties,
which is the point where the rival parties usually fuse into one. In
Britain committees to prepare bills consist of the members of the party
in power, which takes responsibility for policy.

Either house of Congress can of course vote out of committee a bill
that is being stalled by the committee chairman or a majority of the
committee. But such action involves delay and perhaps a protracted
fight on the floor and is avoided apart from exceptional circumstances.
Again, Congress is always reluctant so to vote, for it is an infringement
of the prerogative of the committee chairman and also requires much
exertion and vexation. It will not do so unless it is feeling a great deal
of "heat" from some quarter. Furthermore the committee chairman
and his old-line allies—all long-time incumbents—still retain much power
of maneuver on the floor with respect to getting a bill sidetracked. It
can be amended in undesirable ways, requiring a hard-to-get full-dress
vote to kill the amendments. It can be talked to death. What happens
depends upon how much "muscle" the majority is willing to put into
the business, which usually is not much.

Each house of Congress is composed of cliques which on different
issues shift their internal structures and external alliances. The House
is so composed to a greater extent than the Senate. The individual
members find the cliques indispensable to getting things done. But each
individual is fundamentally alone, answerable only to his constituency.
In shopping around for support on bills, the members trade, tit for tat,
and if one declines to support the bill of another member he cannot
expect the other's support. Thus a member may reasonably hesitate to
support what is patently an expensive boondoggle for some sparsely

settled region. The proponent of the boondoggle will then decline to support his colleague's bill for a needed sewage treatment plant in a densely populated, badly polluted region. As a result every vital appropriation carries with it, either internally or in its wake, highly dubious projects, expensive to all taxpayers and burdensome to the economy. Nor is this occasional. It goes on all the time and is cumulative. The same procedure takes place in all the larger states. Meanwhile the national debt inexorably rises.

The district constituencies for their part are like ponds of hungry carp, judging their representative by what he can concretely "deliver" for them. Most of the constituencies believe that incoming federal projects or contracts are gratis to them, to be paid for by the whole country—by others. They fail to realize however that all the constituencies are getting analogous projects, over the years evenly distributed, so that the citizens are caught in a steadily rising tide of "pork barrel" expenditures which everyone must defray directly or indirectly. Nothing whatever that comes from the government is "free" and there is especially nothing in existence like free public education or free public libraries or free public services in general. Such are only part of the myth.

Everything else failing, bills in Congress are amended, sometimes emasculated with amendments, sometimes swollen grotesquely. The members of Congress also freely use irrelevant amendments tacked on to vital bills in order to foist upon the country expenditures for strictly parochial purposes, often little more than ornamental or of restricted local benefit. Omnibus bills are also frequently passed, filled with disparate items.

The President of course has the power of veto but he does not possess an item-by-item veto, for which many persons have long clamored in order to shrink the congressional "pork barrel". For Article VII, Section 1 of the Constitution stipulates that the presidential veto applies simply to "bills", not to parts of bills, and on details like this interpretations are strict. But in recent years Presidents have increasingly impounded instead of expended some funds appropriated by Congress although the Constitution confers upon them no such power of impoundment. So we see that with respect to the Constitution as in other affairs there is more than one way to skin a cat.

The rule of seniority in Congress is as mechanically mindless as the rule of hereditary succession in kingdoms and was adopted for much the same reason: there was no suitable method available in the situation for uncontroversial rational choices to be made.

Each member of each house is there strictly as a freelance operator, responsible only to a majority of the political actives of his home district, not to any party leadership. And each member has exactly the same rights and privileges in his house as every other, the most venal as well as the most honest, the stupidest as well as the brightest. As there is no party authority to decide who is to take up each task, and in fact no genuine political party in existence, matters must be decided among equal individuals on the floor. Prior to the adoption of seniority rules, chairmanships and other perquisites were decided by wheeling and dealing, which led to many complications and much cankerous bitterness on the part of the losers. The vicious infighting in the jockeying for positions poisoned the working atmosphere and impeded operations. To solve this serious problem, following a period when the House Speaker dictated choices, the rule of seniority was introduced. Preferred positions were thereafter dispensed automatically, more of them than not to low-grade mentalities. The quality of the man makes no difference in the apportionment of assignments. In fact, in the recent case of Representative L. Mendel Rivers of South Carolina, an extreme alcoholic was for many years left in charge of the House Military Affairs Committee, what is regarded as a hyper-sensitive assignment, the target of hostile foreign agents. Varying in content, there are many similar cases.

Rivers was a Congressman from the first district of South Carolina for thirty years until his death in 1970. In this capacity, and as chairman of the Armed Services Committee, he was able to funnel so much defense money into the district that 35 per cent of its payrolls depended on military installations or defense industries. Upon his death he was succeeded by his godson, Mendel Davis. (Political office in the United States is often a family affair, son, grandson, nephew, cousin or brother stepping into the shoes or the jurisdiction of a predecessor.)

Like Rivers, long-term chairmen of congressional committees often funnel a disproportionate amount of federal funds into their out-of-the-way districts, making themselves the objects of prolonged hosannahs from the local constituency. The ability so to direct funds in itself promotes greater seniority.

Congress, in each house, is as a matter of fact operated very much on a catch-as-catch-can basis, almost anything being tolerated that is not to the disadvantage of the group as a whole, and each member within very broad limits a law unto himself.

The fact that the United States has been unable to develop effective political parties—that is, parties that are more than multi-voiced electioneering frameworks—can hardly be laid at the door of the Constitution. What has prevented this development is the size of the country and the disparities of economic and other interests of its various unlike regions. The political actives of the various regions vis-a-vis each other have been unable to develop hard and fast shared principles, and what has seemed necessary to one region has been an abomination to other regions. But within the phantom parties, and across party lines, the regions have been able to co-operate spasmodically on specific issues. This political fracturing of the country by disparate regions has worked against the development of the integrated political parties organized on clear principles and able to exercise some authority over office-holders. These latter, apart from local demands, are all very much on their own, every man for himself, lone wolves all.

Meanwhile many millions in the populace believe there are significant differences between Republicans and Democrats and vote and register accordingly although in recent decades an enlarging middle group of disgusted voters declare themselves to be "independents". So declaring themselves results in no gain for them, merely serves notice that they cannot be counted on to vote according to party labels. As they nearly always have no one to vote for except labelled Republicans or Democrats, unless they plump for ineffective splinter-party candidates, they are essentially back where they started from, on the same constitutional merry-go-round as everyone else.

Seven

COURT OVER
CONSTITUTION

The part of the Constitution establishing the Supreme Court, Article III, is the briefest by far of any designating divisions of the government. All it says is that "The judicial power shall be vested in one Supreme Court, and in such inferior courts as the Congress may from time to time ordain and establish. The judges, both of the Supreme Court and inferior courts, shall hold their offices during good behavior, and shall at stated times receive for their services, a compensation, which shall not be diminished during their continuance in office.

"The judicial power shall extend to all cases, in law and equity, arising under this Constitution, the laws of the United States, and treaties made, or which shall be made, under their authority; to all cases affecting ambassadors, other public ministers and consuls; to all cases of admiralty and maritime jurisdiction; to controversies to which the United States shall be a party; to controversies between two or more states; between a State and citizens of another State; between citizens of different States, between citizens of the same state claiming lands under grants of different States, and between a State, or the citizens thereof, and foreign states, citizens or subjects."

This is all, apart from an additional paragraph that gives the Supreme Court original jurisdiction in cases involving diplomats and those to which a state may be a party, and that "the Supreme Court shall have appellate jurisdiction, both as to law and fact, *with such exceptions, and under such regulations as the Congress shall make.*"

The preceding twelve words are emphasized because they are rarely alluded to in discussions about the Court. They bring out that, under the Constitution, the Supreme Court is subject to regulation by Congress, which may make exceptions among the types of cases heard, individually or by categories. Congress, in short, is explicitly empowered by the Constitution to regulate the Court, not *vice versa*. Yet the Court more often seems to regulate Congress.

Why is this? First, as already indicated, Congress finds it convenient to allow the Court rather than itself to take the blame for unpopular decisions; judges can be removed only with great difficulty and for cause whereas Congressmen are easily removed by the volatile and often quixotic electorate. Second, although individual Congressmen and groups of Congressmen are often volubly wrathful about Court decisions, such wrath being relished by frustrated constituents, it would ordinarily be difficult among 435 members of the lower house and 100 members of the Senate to mobilize enough votes to intervene against the Court. Congressmen are fully sensible of the value of the Court as a scapegoat, deflecting public censure from themselves, and they are in any event usually in great disagreement among themselves.

Only once has Congress seriously moved to trim the claim to final power assumed by the Court, a claim that is itself subject to exceptions. This was in 1868 when the Judiciary Committee of the House reported a bill that prescribed that in any case involving the validity of an act of Congress, two-thirds of the judges must concur in any opinion adverse to the law. Congress could in fact require a unanimous opinion. The bill was passed by 116 to 39. The fear in Congress was that in a pending case the Court was about to hold the post-war reconstruction acts invalid. The bill died in the Senate. While there was much support for the measure in the country, there was also heated opposition from conservatives. The same year there was another House venture, this one successful, to limit the Court. A Senate bill to extend the Court's appellate jurisdiction to customs and revenue cases came to the House. To it was then tacked an amendment completely repealing the appellate jurisdiction of the Court under the Habeas Corpus Act of 1867 and prohibiting the exercise of any jurisdiction by the Court in this respect on appeals. Back in the Senate the amendment was concurred in with no debate on March 12, 1868, by 32 to 6. The bill was vetoed by President Andrew Johnson but was then repassed over the veto.

The Supreme Court meanwhile delayed hearing what was known as the McCardle case, the one which had provoked the strong reaction in Congress. On March 19, 1869, the Court took up the case again on the question of the power of Congress to prohibit it from deciding a pending case and in April unanimously decided that Congress by its statute had in fact, and constitutionally, taken away its jurisdiction in the case and that it could not pronounce judgment.

"Judicial duty", said the Court, "is not less fitly performed by declining ungranted jurisdiction than in exercising firmly that which the Constitution and the laws confer." Although appellate jurisdiction did not stem from acts of Congress but from the Constitution, it said, yet it was conferred "with such exceptions and under such regulations as Congress shall make." [1]

By reason of its power to regulate the Court, only once used, it is clear that the last word in any showdown with respect to the supremacy of Court or Congress under the Constitution lies with Congress, not with the Court. Congress, for its part, is in closer contact with the active political elements of the country than is the Court.

One might say on the basis of what has been said thus far that practically, in nearly all questions, the Court is supreme. Yet even this is not unqualifiedly so. For, contrary to common supposition, the rulings of the Court do not always produce a general rule that is thereupon dutifully followed by everybody. The decisions of the Court apply only to a specific case and may or may not be more broadly applied. Many of its rulings with respect to a single government department for example are simply ignored, not applied, by other government departments. It would be necessary for someone to file another lawsuit in order to get the benefit of the decisive ruling, a tedious proceeding that is not often resorted to, one of the many delays built into the system. The Court cannot direct the entire government.

The country in the case of *Brown v. Board of Education* was shown how an original ruling of the Supreme Court in a controversial case must be followed by a long succession of further court proceedings and peremptory court orders, plus police and military action through a willing executive branch, in specific instances throughout the country. In fact, under *Brown,* the courts, against sullen popular opposition, have had to monitor and direct very precisely the school systems with respect to race in various parts of the country. In many other matters, too, federal judges have taken over the direction of state governments, as in Alabama and elsewhere, with respect to the operation of jails, asylums, shelters and other public facilities where, in the name of local economy or just plain orneriness, the ordinarily decent treatment of inmates has been found violated in wholesale fashion.

Where such stringent judicial or legislative follow-ups are not undertaken or where a ruling is not spontaneously embraced all around, a court decision manifestly applies only to the case in question. No general rule is made operative by it.

Many laws on the books, as well as court decisions, are thus much like beautiful roads that extend a distance and then suddenly end on the edge of a desert or a wilderness. They lead, as it is said, to nowhere except in one case where an accommodating path is marked out. Additionally there are equivocal laws, which seem to say one thing but carry within self-cancelling provisions. One example among many such legal mirages was the Corrupt Practices Act of 1925 which, according to the obvious intention of its framers, did not prevent any corrupt practices. It was no more than complicated window-dressing for the naive.

As to what is called judicial review on the part of the Supreme Court, there is no mention of it in the Constitution nor was it authorized by the constitutional convention. A few of the members, **judging** by their remarks, obviously favored it, and they were not all nationalists. Others were adamantly opposed and said so.

Judicial review is derived by deduction and construction from two separate parts of the Constitution. Article VI, Section 2, three paragraphs from the end, says, "This Constitution, and the laws of the United States which shall be made in pursuance thereof, and all treaties made, or which shall be made, under the authority of the United States, shall be the supreme law of the land; and the judges in every State shall be bound thereby, any thing in the Constitution or laws of any State to the contrary notwithstanding." Combining this section with Article III, Section 1–"The judicial power shall extend to all cases, in law and equity, arising under this Constitution," etc.–one has the implied basis, constitutionally stated, for judicial review.

Not many persons at the time the Constitution was up for ratification saw the connection. But Judge Robert Yates of New York, a member of the constitutional convention, writing as an experienced jurist under the name of "Brutus", did see it and spelled out what he saw as the dire consequences in a series of notable newspaper articles that impressed Hamilton at least. Under such power to interpret and apply what was a piece of formally unauthorized prior legislation, namely the Constitution, appointed lifetime judges would have a power unprecedented in history: to nullify joint acts of the legislature and the executive made on behalf, theoretically, of the broad constituencies they represented.

A few of the observations made by Judge Yates were as follows:

With respect to the Constitution, "the courts of law, which will be constituted by it, are not only to decide upon the constitution and the laws made in pursuance of it, but by officers subordinate to them to execute all their decisions. The real effect of this system of government, will therefore be brought home to the feelings of the people, through the medium of the judicial power . . ."

Those who are vested with this power

> are to be placed in a situation altogether unprecedented in a free country. They are to be rendered totally independent, both of the people and the legislature, both with respect to their offices and salaries. No error they may commit can be corrected by any power above

them, if any such power there be, nor can they be removed from office
for making ever so many erroneous adjudications . . .

This part of the plan is so modelled, as to authorize the courts,
not only to carry into execution the powers expressly given, but where
these are wanting or ambiguously expressed, to supply what is wanting
by their own decisions . . . A number of hard words and technical
phrases are used in this part of the system, about the meaning of which
gentlemen learned in the law differ . . .

The cases arising under the constitution must include such, as bring
into question its meaning, and will require an explanation of the
nature and extent of the powers of the different departments under it.

This article, therefore, vests the judicial with a power to resolve
all questions that may arise upon the construction of the constitution,
either in law or in equity.

The courts are also given authority

to give the constitution a legal construction, or to explain it according
to the rules laid down for construing a law.—These rules give a certain degree of latitude of explanation . . . they are empowered to
explain the constitution according to the reasoning spirit of it, without being confined to the word or letter . . . The opinions of the
supreme court, whatever they may be, will have the force of law;
because there is no power provided in the constitution, that can correct their errors, or control their adjudications. From this court there
is no appeal . . . The legislature must be controlled by the constitution, and not the constitution by them . . .

Most of the articles in this system, which convey powers of considerable importance, are conceived in general and indefinite terms,
which are either equivocal, ambiguous, or which require long defini-
tions to unfold the extent of their meaning. The two most important
powers committed to any government, those of raising money, and
of raising and keeping up troops, have already been considered and
shewn to be unlimited by any thing but the discretion of the legislature. The clause which vests the power to pass all laws which are
proper and necessary, to carry the powers given into execution, it has
been shewn, leaves the legislature at liberty, to do everything,
which in their judgment is best. It is said, I know, that this clause
confers no power on the legislature, which they would not have
had without it—though I believe this is not the fact, yet, admitting it
to be, it implies that the constitution is not to receive an explanation
strictly, according to its letter; but more power is implied than is
expressed. And this clause . . . is to be understood as declaring, that in
construing any of the articles conveying power, the spirit, intent and
design of the clause, should be attended to, as well as the words
in their common acceptation.

[The courts] will be interested in using this latitude of interpretation. Every body of men invested with office are tenacious of power; they feel interested, and hence it has become a kind of maxim, to hand down their offices, with all its rights and privileges, unimpaired to their successors; the same principle will influence them to extend their power, and increase their rights; this of itself will operate strongly upon the courts to give such a meaning to the constitution in all cases where it can possibly be done, as will enlarge the sphere of their own authority. Every extension of the power of the general legislature, as well as of the judicial powers, will increase the powers of the courts; and the dignity and importance of the judges, will be in proportion to the extent and magnitude of the powers they exercise. I add, it is highly probable the emoluments of the judges will be increased, with the increase of the business they will have to transact and its importance. From these considerations the judges will be interested to extend the powers of the courts, and to construe the constitution as much as possible, in such a way as to favour it; and that they will do it, appears probable.

Because they will have precedent to plead, to justify them in it. It is well known, that the courts in England, have by their own authority, extended their jurisdiction far beyond the limits set them in their original institution, and by the laws of the land.

This power in the judicial, will enable them to mould the government, in almost any shape they please.—The manner in which this may be effected we will hereafter examine.

Yates by his precisely insightful analysis produced in the "Brutus" articles, published in a New York newspaper prior to the ratification of the Constitution, what amounted to a blueprint of actual future governmental developments under the Constitution.[2] Yates, in brief, wrote much of the scenario for the future, much more so than any other pre-ratification critic or proponent of the Constitution. What he said was publicly denied by pro-ratificationists.

Marbury Versus Madison

About this applied judicial power, first clearly asserted by the Court in *Marbury v. Madison* (1803), there was from the beginning much controversy and objection. The controversy recurs from time to time and depends in its magnitude more on the content of each disputed ruling than on the elitist principle of judicial review. Those who approve or benefit from a ruling of the Court believe, for the moment at least, that judicial review is an excellent method. Those who disapprove often go so far as to assert that the Court has usurped its power. They go further and charge that the Court often invents laws, which indeed it does. Approval or disapproval of the work of the Court depends upon whose ox is being gored, which usually leaves the Court in a strong public position as it always has a large or influential section of the public on its side.

The decision of the Court in *Marbury v. Madison,* written by Chief Justice John Marshall, was expressed in a very serpentine way. The apparent issue, about which the new Jefferson administration was unduly excited, concerned the last-minute appointment by outgoing President John Adams under the Judiciary Act of 1801 of some Federalist judges. One of these, William Marbury, was appointed justice of the peace of the District of Columbia. Newly elected President Jefferson ordered Secretary of State James Madison, now very much on his way up in the government, to withhold from Marbury the sealed commission of his appointment, signed by Adams. Here was one President refusing to recognize the legal act of a predecessor.

Marbury sued for a writ of mandamus compelling delivery of the commission. To comply with the request would have brought the Court into a direct confrontation with the irate President and his militant popular party, which was the chief opponent of the Federalist Party to which both Adams and Chief Justice Marshall belonged. In the means he employed to avoid this confrontation, which might well have undermined the Court, Marshall formally placed it on the high theoretical elevation it still enjoys. Marshall declared that Section 13 of the Judiciary Act of 1789, empowering the Court to issue such a writ, was contrary to the Constitution and therefore invalid. He denied Marbury the writ.

In so doing he produced, as it were, a bundle of political dynamite with a long time-fuse attached. But the Jeffersonians were too elated by their victory with respect to Marbury to more than growl, and moved on to have repealed the entire Judiciary Act of 1801 which, in addition to providing more judges also excused Supreme Court judges from doubling as trial judges on circuits, a chore they all found distasteful. The Judiciary Act of 1801 lasted little more than a year and circuit-riding by Supreme Court judges continued for a long time.

What Jefferson got out of the decision was very little. What Marshall and the Federalists and post-Civil War Republicans got was a great deal: a claimed brake on Congress and the President, both elected by the sacred people, although it was far from being the absolute brake that Court cultists at times erroneously make it out to be.

The most interesting aspect of Marshall's decision is that Section 13 of the Judiciary Act was not in fact out of harmony with the Constitution, and Marshall and the Court could have denied Marbury the mandamus he sought simply on the basis of Section 13. But by doing that Marshall would not have obtained what he sought: a precedent of record for declaring an act of Congress and the President void.

Sitting in the Senate when the Judiciary Act was written were twelve out of twenty-four Senators who had been members of the constitutional convention, including outstanding participants such as Ellsworth and Johnson of Connecticut, Paterson of New Jersey, King of New York, and linchpin Robert Morris of Pennsylvania. Eight out of fifty-eight members of the House were recent members of the constitutional convention, including stalwarts Roger Sherman of Connecticut and Madison. And President Washington, chief officer of the convention, signed the act. Epigones such as Marshall and his Court, which included one framer, Paterson, certainly had no better understanding of the Constitution than these men.

The reader may judge for himself whether these men in Congress had inadvertently lapsed from the Constitution they had just put together. Section 13 of the Judiciary Act says that the Supreme Court "shall have power to issue writs of prohibition to the district courts when proceeding as courts of admiralty and maritime jurisdiction, and writs of *mandamus*, in cases warranted by the principles and usages of law, to any courts appointed, or persons holding office, under the authority of the United States." [3]

What Chief Justice Marshall could easily have done was to deny Marbury his request on the ground that his case was not one where a mandamus was "warranted by the principles and usages of law". And this was strictly true as the Supreme Court was an appellate court except in constitutionally designated rare cases where it was a court of original jurisdiction. The writ of mandamus in a court of original jurisdiction is a settled part of the legal routine, and the case brought by Marbury did not fall under one of the classifications allowed by the Constitution as conferring upon the Supreme Court original jurisdiction. Beyond this, at no time in English or American history had a court of any kind been empowered to direct the head of a government in a matter of his official duties. In brief, the mandamus could have been denied simply on the ground that the case was one where the Court had no constitutional jurisdiction. Or, the case need not have been heard at all. But by so adjudicating, the arch-Federalist Marshall would not have been able to make his point about the power of the Court to nullify an act of Congress.

Such a staunch adulator of Marshall and the Court as the historian Charles Warren admits:

> it would have been possible for Marshall, if he had been so inclined, to have construed the language of the section of the Judiciary Act which authorized writs of mandamus, in such a manner as to have

enabled him to escape the necessity of declaring the section unconstitutional. The section was, at most, broadly drawn, and was not necessarily to be interpreted as conferring original jurisdiction on the Court . . . Marshall naturally felt that in view of the recent attacks on judicial power it was important to have the great principle [of judicial review] firmly established, and undoubtedly he welcomed the opportunity of fixing the precedent in a case in which his action would necessitate a decision in favor of his political [sic!] opponents. Accordingly, after reviewing the provisions of the Constitution as to the original jurisdiction of the Court, he held that there was no authority in Congress to add to that original jurisdiction, that the [section of the] statute was consequently invalid.[4]

In the United States at the time, the ultimate supremacy of the Court was an unusual claim and had been advanced for a number of years only by a small but growing coterie of lawyers, not all of whom were Federalists. The anti-Court Jeffersonians had earlier clamored to have the Court declare the Alien and Sedition Acts unconstitutional, but these had now changed their tune about the power of the Court.

The Idea of Judicial Supremacy

How the unusual idea of judicial review came to arise at all, an idea that makes the United States Constitution as officially interpreted unique, is itself interesting. There were eight cases of judicial review in the states of the pre-constitutional Confederation—one each in Massachusetts, North Carolina, Rhode Island, Connecticut, New York and New Jersey, and two in Virginia.[5] Such action by these courts however was nowhere formally authorized, just as the legislatures themselves were not formally authorized. Both were *ad hoc* by-products of revolt and secession, the creations of revolutionary juntas.

Where had at least some of the newly independent colonists come upon the idea that a legislature could be judicially overruled? Prior to 1776, in the colonial period, all colonial laws repugnant to English laws were invalid.[6] Here was the very essence of colonial subordination, detested by the revolutionists. Such colonial laws were subject to *administrative* review by the British Board of Trade and by colonial governors, who held office at the pleasure of the King. Hence, at the last resort, all colonial laws existed at the pleasure either of the King or of Parliament, which ruled the Board of Trade. No fewer than 8,563 acts of colonial legislatures were given such review and 469 or 5.5 per cent of them were disallowed.[7] But this was by no means judicial review.

Review in Britain by the Board of Trade began in 1696, prior to which the task fell to the King's Privy Council although that body did not perform it systematically until after 1660. It is thought by many scholars that in this process of essentially foreign administrative review, ideas and principles were developed that in many ways prepared the American mentality for review by permanent judges under the United States Constitution.[8] The judges take the place of the old-style English king and his henchmen.

In a very few cases colonial courts declined to enforce an order of His Majesty in Council because it contradicted the colonial charters, which many colonists, especially lawyers, looked upon as their Constitution. Two such cases were heard in Massachusetts—*Frost v. Leighton* and *Giddings v. Brown.*[9]

The original basis for judicial review, often cited by its proponents, was the pre-colonial decision of Lord Chief Justice Edward Coke in Dr. Bonham's case (1610). The Royal College of Physicians in England had imposed a fine for the illegal practice of medicine and Coke held that according to common law no man can be a judge in his own case.

In the course of his decision he threw out this *obiter dictum*: "It appears in our books that in many cases the common law will control acts of parliament and some times adjudge them to be utterly void; for when an act of parliament is against common right or reason, or repugnant or impossible to be performed, the common law will control it and adjudge such act to be void" (8 Coke 118a).

Leading lawyers of the revolution liked to cite this decision.

In the case of *Rawles v. Mason,* Coke said, "If there be repugnancy in statute or unreasonableness in custom, the common law disallows it and rejects it." [10]

And how does one discover what the common law is, as it is not anywhere recorded? Judges have this pleasant task. As defenders of common law put it, the judges "find" the law in reasonable customs of the people. As critics put it, the judges invent the law, sometimes out of the whole cloth.

Coke as a devotee of the common law was manifestly laying out a large role for judges and has therefore always been an object of admiration by the generality of the legal profession. For very similar reasons Chief Justice Marshall is similarly admired.

At the time of the Bonham case, Coke was in controversy with the repressive Stuart monarchy, which controlled Parliament. He was then, although not always in his career, on the popular side and was the originator of what came to be called "the myth of Magna Carta".[11] Coke, in an age when few people could read and few had access to any books, enjoyed an exaggerated reputation for profound learning in the law; he was not nearly as learned as he professed. Many of his historical doctrines have been found by scholars to be unsound and

Coke did not hesitate to invent supposed ancient laws to his own purposes of the moment, some of them personal and profitable. In this respect he was completely unscrupulous and high-handed.

But in 1776 hardly any Americans, high or low, believed in judicial review. "A fact which contributed greatly to the early supremacy of the legislatures was the general assumption during the years 1776-87 that they were the sole judges of their own constitutional powers," says an esteemed Establishment historian. "Few Americans believed that any State court had the right to declare an enactment invalid on the ground that it violated the Constitution. New York, in creating her Council of Revision, implied that whenever a legislative enactment was approved by the Council, it was thenceforth subject to no question . . . The Massachusetts Constitution of 1780 also showed that the State courts were in no instance expected to annul a statute, for it provided that in 1795 there should be a popular vote upon the calling of a Convention to remedy any transgressions of fundamental law . . ." [12]

Nor had public attitudes much changed at the time of the constitutional convention. In the convention opinions were sharply divided on the point so that nobody can cite for his preference what the sacrosanct Founding Fathers thought. Both Madison and James Wilson, chief theoreticians of the convention, were zealously opposed to judicial review and fought for a council of revision that would give prior certification of the constitutionality of every law, thus avoiding the tangle of later expensive litigation with which the country has since been beset. If either judges or President objected to such a certification, it would be subject to overrule by two-thirds vote of Congress; if both judges and the President objected, by three-fourths vote. Delaware, Maryland and Virginia supported this procedure, which was voted down 8 to 3, mainly on the ground that judges should have no hand in legislation.

Charles Pinckney of South Carolina "opposed the interference of the Judges in the Legislative business", Mercer of Maryland "disapproved of the Doctrine that the Judges as expositors of the Constitution should have authority to declare a law void", Dickinson of Delaware "thought no such power ought to exist", and Sherman of Connecticut "disapproved of Judges meddling in politics and parties". Gouverneur Morris of New York however disagreed and so apparently did Elbridge Gerry. [13]

The convention thereupon, after denying judges participation in the presidential veto, simply made no provision for judicial review of any kind. The absence of any explicit prohibition of something so eccentric as judicial review certainly does not argue that it may be resorted to. For if a constitution had to mention everything not permitted, it would be endless.

Judicial review, then, is just one of the usages of the Constitution that has sprung up in the course of jockeying among the divisions, personalities and factions of the government. It has no sanction from the founders. It was not provided for by the framers in so many words and will be tolerated only as long as it seems useful to political managers or does not produce persistent public objection.

That Marshall was impressed by the growls of disapproval over his pronouncement on Section 13 of the Judiciary Act, which had no immediate practical effect, is suggested by the fact that he never again made a finding of unconstitutionality about an act of Congress although later Courts have found acts of the period unconstitutional. It was not until 1857, or 54 years after *Marbury,* that the Supreme Court again used the shotgun Marshall had loaded—with disastrous repercussions upon itself and the nation.

In this case, as in *Marbury,* the main issues lay below the manifest case being decided. Although this case has been written about *ad nauseam,* it is worth recapitulating to show how the Supreme Court goes about finding an authentic and entirely constructive act of Congress invalid. Section 13 of the Judiciary Act was also such a wholly constructive effort. In other words, there was nothing malicious or underhanded about the acts of Congress in either case—nor anything out of harmony with the Constitution.

The Dred Scott Decision

Dred Scott, a Negro slave belonging to Dr. John Emerson, an army surgeon, was taken in 1834 by his owner from St. Louis, Missouri, to Rock Island, Illinois, and later to Fort Snelling in Wisconsin Territory. In Illinois slavery was forbidden under the pre-constitutional ordinance of 1787 and in Wisconsin Territory by the Missouri Compromise of 1820.

Under this compromise slavery was prohibited north of the line 36° 30′ in the territory of the Louisiana Purchase. Missouri was admitted by Congress to the Union as a slave state and Maine as a free state, thereby preserving the political balance among the states of which eleven at this time were slave and eleven free. The slave-based southern political bloc insisted upon preserving its fifty-fifty voting power in the Senate although it was outnumbered in the population-represented House. Hence the compromise in Congress.

In 1846 Scott sued for his freedom on the ground that he had been four years in a free state and on free territory under congressional jurisdiction and was in consequence a free man. He won in the lower court but was overruled in 1852 by the Missouri supreme court. Appealed to the federal district court and then to the Supreme Court, the case now embodied three main issues: (1) whether Scott was a citizen of Missouri and thus entitled to sue; (2) whether his stay on free soil had given him a title to freedom still valid on his return to Missouri; and (3) whether the long-standing Missouri Compromise was constitutional.

Each Justice of the Court handed down a separate opinion. A majority, including Chief Justice Roger B. Taney, a southerner, held that Scott (and therefore all slaves or their descendants) was not a citizen of the United States or Missouri and so was not entitled to sue in federal courts. In so saying, the Court in effect refused jurisdiction. The majority also held that Scott's residence on free territory had not conferred freedom on him that was retained when he returned to Missouri, because his status, it decided arbitrarily, was determined by the laws of the state in which he resided when he illegitimately raised the question of his freedom. If true, this meant that any black from a free state might be unfree or at least a non-citizen upon taking up residence in a slave state. Finally, the majority held, 6 to 3, that the Missouri Compromise was unconstitutional because it violated the Fifth Amendment to the Constitution which prohibited depriving persons of their property without due process of law, and Scott was someone's property. This principle of due process had been first put forth in connection with a state law respecting property in *Wynehamer v. The People* (13 N.Y. 378, 1856).

Two dissenting Justices held that free Negroes were in fact citizens of the United States and that Congress was constitutionally empowered under Article IV, Section 3, Paragraph 2, to regulate slavery in the territories. This paragraph plainly reads, "The Congress shall have power to dispose of and make all needful rules and regulations respecting the territory or other property belonging to the United States . . ."

In territory under the direct jurisdiction of the federal government north of 36° 30′ everyone was free and Congress was the sole rule-maker for such territory. Once free, a man cannot constitutionally be made unfree unless conscripted or convicted in a court of law of some crime. An owner for example could not have brought a slave to Great Britain or Canada and have retained him as a slave. The slave would have been automatically free.

The fundamental issue, then, related to the power of Congress as clearly stated in the Constitution and did not concern whether somebody's property was in danger of being confiscated. The last was of incidental consideration. For if Scott was a free man through having been brought under the direct jurisdiction of the United States in free territory, there could be no question of confiscation or his right to sue. Scott was certainly not legally a slave—that is, a piece of property—while in Illinois and Wisconsin.

The serpentine decision of the Court, as serpentine as Marshall's in *Marbury* and as unsound intellectually, caused an uproar in the North, and not only among abolitionists. Constitutionalists too were affronted. The decision is considered by many historians as having raised a road-block to the peaceful solution of the slavery question, thus paving the way to the disastrous Civil War.

A long line of mischievous Supreme Court decisions was still to come when the Republicans moved into the ascendancy, coming to an end only in the face of presidential and public opposition during the economic (and legal) collapse of the 1930s.

Judicial review, although not without merit, is far from the great procedure that its devotees, mainly lawyers and political conservatives, claim it to be. As often as not its deliverances are unsettling on the spot or productive of deferred profound difficulties. The main objection to it is that it is politically "unnatural", amounting to a basically arbitrary censorship and rescription of the legislative and executive power. A majority of a few judges are no better readers of the Constitution or devisers of legislation than are legislators, presidents or scholars, as the Marbury and Dred Scott cases show. More of whatever the country has to mobilize in the way of wisdom is directed at the legislature than at the courts even though, true enough, a legislature does not always choose the way of wisdom. Nor, as the record shows, do the courts.

The Income Tax Case

Despite the intellectual fragility of the positions it took in the Marbury and Dred Scott cases the Court was yet to do worse. Perhaps the worst it ever did from every conceivable point of view was in the case of *Pollock v. Farmers' Loan and Trust Co.* (158 U.S. 601, 1895). The case concerned the validity of the income-tax clause of the Wilson-Gorman Tariff Act of 1894. By 5-4 the Court invalidated the tax on the ground that taxes on personal property were direct taxes and that these were forbidden by the Constitution (Article I, Section 9, Paragraph 4) unless laid "in proportion to the census". It will be recalled that at the constitutional convention nobody was able to answer the question of what a direct tax was as distinct from a non-direct tax.

As the careful scholar Corwin observes, "All things considered the decision in the Pollock Case was the most disabling blow ever struck at the principle of *stare decisis* in the field of constitutional law, which means that it was one of the most powerful blows ever struck for transforming the Court's reviewing power into that of a super-legislature." [14]

One anonymous judge moreover changed his vote from an earlier decision in the same case that had sustained the law.

"The real motive of the Court in the Pollock Case was to convert the 'direct tax' clauses into *positive protections of wealth*," Corwin remarks. The italics are his.[15]

As Corwin demonstrates very clearly, the decision in the case was unhistorical, striking down earlier decisions of the Court, and illogical—which later fact showed that as a considered act it was predetermined, violative of the premises laid down.

First, the suit was brought in violation of section 3,224 of the revised statutes which forbade the maintenance in any court of a suit "for the purpose of restraining the assessment or collection of any tax". The suit itself was therefore unconstitutional because illegal. Years before, Justice Miller had observed in *Cheatham v. United States*, "If there existed in the courts, state or national, any general power of impeding or controlling the collection of taxes, or relieving the hardship incident to taxation, the very existence of the government might be placed in the power of a hostile judiciary" (92 U.S. 85,89).

There was furthermore a long line of antecedent cases pointing in the opposite direction from that taken by the Court in *Pollock*, from *Hylton v. United States* (1796) to *Springer v. United States* (1880), and all had been endorsed by every outstanding generally accepted writer on constitutional law including Kent, Story, Cooley, Miller, Bancroft, Pomeroy, Hare and others while nobody of any significance high or low, left or right, had demurred until the Court decided *Pollock*.[16]

In *Hylton* the case involved a question of whether a tax on carriages was an excise or direct tax. The Court then held that *only* land and capitation levies were direct taxes, so that the carriage tax was indirect and therefore proper. If what the Court said then was true, a graduated income tax was surely an indirect tax as it did not fall with direct determination on anyone, was neither a land nor capitation levy. At the time of *Hylton* the Court included two former members of the constitutional convention and two members of state ratifying conventions, all Federalists, who might be presumed to have more than passing insight into the bearing of the Constitution. Moreover the tax in question had been enacted by a Congress liberally staffed with members of the Philadelphia convention and the state ratifying conventions and had been signed into law by no less a personage than George Washington.[17] In overruling *Hylton* the Court was rebuffing the top man in the American pantheon and his aides.

So, it is evident, the Court decides in whatever way it is temperamentally inclined to, like Congress and the Presidents, anything in the Constitution to the contrary notwithstanding.

The decision in *Pollock* was finally nullified by the passage of the Sixteenth Amendment to the Constitution, which took effect February 2, 1913. The Court had gained nearly eighteen years of tax-free bliss for its patrons although it was shown to be out of harmony with the thinking of the country as well as that of the framers, previous Courts and legal scholars—and the Constitution. It was, at the time, very much a law unto itself, with the tacit concurrence of Congress.

Court versus Congress and President

Up until 1970 the Court had held void in whole or part ninety-two acts of Congress, most of them signed by a President.[18] Except for *Marbury* and *Dred Scott*, all were decided after March 9, 1865, and most during the repressive ascendancy of the Republican Party nationally and with mainly Republican appointees on the bench. The reckless use of the Court's power on national and state legislation, then, can be termed a largely Republican political tool and one lavishly employed only when nominees of the Republican Party, risen through the Civil War, had almost continuing control of Congress and the Presidency. The Republican Party of the period, soon abetted by southern Democrats in return for a free hand with Negroes, was the heavily financed political tool of the "Robber Barons", the newly rich industrial entrepreneurs of the post-Civil War period, most of whom had themselves risen from the lower uneducated classes of society. It was these who financed Republican political campaigns and indeed carried elected officials on every level—municipal, county, state and national—on their secret payrolls. It was very much a political Mafia. On the Supreme Court they had their own lawyers, placed there by subservient Presidents and a fawning Congress.[19]

Over the entire period, beginning in 1809, no fewer than 796 state statutes and ninety-three local ordinances were held unconstitutional. There is no question of the authority of the Court, under the Constitution, to review and, if it seems advisable, to nullify state and local acts although the constitutional grounds for many of the state decisions of the Court during the Republican ascendancy were as shaky as many of its decisions with respect to acts of Congress. During the Republican ascendancy the Court aimed mainly to strike down on specious grounds socially ameliorative state legislation that gave trouble to corporations or was disliked by the more affluent classes because it made them liable to local taxes. The Court in this period was, otherwise put, very much of a wild-cat Court, the chosen instrument of plutocracy, and very clearly out of harmony with the literal Constitution. The Court, in consonance with all the divisions of the government, said and did whatever it thought expedient within its partisan outlook, mainly by way of striking down social legislation and inventing law for the benefit of corporations. It could do this because it had little to fear either from Congress or the President or, for that matter, from most newspapers, themselves increasingly corporate tools and indeed corporations themselves.

At the time there was not much of an educated class in the country so that there was no effective way by which the public at large, had it been interested or capable of focussing on the issues, could be made aware of what was happening. Although the governmental actions taken were public, the generality of citizens did not understand their significance, were bemused by meaningless Republican slogans like "The Full Dinner Pail".

Not only has the Court been shown to have arrived at clearly unconstitutional decisions in a long line of cases, many of which have since been overruled, but, for the benefit of those who think the Court is invariably right, it as early as 1810 took to overruling its own earlier decisions. While the rectification of one's own errors is a virtue, the fact that the Court can overrule itself certainly shows it cannot be as infallible, or final, as many Court devotees suppose it to be.

Up to 1970 the Court overruled itself in a large number of cases— expressly in some, by implication in others. Where it overruled itself by implication the conclusion is derived variously by Justices Brandeis and Douglas and by Profs. Emmet E. Wilson, Albert R. Blaustein, Andrew H. Field, Edward S. Corwin, Norman J. Small and Lester S Jayson.[20] By its own admission it overruled itself in one hundred cases. In the entire compilation from all sources, it overruled itself 143 times. Among overruled cases are several from the highly touted Marshall and Taney Courts.

What is most significant to a broad public that misunderstands the nature of law and law-making, the Court often divides in its decisions by 5 to 4. Law, in the popular view, should be so clear-cut that every right-minded man would be in agreement. And not only are four Justices often in disagreement but, historically, those judges deemed most competent are often on the losing side, the run-of-the-mill political types in the majority.

Supreme Court Justices Rated

Who the best judges have been was determined semi-authoritatively in 1970 by sixty-five law-school deans, professors of law, history and political science who were asked by two leading law professors to evaluate and rate the ninety-six Justices who had until then served.

The findings were reported in *Life* magazine of October 15, 1971, and in the American Bar Association *Journal* of November 1972. The categories assigned were "great", "near great", "average", "below average" and "failures". As the specialists polled were all academicians, their ratings can be better understood as A, B, C, D and F.

In the top category were twelve Justices of whom only one got the votes of all participants. He was John Marshall, who shaped the Court, established its power and showed how broadly it could operate. But seven of the twelve were what is known as dissenters, conspicuously found on the negative side in major decisions or striking off in major new directions. These were John Marshall Harlan I, Oliver Wendell Holmes, Louis B. Brandeis, Harlan Fiske Stone, Benjamin Cardozo, Hugo L. Black and Earl Warren. Included in the full roster were Joseph Story, Felix Frankfurter and Roger B. Taney of Dred Scott fame.

Eight of the fifteen in the second tier also made their mark as conspicuous dissenters. Fifty-five were rated "average", six as "below average" and eight as "failures", including Chief Justice Fred Vinson. While none of this proves anything conclusively, it does represent the opinion of certified scholars and shows that most of the top-rated judges are men who made their mark with deviant findings on the law. What was stated as official legal doctrine, in other words, in crucial cases did not always meet with the approval of these stars.

While the meagerly instructed public is justified in feeling baffled, this justification rests on ignorance of the nature of law as well as of the judicial process. The public supposes a judge to be one who compares the law with the facts and draws the inevitable conclusion. They have no less than John Marshall as authority for this view, although Marshall surely knew better.

"The fact before which the doctrine of judicial automatism crumbles is not the fact that judges have viscera and emotions," Corwin observes. "Nor is it the fact that courts have frequently given approval to shockingly bad pieces of logic, indicative as this may be of predetermination. The judicial function is essentially a syllogistic one, and 'freedom of judicial decision' is something vastly more important than freedom to argue badly from accepted premises. It is, rather, freedom to choose, within limits, the premises themselves; and hence asserts itself not *after* but *before* the juristic grounds of a decision are determined upon; and the rules of formal logic are its usual ally, not its usual enemy.

"What gives the *coup de grâce* to the idea that—in the words of Chief Justice Marshall—'courts are the mere instruments of the law and can will nothing,' is the simple fact that most so-called 'doubtful cases' could very evidently have been decided just the opposite way to which they were decided without the least infraction of the rules of logical discourse or the least attenuation of the principles of *stare decisis*." [21] Here, surely, is something to ruminate over.

Courts in general, and the Supreme Court in particular, can take any line they choose and bolster it with a long procession of principles or decided cases, one array negating the other. As to the high court, "alternative principles of construction and alternative lines of precedent constantly vest the Court with a freedom virtually legislative in scope in choosing the values which it shall promote through its reading of the Constitution." [22]

Should the Constitution be construed "strictly" or "broadly"? Should the terms in it be given an "inclusive" or "exclusive" construction? Should the document be adapted to changed circumstances or not adapted? Should the Court's own precedents be respected or swept aside? What are the priorities of the Constitution? Judges alone decide such questions, pretty much according to their feelings of the moment. And over the years even the feelings of judges change so that what they say in one instance they cancel in another. Judges, in other words, can throw a case either way, and on defensible grounds. All this being so, it is evident the Court has as much autonomy as has Congress or the President. And the autonomy of them all in combination rests on whatever they are able to work out among themselves or which one seizes and holds the initiative. At doing this last the President is in the most favored position.

British Views on the Constitution

This difference of opinion at the very top shows that the American process of laying out and applying its own law leaves much to be desired. From beginning to end too many cooks, standing on different bases, are involved in making the soup for an often baffled citizenry.

In Great Britain matters are handled much more deftly. If the courts there find any incompatibilities in the law or Constitution, the final resolution is left to majority vote in Parliament. If the country is sufficiently displeased by the parliamentary decision, it can reconstitute Parliament and get the decision it desires. A precept with most of the nation self-consciously behind it is obviously good law, whatever outsiders may think. But precepts over which jurists certified as excellent by critics and peers express strong doubts and which officials freely violate certainly seem like doubtful law. The United States is immersed in such doubtful law, always subject to argument. The result is much confused churning about.

In Britain, for one thing, there is not a continual wrangle over what the Constitution means as Parliament at any point is the court of final resort on meaning. There have been times when American notions have been proposed for inclusion in British legislation, only to see them rejected emphatically. For example, Gladstone in 1893 proposed a clause about life, liberty, property and due process of law for the Irish Home Rule Bill of 1893, only to see it fail. Waldorf Astor, American expatriate member of Parliament, proposed the same clause in the Home Rule Bill of 1912 and saw it publicly slated to death.

Prime Minister Asquith remarked at the time that American experience alone warned against such a measure. For the language was "full of ambiguity, abounding in pitfalls and certainly provocative of every kind of frivolous litigation . . . What is 'equal protection of the laws'? What is 'just compensation'? Questions raised by these phrases are really matters of opinion, bias, or inclination and judgment, which cannot be acted on under anything like settled rules of law."

If the American system were introduced, said the liberal *Manchester Guardian*, it "would choke the courts with litigation. No sooner would a law be enacted than lawyers would grow rich by resisting its enforcement upon constitutional grounds"—a spectacle familiar in the United States. Said the *London Chronicle*, "All administration would be checked in the American fashion, while laws were tossed from court to court for years in a vain effort to ascertain whether or not they need be enforced. The trouble with the Constitution of the United States . . . is that nobody has ever been able to find out what it means."

The *London News* said, "No act of Parliament could be passed which might not be taken before the courts for them to decide whether or not it was constitutional. The courts would in Ireland, as they are in the United States, be the supreme legislators, for the whole field of social and economic life . . . Judges are not trained for that kind of function by American judges but all will agree that it would erect one of the most galling of all possible tyrannies." [23]

Between the Dred Scott decision and 1889 the Court invalidated only 15 national statues, 127 state statutes and 7 municipal ordinances. Beginning in 1889 however, and until 1936, it struck down by far most of the legislation it condemned in its history, being halted in the carnage only by the political counter-attack of President Franklin D. Roosevelt calling for the retirement of superannuated judges. Thereafter the Court trod far more cautiously, practicing a good deal of what Frankfurter called "judicial restraint".

The Fuller Court of 1889-1910 invalidated 13 national laws, 63 state laws and 14 municipal ordinances—a total of 90. It overruled 4 earlier Court decisions. The White Court of 1910-21 invalidated 10 national laws, 117 state laws and 18 municipal ordinances—a total of 145. It overruled 6 earlier decisions. The Taft Court of 1921-30 and the Hughes Court until 1932 overruled 15 national laws, 154 state laws, and 11 ordinances—a total of 180—and overruled 8 earlier decisions. In its over-rulings the Court contradicts itself on the historical record so that from the standpoint of fixity in the law it is a matter of anyone's opinion which time it was right.

The Court ran into the most criticism of its career, however, after 1932 when it struck down, one after the other, key statutes of the Roosevelt administration designed to cope with the economic collapse of the 1930s, the culmination of one-sided Republican Party corporation policies since the Civil War. Here the Court was confronted more by a condition than a theory and in the upshot had to submit to political forces far stronger than itself—proof that the Court is far from being the paramount factor many think it is in the constitutional system. With the country itself crumbling under the legal structure it had itself invented, it was obviously time to back off.

The Supreme Court from the very beginning, and especially during Marshall's long leadership, handed down a great number of crucial rulings, most of them economic in nature. It is usually said by political scientists that government is basically concerned with the maintenance of internal order and external defense, which is true but incomplete. Economic affairs, relating to property and labor, is integral and essential to both. Without economic structure, in fact, there would be no point either to internal order or external defense.

Labor Alone Creates Property

Although in law most of the emphasis is on property, with slight emphasis on labor, of the two labor is temporally and efficiently primary. For labor, and labor alone, creates property.

Here it may be suspected that I have taken a deep plunge into the whirlpool of Marxism, which does not disagree with this fundamental axiom—in fact subscribes to it. But it was recognized by acute thinkers long before Karl Marx was born that the wealth of any country, and hence its property, comes from labor and from labor alone.

David Hume, writing in 1751 as among the earliest in a long line of savants to reach this conclusion, remarked that

> Sovereigns must take mankind as they find them, and cannot pretend to introduce any violent change in their principles and ways of raising and cultivating them. It is his best policy to comply with the thinking . . . the less natural any set of principles are which support a particular society, the more difficulty will a legislator meet with in

common bent of mankind and give it all the improvements of which it is susceptible . . .

Where manufactures and mechanic arts are not cultivated, the bulk of the people must apply themselves to agriculture; and if their skill and industry increase, there must arise a great superfluity from their labor beyond what suffices to maintain them. They have no temptation, therefore, to increase their skill and industry, since they cannot exchange that superfluity for any commodities which may serve either to their pleasure or vanity. A habit of indolence naturally prevails. The greater part of the land lies uncultivated . . .

Everything in the world is purchased by labor, and our passions are the only causes of labor. When a nation abounds in manufactures [literally hand-made things] and mechanic arts, the proprietors of land, as well as the farmers, study agriculture as a science and redouble their industry and attention. The superfluity which arises from their labor is not lost, but is exchanged with manufactures for those commodities which men's [love of] luxury now makes them covet. By this means, land furnishes a great deal more of the necessaries of life than what suffices for those who cultivate it. In times of peace and tranquillity, this superfluity goes to the maintenance of manufacturers [literally ones who make by hand] and the improvers of liberal arts. But it is easy for the public to convert many of these manufacturers into soldiers and maintain them by that superfluity which arises from the labor of farmers. Accordingly we find that this is the case in all civilized governments. When the sovereign raises an army, what is the consequence? He imposes a tax. This tax obliges all the people to retrench what is least necessary to their subsistence . . . And to consider the matter abstractly, manufactures increase the power of the state only as they store up so much labor, and that of a kind to which the public may lay claim without depriving anyone of the necessaries of life. The more labor, therefore, that is employed beyond mere necessaries, the more powerful is any state . . . The greater is the stock of labor of all kinds, the greater quantity may be taken from the heap without making any sensible alteration in it. . . Trade and industry are really nothing but a stock of labor [sic] which, in times of peace and tranquillity, is employed for the ease and satisfaction of individuals, but in the exigencies of state may in part be turned to public advantage . . . [that is, to defense/offense].

. . . A too great disproportion among the citizens weakens any state. Every person, if possible, ought to enjoy the fruits of his labor in a full possession of all the necessaries and many of the conveniences of life. No one can doubt but such an equality is most suitable to human nature and diminishes much less from the happiness of the rich than it adds to that of the poor . . . where the riches are in few hands, these must enjoy all the power and will readily conspire to lay the whole burden on the poor and oppress them still further, to the discouragement of all industry . . . Where the laborers and artisans are accustomed to work for low wages and to retain but a small part of the fruits of their labor, it is difficult for them, even in a free government, to better their condition or conspire among themselves to heighten their wages; but even where they are accustomed to a more plentiful way of life, it is easy for the rich, in an arbitrary government, to conspire against *them* and throw the whole burden of taxes on their shoulders.[24]

Jefferson regarded Hume as a Tory, a serious mistake on his part. But Hume, an acute thinker, was also very far from being a political radical or sentimentalist. He was very much the detached judicious appraiser.

As to the volatile Marx, moving from the idea that labor creates all value, he rashly concluded that the least skilled laborers, factory workers and the semi-skilled, were destined to establish their own government in the image of a fond parent, staffed by high-minded selfless men, and wrest all power from those who had come to possess property either by their own labor, by stealth and fraud, by inheritance or by outright legally protected theft of other men's labor. In this socialist Utopia private property would be made public—that is, government-owned—and would be administered for the benefit of the workers, supposedly. One sees the sad result in the Soviet police state and its imitators.

What is most remarkable about the people who work for their money is the ease with which most of them are separated from it beyond the calls of necessity, comfort or convenience. It is as though many workers, in the way they expend their money, wish to deny the crude means by which they acquired it. For they spend it freely, like nabobs, on a great variety of frivolous embellishments. Merchants, on the other hand, will trade anything whatever for money, which amounts to a distillation of property, easily exchangeable for other forms of property. The result is that the lower order of laborers, at least, leave themselves with nothing but baubles while the propertied constantly increase their stake—the capitalist outcome.

One is reminded in the reckless spending of their wages by most workers of the way Indians and Africans traded articles of genuine value for beads, rum and antiquated weapons. In return the traders received ivory, slaves and furs, reaping vast profits. A multitude of workers, seduced by the siren song of advertisers, are precisely like primitive Indians and Africans and are to a great extent self-chained to their treadmills. One could live forever, quite happily, without much of what workers today freely trade their labor for in the Consumer Society. To begin with, automobiles . . .

In any event, the workers work, and this is of basic interest to all developed governments. The last is shown clearly in rudimentary societies that aim at independence. Newly established governments, as one sees in Africa, are most interested in putting an often uncomprehending population to work, and if necessary in Marxist regimes will do it at bayonet point as in the Soviet Union.

For effective work to take place the means must be provided and here government plays a large role by securing private property, which amounts, as I have shown, to accumulated labor. From the very beginning the United States government, by means of the Constitution and its system, was concerned about encouraging the development and security of property. It had, to begin with, a great deal of unworked land, part of the public domain, which it sold to buyers with cash for development by labor. Titles and contracts needed to be made secure, which was done through a series of notable Supreme Court decisions. The Marshall Court owes its fame to this achievement.

Some Key Court Decisions

It is necessary to read a detailed history of the Supreme Court to obtain a full idea of how this was done. But a few outstanding cases will illustrate.

Fletcher v. Peck (6 Cranch 87). This case, decided in 1810, stabilized the law of property rights, especially with respect to contracts for the purchase of land. An admitted corrupt legislature in Georgia sold tremendous tracts of Yazoo River land taken from Indians to a group of speculators, who resold the land in parcels to third parties for easy profits. A succeeding legislature cancelled the grant, which cancellation was challenged by a victimized buyer from the speculators. The Court held that the legislature had the legal right to make the sale but that the subsequent legislature might not cancel it, whatever the corruption involved, because to do so was a violation of the constitutional clause against the impairment of lawful contracts (Article I, Section 10, Paragraph 1, which reads, "No State shall . . . pass any . . . law impairing the obligation of contracts . . ."). It was the second state law held invalid by the Court.

There was great outcry that corruptionists should thus be allowed to profit but Georgia, if it had wished, could have taken other steps against the corrupt. What the Court did was to put a floor of legitimacy under the challenged titles. Courts proceeded similarly in other dubious title cases, notably later in the vast tract of the Louisiana Purchase. Just about all the land in the United States was originally acquired in ways morally painful to look into and the courts had the task of indicating where unchallengeable legitimacy began. Unless they had done this the country would be endlessly seething with wrangles about property titles. Nobody then could feel sure about land ownership.

Dartmouth College v. Woodward (4 Wheaton 518). Decided in 1819, the Court held that charters of private corporations were contracts and as such were protected by the contract clause. Although unimportant in itself, the case provided stability for corporate charters and public grants and franchises to corporations, which could not be disturbed thereafter by a state outside their terms. One might call the decision the Magna Carta of American corporations.

The issue in the case was simple. Dartmouth College had been chartered by the Crown in 1769 but in the course of time its president and Federalist-Congregational trustees found themselves at odds with a New Hampshire state legislature made up of Jeffersonian Republicans and Presbyterians. In 1816 these latter changed the name of the college and transferred control to other hands. The Court held, for the college, that as it was a private institution the legislature could not do this under the constitutional contract clause.

McCulloch v. Maryland (4 Wheaton 316). In the same year the Court held that a state might not tax the branch of a bank established by an act of Congress—in effect, any instrumentality of the federal government. It here invoked the national supremacy clause (Article VI, Paragraph 2) to nullify a state law. All the national banking agencies, including the Federal Reserve System, trace their freedom from local supervision back to this case.

Gibbons v. Ogden (9 Wheaton 1). In 1824 the Court ruled in this case, asserting the supremacy of the United States over the states in the regulation of interstate commerce. New York State had granted a monopoly to a group of ship operators to navigate in the waters of New York State. These waters touched other states and the monopolists soon found it profitable to operate outside of immediately adjacent waters. Other states retaliated with laws against out-of-state steamboats. An intruder from New Jersey into New York waters, operating under the Federal Licensing Act of 1793, was one Gibbons and he was challenged by one Ogden, licensed by the New York monopoly. The Court held after hearing the dispute that a state had no power so to regulate or restrict interstate commerce as the power belonged to the national government under the commerce clause of the Constitution (Article I, Section 8, Paragraph 8, which reads, "The Congress shall have power . . . To regulate commerce . . . among the several States . . .").

The decision, quelling interstate regulatory rivalry, is the basis of the national regulation of commerce among the states and was first broadly codified in the Interstate Commerce Act of 1887.

Under Chief Justice Taney there was some modification of the tendency underlying these decisions by the Marshall Court although no great change. Two modifying types of decisions were *Charles River Bridge v. Warren Bridge* (1837) and *Cooley v. Board of Wardens* (1852).

By reason of the Marshall and Taney decisions, and others later, the Court has been held by liberals and radicals to be the unique support of corporations and their owners in the American system, which is not true. All divisions of government, at the federal and the state level, have most of the time done everything in their power to promote the growth of the corporation, an entity of pooled individual capital.

"Despite the prevailing orthodoxy, government intervention in economic life was supported by leading political figures, and public policy took the form of local, state, and federal subsidization of the transportation revolution, federal creation of two national banks, and manipulation of the economy through Treasury fiscal operations, the deliberate use of the tariffs to divert the allocation of resources into desired lines of development, and government subsidies to certain industries (fishing, small arms, and, at a state level, agricultural bounties on grain and silk production)." [25] This was the case throughout, before and after the Civil War.

"The myth to the contrary notwithstanding, government intervention in business affairs—to *help*, be it noted, not to regulate—was the norm of early American history. Never has laissez-faire been used as a means of prohibiting aid to business. What the Supreme Court did by way of eliminating adverse state regulation of commercial affairs was buttressed, moreover, by state courts using common-law doctrines to outlaw budding movements of workers to organize into trade unions . . . American capitalism, in other words, owes more to the avowedly political branches of government than to the judiciary for its early development . . . What is known is that economic growth did take place, government did affirmatively help, and the Supreme Court participated in the development by striking down adverse state regulations . . . business enterprise in this country has never been wholly private. The line between private and the public action is blurred, and always has been blurred . . .' " [26]

Government and Entrepreneurs

The United States government in all its branches and on all levels has always favored the money-hungry entrepreneur as the catalyst in the economic process and the one through whom more torpid non-farm elements would be provided with employment. At times this favoritism has attained extravagant lengths but without it the country would still be back in the Jeffersonian Utopia of small farms, handcrafts and horse power. Benefits derived by the lower orders from the corporate structure are referred to disparagingly by liberals and radicals as outcomes of "the trickle down theory". And not too much trickles down. For a direct benefit outcome to be the dominant feature of the economic system, individual ownership of small producing properties would need to prevail or else some form of government-nurtured co-operative economic organization. The old form of individual operation was unable to finance the widespread installation of machinery, for which a pooling of capital in corporations was necessary. And it was on the basis of powered machine production under corporations that United States industrialism, whatever its boons and drawbacks, was erected.

Judicial decisions and congressional-presidential actions favoring this trend have been numerous and overwhelming. Even an expository winnowing leaves a densely packed account.[27]

Marshall, as he had shown in *Marbury,* for all his careful parsing of the Constitution for the benefit of political infidels, was quite capable of being autocratic. He showed this in 1833 in *Barron v. City of Baltimore* (7 Peters 243) where he held for the Court that the first ten amendments, called the Bill of Rights, were binding only on the federal government, not on the state governments. He thereupon opened the door to a continuing reign of harassment by state police officials of anyone they considered "out of line", a reign that was not brought under control or at least damped down until in the 1950s and 1960s. The decision also led to the nonsensical later notion of "dual sovereignty".

Intellectually the decision won't bear examination and illustrates very well that the government divisions, including the Court, dispose of matters as they wish. True, there never was, and still is not, any great popular support for individual civil rights. Most of the public is as ready to deny them to its devils-of-the-moment as any oafish official. College students often hoot purveyors of dissenting views off campuses —at Yale, for example.

The decision was clearly unconstitutional *per se*. Amendments are an integral part of the Constitution, obtained by the constitutionally stipulated amending process. An amendment is not something that is separable from the main body of the document although Marshall arbitrarily separated the two. "This Constitution", says the document in Article VI, Paragraph 2, ". . . shall be the supreme law of the land . . . any thing in the Constitution or laws of any State to the contrary notwithstanding." The last is called the *nil obstante* clause and traces its incidence back to ancient papal documents. Amendment X, true enough, says, "The powers not delegated to the United States by the Constitution, nor prohibited by it to the States, are reserved to the States respectively, or to the people." Just what these powers may be nobody has been able to say in view of the fact that the supreme power belongs to the national government. Amendment X is meaningless, adds nothing to the Constitution, and has been so held by the Court (*U.S. v. Sprague,* 282 U.S. 716, 733, 1936, and *Knapp v. Schweizer,* 357 U.S. 371, 1958).

Bill of Rights in Abeyance

With the Barron decision all of the Bill of Right's verbal safeguards were swept into the discard with respect to the states, where there was steadily increasingly free resort down through the years to illegal searches, seizures, arrests, detentions, questioning and beating of prisoners, confessions exacted under torture, trials without defense counsel— all directed against stragglers, drifters, local malcontents, vagabonds, visibly discontented workers, unsubmissive aliens, labor organizers, ideological deviants, blacks, Indians, and the like. Most of these were from the lower classes of course. Whoever in any jurisdiction did not fit in with local officialdom's idea of a proper person was subject to official harassment or was even proceeded against on fabricated grounds. Most police powers were in the jurisdiction of states. Police officers in many places carried about with them sheaves of "John Doe" and "Jane Doe" warrants, signed by subservient local judges and giving entry to any opportune premises. Many people were ordered to "leave town" or "move along" in a regular routine.

The Court in *Barron,* as in *Marbury,* need not have ruled as it did in order to attain the specific end desired in the case. It need not have scuttled the Bill of Rights with respect to state application. One Barron, owning wharfage rights in Baltimore, had sued the City of Baltimore under the Fifth Amendment, claiming that he had been deprived of his property without due process of law. The city had built new streets and roads in the vicinity of the wharfs and these avenues in time allowed rainwater to carry surface dirt down to the wharf, raising the level of silt below the wharf. This made the wharf unusable. The Court, had it been so disposed, could merely have held that all this was the consequence of the uncontrollable action of nature—the notorious act of God—and the city was within its rights in constructing roadways. Such a decision however would not have been very far-reaching and Marshall, and the Court he fashioned, liked decisions to have far-reaching applications: statesmanship but not law.

In his decision Marshall pointed out that the First Amendment begins with the words "Congress shall make no law . . .", so that it was merely Congress that was restrained from acting. But these words apply only to the First Amendment and to no others and it was the Fifth Amendment that was under discussion and not all ten amendments or the First. True, the Senate at the time the amendments were being shaped in Congress declined to make them specifically and pointedly applicable to the states. Whether they were so applicable or not was left unstated but the contextual implication was that they applied generally. Clearly if the Constitution is supreme and if the amendments are part of the Constitution, they apply to the states, over which Congress as well as other branches is part of the supreme power.

But as Roger Sherman of Connecticut observed, only those civil rights are operative which any government is willing to concede and uphold. Any notion that they stem from some document, and that such a document has in it some magic power to restrain a government or its officials or transcends a government in action, is childish but is a part of the constitutional myth.

Marshall, though, nevertheless had a practical point in mind and the Court, behind its reasonings, usually does. The country then, in the interval since then and even now, contained and contains many uncouth elements from various sub-cultures, native and foreign. Some of these, only semi-socialized, are a threat to public safety, some are merely perceived by some people as such a threat, but all such nevertheless leave many people uneasy. The decision in *Barron* left all such misfits, genuine or supposed, to the discretion of the state authorities which in many places took it as a mandate to harass anyone they didn't like for whatever reason. Unquestionably many thousands of uneducated lower-class persons in the states over the decades have been erroneously or maliciously convicted and made to serve long prison terms or have even been executed. Local racists had a long field day. Due process of law, in other words, has often been a farce, especially for the man without funds.

Not until the Fourteenth Amendment was passed in 1868 was the legal basis (knocked out by the Court in *Barron*) reintroduced for making the Bill of Rights applicable to the states, and not until very recently were cases actually decided making all the amendments applicable to the states.[28]

Misapplication of Fourteenth Amendment

What the Court decided between 1889 and 1932 however made all its past rulings seem the essence of reason. The basis of the new line of pro-corporation rulings was the Fourteenth Amendment, passed after the Civil War to accord civil rights to blacks but vigorously applied instead for many decades as a special way of obtaining for corporations freedom from state regulation. As there was no federal regulation of corporations, this left corporations in a non-regulatory no-man's-land, a paradise of laissez-faire except for subsidies, franchises, land grants and lax enforcement of existing law by readily purchased officials at all levels from top to bottom.

In 1870-71 the Court, injected with two new appointees, made a sudden about-face in the Legal Tender cases. By 5 to 3 it first held unconstitutional the Legal Tender Acts of 1862-63 with respect to payments made on pre-existing contracts with wartime paper money (*Hepburn v. Griswold*, 8 Wallace 603). It reversed the ruling in *Knox v. Lee* and *Parker v. Davis* (12 Wallace 457). In the first case it held that the obligation of contract and due-process clauses had been violated, which was surely true, but in the second case such action was held justifiable in any time of emergency, not limited to wartime. By this decision the government was conceded the right to ignore any specific limitation in the Constitution in the name of an emergency although the Constitution has no provision for suspending any provisions in emergencies. As any point in history can arguably be construed as an emergency, all that is necessary at any time, judicially, is to convince the Court that an emergency exists in order to allow the legislature and executive to act lawfully outside the restrictive stipulations of the Constitution. And this surely makes good sense although it is not the way most Americans think of the Constitution.

What are called the Slaughterhouse cases of 1873 (16 Wallace 36) are important as producing the first Court decision on the Fourteenth Amendment although the Court was soon to reverse its position. A monopoly conferred by the Louisiana legislature to maintain abattoirs was contested as a violation of the privileges and immunities clause. By 5 to 4 the Court held that it did not infringe the amendment, which reads, "No State shall make or enforce any law which shall abridge the privileges or immunities of citizens of the United States . . ." The Court held, following Marshall in *Barron*, that the amendment protected only rights stemming from federal citizenship, with most civil rights under the dubious protection of the state governments. The Court also refused to consider the due-process clause of the amendment as a substantive limitation on the regulatory powers of the states and held

that the equal-protection clause applied solely to state laws that discriminated against Negroes. The dissenters held that the amendment
did apply to state violations of the privileges and immunities of United
States citizens and that impairment of property rights by statute especially violated due process.

In 1890, in *Chicago, Milwaukee and St. Paul R.R. Co. v. Minnesota*
(134 U.S. 418), the Court laid down its new position on due process
under the Fourteenth Amendment. It upset a recent Minnesota law that
provided for a rate-setting railroad and a warehouse commission to fix
final rates without permitting an appeal to the courts. The Court said
that denial of recourse to the courts was, substantively, deprivation of
property without due process of law. At the time throughout the country
there was great public outcry, especially from farmers, against allegedly
extortionate rates charged by the railroads and grain elevators. After this
decision the federal courts became the final rate-setting authorities for
a long time and these usually saw eye to eye with the railroads and
other public utilities and all the way up to the Supreme Court were
often staffed by former lawyers for the corporations involved. One
hand of the same interests washed the other hand.

Due process of law came into the equation through a significant
decision of 1886—*Santa Clara Co. v. Southern Pacific Railroad Co.* (116
U.S. 138). In this case Roscoe Conkling, counsel for the railroad and
ex-senator from New York, maintained that in the congressional committee drawing up the Fourteenth Amendment the word "persons" had
been chosen to extend the protection of the due-process clause to legal
persons or corporations. Had such been the intent, it would have been
easy to write "nor shall any State deprive any natural or legal person
of life, liberty, or property, without due process of law . . ." The Court
uncritically accepted Conkling's argument, thereby encouraging the
substantive interpretation of the due-process clause as a defense of
corporate property rights.

The Court in effect invented substantive due process. Hitherto due
process had figured in English and American law as a protection of
purely procedural rights in court actions, what is loosely called a fair
trial. It was so held in the Slaughterhouse cases and in 1877 in *Munn v.
Illinois* (94 U.S. 113) the Court held that the question of due process
was not a restriction on the power of a state to fix public utility rates.

Substantive law is law that creates, defines and regulates rights as
contrasted with "adjective" or remedial law, which prescribes the method
of enforcing rights or obtaining redress for their invasion. In bringing
the question of substance into play the object of the Court was to
invoke for it the protection of the adjectival due-process clause. Hence-
forth any regulation that affected adversely the substance—that is, the

value—of property was to be reviewable in the federal courts, which uniformly took a more lenient view than on-the-spot duly elected state regulators. The basis of the properties in question moreover had been largely created through the bounty of the government, by land grants, franchises, charters or other accommodations. Much of their value stemmed from the government, in short, which might not now affect it adversely in the market by regulation without a long and usually losing court proceeding. What was in play was the usual story down through history—government of, by and for *some* of the people.

To go through all these cases, while interesting, might be tedious. The upshot of the Court's work over the years was that corporations were given a free hand (laissez-faire), Negroes and labor organizations were severely put down and restricted, and civil liberties were in general ignored, left to state officialdom.

Negroes Shown Their New Place

Negroes found out where they stood in two notable cases. In 1883 the Civil Rights cases (109 U.S. 3) were decided. Five blacks had been refused equal accommodations and privileges, allegedly in violation of the Civil Rights Act of 1875. The Court called this act unconstitutional because it protected social rather than political rights, here making one of its many convenient off-the-cuff distinctions. The Court held that the Thirteenth and Fourteenth Amendments merely forbade invasion *by the states* of civil rights but did not protect the invasion of such rights *by individuals*. This ruling opened wide the door to aggressive discrimination against blacks by privately owned publicly licensed premises—restaurants, hotels, barber shops, hospitals, stores, transportation lines and stations, and the like. Given such encouragement by the Court, multitudes of whites revealed their true ignoble natures.

Under any authoritatively stated permissiveness people may take the low road or the high road. Historically most take the low road—first because at least half are inherently inclined this way and next because this solid mass exerts a gravitational pull on a portion at least of the other half. On any choice left open to the masses between favoring their animal appetites over the cultivation of their more refined potentialities, one will always find the majority on the side of giving the appetites full play. One sees this every day on every hand.

In 1896 the Court flatly approved discrimination against Negroes in public places in *Plessy v. Ferguson* (163 U.S. 537). Here the Court upheld a Louisiana law that *required* segregated railroad facilities. But the Court went on to indulge in one of its far-reaching extrapolations, holding that as long as equality of accommodation existed segregation did not constitute discrimination and Negroes were not thereby deprived of equal protection of the laws under the Fourteenth Amendment. In the South particularly the dominant whites immediately moved to see that Negroes were given separate facilities of all kinds although they were far from equal as thousands of run-down Negro schoolhouses in time attested.

What was illustrated here in a big way was the ability of government to take plain language and "interpret" it so as to achieve the opposite of the ostensibly intended result and in effect to do precisely what it wanted to do. For all the Court decisions were concurred in by Congress and all the Presidents. Nothing in the Constitution gives the government power to segregate anybody except convicted criminals, the infectiously diseased or the dangerously disordered.

Court Goes Hog Wild

The Court was even wilder than all this indicates. It held the New York Workman's Compensation Law unconstitutional on the ground that it took property from the employer without due process of law whereas in fact the expense would have been placed on the consumer as part of the cost of production. Congress, it held, might prohibit lotteries (188 U.S. 321, 23 Sup.Ct. 321, 1903) but not regulate life insurance (*Allgeyer v. Louisiana,* 165 U.S. 578, 17 Sup. Ct. 427, 1897); might not regulate transport of goods made by child labor (*Hammer v. Dagenhart,* 247 U.S. 251, 1918) but might order railroads to install safety devices (*Southern Railway Co. v. U.S.,* 222 U.S. 20, 32 Sup. Ct. 2, 1911) and might not prohibit railroads from discharging workers for joining unions (*Adair v. U.S.,* 208 U.S. 161, 28 Sup.Ct. 277, 1908).

States were held to have no right to prohibit bakers from working more than ten hours a day (*Lochner v. N.Y.,* 198 U.S. 45, 25 Sup.Ct. 539, 1905) but did have the right to prohibit miners from working more than eight hours a day (*Holden v. Hardy,* 169 U.S. 366, 18 Sup.Ct. 383, 1898). The States had the power however to prohibit women from working more than ten hours a day (*Muller v. Oregon,* 208 U.S. 412, 28 Sup.Ct. 324, 1908) but had no power to prohibit them from working for less than a minimum wage (*Adkins v. Children's Hospital,* 261 U.S. 525, 43 Sup.Ct. 394, 1923).

Such waywardness surely demonstrates conclusively the waywardness of the basic law, the shaky theology of the United States government as given Talmudic and scholastic interpretation. Behind all the verbiage one can readily discern that it is men who are imposing their fluctuating will on the country under technical-sounding language, baffling to ordinary minds.

Among other matters the Court in a succession of decisions vitiated the Sherman Anti-Trust Act of 1890 so that in the United States today trusts or combinations in restraint of trade are forbidden by law but nevertheless flourish in various forms. The chief case was *U.S. v. E. C. Knight Co.* (156 U.S. 1, 1895) which had the result of placing most monopolies outside of federal control. But—surprise! surprise!—labor unions might be conspiracies in restraint of trade in violation of the Sherman Act (*Loewe v. Lawler*, 208 U.S. 274, 1908). In 1911 it gave its flat blessing to monopolies when it upheld the dissolution of the Standard Oil Company of New Jersey (221 U.S. 1) on the ground that it had transgressed the "rule of reason" in such matters but exempted monopolies that conformed to this vague, indefinable and newly invented rule. The decision was denounced by Justice Harlan as judicial usurpation. He had also denounced the *Plessy* decision as constitutionally unwarranted and was unquestionably right in both instances. The Court has not been without able men of outstanding character but they have been a conspicuous minority. Most members of the Supreme Court have been career politicians, "flexible" of mind, placed on the Court because of their personal or political connection to some President or their known adherence to a certain point of view.

In 1911 the Court ordered the reorganization of the "tobacco trust" rather than its dissolution, on the basis of the "rule of reason" (*U.S. v. American Tobacco Co.*, 221 U.S. 106).

Accommodating to monopoly corporations, the Court kept hot on the trail of labor unions. Although the Clayton Act, passed to strengthen the Sherman Anti-Trust Act, had incorporated a provision against labor injunctions, the Court held that secondary boycotts were still enjoinable as illegal obstructions to interstate commerce and violations of the anti-trust laws (*Duplex Printing Press Co. v. Deering*, 254 U.S. 443, 1921). In the same year it invalidated a state statute that prohibited the granting of injunctions against labor picketing as violative of the due-process and equal-protection clauses of the Fourteenth Amendment (*Truax v. Corrigan*, 257 U.S. 312).

The best succinct summary of the work of the Court down through the decades to the 1940s that I have been able to find is by Prof. Benjamin Wright of Harvard University School of Law. With reference to the twelve New Deal statutes held unconstitutional between January 7, 1935, and May 25, 1936, a period of seventeen months, he says, "In the entire preceding history of the Supreme Court there had been relatively few decisions in which statutes of broad general interest had been invalidated."

Moreover, those that were "checked attempts by Congress to extend national protection of civil liberties, to stop the spread of slavery in the northern territories, to impose higher taxes upon the wealthy, or to improve the condition of laborers." [29] Whatever a preponderant popular sentiment favored, the Court was usually *against*.

Civil liberties as laid out in the Constitution were most of the time a dead letter until the Court gradually approached them in the 1930s in a few cases, although it wobbled from time to time. But in various civil-liberties rulings the Court did go against legislative majorities, state and national, and also against the inclination of federal, state and local executive branches. The greatest assault there had ever been on civil liberties was carried out by the executive branch in the latter stages of the Wilson administration and continued into the 1920s. Executive authorities were apparently emboldened by the Court's having sustained the Espionage and Sedition Acts and Selective Service Act (military conscription) of the World War I period.

The Court at least was trying to free itself of the fetters of the position of Chief Justice Marshall in *Barron v. Baltimore* (1832) and in 1937 held, with only a single dissent, that the first ten amendments are not automatically protected by the Fourteenth and must be directly considered (*Palko v. Connecticut,* 302 U.S. 319, 327). Then, very, very gradually in the decades after the New Deal years the Court was led to declare that the first ten amendments applied to the states through the Fourteenth Amendment, literally a judicial revolution in a special but important area.

Down through the years the preoccupation of the Court was mostly with economics, property and who benefits most from it. The Court did become concerned after the Fourteenth Amendment was written with the "rights of persons", but "persons" in its application was largely a code-word for corporations, which are persons by legal definition, a fiction. Persons, to the Court, seldom meant living people until much later. "Between 1899 and 1937 there were 212 cases in which state legislation was held to be unconstitutional for failure to preserve the guarantees of the Constitution regarding the rights of persons" but 184 of these concerned "persons" in the form of corporations.[30]

Until near the end of the nineteenth century the contract clause as interpreted by the Marshall Court had been mainly used to protect property from regulation. "But because of the spread of the practice according to which the states reserved the right to alter or rescind charters or grants of tax immunity, and, to a lesser extent, because of the growth of the principle that there are certain powers which the states may not contract away, the usefulness of the contract clause as a bulwark of vested rights declined." [31]

The Court thereupon in the 1890s freely applied its new substantive interpretation of due process. "To an unprecedent degree the Court became a censor of legislative reasonableness and rationality. States could not reserve powers as against the expanding concept of due process." [32]

Of the 184 cases alluded to, Prof. Wright points out, there were 159 decisions under the due-process and equal-protection clauses in which state statutes were held to be unconstitutional, plus 16 in which both the due process and commerce clauses were involved, plus 9 more involving due process and some other clause or clauses.

"As a result of Marshall's interpretation of the contract clause the Court gave an amount of protection to corporations which had not been anticipated, save possibly by Hamilton. As a consequence of the expansion of due-process and equal-protection clauses the corporations were again the beneficiaries, a result anticipated by those who advocated the expansion. A good many of the decisions are difficult to classify in these terms, but approximately three-fourths of them are concerned with the rights of corporations. Nearly a third involve public utilities . . . Such a summary view may convey an impression of the scope and character of the Supreme Court's work in protecting the rights of property against the state and national legislatures." [33]

The various ideational clauses of the Constitution—contract, due process, commerce, equal protection—are like spigots which courts can turn on or off as it suits their inclinations. They also can be given new meanings. In other words, it is always men at work, not an impersonal mechanism of laws.

Although the due-process clause was present in the Fifth Amendment since 1791, it involved only one case before 1868, when the Fourteenth Amendment took effect. That case was *Murray v. Hoboken Land & Improvement Co.* (18 Howard 272, 1856). No substantive right was considered in this case, only procedure. And due process in the history of law had always been concerned with procedure only.

But soon due process became one of the burning concerns of the Court, with its hitherto unheard of application to substantive considerations through the mediation of the Fourteenth Amendment.

While there were only two instances before the Civil War in which acts of Congress had been declared unconstitutional, "Between 1790 and the end of 1898 there were 23 cases in which Congressional statutes were held contrary to the Constitution. From 1899 to 1937 there were 55. In the same [latter] period there were 401 decisions invalidating state legislation, a figure considerably more than twice as large as that for the preceding thirty-eight years, and over six times as great as that for the first seventy-five years of the Court's history." [34]

To this massacre of legislation there was hardly any formal objection by Congress or the Presidents, who in effect concurred. Here and there individuals objected, as did some members of the Court. But in general the outlook of the Court suited the executive and legislative branches.

The Supreme Court has always been composed of lawyers although no provision of the Constitution requires lawyers on the Court, which could with no constitutional violation consist of philosophers, political scientists, logicians, semanticists, historians or documentary scholars. But appointments to the Court must be approved by Congress, which in turn has always from the beginning been preponderantly composed of lawyers. Although congressional lawyers are not considered by lawyers to be the cream of the profession, they have all had some training in how the lawyer mentality works. This in fact is the mentality of most Congressmen.

Lawyers as such, however well trained, have no special professional expertise for understanding the Constitution. What for example is justice? Lawyers have no comprehension of the word extending beyond what philosophers and linguists give them although it is the first important concept mentioned in the Constitution. Nor does one go to lawyers to discover the meaning of words like tranquillity, defense, welfare, liberty and posterity, or words like commerce, equal protection and law. And one would not go to lawyers for insights into logic and syntax.

That lawyers are all over the scene, then, and mainly lawyers at loose ends for employment, just happens to be a brute fact. But it is a highly significant fact because lawyers represent in the main only those who can pay them, which makes them servitors in the main of the upper economic classes. As it is their necessary role to serve these classes, who alone can pay, lawyers acquire the point of view of their clients and inevitably transmit it in their pleadings and everyday judgements. So, while men, not laws, control the government at all times, most of the men are lawyers, yielding what might accurately be called a government of lawyers rather than ordinary men. That is to say, a government of casuists.

In any event, the fact that lawyers are always at the central points does much to explain how the Constitution is officially interpreted in any instance. A philosopher or a semanticist would not confuse persons with corporations or rights of persons with property rights mainly.

But it was Congress, not the Supreme Court, that pulled the courts off the back of labor in 1932 with the Norris-La Guardia Anti-Injunction Act, which forbade injunctions to sustain anti-union employment contracts or to prevent strikes, boycotts and picketing. For years the courts had seen eye to eye with employers, who in most cases were from the class of former clients.

The Corporate State

And so the situation stood until the advent of the New Deal in 1932. All along, the courts at every level, sustained by the Supreme Court, were the main line of defense against organization by workers although the right of the propertied to organize in corporations and trade associations was freely conceded, encouraged and aided. Various grounds were cited—in the state courts the ancient common-law rulings harking back to the master-servant concept and in the federal courts reference to interference with interstate commerce, failure to allow due process, deprivation of property, no equal protection of law, undercutting of legal privileges and immunities, threats to the general welfare and others of the very few imprecise or ambiguous phrases of the Constitution that occupy most of the attention of the courts. Most of the wordage of the Constitution, it is worth noticing, is never adverted to in courts.

All of which has led, through favoritism toward corporations, to what Prof. Miller calls the Positive State, which "is a shorthand term for the express acceptance by the federal government—and thus by the American people—of an affirmative responsibility for the economic well-being of all. It involves a societal shouldering of a duty to take action to create and maintain minimal [sic] conditions within the economy—of economic growth, of employment opportunities, of the basic necessities of life." [35]

And this Positive State is but a generalized aspect of the Corporate State wherein "Corporations are the recipients of delegated power from the state. They act as administrative organs for the state." [36]

Although all this is happening, it is as unknown to the broad public as is the Constitution, which might just as well, along with court decisions, be written in Sanskrit as far as the public is concerned. As Prof. Miller observes, "The United States today is a corporate society rushing ahead pell-mell with advancing technology and populated by people many of whom [I would say "most of whom"] have belief-systems based on long-vanished social conditions. In substance, those belief-systems postulate an individualistic economy and law, predicated on the bedrock principles of private enterprise and freedom of contract and on the assumption that the power exerted by the units of society is roughly coequal. That these notions no longer reflect reality is the essential lesson to be learned from the advent of corporate America. (How real they actually were in the past is also debatable; it may well be that they existed mainly as ideals rather than as descriptions of societal actuality)." [37]

As to the "many" people so adhering to inapplicable beliefs, the number must be considerably more than half the population. For survey polls show more than 75 per cent of the populace with a cosmic outlook that postulates, with not the slightest evidence of any kind to support it, the existence of a supernatural realm transcending the realm of nature. Millions upon millions are devotees of astrology. People so oriented are obviously as naive and readily manipulable by political operators as are desert nomads.

What is more, the basic acumen of the populace is not placed very high by experts in such matters, who find that "about 67 per cent of the population when tested on a commonly used test of intelligence obtain IQ scores between 85 and 115." [38] This, even though the concept of a generalized IQ is today suspect, surely does much to explain the types regularly elected to Congress, the state legislatures and other public offices. And 17 per cent test below 85. IQ scores for young children range from 0 to 200.

"The people", in brief, are not overly bright and never have been, and this by tests other than controversial IQ surveys—an additional reason the government may at any time do whatever it wishes and also the explanation of why the myth thrives of an impersonal Constitution, containing the sibylline answer to all questions and in full force and operation.

With the rise of the large corporation under the ministering hand of government officials, especially in the courts, there came into view the wealthy dynasties of successful corporate entrepreneurs, insuring a line of descendants of the "Robber Barons". Although the Constitution forbade the granting of titles of nobility, these people, as it turned out, possessed all the material substance pertaining to European nobility. Money *per se* was ennobling in the American scheme. The grant of a title in England was not the grant of an empty honor but usually carried with it, especially in the days before the Constitution was written, grants of estates. The estates were the substance of the title, what made the title worthwhile, gave it something more than panache.

A small class of Americans, the most prominent of them with names well known to the American public, therefore came into possession of vast estates that made most ducal holdings in Great Britain in its heyday seem by contrast like child's playthings. The revenues of the corporations that constituted the estates greatly exceeded those of many of the states of the Union. It would have taken many states together to measure up in value to Standard Oil or a number of other corporations, all the consequence basically of applied mass labor.

The spectacle then took the form of what politicians, and a large number of professors, term the great American democracy, a democracy which has at its core a small and puissant aristocracy of money. What gives this aristocracy (or plutocracy as some malcontents called it) an especial aura is that all its progenitors spring from recently poor common people, many barely able to read. There is, then, hope for everyone—what ideologues termed "the promise of American life". In the process the United States presents to an astounded world—a democratic plutocracy!

Gross disparities in income and personal wealth today are largely traceable to the same historical complex. One would expect among people of many differing talents that income and personal wealth would vary. One's expectation, taking no unusual interference into consideration, is for both to distribute more or less according to the normal bell-shaped curve of probability, from zero to very much, with a substantial distribution in the middle. But there is one characteristic of the population of the United States that is wildly out of line with this curve and that is the characteristic of income and personal wealth, and with it the characteristic of veiled political power.

The amount of wealth as actually held distributes in fact according to a curve that is flat most of the way, embracing only a very small percentage of the population at each stage. When the amount of wealth held becomes quite small, the size of the population embraced by the curve becomes very large. When the wealth is great the population in posession is small.

The following Federal Reserve Board chart tells the story. Under the curve is the proportion of the population, shown along the sides, given as consumer units or families, whose wealth-holdings fall below

Distribution of Consumer Units by Amount of Wealth, December 31, 1962

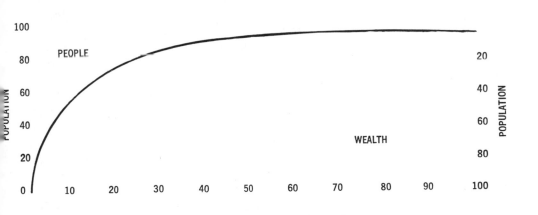

PER CENT BELOW SPECIFIED AMOUNT

PER CENT AT OR ABOVE SPECIFIED AMOUNT

AMOUNT OF WEALTH IN THOUSANDS OF DOLLARS

the amounts specified on the lower line. The percentage of the population holding more than the amounts specified on the lower line appear above the curve up to the column indicated at the top by 0 on the right.[39]

According to this same official source, 11 per cent of the families had negative net worth or were in a position of net debt and 5 per cent had zero net worth while 12 per cent were worth less than $1,000. Beyond this 17 per cent were worth less than $5,000 and another 15 per cent were between $5,000 and $10,000.[40] That gives one 60 per cent of the families.

Those owning the largest chunks of wealth made up such an infinitesimal fraction that it was not given.

By turning this chart upside down one obtains a better idea of the number of wealthholders in each category up to $100,000 and more. At $10,000 or less about 60 per cent of the population is accounted for. As these figures are for 1962 one should make adjustments for changes, especially in market values.

The chart does not show the specific value of levels of wealth beyond $100,000. But as of 1969 it was shown by specialists in the field that ½ of 1 per cent of persons held by net worth 19.9 per cent of the national wealth and 1 per cent held 24.9 per cent. The ½ of 1 per cent held 9.8 per cent of the real estate, 44 per cent of the corporate stock, 32 per cent of the bonds, 9.7 per cent of the cash, 25.7 per cent of the debt instruments, 6.6 per cent of the life insurance and 15.2 per cent of miscellaneous and trusts (which divides into 85.2 per cent of trusts and 7.4 per cent of miscellaneous).[41]

None of this result was achieved by the random interplay of population, even allowing for the fact that the shrewd are usually able to outwit the numerous slow-witted and gullible. The successful wealthholders in almost every case had an omnipotent lever at their service: the government. That is to say, the various common people elected to man the government. One might argue that the free electorate, knowing very little of what everything is all about, was hoisted by its own petard of elections although some of them unquestionably salvaged something for themselves out of the process.

Whatever the effects of inflation on these figures, they have not altered relationships except to compromise much of the wealth held by the less affluent. Government-induced inflation has deflated the middle classes, some to the level of the under-classes.

The levels of income distribution are much the same although the lowest income-receivers do get something. Here it is a question of exchanging money for services, and as long as some service is forthcoming, money is paid. But disparities of income are enormous as between top wealth-holders and the lower employees. Even in the matter of salaries there are wide differentials.

The highest salaries are paid invariably by corporations, ranging up to $1.5 million per year and even beyond. Ostensibly this money, ultimately paid by the consumer, is paid for extraordinary talent. It is doubtful however, even in this period of inflation, that any *individual* pays anyone a salary of as much as $100,000 for the performance of any service. Corporate executive salaries are set by boards of directors, staffed in the main by executives of other companies, and the money is paid— the usual story—out of "other people's money", that of investors and consumers. So the sky naturally is the limit.

In government nobody except the President of the United States is paid a salary in excess of $100,000 and most governmental salaries are considerably below this figure.

All this sudden mention of money is no doubt confusing to some readers but this is what the constitutional story is all about: money and money arrangements—who gets it and how, why, when, where and what for. The constitutional story is definitely not about guaranteeing life, liberty and the pursuit of happiness or establishing justice, promoting the general welfare or securing the blessings of liberty except as these may be interpreted, sometimes oddly, by authorized third parties. The key question is: Who gets the money?

So it is in the distribution of wealth and the nature of the tax laws that one discerns the outcome of the constitutional story. The tax laws, devised by elected leglislatures, as many studies have shown, grossly favor the wealthy and bear down unconscionably on the non-wealthy and have always done so. Efforts have been made to rectify them but an invisible hand in legislative backrooms invariably intervenes to defeat the process. It seems safe to say they will never be rectified.

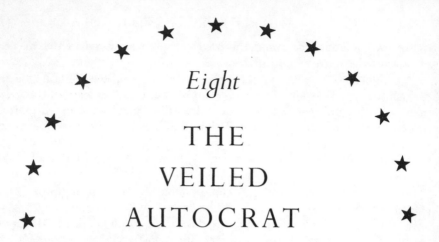

Eight

THE
VEILED
AUTOCRAT

The President of the United States is by far the most powerful formally constituted political officer on earth and stands at the head of the largest industrialized country. Nobody else comes even close to him in stature.

On the formal side he has held his high status since the abolition of Russian czarism and Turkish sultanism, on the practical side since the United States attained its as yet unchallenged economic pre-eminence. The office he holds is inherently imperial, irrespective of the behavior of the occupant.

Multitudes of objectors, I am aware, stand ready to put forward in dissent such names as Lenin, Stalin, Hitler, Mussolini, Franco, Mao Tse-tung as men of more sweeping power. But all of these, while unquestionably wielding more unchallenged authority in their juris-dictions, and more unpleasantly, were never formally installed in a regularly constituted and traditionally sanctioned political procedure. Lenin and Mao seized their power by bloody processes. Franco did similarly as a counter-revolutionist. Stalin and Hitler were, respectively, revolutionary and counter-revolutionary insiders who had to exterminate numerous colleagues in order to rise to unchallenged dictatorial power and thereafter were obliged to maintain an unremitting reign of domestic terror to quell always-feared insurgency. The vast power of the President, by contrast, is formally conferred, handed over.

As for Leonid Brezhnev, as far as can be ascertained he is the spearhead of a collective self-constituted leadership centered dually in the Soviet Politiburo and the Central Committee of the Communist Party of the U.S.S.R. In most of the regularly organized stable governments of the world, especially the British, the executive is a collectivity. The United States consequently is absolutely unique, and dangerously vulnerable in many ways, with a one-man executive. The American President stands in a position midway between a collective executive and an absolute dictator. In time of declared war he becomes in fact, quite constitutionally, a full-fledged dictator.

"The Executive Power Shall Be Vested . . ."

The essence of presidential power is concentrated in the single sentence, lightly skipped over by blithe readers of the Constitution, that opens Article II, Section 1—"The Executive power shall be vested in a President of the United States of America." This portentous line needs to be dwelt upon.

The major difficulty for most people about the Constitution is the way it is usually read. For all parts of the document should not be read at the same pace, at the same elevation of voice or with the same stress. It has been said that the Constitution can be read in twenty to thirty minutes. This is precisely not the way to read the document if understanding of its operation is the goal.

The proper way to assimilate the Constitution most briefly—there are other, perhaps better and longer ways—is to look upon it as a symphony. Some passages should be read, or played, more lightly and softly than others, some more loudly and repeatedly. For they are not all "played" by government as of equal weight. In this approach the Preamble, for example, may be imagined as given out, cheerfully, with chirping flutes and piccolos. Actually, pleasant trivia, mood-setting.

The full orchestra now gives forth with one of the big themes: "All legislative powers herein granted shall be vested in a Congress of the United States", etc. (Article I, Section 1). Brisk variations of this theme now take place, occasionally sounding anticipatory parts of coming themes relating to the President and the Supreme Court, some parts more loudly, some more softly, some rather vaguely. And some more rapidly. On the whole, although tempi would vary, the pace would be *moderato*. The main business, in a gradual crescendo, is Section 8, after which the orchestra gradually quiets down through Sections 9 and 10.

The fundamental portion of the symphony comes with Article II, Section 1—"The Executive power shall be vested in a President of the United States of America." Here is the main theme. It should be stated slowly and loudly, first by full orchestra and then repeated by each section of the orchestra and finally re-stated by the full orchestra, with heavy rumblings of a big tympani section. The tempo is *maestoso*. Variations on the theme follow, some more softly, some more loudly.

One should, in short, repeat this line many times in reading, perhaps up to ten. Doing that fixes its absolute centrality in the mind.

The final movement, beginning with "The judicial power", etc., would be a *scherzo*, varied in content, at times mocking and contradictory. This *scherzo* would take in the amendments. But the listener would be fully aware that in the second movement, and parts of the first, had been delivered the big message.

Alternatively to this fanciful approach, no doubt nonplussing to lawyers and judges, one can give the document close analysis, bit by bit, as Edward S. Corwin does in the treatise *The Constitution and What It Means Today* (1973) and the *Annotations*.

In any event, in order to understand the inner nature of the United States government it is necessary to pause long over the first line of Article II and ponder deeply the question "What is executive power?"— aware all the time that it is concentrated in the hands of one man. Leave executive power out of the system and the whole affair is instantly inert. Congress becomes an aimless discussion group and the Supreme Court purely academic. This question—"What is executive power?"—is an essential guide in an analysis of the Presidency. It will be seen to contain the entire substance of the office, the mainspring of the system.

Article II, almost immediately and deceptively taking leave of the portentous theme of executive power, goes on to more or less babble about a number of subordinate matters. The President, native-born, shall hold office for a term of four years with a Vice President of practically no prescribed duties for the same term, both repeatedly electable. Amendment XXII, proposed in 1947, pushed through to ratification in 1951, limits any President to two terms. This amendment, which makes every President a completely free agent in his second term and bars the country from continuing further in office a superior person who commands the confidence of an electoral majority, was a retrospective act of petty symbolic revenge against the recently deceased Franklin D. Roosevelt and his "New Deal" on the part of Republicans and dirt-level Democrats.

Again, now knowing that he will never be allowed to stand for re-election after a second term, an ill-disposed President may plan to ride roughshod over his political enemies, as President Nixon indeed is known to have intended upon his re-election in 1972. A wild-card President in his second term knows that nothing whatever threatens him except a highly unlikely impeachment.

Far from limiting the power of the office, which is always there for any incumbent to use or abuse, the amendment merely denies the electoral majority an opportunity of exercising its judgement on the basis of a man's performance. It cannot keep a superlatively effective

President in office. It is hardly likely that such a majority would ever be likely to give more than two terms to a palpably bad man. And Roosevelt, rated by virtually all political scholars as the third-greatest President in the history of the country, was never this. The amendment merely shows how distrustful American conservatives are of the American electorate, perhaps not entirely without justification in view of the frequency with which mindless conservatives have won office.

One can easily visualize the following contingency arising under the restrictive amendment. A President of demonstrated superior capacity and vigor is in his eighth year of office when a tremendous emergency promising to be of great duration arises. Nobody else commanding the confidence of the populace and of tested ability is in sight to confront the situation. Such a man must, in the presence of Amendment XXII, step down to make way for either one of two obvious lightweights. A Washington or Lincoln must make way for a Calvin Coolidge, Buchanan or Gerald Ford.

I wouldn't advise anyone to lose any sleep over this prospect. If the critical situation should ever arise, one may be sure that Amendment XXII would be rapidly rescinded or some irregular way found to keep the indispensable man in the government, perhaps in the Cabinet, with the elected President subordinate to him. Such impromptu cadenzas have been frequent in the history of the Constitution. History, contrary to Constitution worshippers, is not governed by instructions on a piece of paper.

Still dealing purely with the election of a President, not his operations, Article II continues by telling how he shall be chosen in an Electoral College, which never assembles to make a choice but is spread through all the states. This system has never worked except in the unanimous choice of Washington, even as supplemented by Amendment XII in 1804. The President is never in fact nominated and elected as the Constitution stipulates. He is instead nominated and elected by unprescribed irregular processes, one of numerous extra-constitutional formally unsanctioned usages.

If the Electoral College, which literally consists of political dummies, were in fact operational, its elected members would all meet in one place, much as the College of Cardinals meets to deliberate and select a Pope. They might be elected through parties and committed to certain candidates but the actual choice would be by majority collegiate vote. Amendment XII however stipulates that the electors must meet in their respective states. They never consult together, a farce all the way. The Electoral College is a long-acknowledged constitutional anomaly, one of many.

The remainder of Article II, Section 1, tells who is eligible in terms of birth and age to be President, what shall be done if he vacates office, how he shall be paid, and prescribes the oath he shall take, of which the significant words are "I will faithfully *execute the office* [emphasis added] of President of the United States" and will "preserve, protect and defend the Constitution of the United States". That is, always as he and his personally chosen advisers understand it.

Presidential Power

To "execute the office" is itself a sibylline phrase. Some of its duties appear in Section 2 of the same article where, introducing a vast power, the President is named the generalissimo of the armed forces, is allowed to require the opinion in writing of the officers of each executive department which he himself appoints (all such departments are established by Congress), and is given the authority to grant reprieves and pardons for offenses against the United States except in cases of impeachment. He is also given authority to make treaties with the advice and consent of two-thirds of the Senate (not with Senate ratification as commonly supposed), and with only a majority of Senate approval to appoint diplomats, judges of the Supreme Court and all other officers not otherwise constitutionally authorized, with power to fill vacancies during any Senate recess. But Congress is given the authority to vest the appointment of inferior officers in the President alone, in the courts or in the heads of executive departments. As these latter are subject to instant dismissal by the President (several have been so dismissed) they would not be likely to appoint anyone displeasing to him. Most presidential appointments to the executive branch are routinely approved by Congress as a matter of constitutional usage, for the President is felt to have the inherent right to choose members of his administration.

In the passages just touched upon we see emerging some of the President's great power. As generalissimo he is completely autonomous, in war and peace. In time of peace he can locate the armed forces and the weaponry wherever he likes. For discharging this duty there is no lead given in the Constitution nor any dependence whatever related to Congress. He can, in fact, fly in the face of Congress—and has done so.

The Senate early in 1917 filibustered to death a proposal by President Wilson to arm American merchant ships carrying military supplies through submarine-patrolled waters to England and France. Wilson thereupon issued an executive order to arm the ships, which was done, a step in the steady progress of the administration to involve the United States in World War I.

The President may, in short, induce or wage war in any way he decrees, or take subtle steps leading inevitably to war (as Wilson did), and grant reprieves and pardons to anyone he selects, for whatever reason, without consulting anyone. Pardons historically have gone to politically connected persons in the main. With respect to limitations on presidential treaty-making powers, there are ways around these as part of the broad category of "executive power".

How Presidents interpret the Constitution so as to yield them broad prerogative powers to act alone in genuine or purported emergencies is given close and detailed attention in a masterly study by Prof. Richard M. Pious, political scientist of Columbia University. Very much like the Supreme Court they construct syllogisms by arranging isolated clauses of the Constitution in a variety of ways as premises, leading to conclusions which state that they have the power they wish to exercise. Whatever the Constitution does not expressely forbid, and it forbids very little, they may do. But whatever the Constitution does not expressly command, they with a little ingenuity deduce.[1] It is obvious that by rearranging sentences and words, and taking some out of context, one can make almost any substantial text mean whatever one wants it to mean. It is by such rearranging that all branches of the United States government derive their steadily expanding authority, which collectively at least is unlimited. Presidential authority, unless effectively, by action, nullified either by Congress or the Supreme Court—a very rare event—is thus practically plenary.

In time of war the President may, disregarding the generals, make ultimate strategic decisions. Lincoln ordered a cautious General McClellan to make a general advance in the field, eventually summarily removed him. Wilson decreed that American forces in Europe in World War I be kept under unified American command, not distributed as replacements in French and British regiments as the French wanted. He also decided to send American troops to Russia in support of a tottering czarist government. The United States was not at war with Russia or any segment of the Russian people. In 1918 he concluded a European armistice. Franklin Roosevelt waged naval warfare against Germany well before Pearl Harbor. Truman ordered the dropping of the newfangled atomic bomb on Japan, vengeance for Pearl Harbor. He later also summarily dismissed General MacArthur, long infatuated with himself, for disputing presidential instructions in Korea. Where, when, how and with what to attack lies finally with the President and the President alone.

As to the presidential power to make war at any time on his own initiative, the State Department (which is merely one of the President's many masks), in an official memorandum submitted to the Senate Committee on Foreign Relations on March 8, 1966, held that President Johnson was under no obligation at all to consult Congress before attacking North Vietnam on February 7, 1965, even if he had not obtained broad permission of Congress in the Tonkin Gulf Resolution of August 10, 1964.[2] The Tonkin Gulf "incident" was either wholly imaginary or something blown up out of very little to vast propaganda proportions by a President intent upon war to the hilt. The State Department memorandum ominously stressed that "Since the Constitution was adopted there have been at least 125 instances in which the President has ordered the armed forces to take action or maintain positions abroad without obtaining prior Congressional authorization, starting with the 'undeclared war' with France (1798-1800) . . ."

So much for the widespread popular enchantment with the idea that Congress alone has the power "to declare war". In passing, it should be remarked that virtually all popular beliefs about the Constitution, as the consequence of persistent propaganda, are either completely false or properly subject to vast qualification. The document does not function as most people think it does.

A symphonist might score Section 3 largely for singing harps, with perhaps a low growl from the trombones at the end. It rather innocently stipulates that the President shall give Congress information on the state of the Union, recommend measures to it, call extraordinary meetings of one or both houses of Congress and adjourn such meetings, receive diplomats, commission all officers of the United States and "take care that the laws be faithfully executed"—the fateful line that abruptly tripped up President Nixon.

One thing the President may not do, at least openly, is to violate the law deliberately although, independently of the Supreme Court, he may interpret it within broad limits, and what he and his henchmen do in secret nobody usually knows, least of all Congress or the press. There is no agency at all to give the executive close surveillance. The Watergate revelations gave the country a unique view of operations inside the White House—gamy business all around. That all this was peculiar to Richard Nixon is something no political sophisticate can believe. A preliminary study, which needs to be fleshed out and deepened, traces similar publicly unpalatable doings unbrokenly back to the Roosevelt administration.[3] There is much evidence that from time to time the same sort of high-handedness went on under Wilson and Theodore Roosevelt as well. The scandals of the Harding administration of course are part of the same tissue.

The Watergate episode brought in its train a flood of books detailing widespread delinquency in the government, but these had been foreshadowed by another long train of earlier volumes on the same theme, which were largely ignored by press and public. It took the spectacular

Watergate affair itself to alert the reading public to what was really going on. A pre-Watergate book by a lawyer, titled *How the Government Breaks the Law,* detailed proven law-breaking as a steady preoccupation at every level of government—municipal, county, state and federal. The book showed that, at the executive level, government proceeded pretty much *ad libitum* outside the stipulated rules at all levels.[4]

Lawlessness in American government is nothing new. The Arno Press, a subsidiary of the *New York Times,* has published a catalogue titled *Politics and People: The Ordeal of Self-Government in America* that lists reprints of 58 books published since 1873 on governmental lawlessness—and these are merely a sampling of all that are of record.

Richard Nixon, then, was not the inventor of playing fast and loose with constitutional precepts. He was merely the biggest fish incontrovertibly caught in the act. As to it all being a phenomenon associated with self-government, there is this to be said: it has nothing to do with self-government, everything to do with government by light-fingered, silver-tongued up-from-nowhere *officialdom,* unrestrained by any agency or inner mechanism.

Governments, like other institutions and persons, enjoy a secret life of their own, quite at variance with their public masks, which are the basis of their outward images. The psychoanalysis of a government would bring as much strange material to light as the psychoanalysis of an individual. Only very naive mentalities take governments, especially "democratic" governments, at face value.

As the President is given the power alone to appoint his own and to receive foreign diplomats it is clear that the entire range of foreign affairs, except as qualified by Senate-approved treaties, is an open-ended sphere of operations for him. So it is evident that he has the ultimate decision on foreign policies as well as in any war that may be engendered by them.

That is all this article says about "executive power" although it is by no means the entire story.

The article concludes with the misleading reassurance that the President and all other civil officers may be removed by conviction of two-thirds of the Senate after impeachment by a majority of the House of Representatives. The impeachment theme is given unduly heavy emphasis in many schools, where teachers often say, "Just think, children, the President may be removed from office by Congress if he doesn't behave."

Actually, it is almost impossible to remove a President once he is installed. Since 1789 there have been, to date, thirty-nine Presidents and none has been removed by the process although quite a few framers seemed to think it would happen rather frequently. An attempt by

Congress to convict one, Andrew Johnson, failed by a single vote although he had blatantly refused to enforce several laws passed by Congress. Congress, for its part, disregarding this nonfeasance, impeached him for disregarding an arguably unconstitutional law it had passed, the Tenure of Office Act.

The Constitution requires that two-thirds of the members present of the Senate must vote to convict (Article I, Section 3, Paragraph 6) and that impeachments must be brought in the House (Article I, Section 2, Paragraph 5), which proceeds by majority.

Richard Nixon resigned in 1974 under the threat of almost certain impeachment, the only President to relinquish office during his term. As the chief evidence against him that he had broken the law he had sworn to enforce consisted of his own words on electronic tapes, it was evident that not many Senators, much as they might have wished, could with any plausibility have voted to acquit. To do so would have made them publicly ridiculous.

The grounds for conviction after impeachment are solely "treason, bribery, or other high crimes and misdemeanors" (Article II, Section 4). Nixon, although never convicted of anything, was subsequently given a blanket pardon by President Ford, his own appointee to Vice President —straight farce all the way. Subsequently Nixon drew a generous presidential pension, with perquisites, for life.

There are many good reasons for ridding oneself of a Chief of State —demonstrated incompetence, physical or mental incapacity, serious illness, failure to command the confidence of the nation, habitual drunkenness or inexplicable eccentricity and the like—but unless they can be construed as crimes or misdemeanors they will not supply adequate constitutional grounds. However, as Congress throughout is the sole judge of what is fitting, it theoretically could but hardly ever would remove for anything but the clear-cut stipulated reasons. It failed by one vote to convict Andrew Johnson in what boiled down to differences between Congress and the President over the policy of reconstruction after the Civil War. Johnson wished to pursue Lincoln's conciliatory policy, which no doubt would have prevailed had Lincoln not been assassinated. The assassination in itself inflamed Congress, many members of which all along wanted to treat the South punitively as conquered territory.

As John Adams commented in July, 1789, on the new Constitution, "The Executive [is] not punishable but by universal convulsion, as Charles 1st." [5] Charles I, King of England, Scotland and Ireland, was beheaded in 1649, the only British king to be dealt with so summarily.

While preparations were being made for the impeachment of Richard Nixon there was much public hand-wringing and groaning about the "ordeal" to which the country was about to be subjected, perhaps for months, with the two top branches of the government monopolized in the process, everything else in a volatile world neglected. Nixon's last-ditch defenders called upon the accusers to produce "the smoking pistol"—that is, incontrovertible evidence of criminality. They subsided only when the fatal tape was reached. Andrew Johnson fought back against overwhelming odds to defeat opponents in a Senate trial that consumed three months from impeachment to acquittal and left a shaken President in office—and, for a long time, a shaken Presidency.

So Adams was correct. It takes a national convulsion to get rid of a President by the impeachment process. And there is about it no certainty of success, leaving in office a badly wounded chief executive, a shaken office for successors, and frayed tempers throughout the land. Impeachment of a President is like using an atomic bomb to treat an infection in a tooth.

A far better method of getting rid of an unwanted President, unwanted for whatever reason, would be for two-thirds or three-quarters of each house of Congress to vote him out of office simply on the ground that they have lost confidence in him. Unsettling though this might be, it would be less unsettling than the impeachment route.

The President is consequently far more secure for his term of office than is the chairman of the Soviet Central Committee and Politburo. Nikita Khrushchev, by mere vote of the body in his absence, was abruptly deposed, apparently much to his own surprise. In effect, it is virtually impossible to remove a President. His security in office for his term is but one facet of his power.

Vast Prerogative Powers

Other powers of the President are mingled with those of Congress, for every bill passed by Congress is subject to presidential veto (Article I, Section 7, Paragraph 2). Although the bill may be repassed over his veto, it requires only one-third plus one vote of either house to sustain the veto—at most 34 in the Senate or 146 in the House.

As a quorum by constitutional definition consists of a simple majority in either house, the minimal vote with a bare quorum in the Senate to sustain a veto would be 17 members, in the House 73. So it is evident that with only very weak legislative support a presidential veto can stand.

The veto has an innocent sound to most of the public. It features rather blandly in the news from time to time and is far less enthralling to read about than whatever interests most people. Few people therefore are aware of its true power or that it is a modified survival of the long-abandoned, often patriotically damned British royal prerogative, inoperative since 1688. Under the prerogative the King simply squashed proposed legislation. The veto, in truth, is like a lightning bolt thrown at a house of cards.

Statistics make this plain. From the inception of the Constitution through the Ford administration, Presidents have employed the veto 2,360 times. They were overridden by a paralyzed Congress only 92 times, or in precisely 4 per cent of the instances.[6] The veto, then, is 96 per cent effective in stopping legislation the President finds undesirable. This is indeed power. Anyone who prevails 96 per cent of the time in large ventures must surely be considered a powerful person. For nearly three hundred years no British monarch has had available to him such authority.

John and John Quincy Adams, Jefferson, William H. Harrison, Taylor, Fillmore and Garfield emitted no vetoes. Taylor and Garfield were in office only briefly. Washington issued only two vetoes, Madison only seven and Monroe only one. Jackson vetoed twelve bills. All these early vetoes, made on purely constitutional grounds, were sustained. Jackson was the first President to veto for reasons of policy. The first President to see a veto overridden was John Tyler (1841-45), who issued nine vetoes, eight of which were sustained. With the outbreak of the Civil War, Tyler, a Virginian, joined the Confederacy and was elected to the Confederate Congress. Lincoln issued only seven vetoes, all sustained. By percentage the embattled Andrew Johnson saw most of his vetoes overridden, 15 out of 29, or more than 50 per cent.

The most massive use of the veto, now an instrument of policy, came immediately after Johnson. Grant vetoed 93 bills, was overridden only four times. Cleveland, the first Democrat elected after the Civil War, in his first term sent down 414 vetoes and was overriden only two times. In his second term he vetoed 170 bills, was overridden only five times. McKinley, with a docile Congress before him, vetoed 42 bills, was never overridden.

The greatest number of vetoes issued by any President is credited to Franklin D. Roosevelt, who served a record three-and-a-fraction terms. Out of 631 vetoes he was overridden only nine times, or 1.5 per cent. Truman registered 250 vetoes, was overridden only 12 times, or 5 per cent. Eisenhower issued 181 vetoes, was overridden only twice. Presidents whose vetoes were never overridden were Washington, Madison, Monroe, Jackson, Polk, Buchanan, Lincoln, McKinley and Harding.

It is evident that the veto is a powerful presidential weapon. But it is by no means the end of presidential powers. It is merely the big executive negation of congressional willfulness.

Congress, it may be contended, is equally powerful as it may reject or modify presidential proposals for new legislation. While this last is true, it is also true that all the legislation passed by Congress in its history and retained on the books amounts to an enhancement of presidential authority. Whenever Congress passes any sort of valid statute, it is increasing or holding steady the level of presidential authority. For it is the President who must carry the statutes into effect—or give them only symbolic enforcement.

The President also possesses singlehanded affirmative powers in the form of executive orders. Up to December 31, 1975, the Presidents had issued 11,893 such orders, an average of 64 per year.[7] Many of these are extremely consequential.

Just what are these? They are one-man decrees, often far-reaching, the authority for which the President's law officers deduce by selecting suitable premises from the Constitution, standing Supreme Court decisions, a long line of statutes in force, precedents set by long-gone Presidents, new interpretations of their own or combinations of these.

The issuance of one-man decrees took place under the British Constitution as it stood in the late seventeenth century, was part of the royal prerogative. It was defended by John Locke in his *Second Treatise of Government* (chapter 14), which is cited by defenders of the practice by the President. But the writings of John Locke are not part of the American Constitution, which nowhere implicitly or explicitly gives a President this power of making new law. Nor are most Americans made aware by most commentators or by the communications media that a President wields such autocratic power without explicit constitutional sanction.

Locke addresses himself particularly to the question of what is to be done if wrong use is made of this power. In such a case, he says, "The people have no other remedy in this, as in all other cases where they have no judge on earth, but to appeal to heaven"—that is, revolution. And this is precisely the road dominant Americans took in 1776.

But this is by no means the only known way out of the difficulty. As Machiavelli says (*Discourses*, vol. 1, p. 34, Walker-Richardson translation), "The republic of Venice, which ranks high among modern republics, has reserved to a few of its citizens authority to deal with urgent questions with regard to which, if they all agree, they can make decisions without reference to any other body. Whereas in a republic in which no such provision is made, it is necessary either to stand by the constitution and be ruined, or to violate it and not be ruined." This was Lincoln's choice under the American Constitution.

If proper provision were made, such unanimously determined decrees could be issued in emergencies by a permanent special committee consisting of the President, the Chief Justice of the Supreme Court and the majority and minority leaders of each house of Congress. The initiator of the decree would be the President alone.

As to statutes in general, it should be noticed that in the course of time presidential power is steadily enhanced by them. For new statutes are designed to embrace and control new situations and additional situations, thus extending the executive power over more activities. A President today, as a consequence of more statutes, a long line of court decisions and presidential precedents, has more explicit unchallenged power at his fingertips than George Washington ever dreamed existed.

It is illuminating at this point to give some indication of the size of the executive division of the government. Indeed, when most people refer to the government, it is to the executive division they refer, not to the comparatively gossamer court and legislative divisions. While the civilian workforce of the government is officially stated at about 2.9 million people, the actual number of people paid with federal funds is probably about 7 million, according to a survey reported in a United Press International dispatch from Washington dated December 23, 1978.[8] The larger figure does not include the armed forces, which bring the total to 10 million. All these, except for the legislative and judicial divisions, are in the special domain of the President.

Civil Service Commission records do not include all these employees, most of whom function under full-time and part-time contracts, sub-contracts and federal grants. The Department of Health, Education and Welfare for example enrolls about 145,000 employees but it pays the salaries of 980,000 additional people in state and local governments, universities, research centers and in the employ of organizations doing contract work for the government.

A large number of government-created special corporations employ hundreds of thousands of full-time employees who are paid with federal funds but are not counted as government workers by the Civil Service Commission.

Although the Labor Department officially lists only 22,377 in its employ, through the Comprehensive Employment and Training Act (CETA) it pays the salaries of 750,000 nominal state and local government employees and of 77,000 state employees who work in employment service offices.

If anything, according to government sources referred to in the dispatch, the estimates given of federal payrolls are too low. People who rail against "big government", using Civil Service Commission figures as a base, have in mind only the very tip of the iceberg.

All this vast domain is under the authority of a single man, the President, which should give readers some idea of the magnitude of his office amid the emerging outlines of the Corporate State.

As outlined above, the President is the sole person vested with executive power by the Constitution, which raises the question of what executive power in and of itself may be. At a minimum it must be the power to act outward from the government. Neither Congress nor the Supreme Court has such power or the means of implementing their decisions by positive outward action. What is the President to do if he senses dangers, disadvantages, embarrassments pressing in upon the nation he heads and the Constitution he is sworn to uphold? Or upon himself? All else failing or seeming unlikely, he acts like a king and issues an executive order, often another lightning bolt. In consequence, he is damned if he does, damned if he doesn't.

Any time Congress doesn't like it, it can always pass a resolution of dissent, a weak response, or can impeach him and put him on trial, guaranteeing turmoil for the country. It can, too, pass legislation nullifying the effect of the executive order, which the President can in turn veto. If repassed over his veto the issue may wind up before the Supreme Court, which may sustain the President's right to issue the order, probably will because it usually does. It is extremely rare for the Supreme Court to condemn a presidential order.

Between the veto and the executive order the President, it is clear, is in a strong and virtually autonomous position and requires only the will to act. But this is still only part of presidential power.

Foreign Affairs—A Presidential Playground

The President alone may make treaties, but for this requires two-thirds of the Senate to support him, clearly a division of authority. A treaty has the internal domestic effect of a statute or a constitutional provision so that by a treaty the President and two-thirds of the Senate can, in effect, extend the Constitution, quite legally if circumlocutiously. Beyond this the President, and the President acting alone, may terminate treaties with a mere announcement, as President Carter in 1978 calmly terminated the mutual defense treaty of 1954 with Taiwan upon announcing the forthcoming recognition of the mainland People's Republic of China. All this was by his sole decision.

As to recognizing or withdrawing recognition from a foreign government, the President may do it by his sole decision. In recognizing the Peking government President Carter, a Democrat, merely took the second step in a process initiated some years earlier by President Nixon, a Republican, who also did not consult Congress. Nixon, too, had for years made political capital out of preaching detestation of Communist China. About this sort of thing individual members of Congress, if so disposed, can only fume and huff and puff. If thoroughly aroused, of course, Congress may impeach and remove the President, at the price of throwing country and government into wild disarray.

In terminating treaties the President is in much the same position constitutionally as in making appointments. These latter, as we have seen, must have the consent of the Senate. But the President may discharge any appointed executive official (although no judge or statutory administrative official), which means such officials are always under his thumb, his creatures. "With well over 1000 treaties submitted by Presidents to the Senate from 1789 through 1971," says Corwin, "it is a good calculation that the Senate amended about 14 per cent, and rejected or so tampered with about 12 per cent that either the President or the other contracting party declined to go on with them." [9] Here the President was 88 per cent, or a shade less, successful.

Most treaties are instruments extending to foreign nationals the rights of American citizens in return for reciprocal treatment of Americans in foreign countries. Additionally, they are part of "the law of the land", on a par with statutes and the Constitution. They affect domestic as well as international relationships, and in a great variety of ways, mostly with respect to property ownership and use.

Short of treaties, the President, and the President alone, may and does make executive agreements with foreign governments as part of his exclusive conduct of foreign relations. Only the President and his subordinates are in direct official touch with some 150 governments of the world. Thousands of such agreements have been made, many of them far-reaching and of the status of treaties.

Just how far-reaching such one-man agreements may be is seen by consulting the case of *U.S. v. Pink,* decided by the Supreme Court in 1942. The agreement, which assigned sequestered former czarist assets, superseded the law of the State of New York and was therefore presumably part of "the law of the land". The agreement was never approved by Congress. The effect of the agreement was to deny assets of a nationalized Russian insurance company to one set of creditors and to give them to another, sponsored by the Soviet government, contrary to state law.[10]

Some such agreements are called congressional-executive agreements when approved by both houses of Congress. In 1951 about 85 per cent of such agreements, for example, were approved by both houses of Congress. But other agreements are never submitted to Congress for approval. These are called presidential agreements.[11] However, if appropriations are required to implement them, Congress gets an opportunity to review presidential agreements. But many involve no appropriations. The Roosevelt-Litvinoff agreement involved in *U.S. v. Pink* did not.

Many of these agreements are momentous and far-reaching, significantly affecting the lives of Americans. In 1817 the Secretary of State exchanged notes with the British Minister to Washington that limited each nation's naval forces on the Great Lakes. The Senate approved it a year later. In 1898 the State Department entered into a protocol with Spain whereby the latter agreed to cede all title to Cuba, Puerto Rico and other West Indies possessions to the United States. In 1899 and 1900 the State Department exchanged notes with various European governments with respect to the "Open Door" in China, by which the United States secured equal access to all parts of that country on a basis of parity with other nations. In 1908 identical notes were exchanged with Japan to the effect that China was not to be taken over or subordinated by either one. In 1907 an agreement was made with Japan to regulate Japanese immigration to the United States.

Additionally, after the termination of the Treaty of Washington in 1885 American fishing rights off the coasts of Canada and Newfoundland were defined for more than twenty-five years by simple agreement; there was a simple State Department protocol in 1901 to end the Boxer Rebellion in China; in 1917 the State Department agreed that Japan had "special rights" in China; the armistice of November 11, 1918, and all the agreements and understandings with American "Associates" in World War I and with "Allies" in World War II were similarly handled on the executive level, without consultation with Congress. The so-called Yalta and Potsdam agreements represented purely presidential action.

"More recently," as Corwin notes, "President Nixon revived and renewed an executive agreement with Portugal allowing the United States to refuel military planes in the Azores and granting $435 million in economic aid to Portugal without consulting Congress." [12]

When the Senate in 1905 declined to approve a treaty that President Theodore Roosevelt had made with Santo Domingo to puts its customs houses under United States control, the President merely changed the treaty into an agreement and carried out its terms. A year later the Senate gave in and ratified the agreement. President Carter indicated he would proceed similarly if the Senate rejected an arms limitation treaty with the Soviet Union (SALT).

The Supreme Court moreover has ruled that an "executive agreement" within the President's authority, which is by Court dictum "inherent", is part of "the law of the land" that the courts must give effect to, any state law or judicial policy to the contrary notwithstanding.[13] So a presidential agreement transcends the laws of all the states.

This manifestly is law by decree, of which a great deal issues from the executive office at all times, whether the President is "conservative" or "liberal". In Corwin's view, this "is going rather far. It would be more accordant with American ideas of government by law to require, before a purely executive agreement be applied in the field of private rights, that it be supplemented by a sanctioning act of Congress. And that Congress, which can repeal any treaty as 'law of the land or authorization,' can do the same to executive agreements would seem to be obvious." [14] Yet Corwin, scholar though he was, was only a private citizen. His informed views on the government had no more operating force than those of a Skid Row derelict.

In the 1950s, when constitutional amendments were being proposed to limit the President's power to make executive agreements, they were rejected by Congress. Congress, it turns out when one comes to the "moment of truth", is no more anxious to restrict the President than it is to restrict the Supreme Court. Congress prefers to leave both with a free hand, reserving the right at all times to blame them if such a tactic fits the mood of the electorate. The electorate, meanwhile, not knowing whom to hold accountable, sinks into apathy, like Pavlov's experimental dogs. In the congressional elections of 1978, it will be recalled, two-thirds of the eligible electorate did not vote. Apparently the knowledge is slowly sinking in that the electorate and what it thinks has little role to play in American government. It was never, from the beginning, intended to have much of a role. Hence the elaborately labyrinthine Constitution. The "tyranny of the majority" was the thing most feared by the framers themselves. A majority, to them, was inherently wrong.

As to the Supreme Court, Congress in the 1950s launched another of its occasional broad attacks upon it with a view to limiting its power but failed by a single vote in the Senate. The vote was on a House bill, the residue of several broader bills. This bill read: "No Act of Congress shall be construed as indicating an intent on the part of Congress to occupy the field in which such Act operates, to the exclusion of all state laws on the same subject matter, unless such Act contains an express provision to that effect, or unless there is a direct and positive conflict between such Act and a State law so that the two cannot be reconciled or consistently stand together." It was defeated by the Senate 41 to 40, a close call. Corwin opines, however, that there is good reason to believe that the closeness of the vote induced the Supreme Court to "pull in its horns".[15]

Five bills to limit the authority of the Court had been passed in the House and Senate bill 2646, which was dropped in favor of H.R. No. 3 quoted above, was the broadest of all. It would have limited the appellate jurisdiction of the Court in cases arising out of contempt of Congress, the federal Loyalty-Security program, state anti-subversive activities statutes, regulations of employment and subversive activities in schools, and admission to practice law in any state.[16]

There is no express constitutional sanction for executive agreements, but the authority has been stated by the Supreme Court to exist as an "inherent" power of sovereignty.[17] In other words, if the United States has sovereignty, by elementary deduction it has all powers attributable to sovereignty, and the President as the sole possessor of executive power may exercise them even if the Constitution makes no overt reference to them. The President, in other words, is virtually a sovereign in his own person.

In the period of writing this section I heard one of the more intelligent and apparently well-informed television news commentators refer to the United States government as one of limited powers, which notion is part of the common myth about the government as taught in the schools and echoed faithfully in all the news media. In response to this it is only necessary to say that the United States has a government of absolutely unlimited powers, which at the point of execution are solely in the possession of one man, often solely at his discretion, the President of the United States. Any denial of this, no matter by whom, is so much nonsense. If all the law professors unanimously joined in denying it, it would still be nonsense. The power of the government, in most particulars of the President, is plenary although this is a fact concealed from most Americans because it is plainly in view, like Edgar Allen Poe's purloined letter. Most Americans do not want to see and recognize this, perhaps because it puts them into proper perspective as political Lilliputians, of little account. They are still afloat on a tide of untenable eighteenth-century Whig notions.

But the television commentator referred to above had high authority for his remarks, no other than Chief Justice John Marshall of the United States Supreme Court. Speaking for the Court in *McCulloch v. Maryland*, a key case (4 Wheaton 316, 1819), Marshall said, "This government is acknowledged by all to be one of enumerated powers . . . If any one proposition could command the universal assent of mankind, we might expect it would be this—that the government of the Union, though limited in its powers, is supreme within its sphere of action."

Marshall and other government men, such as Madison and Hamilton in *The Federalist*, as it turns out are the main sources for erroneous beliefs about the United States government and its operations. Writers on the Constitution continually cite Marshall, always respectfully but often with some indication of disbelief as with respect to his remark that "Judicial power, as contradistinguished from the power of the laws, has no existence. Courts are the mere instrument of the law, and can will nothing" (*Osborn v. U.S. Bank*, 9 Wheaton 738, 1824). Nobody at all familiar with the law and the courts believes that. It is a fairy tale put out for the naive.

Not only is the entire constitutional operation completely in the hands of the government (and not "the people") but, as it happens, what most Americans believe about the Constitution and how they describe it amounts to parroting what they have heard from government men, who in turn in most cases are built up to over-sized intellects by the propaganda of political partisans. The government people are like playwrights and actors who live in a special world where they are allowed to write their own reviews and then happily find the reviews widely quoted as gospel. Naturally they give their own script and acting splendid evaluations.

The idea that the United States has a limited government stems from the fact that there are indeed limits on minor details, set in the Constitution. These limits do not apply to major powers of government. They do, however, forbid bills of attainder, the taxing of exports (although exports, as well as imports, may be collectively or selectively forbidden), the passage of ex post facto laws, taking property without due process, granting titles of nobility, etc. Elective terms of office are also limited to two, four or six years. The power of individual states, however, is severely limited, to the point of extinction (Article I, Section 10). These and other limitations amount to a determination of the internal *etiquette* of the government.

None of these or similar stipulations places the slightest limit on the national government with respect to any power peculiar to sovereignty. With respect to all sovereign powers, the government is constitutionally unlimited and may go as far as it likes or finds expedient. The notion, then, that the United States government is somehow limited in the exercise of traditional governmental powers is simple nonsense of the first water.

The executive agreement usually consists of an exchange of notes between the Secretary of State and the head of a Foreign Office or chief diplomatic officer of a country. At least one has been signed by a President.[18] Although the Supreme Court has found the authority for such agreements in the "inherent" powers of sovereignty—which, baldly stated, is merely what governments in general habitually do—one can derive it from Article II, Section 3, empowering the President, and him alone, to "receive ambassadors and other public ministers". The President is obviously not expected to receive ambassadors to stage pleasant chats or to pray together but to "preserve, protect and defend the Constitution of the United States" in ways that are not specified. He is the only constitutional officer empowered by himself to do this or to "take care that the laws be faithfully executed". The Constitution does not specify how one "takes care".

Most of the people who read the Constitution carefully, especially political disputants, are legalists. That is, they are hunters after some word, phrase or clause, or combination of such, that to them gives positive permission or sets up some verbal inhibition. Owing to the influence of the legalists, most citizens have the same attitude toward the Constitution. To such the Constitution is a cookbook. But this isn't the way it works except on rare occasions.

To top all of the foregoing—a deluge of vetoes, executive orders, foreign agreements, singlehanded termination of treaties and dismissal of officials, appointments, recommendations of new measures to Congress—in recent years Presidents have taken to impounding money appropriated by Congress, not without congressional protests. Congress alone has the constitutional power of appropriating money. But the President, and the President alone, has the power of releasing it for spending by the executive branch or, as it turns out, not releasing it. What Congress or individual Congressmen may do in response is to denounce him or impeach him on the ground that he is exceeding his constitutional powers, construable as a crime. For the Constitution says nothing about anyone impounding money.

The President and Congress

The power of recommending measures to Congress in the hearing of the entire country is itself an instrument of power although the President may get desired measures before Congress in many other ways—through a friendly Congressman, by apparent demand of some influential outside group, etc.

Every President has a certain number of rock-bottom political friends in Congress, more perhaps than any other individual. Apart from the merits of what he proposes, his power of appointing higher officials and of directing appointments throughout the executive branch is an inducement to many Congressmen to go along with him. Promises of appointments to come may sway key Congressmen to his side who have great influence among colleagues. All this stems from the patronage power, which is solely at the President's disposal. Careers have been made and broken by it. By reason of the great volume of external federal programs now in force, low-level and middle-level patronage is now far greater than it ever was in the past.

In their approaches to Congress many Presidents, much of the time, are engaged in something very much like a game of chess or cat-and-mouse. In this game the President and his advisers enjoy the advantage of strategically superior positions. The outcome of course may depend upon the adroitness of moves by either side. But on the President's side the moves depend upon his decision alone, presumably after listening to good advisers. The responsive move in Congress, on the other hand, must be decided by a majority of 535 members, who often fall to quarreling among themselves. Congress is a divided and sub-divided force, often little more than a rabble.

Congress, as we have noticed, is more than a simple two-party structure with everybody accounted for in advance. It is at least four parties and by expert analysis fully six parties. The four-party division is arrived at by counting the conservative and liberal wings of each party. More tenably there are six broad divisions in Congress today, two among the Republicans and four among the Democrats. The Republican division is between Main Street and Wall Street Republicans, or traditionalists and modernists. The Democratic divisions consist of "New Left" Democrats who favor what is called affirmative social action; the traditionalists who are closely linked to the labor unions, are concerned about Soviet policy and defend the welfare state while indifferent or opposed to affirmative social action; the racist states'-rights Wallace-ites and the ambiguous coalition of Carterites who deal across all lines, issue by issue.[19] These latter, from President to President, might be regarded as the White House party. One can detect splits also among the Main Street and the Wall Street Republicans, such as western progressives and eastern liberals vis-a-vis self-styled moderate and extreme conservatives. Furthermore, Congress is divided into two houses, each with different constituencies and very different tenures. Either house may veto the other, and often does.

Against such a divided array a President who knows what he is doing can usually prevail, either wholly as President Carter prevailed with the loudly resisted Panama treaty in the Senate and as he at least partly prevailed with his energy proposals. Most of the leverage is on his side. What the President cannot get from Congressmen on the merits of a proposal or through ideological affiliation he can often obtain by wielding the carrot-and-stick of his enormous patronage power which, despite all talk of civil-service rules, extends to all levels of the executive branch. And patronage for friends is one of the big props of Congressmen in their home territories, often making the differences between re-election and defeat. Many social programs are patronage game preserves. The President is the dispenser.

Although all Congressmen are provided with small staffs, at public expense, which work to forward the fortunes of their chiefs, the President in the White House is provided with the largest personal staff of anyone in the government. This staff functions very much as a Praetorian Guard, to protect and to advance the governmental and political fortunes of its chief at all times. Its members are the absolute creatures of the President. They will often do anything, legal or illegal, moral or immoral, as clearly revealed in the Nixon administration, to enhance the actual as well as the apparent standing of the President.

When it comes to lobbying Congress, the President heads the largest lobby group in or out of government. To draw upon he has, first, members of his personal staff, some chosen for their lobbying skills. He also has all his departmental heads and their sub-chiefs and the various permanent departmental experts. Whenever he deems it necessary he can, working every conceivable approach, flood Congress with this array and can recruit federally funded experts from around the country by simple invitation. Hundreds stand ready to respond.

The President also has various known stand-by forces at his call. The chief prosecuting officer of the nation, the Attorney General, is his appointee, usually a close political associate. It is this officer who from time to time procures the indictment and prosecution of law-breaking Congressmen of whom, lamentably, there is always a considerable number.

Most Congressmen are mainly interested in two things: votes in their home territories and money contributions to support re-election campaigns. These latter come mainly from corporations, directly or indirectly. A considerable number down through history have also been interested in building personal estates, by means both legal and illegal. All this is in harmony with the Constitution (except for illegal practices of course), which in several places stresses that it is establishing offices of "honor, trust or profit" that yield "compensation for services" and "emoluments".[20] The Constitution is very positive on the theme of rewards for government officials.

There was considerable discussion at the constitutional convention about compensation, with some members suggesting that certain officials, such as Senators and Presidents, not be paid. While low compensation or no compensation was politically popular at the time, and always is, it was clear that with any uncompensated office only a wealthy man could serve or an invitation to corruption would be implied. The door was therefore left open to generous compensation, suggested in the term "offices of profit". That this is not enough for many officeholders is something that cannot be helped.

While the great amount of corruption in American government does not stem from any specific constitutional fault, it is encouraged by the tripartite structure of the constitutional government and the resulting labyrinth. The framers were voluble in their dislike of corruption and lambasted the British for freely resorting to it. And since that time Parliament has thoroughly cleaned its own procedures.

The framers assumed, unwarrantably, that Congress would pass effective laws to keep corruption at a minimum, but Congress, the center of most demonstrable corruption in national government, has steadily refused to do so. And with respect to this reluctance on the part of Congress any President is in a delicate position. Dependent upon Congress for support in many ways, he cannot instruct Congress how to regulate itself or its members—an outcome of the vaunted separation of powers. Presidents consequently do not make recommendations for establishing barriers to corruption, which private citizens instead from time to time recommend. In response, to date, Congress at most has passed intentionally ineffective measures.

While appointees in the executive branch have often been found to be corrupt, the only two Presidents for which cases of corruption could be clearly made out were Lyndon Johnson and Richard Nixon. Vice President Spiro Agnew was forced to resign upon being shown to be corrupt. And while corruption in the state courts is comparatively "oceanic", in the federal courts at all levels it is extremely rare with only 55 documented cases on record. Of these, 8 judges were censured, 17 resigned and 19 were either absolved or their cases died in committee. Only 8 were impeached, of which 4 were convicted and removed from office. Three were put on criminal trial, of which 1 had his case quashed after juries twice failed to agree on a verdict, 1 was acquitted and 1 was found guilty and served nineteen months in the penitentiary.[21]

What makes judges vulnerable to detection and therefore circumspect is the fact that they deal with lawyers, who don't like to lose cases for occult reasons. Congressmen however are not as exposed to close scrutiny and have often been found involved in corrupt arrangements although not as often as they would be if congressionally passed laws were more precise and searching. The Constitution leaves it strictly up to Congress to deal effectively with corruption, and the response of Congress is distinctly puckish.

Whatever reinforces a Congressman's standing enhances his position, and the President is the one man in the government most able to distribute boons.

Such is the mere weight of the presidential office that the simple presence of a President, however undistinguished personally, can be a great help to a Congressman in his home district during an election period. The President comes in with a large personal entourage—Secret Service men, hordes of newspaper people and photographers and assorted assistants, camp-followers and technicians—much like an English monarch of the old days on a royal progress through the land. With him goes a vast communications and aeronautic apparatus designed to keep him in touch with the world at all times. Bleakville, U.S.A., the home town of a lowly Congressman, becomes the center of the world. The splash of activity alone focusses attention on the lucky Congressman, which attention he needs to alert his lethargic constituents to his existence. All indeed a President need do to start tongues wagging in a congressional district is to refer in a press conference to the incumbent as "My good friend, Congressman So-and-So". The news media quickly disseminate such gems.

So none except an already discredited President ever comes crawling to Congress on broken legs. The President, in brief, is a constitutional lion and everyone in Congress knows it, shows it by standing when he appears before them. Many would be happy to kiss his feet.

The President too has more direct and more commanding access to the public than any Congressman or group of Congressmen. He can hold regular press conferences, and through these can get saturation press attention. He can at any time command all radio and television channels for stating his case.

It is often said that the three main divisions of the government are co-ordinate and co-equal. Conceding for the moment that this is true (although it is not), the same is not true for individuals in each division.

A President holds 100 per cent of the authority in the executive branch. Each Congressman, on the other hand, wields $\frac{1}{535}$th of the authority in Congress, which never stands at 100 per cent together on a single issue. Each man on the Supreme Court wields no more than $\frac{1}{9}$th or 11 per cent of the authority, which requires by custom at least $\frac{5}{9}$ths to carry whatever the authority of the division is. The Constitution says nothing about decisions by a divided Court.

The voting authority of individual Congressmen turns out on computation to be one hundred and eighty-seven thousands of one per cent. It is only by bunching the votes of many Congressmen that one can obtain substantial percentages.

To bring out the disparities in another way, imagine each branch to be worth $2 million, evenly divided among its various members. At this rate the President has a net worth of $2 million. Each member of the Supreme Court has a net worth of $222,222.22. Allotting $1 million to each congressional house, as they claim to be equal, each member of the lower has a net worth of $2,300 and each member of the upper house a net worth of $10,000.

This sort of fanciful computation serves to bring out the *positional* strength of each individual in the government. It is not to be denied that a fumbler in the White House, faced by one or more capable men in Congress, may be unable to bring the full weight of his position to prevail, just as not every wealthy man has the personal characteristics to match his wealth. But in either case the wealth is there at any starting point, a strong base.

Members of Congress and the President all have different constituencies. The presidential constituency is national and is more deeply affected by presidential actions than by actions of Congressmen. As long as the President commands something around 50 per cent of electoral approval as shown by public-opinion polls, he is in a strong position.

Most members of Congress, on the contrary, have different constituencies, demanding contradictory measures. As each two members of the Senate from the same state have the same constitutency, the Senate constituency divides into fifty parts, broadly similar by region but different even in contiguous states. As Senators of the same state sometimes vote oppositely, this reduces the state to zero influence on a measure. Sometimes a lower-house delegation similarly divides. The outlook on the world of the Northwest, for example, is very different from that of the Southeast, and both are very different from the Northeast or Middle West.

The differences are even greater in the House of Representatives, composed from 435 congressional districts.

Only the President speaks single-mindedly to and for a cross-section of all these constituencies.

When it comes to opposing a President, the members of Congress are very much in the position of a man attempting to fashion an opposition movement out of the scattered pieces of a wriggling jigsaw puzzle. The President presumably knows what he wants to do to meet some problem that everyone concedes exists and must be dealt with. It is not enough merely to oppose him. One must also out-think him and his advisers, come up with some better way. Even resourceful Congressmen usually have difficulty doing this.

The constituencies of Congressmen are necessarily parochial. How some measure will affect congressional districts and states is the question that weighs with Congressmen. If they cannot show some clear-cut adverse or favorable result—and usually they cannot—they cannot count on much interest at home. Furthermore, most members of the electorate don't understand the ramifications of what is being talked about and a great many, engaged in non-political distractions, don't care one way or the other.

Because, in democratic theory, everyone should be interested in government, it is widely assumed in the United States that everyone *is* interested in government. Most Americans in fact are not at all interested in government and even less in the Constitution, which is taken on faith as represented. To a vast majority both are extremely boring subjects, of interest only when presented in terms of conflict, scandal or impending hardship.

The President under the Constitution, in other words, is ultra-powerful, far more powerful than is commonly thought by the general populace or many news commentators. Congress most of the time is a paper tiger, easily soothed or repulsed.

A President who knows what he is doing—and many Presidents, perhaps most, have not had a clear idea of how to handle the unnecessarily difficult office—can pretty well have his own way with Congress, provided of course that he doesn't propose too obviously drastic departures from the past. While it can be done, as Franklin D. Roosevelt showed, it cannot be done under all conditions because for such measures to succeed a President needs a substantial section of the politically alert sections of the populace on his side. Roosevelt had this. Also needed are favoring circumstances, which Roosevelt also had. And the President himself needs acumen, which Roosevelt also had.

As, despite all of the foregoing, presumably sage commentators have been heard on television to echo a widely propagated notion that the President *really* has little power under the Constitution (to say nothing of what he and his henchmen may do in secret outside it), I shall at this point introduce the man whom lawyers call an expert and highly qualified witness—none other than outspoken John Adams.

Adams felt that the prescribed power of the Presidency was practically plenary when pushed to its limit. According to his grandson, Charles Francis Adams, after editing the writings of his grandfather in 1859, "There can be no doubt, that John Adams regarded the constitution of the United States as forming a government more properly to be classed among monarchical than among democratic republics, an idea, suggested at the outset by Patrick Henry in America, and by Godwin in England, which has reappeared in some essays in late years.

"And the truth or falsity of this construction cannot be said, by any means, to be established by the mere half century's experience yet had of the system. For, although in practice the action of the chief magistrate has thus far conformed with tolerable steadiness to the popular wishes, this does not seem to have arisen from any power retained by the people to prevent him, had he inclined otherwise, so much as from the moderate desires of the men who have been elected to the post.

"It is a remark of M. de Tocqueville, respecting the United States, that there are multitudes who have a limited ambition, but none who cherish one on a very great scale. This may be true now, in the infancy of the country, and yet time may finally bring it under the influence of the general law of human experience elsewhere. Assuming the main check which existed for forty years, the chance of reelection, to be definitively laid aside, it is not easy to put the finger upon any clause of the constitution which can prevent an evil-disposed president [or one merely self-willed and contemptuous of the electorate] for four years from using the powers vested in him in what way he pleases, without regard to the people's wishes at all.

"Indeed, it is possible to go a step further, and to venture a doubt whether an adequate restraint can be found against the corrupt as well as despotic use of his authority—the sale of his patronage, as well as the perversion of his policy. The only tangible remedy,—that by impeachment,—is obviously insufficient." [22]

Adams goes on to point out that the impeachment process is sluggish, much time and effort are required to accumulate proof and in the meantime a President with the bit in his teeth is wielding the sweeping powers of his office.

When this was written Lincoln was still to demonstrate the limitless power of the office by quite literally salvaging the Union from militant internal foes with actions that were clearly unconstitutional in detail. Still to come were twentieth-century Presidents who would with rising emphasis show the vast power of the office for unsuspected mischief— Theodore Roosevelt, Woodrow Wilson, to some extent Franklin D. Roosevelt, and then with rising emphasis Kennedy, Lyndon B. Johnson and Nixon.

There eventually arose the notion that an imperial Presidency had been created by the perverse nature of the men holding the office, whereas the fact is that the office itself as constituted is imperial. That other Presidents did not utilize its powers as these just named did proves nothing. Many emperors down through history simply lolled in office, failed to use all their powers, were pussy-cats.

The powers are there, as the Presidencies of these men amply prove. The powers are not seriously limited in nature or scope. This fact poses a fundamental dilemma for every member of the electorate. If the President in question is one whom one supports and admires and feels is essential to the well-being of the nation, it is clear that he bears a crushing burden and responsibility. For so very much depends upon a single mortal. If, on the other hand, the President is one who arouses deep uneasiness and distrust, as many distrusted Nixon and Lyndon Johnson while they kept the nation for more than seven years in a pointless and disastrous presidentially decreed war, then the citizen must realize he is helpless under the constitutionally rigid leadership of a very undesirable person who cannot be got rid of save by explosive means.

Either way, whether he approves or disapproves the President, every citizen lives under a constitutional sword of Damocles. Or, put another way, he is like a rat in a constitutional trap. In no other constitutional system does so much depend upon one man, whether saintly or evil.

The consequences of the violent removal of an excellent and widely trusted President were shown after the assassination of Lincoln, which brought an incalculable amount of avoidable travail upon the nation for many decades. Some of these consequences were the harsh treatment of the South after the Civil War, the retaliatory harsh treatment by the South of the freed slaves, the impoverishment of the South economically and culturally for more than seventy years, and the deep blot on the nation's international image produced by its resultant highly popular racism—grass-roots democracy in action.

The assassination of President Kennedy may have had similar unwelcome consequences on the theory of his associates that he would not have pursued the Vietnam involvement, though he began it, as fanatically, remorselessly and destructively as the crude, simplistic and insensitive Johnson and Nixon.

The assassination of a British Prime Minister could not have such ill effects on public policy, as the British government consists of a Cabinet nearly every member of which is capable of functioning as Prime Minister. In any event, the policies for which a Prime Minister speaks are not his own but belong to a collectivity put up by a parliamentary majority elected by a popular majority. There is no such majority policy under the American Constitution. It is all *ad hoc* patchwork.

With four Presidents assassinated and four attempts which miscarried against three others, assassination must be considered part of the American constitutional process, a constitutional usage. It is clearly a process far more often successful than impeachment. And in three out of four instances it altered national policy. The assassination of McKinley, which enthroned Theodore Roosevelt, brought in its train vast presidentially induced changes in national policies.

As a consequence of these misdeeds the President is today one of the most heavily guarded constitutional officers in the world, at great cost to the taxpayers. Even so he is hardly safe.

High-rated Presidents

Instead of looking into the Constitution for the sources of the presidential power it would be well to consider some of the times when the President has acted unilaterally, in defiance either of Congress or the Supreme Court—or both—and of the plain language of the Constitution.

The stellar case concerns Lincoln, rated by appropriate experts as the stellar President in the history of the country. While some give the laurel wreath to Washington, most find Lincoln their top choice.[23] With this choice, for whatever it may be worth, I concur.

The ratings referred to were given in 1962 by seventy-five scholars, of whom fifty-eight were historians (an over-weighted category by an editor who was a historian), six political scientists (a category that should have been more heavily represented), three historian-political scientists, two journalists and six of miscellaneous occupation. Knowledgeable journalists, too, rather than historians might well have been more heavily represented.

Only five Presidents were considered "great" or given an A rating for performance in office—Lincoln, Washington, F. D. Roosevelt, Wilson and Jefferson, in that order. "Near great" or B were Jackson, T. Roosevelt, Polk, Truman, John Adams and Cleveland. In my view, Wilson and Jefferson too should be placed in this second category—Wilson because, while he had in him the makings of greatness, he really failed the country and Jefferson because his performance was far below that of the first three. Jefferson, despite many internal confusions, was unquestionably a great public man, but not a great President. All of the "near greats", one senses, had about them the capacity for being "great" but somehow missed.

The rest were "average" or C, a total of twelve, six below average, and two were rated failures—Grant and Harding. To these failures, it would seem, should be added more recently Lyndon Johnson and Nixon, with Ford possibly in the below-average group. As Kennedy clearly does not qualify for A or B rating, and was hardly "average", he seems to fall into the below-average group too.

Historians seem peculiarly susceptible of confusing the magnitude of an office and large events with greatness in the office-holder. There is too the insensible national pressure to cater to the wish of the populace that it is governed by great men, of the stamp of Washington. Nobody likes to feel that the country is governed by shabby characters although it often is, thanks to its loose selection processes. The totals given do not add up to the full number of Presidents because two are omitted owing to the extreme brevity of their service—William H. Harrison and Garfield.

American historians as a general rule have levelled their heaviest critical guns on four men, on whom there seems to be a perpetual historians' open season: Benedict Arnold, Aaron Burr, Grant and Harding. The critical acumen of the historians appears to flag with most others. A case in point is Wilson, who is generally vastly overrated, his potentiality confused with his calamitous foreign-policy blunders and wholesale civil-rights violations.

The reason Wilson is invariably rated so high, I surmise, is that so many people and institutions of continuing influence were implicated in his disastrous foreign policies and also that he himself was a professor—of political science, no less. I suspect that the professors cannot help but have an unconscious soft spot in their hearts for one of their own in the highest office, the only one in history.

Lincoln, at any rate, no professor, belongs in the American pantheon with Washington. And Lincoln, more than any other President, and justifiably, was the boldest, with the surest touch, in his extrapolations of the Constitution.

While he waited after the election of 1860 to be inaugurated on March 4, 1861, seven states of the Deep South announced they had seceded from the Union. *There* was a cruncher for any new President to deal with. Outgoing President Buchanan, rated by our scholars as the bottom-most of the below-average Presidents, opined that he could find nothing in the Constitution forbidding secession, a maneuver that had often been toyed with by ambitious state politicos since 1812. The clamor for it first arose in New England, not in the supposedly hot-headed South. Nor, if he had searched ever so hard, would Buchanan have found anything that gave warrant to form any government at all.

Such punctilious childishness had no appeal for Lincoln. Here he was, the chief executive officer of the country, sworn to preserve, protect and defend the Constitution and to enforce its laws. What should he do?

The North, and Congress, contained southern agitators and sympathizers—secessionists or general mischief-makers all. Half the Senate was allotted to the South, if one counts the so-called Border States. And there was an urgent need to act rapidly.

But the relevant constitutional powers were all allotted to Congress —suspension of habeas corpus in the event of rebellion (Article I, Section 9, Paragraph 2), the authority to call forth the militia to suppress insurrections (Article I, Section 8, Paragraph 15), the power of governing militia called into the national service, the power to borrow money (Section 8, Paragraph 2), and so on. What to do when a large section of Congress is traitorous?

Five weeks after the inauguration, a period of watchful waiting, South Carolina militia in a surprise attack opened fire on Fort Sumter in Charleston Harbor and forced its surrender. Here was armed violent rebellion. Lincoln on April 15, 1861, on his own authority, called for 75,000 volunteers, thereby leading five other states to secede, and went on to enlarge the army and navy, commandeer the railroad between

Washington and Baltimore, declare the suspension of the writ of habeas corpus along the line and eventually up to Boston, and in 1862 went on to establish conscription (to match southern conscription) which constitutional "authorities" such as Daniel Webster had long ago maintained was unconstitutional. Nothing whatever in the Constitution bars conscription, of men or even women—or children. He also then suspended the writ of habeas corpus for all persons suspected of "disloyal practices", surely a vague charge.[24]

His actions under these decrees, ultimately ratified by a Congress purged of doubtful elements, brought Lincoln almost at once into conflict with the courts.

Without habeas corpus available a person may be arrested and detained indefinitely without recourse to due process or a presentation in court, a situation analogous to the establishment of dictatorship. For dictators simply have people arrested and jailed, with or without being charged.

John Merryman, a Baltimore secessionist, was among others seized in 1861 by the military. He petitioned Chief Justice Taney of the Supreme Court, sitting as a circuit judge, for a writ of habeas corpus, which was granted. The writ was spurned by the military commander in charge and Taney cited him for contempt, holding that the power to suspend the writ was vested in Congress, denying that the President had the power to suspend the writ and condemning the suspension of constitutional rights by military order.[25] The President held to his position, retained Merryman. The commander did not stir.

As to all this, Taney was formally correct. But Lincoln was also correct. Waging war against a federal fort was illegal. The President had the explicit duty to "take care that the laws be faithfully executed". Moreover, he was the only person authorized by the Constitution to wield executive power. Nobody else could act. Congress was in disarray, harbored southerners and southern sympathizers, and it was difficult for a time to tell precisely who was for the Union and who against. It was a clear defect in the Constitution, one of many, that assigned the relevant powers to Congress alone, that segregated governmental powers in different compartments.

Lincoln simply "executed the office" of President of the United States. Taney condemned the *means* Lincoln took upon himself to use; history has vindicated Lincoln for attainment of the *ends,* the preservation of the Union, which the Constitution in its Preamble dedicates itself to.

Which was more important—the etiquette of the defective Constitution or the substance of the perilous situation? Had Lincoln waited for Congress to pull itself together the Civil War might have been over in a few weeks (as the South believed it would be) and secession would have succeeded. The South did not believe the North would fight for something so intangible as mere Union.

The contest between Lincoln and Taney illustrates that it makes a difference what premises one selects from the Constitution for one's syllogisms. Premises can be chosen freely, wherever the inclination of the chooser dictates. In other words, the choice devolves upon men, not laws. It is this that gives officials, notably the President, a free hand.

As to Congress, resentment in it arising from personal pique at Lincoln's assumption without congressional authorization of what are now known as "war powers", led to the establishment by the radical Republicans of a joint committee on the conduct of the war which by its blundering activity impeded the proper prosecution of the war and probably prolonged it, a sample of representative democracy at work under a defective system. There was no question that Lincoln in what he did acted for any ends of his own, personal or political.

With Lincoln having shown the way by setting precedents in an emergency, there is no need to examine in detail the autonomous actions of later Presidents that stretched the Constitution beyond mechanical legalistic and schoolroom preconceptions. In most instances such actions are taken by Presidents under color of an emergency, sometimes fictitious. The Constitution makes no mention of allowable departures from constitutional etiquette under emergencies. The emergencies cited by Presidents do not all withstand critical scrutiny. Lyndon Johnson and Richard Nixon, victims of egocentric afflatus, created "emergencies" out of thin air. Nixon, who frequently invoked the name of Lincoln, appealed vaguely to alleged dangers to the national security in extenuation of numerous misdeeds perpetrated in his own political and financial interest. Franklin D. Roosevelt had a genuine economic emergency to contend with upon taking office, and then a wartime emergency, and took great constitutional liberties in a variety of directions. The costly Manhattan Project that produced the fateful atomic bomb was the product of a simple executive order. Nobody at the time, least of all the President, understood the full historical implications of the action.

The first steps toward building a free-wheeling intelligence apparatus for the United States were taken by means of a secret executive order from President Roosevelt in 1936, at first directed at the German Nazis and their supporters in the country, later at Communists and their fellow-travelers, native and Russian. All the subsequent steps in creating widespread intelligence services, from the Office of Strategic Services to the Central Intelligence Agency, were presidentially initiated and supervised. The American intelligence apparatus is wholly an arm of the Presidency, with Congress carefully keeping as far as possible away from it apart from blindly voting funds.

Now, the world being what it is and Russia long a virtuoso practitioner of the black art of espionage, the United States obviously needs an effective intelligence service. To suggest anything different is to stamp oneself at best as utterly naive. But from the 1950s onward this new apparatus, including the Federal Bureau of Investigation and the intelligence services of all the armed forces, was increasingly directed, and provocatively, at disaffected domestic political groups, many of them merely eccentric, and under Kennedy, Johnson and Nixon in the 1960s against political opponents and general nay-sayers. Martin Luther King came under intimate surveillance under the Kennedy administration.

Anything that wasn't straight Republican-Democratic pork-barrel politics was suspect by intelligence voodoo men as of hostile foreign derivation, part of a world plot to subvert the cloud-cuckooland American Dream. The White House itself was always the main impetus for illegal actions. And the literature dealing with this perverted underground government activity, already large, is steadily growing.

For the main enemy of the politicians was among the illusion-saturated populace, its ears still ringing with the campaign slogans of 1776.

All the actions of Presidents, unless rejected by a vociferous public opinion, usually lacking, become precedents for subsequent Presidents. Power accumulates, waits in storage, as it were, for future use. But Presidents alone in the American system are in a position to perform such actions, whatever they are, and without consulting a single soul.

So powerful have Presidents shown themselves to be that presidential government has become a world-wide term used in contrast with parliamentary government, and most of the present-day dictators of the world style themselves presidents, not kings or emperors.

What it all shows of course is that one is, always, governed by men, not by prefabricated laws. It also shows that laws and minutely prescriptive systems of government cannot be devised that will anticipate all events.

According to prevalent theory, if Congress and the President together enact a law that is not in harmony with the Constitution as read by lawyers, the Supreme Court will disallow it and it will fall by the wayside. Franklin D. Roosevelt, again showing the power of the Presidency, shot holes in this theory.

To deal with the economic emergency of the Depression, Congress and the President in the 1930s enacted a series of untraditional laws that were steadily and rapidly held unconstitutional by the Supreme Court.[26]

Returned to office in 1936 by a popular landslide that left him losing only two minor states, the President proposed to Congress on February 5, 1937, a plan for reorganizing the federal judiciary. It made no mention of the disputed Supreme Court decisions; on the surface it seemed purely technical. The plan innocently asked for an increase in the membership of the Supreme Court from nine to a maximum of fifteen if judges refused to retire at age 70; the addition of not more than fifty judges of all classes to the courts; the sending of appeals from lower-court decisions directly to the Supreme Court; permission for government attorneys to be heard before any lower court issued an injunction against the enforcement of any act of Congress when a question of constitutionality was at issue; and the assignment of district judges to congested areas so as to expedite court business, which Roosevelt misleadingly claimed was greatly in arrears.

Anti-New Dealers, masquerading as devotees of a thrice-sacred God-ordained Constitution, attacked the bill in terms just as devious, accusing the President of attempted "court packing" with subservient judges. Since Washington all Presidents had sought to pack the Court with men of their own political outlook. At one time the Court held only six men. Washington appointed only politically active tried and true Federalists. Here and there Presidents miscalculated and appointed an independent mind. Theodore Roosevelt appointed Holmes and ever after bemoaned the fact. Eisenhower thought his appointment of Warren as Chief Justice a terrible mistake. Yet experts rate Holmes and Warren as among the best Supreme Court Justices.

The attack on the Judiciary Reorganization Bill split the Democrats in Congress, many of them, at bottom, mechanical constitutional formalists and traditionalists. Despite the failing prospects for the bill, Roosevelt, unaccountably to many observers in view of his "pragmatism", fought even harder for it. He took the fight to the country, now getting down to the issues at stake. At an inaugural dinner on March 4, 1937, he said that the "personal economic predilections" of the Court had made it impossible for the federal and state governments to deal with serious social and economic problems. In a radio address he charged that the courts had "cast doubts on the ability of the elected Congress to protect us against catastrophe by meeting squarely our modern social and economic conditions" and held that the intention of the bill was to restore the balance of power among the three branches of the federal government.

Extraneous factors contributed to a weakening of support for the bill. The Supreme Court Retirement Act, approved by Roosevelt, came into effect on March 1 and allowed Justices to retire—with full pay—at age 70. The forthcoming retirement of Justice Willis Van Devanter, one of the arch-foes of New Deal legislation, was announced on May 18.

On July 14 Joseph T. Robinson of Arkansas, majority leader in the Senate fight for the reorganization of the Court, died and support for the bill weakened.

Additionally, the Supreme Court, an eye on the recent election returns, had suddenly taken to validating significant New Deal and state legislation—the Frazier-Lemke Farm Mortgage Moratorium Act of 1935, the Washington State minimum-wage law for women, the Social Security Act and the Wagner Labor Relations Act. Anti-New Dealers had been frenzied in their opposition to these measures.

On July 22 the Senate by a 70 to 20 vote recommitted the reorganization bill to the judiciary committee, where it was allowed to die, and on August 26 the President signed the Judicial Procedure Reform Act, a face-saving measure, which altered procedures in the lower courts.

About all this one can read, depending upon the writers, two versions: the first is that the President lost ignominiously in his unholy attempt to "tamper" with the Court and the sacred Constitution, the second that he lost the skirmish but won the war. For in the next four years he filled seven vacancies on the Court with Justices of his own choice, replacing aged mainly Republican appointees who resigned under presidential fire.

What the entire episode demonstrated was the paramountcy of presidential power. Roosevelt unquestionably did not want to undermine the Court permanently or generally, or he would have proceeded differently, would not have persisted in pushing for his oblique plan as he did long after it was obviously dead. All he wanted to do was to clear the way for necessary social and economic legislation, which he did. He brought the Court to heel, sharply.

The magnitude of the President's victory cannot be appreciated unless one notices that since the Supreme Court held unconstitutional the Bituminous Coal Conservation Act of 1936 in *Carter v. Carter Coal Co.* (298 U.S. 238, 1936) it has not to date found invalid a single piece of general national economic or social legislation although much of it has since been placed on the books. Instead the Court has concentrated on the long-neglected area of civil liberties, tardily bringing the first eight amendments to apply to the states through the mediation of the Fourteenth Amendment to the Constitution—"No State shall make or enforce any law which shall abridge the privileges or immunities of citizens of the United States, or shall any State deprive any person of life, liberty, or property, without due process of law; nor deny to any person within its jurisdiction the equal protection of the laws."

The application of these lines alone to hitherto free-ranging state officials, many of whom performed down through the decades like power-drunk storm-troopers under an averted federal eye, amounted to a small revolution.

Prior to the advent of the New Deal the Supreme Court had also made free use of this amendment in a heavily edited version that made it read, "No State shall make any law to deprive any person of property, without due process of law." Under that reading the Supreme Court had freely invalidated state laws written to regulate socially disruptive economic activities and their effects. The Court furthermore had invented substantive due process, of which there was no mention in the Constitution or in law. The Court repeatedly held that social and economic regulation, as heavily subsidized Republican newspapers cheered, was unconstitutional, thrusts at the holy ghost of liberty. Government, on this one-sided reading, which for many decades generally found favor in Congress and the White House, was powerless to act in economic and social matters. Laissez-faire prevailed for business and property interests but, oddly, for nobody else. As a consequence, the rich became richer—the old, old story.

It is as an illustration of latent presidential power that the "court fight" is constitutionally significant. It demonstrates that one should never under-estimate the power of the President under the Constitution, nor over-estimate that of the Supreme Court.

Incidents from the incumbencies of other Presidents—Cleveland, Theodore Roosevelt, Wilson, Truman—buttress this contention, but the performances of Lincoln and Franklin D. Roosevelt alone are sufficient to establish the point. Naturally, no President brings all his power to bear at all times. There is no need for that. But in the face of any need this is where constitutional power lies—in the Presidency. And a President who does not use this power as needed may be as harmful as one who over-uses or abuses it. Under-kill may be as dangerous as over-kill.

The responsibility for the right use of power therefore depends on the judgement of one man alone, more often than not an untried person of circumscribed experience and, as the long run of history shows, often neither perceptive nor knowledgeable.

Single-handed Presidential Actions

A few episodes illustrative of singlehanded presidential power will serve to reinforce the point.

In 1793 George Washington issued a proclamation of neutrality in relation to warring France and Great Britain and warned all Americans to abstain from acts of belligerency against either. Neither the Constitution nor any statute gave Washington the authority to issue such a proclamation. In so doing, Washington undercut anyone in Congress who might have wanted to propose war against either side. Washington, in other words, made a pre-emptive strike against the legislature.

Merely by making an announcement of policy, especially in the sphere of foreign affairs, the President can determine the course of the country, no matter how strong popular or congressional sentiment may be to the contrary. In 1793 popular sentiment distinctly favored France, allied during the war against Great Britain and tied to the United States by the treaty of 1778 which pledged the United States to come to the assistance of France. Washington's proclamation simply nullified this treaty.

In 1940 President Roosevelt turned over to Great Britain fifty re-conditioned naval destroyers. In doing so he violated several statutes plus the Constitution's allotment of power to Congress alone to "dispose property of the United States" (Article IV, Section 3). While the action met with popular applause, it violated the Constitution—trampled on it, in fact.

Under the Jay Treaty with Britain, President John Adams extradited the first fugitive from justice although the law did not specifically allow such action.

In all these instances Congress later, sometimes much later, passed enabling legislation. It did not provide for extradition until 1848. What this serves to point up is that the President often fills interstices in the law. He often acts where there is no law, and Congress later formally makes the law. Or it does not. In this role the President is obviously a one-man legislator. As we have seen, he also violates the law as well as the Constitution on occasion.

Congress or the Supreme Court too may sometimes invalidate a President's action, but as such invalidation usually comes long after the event the original act stands as a *fait accompli*. Congress and the Supreme Court merely lock the barn door after the horses are gone. Thus, after the bombing of Pearl Harbor by the Japanese the President decreed military government for the Territory of Hawaii, which con-tinued throughout the war. In 1946, the issue now moot, a divided Supreme Court ruled that the President had no constitutional power to do what he had done.[27]

Suppositiously a President may now never act similarly under similar circumstances, for the Supreme Court has said what the Constitution "means" in these respects. But, judging by governmental practice, this is not so. A future President may proceed in exactly the same way because the ruling of the Court applies only to the specific cases before it. As lawyers say, different facts enter into different cases and call for new rulings, which may necessarily be delayed until the issue is dead.

Whether or not any law or the Constitution gives explicit sanction for some action, the President alone, one person, possesses constitutional executive power. If he cannot or does not act, nobody can. As to this, the document is absolutely explicit.

While the Constitution in no respect calls for inaction, the way it divides its powers would produce inaction in many situations if constitutional prescriptions were adhered to. Had Lincoln waited for Congress to bring into play the powers allotted to it the Union almost certainly would have been shattered.

The Constitution divides powers the way it does because the precedent colonial and Confederation state governments were so divided. The division of powers is, then, a mere copy of what preceded, no innovation. It is often said that the framers got the idea of a division of powers from Montesquieu's *The Spirit of the Laws* (1748) or Locke's *Second Treatise of Government* (1690). But as the colonial governments had already evolved such a system when Locke wrote, the conception could not have originated with him or Montesquieu although what these men wrote may well have reminded the framers of the notion, given it greater force.

In the colonies the legislatures were elected by the eligible electorate, mainly property-owners. The governor was appointed by the King, and the governor in turn appointed a council to advise on legislation. There was often considerable tension and hostility between the governors and the legislatures as there still often is between Congress and the President and between governors and state legislatures. In colonial times the governors had a clear upper hand, able to dissolve the legislature in most of the colonies.

The judges of the courts, independent of legislature or governor, were also appointed by the King and served during his pleasure. But the judges were usually nominated by the governors. As governors and judges were the King's appointees there was hardly much genuine separation between the two but formally at least the executive was separated from the judiciary and each was separated from the legislature.

The revolutionary state governments adhered to this pattern but concentrated most power in the legislatures, elected by "the people", and made governors, and to some extent courts, dependent upon them— a fact disliked by the framers of the United State Constitution.

Hence the tripartite division of powers and the resultant system of checks and balances, which is supposed to prevent one branch from prevailing by subjecting it to salutary intervention by the others. What is overlooked is that the mechanisms of intervention by Congress and the Supreme Court against the executive are so ponderous and subject to such long delay that the executive most of the time has a very free hand. And if he gets support from one of the other branches, the sweep of his power is practically Napoleonic.

This supposed system of equitable checks and balances does not exist in fact. The main check lies with the President, either on Congress or the Supreme Court. Neither of these in fact exerts much check on the President as I've just shown. True, if Congress could mobilize and discipline itself, which thus far it has been unable to do, it might prevail by constitutional procedures, either over the President or over the Supreme Court. Congress however can exert itself effectively only spasmodically because Congress, like the populace at large, is deeply divided on most questions. It is also liberally interlarded with pecuniary adventurers.

In any event, the separation in the Constitution between the legislative and the executive is wholly artificial, like the supposed separation in individual people between will and action. What an entity *does*, individual or institutional, is its will. The will is not something separate and apart from action, desiring to prevail but unable to act.

Presidents under the Constitution, without giving either Congress or the Supreme Court an opportunity to check them, simply act as action seems necessary to them. If Presidents make a mistake, the country is committed to the mistake and must bear the consequences. Under the British Constitution the powers of a collective executive and the legislature are fused, a fact that Montesquieu did not discern because at that early stage the fusion was not explicit and formalized but was in the process of developing. Montesquieu derived his view from Locke.

Franklin D. Roosevelt during World War II stretched his powers as Commander in Chief to the limit. Industrial relations throughout the war for example were governed by simple presidential agreements made with representatives of employer associations and trades unions. Under the agreements labor, via unions, was pledged not to strike and employers not to use the lock-out. All disputes were referred to the War Labor Board for settlement. This body, appointed by the President, had no legal status; its decisions were purely advisory.

When the board's decisions were not accepted, the President would intervene and bring to bear on recalcitrants the threat of "indirect sanctions". Non-compliant workers were faced with the prospect of induction into the armed forces if they were eligible, and employers holding war contracts would be ordered not to employ those ineligible for military service. Non-compliant employers were faced with being denied "priorities" for materials or having their plants seized by the government under legislation that permitted this when "necessary production" faltered. Just what "necessary production" might be lay within the determination of the President. This was pure dictatorship.

The mere threat of such actions was enough in most instances to obtain compliance with the wishes of the White House. President Truman therefore was not unusually high-handed when during the presidentially decreed Korean War he ordered his Secretary of Commerce to seize and operate most of the steel industry in order to avert a strike of the steel-workers. He cited the requirements of national defense and "the authority vested in me by the Constitution and laws of the United States".

Before the order was executed it was blocked by an injunction from a court which was sustained by the Supreme Court.[28] Here, suddenly, we see a President challenged and the procedure abandoned. Why? Was Truman as far off base as his political opponents maintained? Not at all. The President acted under a vast accumulation of legislation piled up by Congress since World War I and on into World War II. He and his advisers decided for their own reasons against fighting the court order.

As Corwin summarizes them, these accumulated powers allowed the President "to control absolutely the transportation and distribution of food stuffs; to fix prices; to license importation, exportation, manufacture, storage, and distribution of the necessaries of life; to operate the railroads; to issue passports; to control cable and telegraph lines; to declare embargoes; to determine priority of shipments; to loan money to foreign governments; to enforce Prohibition; to redistribute and regroup the executive bureaus; and in carrying these powers into effect the President's authorized agents put in operation a huge number of executive regulations having the force of law; and the two War Powers Acts and other legislation repeated this pattern in World War II." [29]

What the Court did in its *Youngstown* decision was to discern a distinction between a general and declared war and a localized war carried on by simple executive decision, of which latter there have been many in American history.

In the Youngstown case Justice Frankfurter, in a concurring opinion, pointed out that eighteen statutes authorizing such seizures had been passed between 1916 and 1951 and that Presidents, *without specific statutory authorization,* had carried out eight seizures in World War I and eleven in the World War II period. Some of these seizures took place before the opening of actual hostilities.[30]

The War Labor Disputes Act of 1943 validated such seizures by statute—shades of property rights!—and the Supreme Court later upheld this law.[31]

Four justices in the Youngstown case, with three more in partial and varying agreement, thought that the President in the absence of specific restrictive legislation does possess residual or granted authority to deal with emergencies he considers threatening to national security! Says Corwin, "The lesson of the case, therefore, if it has a lesson, is that escape from Presidential autocracy today is to be sought along the legislative route rather than that of judicial review".[32]

But the American legislature, as I have shown, has great difficulty in pulling itself together, especially if faced with presidential opposition. Until the American electorate creates effective political parties (which it has never done), Congress will never be able to direct Presidents, will always be pretty much under their thumb. An effective political party is one able to translate its program into public policy and to keep conflicting programs from becoming public policy. If done democratically, this is done openly and directly, as in Britain, not surreptitiously. It is done in full view in the legislature, not piecemeal in obscure courts and executive backrooms. In the United States, contrary to free-running propaganda, there is in fact little democracy and there are very few actual democrats.

In the absence of legislation by Congress the President is the governor of conquered territory, in charge of the landing of foreign cables in the United States, and may establish military commissions in territory occupied by United States armed forces.[33]

But all is not lost; the power of the President is not absolute. For if an order of the President or one of his subordinates is not according to law (assuming there is a law on the subject), it "will be set aside by the courts *if a case involving it comes before them*" (emphasis added).[34]

What this indicates is that the injured party should get in touch with his lawyers and bring a defensive lawsuit. As perhaps 75 per cent or more of the populace is not aware of the full spectrum of their formal rights and moreover could not afford the great expense of this kind of lawsuit, the remedial action is obviously available only to clearly affluent interests, with respect to which government is most of the time very punctilious in its behavior. With these it carries on like two gentlemen fencers.

As one goes through all the fine print involved—which Corwin presents—the chances of anyone recovering damages is practically negligible.

So the President in the American constitutional system is very much a *de facto* king and is, as such, either good, bad or indifferent according to whatever criteria are brought to bear by the judicious observer.

Nine

THE RISKS
IN ONE-MAN RULE

"It is now the general consensus, and it can be persuasively argued among contemporary justices of the Supreme Court, that there is *no limit* to the Chief Executive's power," said the late Herman Finer, who was for many years one of the leading political scientists of the nation.[1] "For example, in the absence of congressional action, the President may, at his discretion, have all aliens interned, seize for public use all property containing steel, or suspend, as Lincoln did, the procedure of habeas corpus."[2] He can also, should the occasion arise, direct the troops to enforce any order of his own or of the courts.

He may indeed go much, much further than this, depending upon circumstances. He can, as legal proceedings grind on, have whatever category of people one names summarily interned, segregated in concentration camps, on the plea of some threat to national safety, as was done with Americans of Japanese descent after Pearl Harbor. Acting with congressional approval, he can relocate masses of people over thousands of miles of distance as has been done repeatedly for 150 years with native Indians. To be sure, adopting the prevailing popular view, such people "don't count", a touch of grass-roots democray. What all this amounts to, simply, is government at its fullest, which is never a minuet. Many a dawdling taxpayer has learned this the hard way.

Prof. Finer taught variously at Yale, Harvard and the Universities of Chicago and London and subjected the Presidency to intensive analysis in a book published long before Watergate or the outcry about "the imperial Presidency". Added to his penetrating analysis he offered suggestions for constitutional changes that would, while modernizing the office of President, preserve intact the basic outlines and general spirit of the Constitution.

He depicted the President as overweighted with responsibilities and at the same time having lawfully concentrated in his hands the means for rash and irresponsible actions either by himself or by anonymous hired deputies. The Watergate episode proved he was correct. In so far as the President delegates decision-making to underlings or defers to their judgement, both a matter of simple necessity, the American people are to a great extent governed by faceless persons unknown to them. Such even write presidential speeches and decrees.

One could develop a considerable argument that the American people are not really governed by the President, Congress or the Supreme Court but by thousands of the President's deputies, at least in large part. As of 1958 for example, as Finer points out, the President submitted to the Senate the names of 59,079 appointees, since which time the total has risen. No individual can keep track of such a mass.

The basic function of the President (leaving out the ceremonial, the symbolic and the nominal leadership of his always discordant political party), is one of decision-making. There are so many decisions to be made that no single person could make them all, good or bad, so the President must rely on personally chosen assistants.

Not only is the American system of government in consequence extremely problematic but it can be shown to be such merely through the works down through the years of leading political scientists of all colorations—left, right and centrist. The net approach of political science to the American government is to see it studded with internal problems, fundamental and otherwise—all of which is suggested in these pages but largely unknown to the populace.

One could, in other words, compile a treatise, citing only from the works of leading political scientists, that would show the constitutional system, so fulsomely hailed in propaganda directed toward the largely uninterested populace, as full of cracks. In any event, the system as it functions does not function as represented in the lower schools and in the newspapers. That is one dead certainty and the only one I would insist upon. As a result the politicians are free to extemporize, unrestrained by the constitutional pseudo-fetters.

One man cannot make all decisions, even if he is intelligent and quick-witted. In this respect the Presidency is inefficient and irresponsible. All major policy decisions are the President's responsibility, but the decisions themselves are likely to have been made by the President's hired advisers, who in most cases cannot be held responsible, cannot be replaced, and cannot be dismissed by the electorate.[3]

What has happened is that the nation has long ago burst the constitutional straitjacket fashioned by the framers, designed to keep the country on a certain political track. The straitjacket was burst wide open in the Civil War, if not before in less spectacular ways, and has continued to be "let out".

One could cite many instances but let me here, by way of illustration, merely consider the First Amendment, the fetish of all civil libertarians. According to this amendment, "Congress shall make no law respecting an establishment of religion, or prohibiting the free exercise thereof; or abridging the freedom of speech, or of the press; or the right of the people peaceably to assemble, and to petition the Government for a redress of grievances."

As I have shown, the amendments constituting what is called the Bill of Rights were proposed in the early Congress to quell the clamor for a second convention, which would have undone the work of the Federalists in the first convention. As such, they served their purpose. Even at this late date, with many people fully alert, a general constitutional convention would be regarded by all constitutional adepts as a snake pit. It would, like the original one, violate its mandate and go much further than expected. Its authority would be ultimate, subject only to the process of ratification by three-fourths of state legislatures or conventions.

If words have any meaning, Congress, the chief legislative body of the country, may have nothing whatever to say about religion or its exercise, speech, the press, or public assembly—all of which are widely exercised human activities. Simply on the face of it such a prohibition, taken as a guide for future government actions, is foolish and automatically null.

Actually, the amendment as it stands was long ago shot full of holes. And in fact the amendment is not reasonable. If the admendment read, "In so far as public order permits, Congress shall make no law", etc., it would be more nearly in accord with a reasonable approach to realities. But it does not. As it is, Congress has in fact many times made laws breaching the amendment and has been sustained by the Supreme Court in a long line of cases.[4]

In time of declared war, for example, some people—sometimes for good reason—wish to disseminate one of three lines of thought: the government erred grievously in allowing the nation to enter the war; people should do all in their power not to co-operate with the war-making operation; and, a different tangent of objection, the government is not prosecuting the war properly and should mend its ways or be dismissed. No government this side of bedlam is going to tolerate these sorts of political counter-offensive in the midst of savage conflict, no matter what words appear on a piece of paper, and the United States government does not tolerate them as many cases show.

The laws of criminal libel, too, completely negate the provision.

As to religion, the government does in fact make laws "respecting an establishment of religion" and its "free exercise".

"The best-known instance in which public policy was held to limit the practice of certain religious tenets (e.g. polygamy) was in the anti-Mormon cases preceding Utah's admission to statehood. The use of public streets and parks for preaching has been denied, and the denial upheld, where the habit of the sect was to attack other religious sects; and where a license was issued to all, without leaving any discretion to the issuing officer as to when a license was to be granted, the licensing principle has been sustained . . .

"A state law requiring officeholders to affirm a belief in God has been invalidated as a religious qualification under both the 'establishment' and 'free exercise' clauses. But certain religious beliefs other than polygamy have been held in conflict with public policy—e.g., resistance to compulsory vaccination and [to] drug control laws . . ." [5]

No religious tenet against children's being schooled, for example, would be allowed to go unchallenged and unextirpated.

Most striking in the making of laws respecting religious establishments is the grant to them of tax immunity on all church properties, including revenue-producing investments. Such immunity was upheld by the Supreme Court as recently as 1970 (*Walz v. Tax Commission*, 397 U.S. 664).

But in giving tax immunity to church property the Court contradicts several other sections of the Constitution, notably the equal-protection clause of the Fourteenth Amendment as well as the establishment clause itself. If tax exemption is given to one class of property-holders, the burden of taxation is increased for others and in effect a subsidy has been granted to the tax-free institution at others' expense.

Educational and charitable institutions are similarly given exemption but these can be shown to contribute to public well-being in concrete ways. It is unsupported, undemonstrable theory that religion makes such a contribution and the course of history shows that religion is often—very often—a disorder-provoking factor.

In any event, there has been sufficient adherence to an official hands-off policy with respect to religion to allow the mushrooming of pseudo-religious movements that amount to little more than cynical money-collecting and mind-distorting enterprises, all tax-exempt and virtually free of official scrutiny. These segregate their dupes and in various ways intimidate them. But the day of such immunity may have ended with the dramatic disclosures of the sinister and indeed subversive nature of the Rev. Jim Jones's Peoples Temple, which terminated in 1978 with the suicide and murder of nearly one thousand duped Americans in a Guyana commune. The Constitution and its officialdom certainly failed to protect these.

A sign of the times may be seen in proceedings of the State of California against the Worldwide Church of God, founded in 1934 and consisting of 70,000 reported members yielding an income to the church of $70 million annually. The members contribute 10 per cent of their income to the church.

The California attorney general first accused top executives of the church, including an attorney paid a reported $200,000 per year, of looting the assets of the church and living in profligate style, and then had appointed a temporary receiver and barred church executives from church offices and records.

Said one of the church officials of the proceedings, "This is unconstitutional." Said another, "In the annals of the Constitution, these are days of infamy. There have been no blacker days in history." [6] Not only does money talk, it can also scream.

As to the press, in recent years there have been frequent clashes between the right of the press to proceed unhampered in getting certain information and the desire of the courts during trials to learn the sources of such information, which could have a bearing on someone's guilt or innocence. Here one runs into a flat constitutional contradiction—between the right of the press to conceal its sources, because for lack of such concealment possible informants will remain mute, and the right of a defendant to obtain information that may acquit him, the essence of a fair trial. Courts have been inclining increasingly toward upholding defendants' rights, which augers ill for supposed absolute press freedom.

In any event, the press is not always so keen on contending for its absolute First Amendment rights. In time of fully declared war, for example, the press enters into "voluntary" agreements with the executive branch to practice restraint in the dissemination of certain news and—necessarily, as it seems to me—agrees to be guided by the government in much of what it prints, which amounts to clandestine censorship, abhorrent to righteous constitutionalists. Nearly all of the press (excepting in the final stages the *New York Times*) did not know about the Manhattan Project for producing the atomic bomb, nor did Congress or the American people. But the Soviet Union, as it turned out, was well informed through its ubiquitous spy network. Under the screen of wartime censorship, moreover, government can and does conceal a great deal that has nothing to do with the war effort. The courts therefore can interpret away even absolute constitutional prohibitions that give so much reading pleasure to many citizens.

Beyond all this, freedom of the press entails far more than most libertarians suppose. It is double-edged. For under freedom of the press one may elect not to publish something of vital importance or to shade the significance of what one publishes. The post-Watergate revelations relating to the F.B.I., the Justice Department, the C.I.A. and hundreds of corporations brought out much of a seamy nature that the press for many years had ignored even though many preliminary clues and free-lance writings had suggested much might be amiss. J. Edgar Hoover, director of the F.B.I., was long a press hero although as early as the 1950s Fred J. Cook, a respectable freelance writer and well-known former newspaper man had written about him and his bureau in critical terms that should have aroused general press attention.

The press of course aimed to be what it thought was "constructive" —that is, to take officially approved people at face value or a little more. But this, as all history shows, is a thoroughly unsound attitude. Governments, the business world, politics, the legal profession have all particularly shown themselves for centuries as open frontiers along which one cannot be too sure what anyone is up to. None of these environments, to speak of no others, are noted for their proliferation of Nobel laureates or other certified characters, and the press, as an instrument of information, should not assume that, particularly in the areas named, there are many candidates for laurel wreaths. And the hidden story, as Watergate showed, is always more interesting than the gilded, reassuring surface—and more sobering.

A Proposed Executive Group

In order to improve the Presidency, relieve one man of so much responsibility, minimize incompetency or villainy in the office and increase its efficiency, Prof. Finer proposed that a collective and supportive leadership be formed around the chief executive.

The leadership would consist of the President and a Cabinet of eleven Vice Presidents, all elected on the same ticket every four years and without limit on the re-eligibility to office of any one of them. They would be nominated by the conventions of each political party, as at present.

The President and his elected Cabinet of Vice Presidents would have the same term of office as Congress, where the term of the Senate would be reduced to four years and that of the House raised to four years, so that all—President, Cabinet and Congress—would be elected on the same platform. Alternatively, all might be given a concurrent term of five years, thereby soothing diminished Senators.

With one-third of the Senate now elected every two years, the House every two years and the one-man executive every four years there emerges "no clearly visible line of authority, responsibility or concerted policy. It splits the power to make policy, disperses it, obscures it. It splits the voters' acknowledgement of their own duty to accept the consequences of their choices and thus to be sensitive (in anticipation) of their own duty to accept the consequences of the leadership they have chosen, or rather the leaderships, rival and clashing leaderships." [7]

But these disparities in the legislature and executive were precisely what the framers worked so hard to achieve—in order, precisely, to frustrate the electorate.

As a consequence of the shared platform the President and his Cabinet stood on for election along with Congress, the party caucus in Congress would establish a firmer link with the executive, Finer maintains. Party cohesion would become more important.

To be eligible for President or Vice President the candidates, Finer recommended, should have served in either house of Congress for at least four years—this so as to be sure of having men in high office who are familiar with the operations of national government. If it is argued that Congress harbors many of dubious breed, Finer points out that "The character and operation of Congress will improve as its members gain in stature and repute; and this will be so if Congress becomes the one arena in which a man's demonstrated prowess in the tasks of legislation and executive devices and control (in everyday rivalry with fellow members) is the sole access to highest office." [8]

More opportunities for political advancement would be opened to many men by this scheme, Finer argues, and so would tend to bring into politics abler men, replacing many of the traditional dubious operators.

As it is now, Presidents (and no other particular men high in government) have usually been either former Senators or Governors of states, sometimes former Cabinet officers or Vice Presidents. For a lone man to go from one of these modest offices to the Presidency taking with him nobody else of nearly comparable authority or status, amounts to a dizzying transformation that has visibly intoxicated some with feelings of limitless power. To the outward view everyone in politics, back-slapping and hand-shaking all around, seems pretty equal. But the present distance between a President and whomever is judged to be next to him in authority is enormous, almost astronomical. A President at present is a giant among midgets, a veritable potentate.

Prof. Finer would allow the President to name the Vice President who would be his successor in the event of his departure for any reason.

Under the Constitution now the Vice President, as everyone knows, is virtually a nonentity. His sole duty is to preside over the Senate (and most Vice Presidents turn this job over to a substitute presiding officer) and to cast the tie-breaking vote when the Senate deadlocks. In the nation's history Vice Presidents have cast about 200 such votes or an average of about one per year.[9]

While the President under Finer's plan would continue to determine ultimate policy as at present, he would always carry with him the authority of his eleven-man elected Cabinet, each member of which would be responsible for one of the major departments of the government. If any Cabinet member seriously disagreed with some line of presidential policy, he would be permitted to resign and the President would have the power to dismiss any or all of his Cabinet and appoint others from Congress to take their place. But members of a formal Cabinet would always be present, if only as witnesses to presidential decisions.

Prof. Finer would have the President and his Cabinet sit in the House of Representatives and take the lead there, with the First Vice President allowed from time to time to sit in his place. The Senate would be stripped of its special powers over treaties and appointments —enough by itself to make the Senate unanimously against the plan.

While the President would retain his veto power, he could, under Finer's plan, be overruled by 55 per cent of the House. The Senate would have no role in overriding the veto.

But the President and his Cabinet might reciprocally resign en masse, in which case there would be new elections for President, Cabinet members, House and Senate. Congress, in checking a President, would always be forced to consider that it might be obliged to run the gauntlet of an election, face "the people". Congress seldom relishes this prospect.

There is more to Finer's scheme for rather drastic alterations in the executive branch of the Constitution and they are well worth reading. It is noticeable that by it he aimed to make the American government more like the highly responsible British government, without going quite that far, instead of leaving it to operate, as it does now, out of various holes and corners so that nobody can be sure of just what it is doing, playing a cat-and-mouse game with the electorate—and itself! And also failing to devise coherent policies, especially in the important economic sphere.

I present a brief outline of Finer's plan, not because I believe it can or should necessarily be adopted, for as anyone can see it has been ignored by the politicians, was never even given deserved public dis-

cussion. What is interesting about the plan is the implications it con-
veys in the views of an outstanding political scientist about the fulsomely
lauded American government, the laudations always coming from those
having an above-average beneficial interest in it. Such laudations seldom
come from political scientists, who know better. As Finer observes,
"Many scholars have been disturbed by the inadequacy of the Presidency
to discharge the responsibilities with which the office is charged today
and have made various proposals to regenerate the political leadership
of the nation." [10] In an appendix Finer summarizes the proposals of
some of these men, all outstanding scholars—Edward S. Corwin, Charles
S. Hyneman, William Y. Elliott, Charles Hardin and Paul T. David,
variously attached in their time to the leading universities of the
country.[11] The list could be greatly extended, not a radical, subversive
or fanatic in the bunch.

What were Prof. Finer's motives in writing this book shortly before
his death? He gives it as follows: "The cardinal fact that frightens me
in the present situation is that *all* responsibility falls on one man, who
may be inept politicially." [12]

As if to buttress his argument, history capped his book with the
ill-starred Presidencies of Kennedy, Lyndon Johnson, Nixon and Ford.
Finer unerringly analyzed the system that led to the Watergate and
post-Watergate revelations of rampant but well-concealed wrong-doing
and high-handedness.

As to the probability of achieving any of the changes proposed by
Finer and other political scientists in the foreseeable future, that is
reduced to a minimum by the virtual impossibility of amending the
Constitution if there is any discernible opposition at all—another gross
defect. And constitutional changes such as Finer proposes would be
bitterly opposed. While states with only half the population of the
country can put through an amendment, states with only 5 or 10 per cent
of the population can block any amendment.

First, the small states would appose amendments under Finer's plan
because the proposals would reduce the power of the Senate in which
these states enjoy equal power with the large states and have a say
about treaties and appointments and thus a saleable general bargaining
position. This counts with local politicos. And the small states alone can
block any constitutional change.

Constitutional changes of this magnitude are not brought about
through rational discussion as among scholars. Nor was the British government brought to its present high level by rational discussion. It
was produced and developed out of conflict, often in civil strife. But
Finer's critique and proposed reforms do serve to focus the problem for

anyone who is interested in why so many things go wrong with American government, and why officialdom has such a free extemporizing hand.

As matters now stand, nobody knows precisely what is going on in the Presidency or elsewhere in the government. The President can, and does, spring one surprise after the other on the country. Discussions, if any, have been had only with his cronies and personally selected advisers, all members of the palace guard. Without telling anyone of his intentions, not even Congress, the President may be maneuvering the country into a wasting war or ruinous financial straits.

Finer's plan would make the President and his Cabinet of elected and established public men more visible, and so subject to some check, and would place at the President's disposal seasoned political operators who were not hand-picked yes-men. In such a Cabinet a President would be forced to listen to political peers.

And as Finer points out, the strain of the office is too much for one man to bear. He computes the average age of Presidents at death to be 63 years, comparatively young. Again, with the President now not obliged to carry on discussions with a Cabinet of political sophisticates nor to appear in Congress, much about his personal condition and fitness can be concealed from the country and has been concealed by many Presidents. Concealment of condition is fairly standard among Presidents who are below par.

In the present state of the Constitution a President may isolate or conceal himself entirely from the country, and Presidents have done just this at crucial times of great moment to the future of the people. Nixon for example was very reclusive. There is nothing whatever in the Constitution that obliges a President to show himself at any time. He is under no obligation to hold press conferences, appear before his own hand-picked Cabinet (or even hold Cabinet meetings), to make public speeches or appear before Congress. He may communicate entirely by writing, and whether the composition beyond the signature is his, nobody may know outside of his personal circle.

Woodrow Wilson's Secret Incapacity

Owing to this state of affairs under the Constitution President Wilson was able to remain withdrawn in the White House during his last year in office, stricken with such a serious illness that, as his principal biographer says, he was "either gravely ill or severely incapacitated at the time that the country needed his leadership most." [13] To this day there is no certainty about what his condition was or how the high office was handled. Others may have made decisions in his name.

Wilson experienced a severe stroke and paralysis of his left side on October 2, 1919, although this news was not conveyed to the public or anyone else in the government. Just how much responsibility he was able to exercise over his few written communications thereafter, and how much was exercised by his wife or appointed aides, is not even today known for sure.

Pending was the Treaty of Versailles, to which Wilson had committed himself. The treaty was voted on in the Senate on November 19, 1919, and again on March 19, 1920, and was defeated. A group in the Senate insisted upon the inclusion of reservations with respect to the League of Nations. If opponents would not yield, said Wilson in a letter on January 8, 1920, the people would decide the issue in "the great and solemn referendum", the national election of 1920. In that election Harding, a Republican, won and concluded a separate peace with Germany while promising that the United States would never enter the unholy League of Nations.

Whether Wilson, had he been fully himself, would have been able to effect some sort of compromise or come to some sort of terms with opponents of the treaty, one cannot know. In any event, World War I just completed, the curtain had already risen in the Senate on the road to World War II, which would eventuate in a bare twenty years. That the United States in its own interests should have been in the League was shown some twenty-five years later when it took the initiative in pressing for the establishment of the United Nations Organization, a broader successor to the League.

With respect to Wilson the situation, and its constitutional implications, was a great deal graver than is indicated simply by his collapse in 1919. The fact is that Wilson, at least since 1906, had been a bad health risk, a man with a long carefully concealed history of cerebral vascular disease that had many acute episodes, both before and after he became President. As a consequence, the vital factor, his judgement, was impaired. All this, it should be stressed, was carefully hidden at all times from the always great and wonderful American people and indeed from upper-echelon political leaders.

And during Wilson's term of office epochal, literally earth-shattering, alterations were made in long-term United States foreign policy, departing from precepts laid down by Washington and adhered to since then—no entangling European alliances that would drag the United States into the maelstrom of incessant European conflicts.

The full story of Wilson's pathology was first laid out by Dr. Edward W. Weinstein, professor of neurology at the Mount Sinai School of Medicine of City University of New York, in the *Journal of American History*.[14] My attention was called to this key study by the historian David Freeman Hawke.

Dr. Weinstein, after a close study of all available records, found that Wilson had had a "long history of cerebral vascular disease" that brought "alterations in behavior and personality" in the period when he was President. But after the stroke in 1919, with a year left of his term of office, Wilson was not hospitalized, no records were kept of his condition or they were destroyed. As far as Dr. Weinstein was able to ascertain no technical procedures were done after this culminating episode and no tests were made to evaluate mental functioning. To the nation the White House maintained the attitude that nothing was seriously amiss.

Wilson's long history of cerebral vascular disorder, Dr. Weinstein found, carried with it all the typical marks of the progress of this disease. There was a first period, ending in 1896, which manifested itself in bouts of what were then called "nervous stomach" and "tension headaches" with high blood pressure. The condition was already diagnosable as cerebral vascular disease.

Dr. Weinstein terms the ensuing period, up to the stroke in 1919, as the second phase of the disease. The third and culminating episode was "a massive stroke resulting in the left hemiplegia (paralysis of the left face, arm, and leg)." Wilson died in 1924, aged 67.

"The third takes up the remainder of his presidential term when much of his ineffective political behavior can be explained", Dr. Weinstein writes, "on the basis of the changes in symbolic organization that occur after certain lesions of the right cerebral hemisphere."

Wilson's early adult life, Dr. Weinstein found, was marked by episodes of depression, dyspepsia, colds, headaches, dizziness and feelings of dullness with a sense of numbness in the right hand—all diagnosed at the time as neuritis, which in itself can be a serious ailment, a matter of diseased nerves.

But on May 28, 1906, Wilson, then president of Princeton University, awoke to find he was completely blind in the left eye, a fact undisclosed to the world. A blood vessel had burst in his eye, which as Dr. Weinstein remarks was "a manifestation of a more general disease of the arteries, probably high blood pressure." Further, the sequence of episodes of paresthesia in one hand and blindness in the opposite eye is characteristic of occlusive disease of the internal carotid artery, the major supplier of blood to the brain." This is marked by arterial clots which, stationary for a time, may move along, thus relieving the block. Wilson was thereafter episodically blind in the left eye, unknown to the public, and had a recurrent numbness of the right arm which he called "writer's cramp".

What is significant about this is that a President's brain is absolutely central to the American constitutional system and a President with a brain subject to insufficient blood supply should, as the office is set up, manifestly not be President.

The files of Dr. Francis X. Dercum of Philadelphia, who attended Wilson in 1906 and in 1919, Dr. Weinstein discovered, were destroyed under the terms of his will, an unusual procedure, experienced doctors inform me. The usual practice is for such records to be carefully preserved for the information of doctors treating the dead doctor's patients. Dercum was a neurologist, so that the area of medical expertise involved was recognized at least from 1906 onward. Wilson, after 1906, thought he might at any moment die, so that he was fully aware of the seriousness of his condition, as were his attending physicians. He felt a "virtual death sentence pronounced on him in 1906".

Accompanying the progress of Wilson's disorder were personality changes. After 1896 he felt more tense. And after the episode of 1906 he became irritable and impulsive. There were however periods of apparent recovery and he was apparently in good shape when he entered the White House in March 1913. But in 1915 he had several days of "severe, blinding headaches" and many so-called colds, the exact nature of which was not disclosed.

In 1916 Wilson felt increased tension, showed irritability and displayed intolerance toward any opposition, with outbursts of anger over trivia. At this particular time momentous decisions were being made in American foreign policy which had a direct bearing on the future of western civilization and, without entering into this topic here, I agree with those who maintain that the Wilson administration took and held to the wrong course throughout, laying the preliminary foundations of the chaotic world we find today.

Secretary of State William Jennings Bryan, who advocated a course of traditional American neutrality toward the European belligerents, resigned in 1915 as Wilson moved inexorably toward participation in the war on specious grounds. Wilson should instead have mediated an end to the ruinous conflict, which could have been ended as a stalemate in 1916, but chose to ally himself with the all-out war parties of Britain and France, thereby collaborating in the steps that led to the eventual dismantling of these two mighty powers as well as Germany. It was the promise of American participation, with the promise of ultimate victory, that led the leaders of Britain and France to hold out. The consequence was a strictly pyrrhic victory.

Wilson, knowing little about the interminable European quarrels, probably caring less, was a cultural Anglophile and mistakenly felt he was doing England a favor, as well as American bankers who had lent heavily to Great Britain and France with the blessings of the government. While warfare is old in human history, warfare that pits modern industrial nations against each other is insane as far as the prospects of any benefits are concerned. War was obsolete as effective policy a good four decades before the invention of the atomic bomb but many politicians in all countries apparently haven't yet assimilated the message.

Into his second term Wilson's condition, always unknown to outsiders, steadily worsened and he was attended by Dr. Cary T. Grayson, a young navy doctor attached to the White House who became a Wilson acolyte, admirer and medical screen. Presidents are usually attended by doctors from the armed services—that is, by subordinates under their control. Wilson made Grayson a rear admiral in 1916. To the outside world there was no intimation by Grayson of Wilson's perilous condition, for which he prescribed simple rest and relaxation although he later warned the President that his proposed tour of the country on behalf of the League of Nations after the war might cost him his life. Yet Grayson, knowing the gravity of his patient's plight, nevertheless collaborated in averting a move to declare Wilson incapacitated after his stroke and did not then tell Wilson of the extent of his disability. While Wilson himself had initiated the cover-up of his condition, he had now drawn those attending him into the same scenario.

In 1918 Wilson showed the strain he was under when his public language, according to Dr. Weinstein, became "splenetic and petulant", as when he called for the election of a Democratic Congress. The country sent back a Republican Congress.

On April 3, 1919, at the Paris Peace Conference, Wilson became ill with, as Dr. Weinstein reports, "high fever, cough, vomiting, diarrhea, and insomnia," which certainly gave Grayson notice that all was far from well. Some around him suspected Wilson had been poisoned. Grayson diagnosed his condition as "influenza".

The next day blood appeared in Wilson's urine, sign of an internal vascular lesion. It was followed by twitching of his left leg and the left side of his face. Wilson's thought processes were now obviously garbled. He believed the French servants around him were spies and according to one account he thought he was personally responsible for all the furniture in the palace at Versailles.

After his massive stroke, which came on October 2, 1919, after his tour of the United States speaking for the League of Nations, Wilson denied his incapacity, which Dr. Weinstein indicates is a typical sequel for victims of this malady. He became blind to political reality at home, thought Harding would be "deluged" to defeat in the elections of 1920, thought public opinion favored the League. Harding, a cipher personally and politically, and an alcoholic to boot, won decisively. His below-par condition, too, was concealed from the electorate.

In his last year in office Wilson was unable to walk or to make speeches and, as far as can be ascertained, communicate rationally—all unknown to the public or to Congress.

That many strange turns of policy took place in Wilson's administration is therefore no great wonder. The President was a very ill man. And what was in fact the greatest continuous cover-up in American history had been engineered, initiated by the President himself before he became President. As a consequence of the decisions made in this administration the nation and the world are still experiencing deep reverberations.

Critics of Wilson's foreign policy with respect to World War I find his attitudes at best unrealistic and attribute these to his "idealism". As his attitudes all along toward his own condition show, Wilson was in fact emotionally oriented to deny reality, to see events as he wanted them to be rather than as they were. Not an uncommon failing in lesser mortals, in a presumably sophisticated and highly educated person they can only be regarded as delusionary.

During the war the ever-gullible American press, depicting Wilson as a knight in shining armor, portrayed the Kaiser as a military crackpot with a "withered" left arm. Much was made of this arm. The simple fact is there were crackpots at the top in all the big capitals—in Washington, London, Berlin, Paris and St. Petersburg.

Roosevelt's Fateful Secret Incapacity

Another time when the United States and western civilization lost heavily when a President became gravely ill, the fact concealed from the public and everyone else outside the White House, came toward the end of World War II. The fact relates integrally to the failure of the Allied armies to capture Berlin, which they were in a position to do long before the Russians took the city. Instead the Allied armies, British and American, dawdled at the Elbe.

What induced the inertia has been made the subject of intensive research by General James M. Gavin, commander of the famed 82nd Airborne Division, who for many years made it his business to talk about the contretemps with scores of persons involved, military and civilian, Americans and foreigners. He reached the conclusion that, at the time, the American government was simply mysteriously paralyzed at its center—at the State Department, the War Department and the White House. No word came from any of them as the victorious armies, anxious to go, waited inertly at the Elbe. There was no political guidance.

Berlin instead fell to the Russians on May 2, 1945. The war ended in Europe on May 8, 1945, with the Allied armies still inert at the Elbe, to which the Russians now swarmed. But as early as April 15 the American Ninth Corps reported that with the First Corps it was ready to take Berlin, assisted by the British Twenty-first and Twelfth to the north. There were, in fact, four armies, poised and fresh, irresistible. They were ordered simply to "hold", as no other orders came from Washington.

The political charge was later made that President Roosevelt had made a secret agreement with Stalin to allow the Russians to take Berlin, what is now Communist Germany, eastern Europe and the Balkans. No evidence of such a deal has been found and it seems highly unlikely that it ever was made simply because the allegation makes no sense.

The fact of the matter is that in the early months of 1945 the constitutional Commander in Chief of the United States forces was ill and rapidly dying and consequently unable to exercise his judgement to the full. President Roosevelt died, indeed, on April 12, 1945, at Warm Springs, Georgia, precisely as the American and British armies were in readiness to spring forward.[15]

Roosevelt's health began failing in 1941 and was in marked decline early in 1944.[16] With only a year of life left to him, there lay ahead an extremely crucial period during which his condition steadily declined— his campaign for re-election to a fourth term, the second Quebec Conference, plans in incubation for a United Nations Organization, preparations for the reconversion of the country to a peacetime basis, the Yalta Conference, the *coup de grâce* to a battered Third Reich, etc.

At the instance of Vice Admiral Ross McIntire, his personal physician, Roosevelt was scheduled for an intensive medical examination (lightly termed a "checkup") at Bethesda Naval Hospital on March 27, 1944, because everybody, including his family, was alarmed by his enfeebled appearance and slow reactions. Selected to conduct the examination was young Lieutenant Commander Howard Bruenn, USNR, a cardiologist. What he saw wheeled before him was a President with "a blue grape cast to lips and fingernails, quick, shallow respiration supine, a grayish pallor on the face and a noticeable agitation of the hands."

Bruenn's report to McIntire the next day "both written and oral, depicted a very old man with few life-sustaining forces left. He could expire at any time. And yet, with proper care—and granting that Mr. Roosevelt's mental functions were not badly impaired—he might live on for months, maybe a year or two. The prognosis would constitute a medical guessing game, but it wasn't optimistic." [17]

McIntire showed no surprise. He asked Bruenn if he would like to be the President's attending physician, under the tight authority of Mc-Intire, not allowed to discuss the President's condition with the patient, members of his family or outsiders. Bruenn agreed and McIntire, with a phone call, had Bruenn placed on detached service at the White House.

What Bruenn found was that Roosevelt had high blood pressure, rising steadily since examination in 1941; indications of bad conditions in the heart, which was enlarged; fluid in the lungs and a variety of other serious negative signs. The President was experiencing congestive heart failure, which led to a final diagnosis of hypertension, hypertensive heart disease, failure of the left ventricle of the heart, and acute bronchitis along with a generalized degeneration of the vascular system. At 62 the President was prematurely aged organically, owing to the fact that, paralyzed by poliomyelitis from the hips down since 1921, he had been denied normal exercise. With the greatest war in history raging toward a climax, with the United States in it up to its ears, and with vast postwar stakes at risk among mutually suspicious co-belligerents, the Commander in Chief of the United States armed forces was a burned-out matchstick.

Bruenn prescribed two weeks of bed-rest and regular doses daily of digitalis and codeine, but McIntire, who knew his patient, also knew that Roosevelt—who was careful not to inquire about his own condition —would disregard all such instructions even as he continued to refuse giving up smoking cigarettes. For men in the position of Roosevelt, accustomed for years to having their own way and having the world kow-tow to them, seem insensibly to come to believe they are exempt from the laws of nature, imagine they are kept afloat by the power of their own wills—or by an inscrutable fate. So it probably was with Wilson too. Or, what is worse, perhaps they fully understand the position but, like the dog in the manger, refuse to budge.

McIntire, leaving nothing to chance, or to Bruenn, then arranged for a secret conference of six of the leading medical specialists from around the country, also bringing in Bruenn. It was held on March 29, 1944. The specialists heard Bruenn's report and his prescriptions and at once disagreed among themselves but said they wanted to see the President before coming to conclusions. After this examination they were more inclined to agree with Bruenn but were more optimistic than he and advocated a more tentative approach.

Bruenn firmly disagreed, held tenaciously to his original position. In the end they came around to his view but advocated going easy on the medication because "too much medication would arouse the patient's suspicions". For Bruenn had indicated that in addition to digitalis the President should be given ammonium chloride followed by an injection of mersalyl as well as tranquilizers. On the record, Roosevelt was not told of his condition on the theory that to tell him would be unsettling, might worsen his condition. Bruenn was left in charge and all agreed to meet again in two weeks with the President always under close observation.

As the year wore on, various closely associated political people visited the President, and those for whom the question came up advised him not to run for a fourth term simply because he looked as though he were dying although nobody said this. Everybody in the White House who came into contact with him could see that he was dying but he appeared oblivious to the inevitable.

In the course of his rapid decline there were many strong indications that his usual sharp judgement was impaired—his public statement at Yalta that 50,000 German officers should be executed, his initial acquiescence in the Morgenthau Plan to convert Germany into an agricultural country, and various others. Merely his decision to run for a fourth term showed him to be out of touch with reality, which was further shown by his failure to bring Vice President Truman into the White House immediately after the election.

On March 29, 1945, Roosevelt entrained for Warm Springs, Georgia, to die there of a cerebral hemorrhage (the malady that had laid Wilson low) on April 12. Meanwhile the American and British armies, without instructions from the top, idled at the Elbe as the Soviets drove toward Berlin, which they took on May 2. At the same time, with the armies of the western allies standing still as though frozen, the Russians had taken all of Poland, eastern Germany, Hungary, Austria, Bulgaria, Yugoslavia and Czechoslovakia. Immediately or soon after, they established in each country except Austria their own satellite governments, which remain today. A large part of Europe, once in Nazi hands, had now been shifted to Soviet hands with neither Britain, France nor the United States obtaining so much as an acre by way of a consolation prize, or indeed permission to enter for a look around. The Soviets, propped up through the war with an avalanche of American supplies, had taken the jackpot.

What is constitutionally significant about all this is that the White House steadily lied to the country about the President's condition as it always does in comparable circumstances and always will as long as the Constitution permits a President and his personal staff to insulate the chief executive from the country, feeding to the outside world whatever staffers and the President want it to hear and believe. Not only is this the case with a President's illness but also in general, as many administrations, notably those of Lyndon Johnson and Nixon, have shown. The country is fed a line of falsehoods, not only about the

President but about vital public affairs, involving matters of life and death or other ruination for millions. Eisenhower directed that the country be kept "confused" about the dangers of nuclear fallout.

News publications, made aware of the signs of physical deteriorioation in President Roosevelt reported to them by close observers, clamored for specific information. *Life* magazine, which was most pertinacious in its inquiries, was finally given a written answer to questions by Admiral McIntire's secretary on June 6, 1944 (D-Day in Europe). To one question the answer was: "The final checkup on his last physical examination is extremely satisfactory."

The checkup referred to was the one by Bruenn that had brought together like birds of ill omen all the specialists. The implication in the ambiguous sentence is that the checkup was satisfactory to the President (and the country), whereas the actual position was that a thorough checkup, giving satisfaction to medical experts, had disclosed the suppressed fact that the President was in extremely bad condition and liable to die at any time—was in fact unfit to retain office.

Under Amendment XXV, Section 3, of the Constitution, ratified in 1967, it is left to the President to declare in writing his inability to discharge the powers and duties of his office and then he may similarly declare he is able to resume them. If the past is any guide, with the cases of Wilson and Roosevelt mainly in point, no President will ever make such a declaration. If he desired to do so, the members of his immediate staff, who are left essentially in charge, would not allow him to do so but would carry on, as Wilson's staff did, with the President a helpless puppet, a prisoner of his staff. No men have yet surrendered this office, out of thirty-nine to hold it, without being obliged by forces over which they had no control—the end of their stipulated terms, the threat of impeachment (Nixon), or death. This part of Amendment XXV may therefore be considered simply as pure poetry.

Left out of most reckonings about the Presidency is the President's personal staff, which operationally is an extension of himself. Most of its members are obscure but suitably competent people, young rather than old, whose fortunes are tied to those of the President. Whatever diminishes him diminishes them—and their future prospects. If the President dies, their careers are interrupted, possibly blighted. If he is disgraced, as Nixon was, they may be involved and also disgraced, as were the members of Nixon's staff. On the other hand, if he leaves office normally, most move on to higher positions, mainly in the corporate world. They possess a highly marketable commodity: know-how about the inner operations of government.

The presidential staff, then, has two stakes in view: (1) immediate continued participation in national decision-making and (2) prospects of future promotion into higher socio-economic strata. It has no special motivation to be concerned about the public interest or constitutionalism except as these may be (or may not be) served by the President. It should be remembered that not all Presidents are thought to have been devoted to the general welfare. Was Nixon? Was Lyndon Johnson? Was Harding? Was Grant?

Experts find, as already shown, that many men who hold this office are not equal to its demands. The framers of the Constitution thought that through the Electoral College what they called "first characters" of the country would be chosen as Presidents. An arguable case could be made that from Washington through Andrew Jackson such characters were indeed elected. But, since Jackson, nobody designatable as a "first character" at the time of his election was chosen, unless one would call victorious generals like Grant and Eisenhower "first characters". But by no stretch at all can anyone else be so designated, including Lincoln and Franklin Roosevelt. For at the time of their election they were not regarded as among the "first characters" of the land.

But successful handling of the office of President may convert a person into a "first character", as Lincoln, Franklin Roosevelt and a few others were converted. Most men upon being elected are virtual unknowns, their stature inflated through a bath of instant publicity. Mere nomination converts nonentities into veritable giants, and when defeated, they again become nonentities. The naming of defeated presidential candidates is a favorite game at which nearly everybody shows his ignorance. To save their lives most Americans, nearly all Americans, could not name 5 per cent of the defeated candidates and date the election in which they lost.

What is the case, then, is that it is the office itself that converts a few of its holders into "first characters" and shows that the extra-constitutional selection process largely turns up men who are not equal to the office. Many are called, few are chosen, and of those chosen, fewer still are anointed over the long run with the approbation of the nation. The prevailing selection process practically insures that anyone selected for the office will be weighed in the scales of history and found wanting. The presidential selection process is in fact ridiculous, and as long as the country tolerates it it deserves what it gets.

Vacuum at the Top

There is no need here to dilate upon the vast impact on western civilization of the failure of the British and Americans to capture Berlin and contiguous territory and its capture instead by the Russians. Incoming President Truman had no first-hand grasp of the immediate situation,

had too many other matters to attend to in settling into the top position
to give the Berlin situation full attention. The fact is that at this precise
crucial moment there was a dangerous vacuum at the pinnacle of the
United States government and, precisely in accord with the rules, nobody
either at the War Department or the State Department stepped into the
vacuum to give the saving order of command. Had someone taken the bit
into his teeth he might have achieved the status of a hero. But if the
order had brought calamitous consequences, he would have been crushed
—an example of what can happen when an unauthorized person exercises
authority at a crucial moment. The United States in fact had no effective
Commander in Chief at this moment.

Whether it is true or not that Roosevelt's final illness and ill-timed
death was at the root of the paralysis of the Allied armies on the Elbe,
the then situation as a whole points up the dangers of having so much
authority concentrated in the hands of one man, nobody else near him
capable of lawfully exercising full authority. Had there been in effect a
Cabinet-type executive group of the kind Prof. Finer prescribes, high
elected officials closely associated with the President, not remote appointees, would have been available to take intelligent command. The
American and British armies obviously should have moved.

An important feature of the eleven-man Cabinet Finer proposes
is that these men, all elected and all with their own careers to think
of, would by means of constant meetings have the physical and mental
conditions of the President constantly in review. Each member of the
Cabinet would indeed have all the others under review. And the
decline in fitness of any of them would be known to all and conveyed
to the outside world.

This sort of review is not possible with the present Cabinet of presidential appointees, for this group meets only upon the summons of the
President and consists moreover of the President's men, not the nation's.
The nation has nobody at all near the President, an odd circumstance.
Some Presidents do not bring present "Cabinets" together at all or do
not attend their meetings, which in any event cannot come to any
decisions in the absence of the President. And if the Finer-type Cabinet
sat regularly in the House of Representatives, the members of Congress,
too, and the press, would be in a position to make judgements at all
times about the physical fitness and mental acuteness of all, from the
President down the line of Vice Presidents.

In the Presidency as constituted, in other words, the American people
are sitting on a bomb, not timed to go off at any particular time but
liable to explode at any moment. The problem here is not one of an
imperial Presidency but of an anarchic Presidency, a wild-cat Presidency

—or, as it has been termed, a Protean Presidency. The situation comes down to this: anything can happen.

There is, too, the question of general capability. As I have shown, the appropriate experts do not give Presidents equal ratings in ability and in fact rate very few of them high, most of them middling and a great many very low. A country with the pretensions of the United States seems certainly laggard in not providing for better men in such a Protean office or laggard at least in not buttressing the office by others, duly elected and with their careers at stake in how they perform. No sizable corporation for example would leave so much of its destiny in the hands of one man. Nor would it choose its chief executive so nonchalantly as does the United States.

Now, to establish a system the fissures, interstices and cracks of which must be filled by one man acting on his own responsibility is not, in the long view of history, especially original or wise. Yet this is the sort of hit-or-miss system the United States has even as the dervishes of propaganda mindlessly praise it to the skies.

Presidential Illnesses

Wilson and Roosevelt apart, other Presidents have experienced serious illnesses while in office, in some cases known to the public, in others concealed.

President Eisenhower suffered two heart attacks and an attack of ileitis that required surgery while president, and during his periods of recovery, he left executive affairs in the hands of appointed subordinates and immature Vice President Nixon. These illnesses, owing to their spectacular nature, were known to everybody.

President Kennedy was a walking bundle of ailments, the most serious not known to the public—the usual White House story. His back ailments and knee injuries were publicly known, but that he had Addison's disease, a serious glandular malady, and regularly was administered "pep" drugs, was carefully concealed.

Lyndon Johnson, who came to the Presidency by a chain of accidents and was not thought even by those who placed him as a back-country vote-getter on the electoral ticket as Kennedy's running mate to be in any way fit to be President, had experienced a massive heart attack before attaining national office, was never regarded by adepts as physically or mentally sound while President.

As modern medicine is well aware, serious physical maladies bring in their train psychic involvements, and the office of President, the center of decision-making, calls at all times for the utmost mental clarity. No individual whatever can be guaranteed at all times in a highly complex world to bring this degree of clarity to such a demanding office. As everyone knows from his own experience, all human beings are subject to ups and downs, good periods and bad. When this pattern is complicated by easily concealed serious illness, one has a true devil's brew with a solitary ruler in office.

And it is here that Prof. Finer's argument for a regularized collectivity around the President becomes irrefutable. Such a collectivity would be rooted in diverse sections of the country, staffed by men experienced in political give and take, each member aware of the other's weaknesses and strengths. Not to have such a collectivity is to choose to continue with the gamble on a single person about whom, moreover, the nation may and probably will lack vital timely knowledge.

National affairs suffered serious avoidable setbacks with the sudden removal of Lincoln and the illnesses of Wilson and Franklin Roosevelt and possibly also the hidden instabilities of Kennedy, Lyndon Johnson and Nixon. Future setbacks, instead of being merely serious, might well be catastrophic. The United States, in short, with a one-person executive sits on a keg of dynamite or, more delicately put, under a sword of Damocles.

In this atomic age the preceding statement, far from figurative, may turn out to be literally and disastrously true. For the President is the one person, in the current refrain, who has "his finger on the button". The button in question is the one that signals the release of nuclear missiles against a designated foe which, not to be outdone in *schrecklichkeit*, releases a salvo in return—wholesale carnage all around.

Such a responsibility clearly is far too much to vest in the authority of a single person subject like everyone else to a variety of diseases and distempers. I, for one, wouldn't think it a good arrangement even if I could always be sure the President was a Washington or Lincoln. For by reason of invisible organic processes the most rational of men can be unhinged.

While it is true that every President is surrounded by advisers and aides, all of these under the Constitution are chosen by the President, are consequently usually what are known as stooges, mere extensions of the President himself. While men like Washington and Lincoln could tolerate opposition from their Cabinets, and choose their own way, the memoirs are replete with stories of the ill consequences that befell nearly every person who bucked a President or told him what he did not want to hear. While Presidents are of various temperaments, many cannot stand opposition. The atmosphere therefore around such Presidents is one of abject sycophancy, a ballet of puppets.

What is needed around the President very obviously is a group of persons so independently based that their dismissal causes at least more than the ripple that follows the dismissal of a presidential appointee. Not that a collection of independently based people could not come to collectively injudicious conclusions, which just cannot be prevented by any known constitutional device. The British Cabinet for example has made wrong decisions in crucial instances in this century—and the British people have paid for them. But I, for one, would rather go down under a wrong decision arrived at by twelve or so men than by one. The odds somehow seem better in the first alternative.

Were the Framers at Fault?

All of which appears to cast some doubt over the oft-hymned authors of the American Constitution. These men however should be exonerated of fault. The fault lies with those who compose the hymns of constitutional celebration.

The framers of the Constitution and those who pushed it through to ratification, although as a whole not men of unusual wisdom (contrary to legend), unquestionably rendered a great service to the nation, both as it then existed and as it was to become. For they fashioned for the nation something to start with, something to chew on, and anything that gave an effective start toward a unified nation that was eventually to extend across the continent amounted to a very considerable contribution, defective though it ultimately proved to be.

The fact is that the Constitution is like a venerable treasured clock which one can never be sure is giving the correct time. It is erratic in its deliverances, sometimes stops functioning completely.

But the very idea that any group of men meeting in Philadelphia in the summer of 1787 could produce an elaborate and detailed mechanism that would anticipate and provide for every facet and contingency of the future of a nation destined to expand from 3 million to 225 million or more persons is inherently untenable. No group of men could do that at any time, and no group of men before them or after them ever did.

They thought they might have, as the remarks of several showed, but in this and several other aspects they were self-deceived, trapped in the mechanical thought patterns of their own times. That they hoped they were producing a final structure, in need of little change, is shown by the difficult procedures they laid down for amendment. But that they had succeeded many of them doubted. Precisely what these centered their doubts upon they did not all indicate and it would be useless to speculate.

It is this difficulty of amendment that is the chief inducement to the government, especially the President but also the Supreme Court, to extemporize under pressure of necessity or otherwise, giving rise to what some call "the living Constitution". This living Constitution is an adjustable, flexible Constitution—adjustable by officials according to the necessities as they see them. In the process of adjustment words are given new meanings. While it is true that language inexorably changes, it does not change to suit the momentary convenience of whoever uses it. No amount of interpretation can change the meaning of phrases such as "Congress shall make no laws respecting . . ." For Congress either may, or may not, make such laws—no two ways or middle way about it.

What the framers, living in a simpler age, did not see is that governments must act fundamentally according to their own judgement from time to time. For life is not contained in a mold. The only inner prescriptions that may block them must be of their own devising, cannot be a set of *a priori* rules laid down antecedent to experience. Such devising either is according to a regular readily available procedure, as in Britain, or is done irregularly, on a catch-as-catch-can basis, as in the United States. What is constitutional and what is not in the United States is always up in the air, subject to dispute and wrangling that often goes on for years.

The main difficulty about the Constitution of the United States is precisely that it consists of a set of incomplete prescriptions, ostensibly frozen in time except as subject to an almost impossible amending process. These amount to prior legislation. No government can be harnessed by such a net of prescriptions, and experience has shown this in the history of the Constitution. What happens is that one either needs new sets of "interpretations", many of them palpably unreasonable and requiring elaborate and dubious rationalizations, or one falls into a self-defeating constitutional lockstep.

Governments do whatever they feel they can and must either by direct and forthright process, with or without the participation and understanding of the populace, or they proceed by indirection. The United States government, owing to the complexity of the prescribed procedures it operates under, proceeds in many matters by indirection, bypassing or enlarging the prescriptions but claiming not to.

Both the British and the Soviet governments in most of their affairs proceed directly, the British with the participation and understanding of its populace and the Soviet without. The Soviet government takes its actions without consulting anyone outside its top layers. The British government makes its decisions by majority in Parliament, most of the decisions openly debated and analyzed. The prescriptions it operates under are self-imposed and can be changed from interval to interval by open action of Parliament. There is no set of fixed prescriptions outside or above the British government purportedly telling it what it or any of its divisions may or may not do.

It is apparently, but only apparently, otherwise with the United States government. The Constitution tells each divsion what it may and may not do and what its relations shall be with other divisions and how they shall all comport themselves with respect to the populace. But each phrase of the Constitution is subject to interpretation, formally by the Supreme Court but in fact also by the President and by Congress. And the interpretations either extend or modify the phraseology, and change from interval to interval.

In a world of constant flux such a procedure is only reasonable. But it means that Americans are dependent like other peoples on the judgement of officials. And under the American system the operative officials are screened from public view, not responsible for their actions. The American people in fact have little to do with the functioning of the United States government and do not, like the British, staff it at a single stroke but do it piecemeal. They are, as it were, never in the confidence of the government, always suspect outsiders, guessing at what might be going on until moments of often unhappy revelation, most of the time in the dark.

Which of the branches is allowed to have the upper hand at any particular moment depends upon their reciprocal interplay and the state of the public.

As laid out by the framers under the Constitution, Congress comes first and was given the most attention of the three branches in the Constitution. To the generation of 1787 the legislature was the most important body of government. In the grass-roots thinking of the times the executive and the courts were subordinate although the chief framers themselves did not think so.

As it has turned out, however, owing to the structural ineffectiveness of the legislature, the President has emerged as the dominant figure of the Constitution, with the Supreme Court next. Were Congress to make itself effective, which depends upon the behavior of the disorganized populace, it might be different. But the system established by the men of 1787, with Congress elected by stages, divided into two houses and some members representing states and others districts, left Congress structurally weaker than either the President or the Supreme Court. It would take a formidable public mobilization to overcome this weakness. The consequence is that either the President or the Court usually prevails over Congress.

As to the celebrated check-and-balance system, most of the checks are imposed by the President on Congress, as I have shown, and the balance by the Supreme Court (with the possible tacit assent at times of Congress and the President). In one minor showdown with the Supreme Court the Congress prevailed and President Franklin Roosevelt, driven to the wall by adverse Supreme Court decisions, successfully maneuvered so as to alter the entire course of Court decisions. But both these actions required massive effort, not readily repeatable.

On any assumption that Congress is the branch of the government that should prevail or should even hold its own with the executive branch and the courts, the Constitution is totally defective. It is probably true that a majority of the constitutional convention, suspicious as it was of "the people", did not want Congress to prevail short of a virtually total popular mobilization. And that, in view of the internally divided and variegated character of the people, irrespective of constitutional arrangements, is a virtual impossibility.

It will require the development of a distinctive strain of people, a blend of the many strains now in the country, before Americans can be looked upon as a demographic unity in the way the British, French or Germans are. The fact is that the United States is a country inhabited by many different strains of people, and their outlook, by region and acculturation as well as by strain, are as multi-divergent as those of the various peoples of Europe, Asia and Africa. Although the United States has a national government, it does not have a national people, all claims to the contrary notwithstanding. And this fact is reflected in a kaleidoscopic Congress wherein lower-grade types in the confusion readily find a hospitable roost. Few first-class performers are ambitious to sit in Congress.

Conditions Today under the Constitution

What, then, of all the misguidedly patriotic praise one finds heaped upon the Constitution in the schoolbooks? Most of it, it turns out upon analysis, is simple nonsense, pap. Echoes of it in the newspapers are also nonsense. The ascendant politicians, to be sure, have reason to praise the Constitution constantly, as they regularly do, because it is the means by which they hold a place in the world. But the politicians, as the public-opinion polls show, are today one of the most despised groups of men in the country. Their opinions in general weigh little with the public, which is tuned into very different wave-lengths.

Just how is the country at present faring under its constitutional system? The reader is by now familiar with my dissenting conclusions so I shall turn to the *New York Times*, widely regarded as the premier American newspaper. On November 12, 13 and 14, 1978, it published a long three-part survey titled "Governing America".

"The United States", according to the opening paragraph, "is becoming increasingly difficult to govern because of a fragmented, inefficient system of authority and procedures that has developed over the last decade and now appears to be gaining strength and impact, according to political leaders, scholars and public interest groups across the country." As to all this being a development of the latest decade, the readers of this book know otherwise. Divided authority was the basic aim from the launching of the Constitution onward. The inefficiency and ineffectiveness is rooted in the system, was long ago made evident and is operationally cumulative.

Officials, the next paragraph stated, "acknowledge evidence of failure in the Presidency, Congress, the bureaucracy, the political parties and the Federal system of state and local governments." This assertion takes in the entire constitutional system except the courts, which others, including Congress and the President, from time to time criticize.

A Harvard professor was then quoted: "Our political institutions do not match the scales of economic and social reality. The national state has become too small for the big problems and too big for the small problems." Congressman Philip M. Crane of Illinois put the blame on "50 years of big government", so that in his view smaller and less government, not better government, appears to be the remedy. According to Tom Hayden, noted rebel activist of the 1960s, "You can take any issue you want, and the system isn't delivering. There is no glue holding the country together." What he refers to as glue can be nothing other than the fabulous Constitution itself plus its legal system. This, I take it, is the "glue".

This first *Times* article went on to develop the thesis that the trouble arises because of the convergence of a number of new and old forces which "include the organization of political movements around single issues rather than parties, a quantum jump in lobbying and campaign contributions on the parts of the public and special interests, a decline in the moral authority of the Presidency and of government at all levels, enormous growth in centralization of the Federal Government, and decentralization of Congress."

There was a reported consensus among observers "that no coalition of interests is strong enough to get priorities for the overall public good, to effect reforms that have wide public support, to root out inefficiency and corruption in government programs, and to inspire confidence in political leadership."

But some persons correctly discerned the disunity as "systemic"— that is, rooted in the constitutional system or, more properly in the light of what it has become under escalating extemporization, the constitutional non-system. "I'm not sure anybody could pull this Government together," said Representative Morris Udall of Arizona, according to the *Times*.

"The national political parties have continued to decline," said the *Times*, "until they are little more than frameworks for nominating candidates and organizing Congress and some state legislatures." But this limited potency of the political parties was observed long ago, as the readers of this book are well aware. Countless analysts have made the point down through the decades.

The *Times* articles went on to supply details buttressing these themes, without however mentioning the Constitution or raising the question of how all this can be happening if the Constitution is all that it is cracked up to be.

The *Times* quoted Stuart Eizenstat, presidential adviser for domestic affairs, as saying, "We have a fragmented, Balkanized society, with an economic proliferation of special economic interest groups, each interested in only one domestic program—protecting it, having Government spend more for it, unwilling to see it modified." All of which sounds a lot like much-vaunted liberty. Against all this the constitutional powers as laid out are unable to produce harmony.

As to the *bête noire* of special-interest activity, the *Times* quotes a consultant to special-interest groups as saying that no more than 6 per cent of the population is involved in such operations, from the contributors of money to people traveling to Washington and the state capitals to lobby, and on to professional lobbyists. On the direct economic side such groups are mainly interested in price-fixing, subsidies and tax preferences. They take in just about the entire economic spectrum at the managerial level.

"Our political system has become dominated by special interests," said David Cohen, president of Common Cause, a political reform lobby. Actually, it has been dominated by such interests since 1787. The difference between then and now is that now they are more specialized, more numerous and more discernible, their earlier high-flown rhetoric discarded.

Not only do the special interests obtain legislation supportive of their domains but they succeed in killing much reform legislation, thus preserving confusion. And the economic special-interest groups are the main contributors to political campaigns, especially at the congressional level. They are the political providers, the living heart and soul of the system.

According to John Gardner, former Secretary of Health, Education and Welfare and founder of Common Cause, quoted by the *Times*, the federal government "is a collection of fragments under the virtual control of highly organized special interests. In the special-interest state that we have forged, every well-organized interest owns a piece of the rock." His remedy for the situation is public financing of congressional election campaigns in the way that presidential campaigns are now funded, thus eliminating purchased Congressmen. To this remedy Congress thus far has been resistant.

Where have Presidents stood with respect to "special-interest groups"? Despite all political rhetoric, every President has been supported by a varying coalition of special-interest groups, and necessarily so. Government, contrary to a common misconception, cannot exist in a vacuum. It needs roots in society and must make use of such roots as it finds, or must develop some of its own as do totalitarian governments. It cannot turn to Skid Row, Tobacco Road or the slums for support. Nor to the Grove of Academe.

Government, therefore, all political rhetoric to one side, finds or establishes its main roots among people with a demonstrated capacity for looking after themselves. For if people cannot serve themselves first they cannot be capable of doing anything for others, a harsh fact. People with a capacity for looking after their own interests, experience shows, are also people with a capacity for giving support to political people— always on a narrow strictly *quid pro quo* basis. The political support is not given out of idealism, no return expected.

What of people without the capacity for reinforcing their own interests—the lame, the halt, the blind, the diseased, the superannuated, the unskilled, the immature of all ages, the illiterate, the improvident propagators, the mentally below par or disordered and the like? Such, unless supported by able friends or relatives, are dependent on public policy in the absence of their own private funds, become public charges. Although today liberally supplied with self-appointed spokesmen for public money, they are not themselves a political force and are nobody that any elective official can count upon at the polls. Their sole support is public sentiment, which can wear thin as demands intensify.

But although not themselves part of lobby groups, those who represent them or profess to do so are often, and increasingly, professional liberally paid lobbyists who as far as financing is concerned represent what are called the providers of services. These latter—doctors, nurses, therapists, social workers, organizers, teachers, aides, administrators— cater to the needs of the indigent and helpless unfortunate and are paid for out of public funds, which is the political objective.

At least 25 per cent of the population is in this category of helplessness, the figure derived simply by the application of the law of probability to large populations. Concrete statistics, for those who prefer them, support this figure, with another 25 per cent only somewhat better positioned and liable at any turn of the whirligig of circumstance to find themselves in the lower category. For they all, as the record clearly shows, own little or no property.

Much as he might wish to, no President could look to this under-class for political support although he may gain support from their lobbyists and service providers, depending upon how lavish he consents to be with tax-derived money. A President must, necessarily, look elsewhere for support and, if so disposed, do what he can for the under-class, most of which does not even vote and much of which is not even capable of voting. The political field is therefore left to the activists and, more particularly, to the organized activists—that is, the special interests of all kinds.

It is these, according to the final thrust of the *Times* articles, who are tearing the government apart, like ravenous sharks and vultures after carrion. They do not constitute a responsible ruling class, are a collection of overreachers. The *Times* neglects however to point out that the horror story it spreads before its readers is being woven on the loom of the Constitution. For the government acts within the extremely elastic and multi-vocal terms of this instrument.

If Congress is fragmented, the relevant fact is that it was designed to be. If no coherent policy emerges, or emerges only spasmodically and with difficulty, the design itself makes such an outcome practically certain, always has. To cap this, the electorate has never been able to agree upon the establishment of disciplined political parties adhering to a certain set of principles—in part because the Constitution itself gives little support for or encouragement to the establishment of such parties. The framers of the Constitution were explicitly hostile to political parties and factions although they themselves composed one.

The Constitution, as everyone knows, keeps the government divided within itself with the one-man executive alone being able, if temperamentally ready and willing, to act expeditiously. To submit any complex problem to Congress for solution, as every observer knows, is to wait a long time for deliverance—if indeed it is forthcoming at all. A revealing example is found in the fate of President Carter's energy proposals.

What the *Times* reports in its series, then, is simply American government as usual, nothing new added, although the focus is on a decade of inadequate Presidents. It has been the absence since long before 1968 of a sure presidential hand that has led to the situation described by the *Times*. For when the Presidency is in the hands of a weak man, the entire system shudders constantly like an early-model automobile.

The malaise the *Times* is dealing with, without saying it, perhaps without being aware of it, is, first, a constitutional one and, second, the absence of an effective presence in the White House.

The pinnacles of the Presidency, as all experts agree, were attained under Washington, Lincoln and Franklin Roosevelt. But it should be observed that, beginning with Washington, after each of these Presidencies the office, like a declining stock market, began a slow slide downward in the quality of occupants until, having attained an abysmal bottom, it suddenly emerged—by chance—in full luster with the presence of one man.

Sixty-four years elapsed between Washington's departure from office and Lincoln's appearance and sixty-seven years between Lincoln's departure and the appearance of Franklin D. Roosevelt. If sixty-five years is the cyclical interval between superlative Presidents of the United States, the next one is not due to appear until around the year 2010. The downslide after Washington ended with the inept Buchanan and that after Lincoln with the inept Hoover. As it is, since the departure of Roosevelt the Presidency has been slowly sliding downward, in performance and in public esteem, leading one to believe that in tone at least history may be repeating itself.

Without the guidance of intelligent broadly supported parties the United States appears to be dependent upon the insights or lack of them, of one man. And if a capable man does not turn up by chance the country merely wallows until an acute crisis develops and the single savior appears. Unfortunately, the time of severe crisis may some day come with no savior ready to step forward to take the helm.

What favors the "savior" is not that he bears the marks of a great man but that the accumulation of ineptitude is so evident to many people that a majority of the country agrees with him on the need for drastic changes and a reversal of policy. Washington, Lincoln and Roosevelt all stepped into the Presidency at such times. Attitudes that had preceded them, never fully analyzed and addressed by effective political parties, clearly had to be discarded and new ones developed.

If the White House is unable to lead Congress, this body remains merely a squabbling rabble, its members intent only on personal estate-building. There never was a time in American history under the Constitution when Congress, on its own initiative, gave the country effective leadership. It cannot, considering the way it is constitutionally designed, give leadership.

No leadership at all from the White House, to be sure, is better than misguided leadership such as the country got in foreign policy under Wilson and, later, in both foreign and domestic policy under Kennedy, Lyndon Johnson and Nixon. The quietistic administration of Eisenhower was clearly preferable to the fevered and badly conceived activity under his three successors.

But just how well served is any country whose well-being depends so largely upon the pure luck of having one capable man in the executive office?

So, except for its restricted view of the causes of the situation it describes, I concur with the diagnosis by the *New York Times*—as far as it goes. What it sets forth, however, fits perfectly with what I have laid before readers: the United States does not flourish under an effectively constructed political system, all claims to the contrary notwithstanding. For a good system does not get so far out of hand.

Constitutions Are Products of Evolution

Why is it that Americans, indoctrinated from childhood with the conviction that the Constitution of the United States is the most nearly perfect governmental instrument ever devised, nevertheless live in a society that, except for rare intervals, is wracked by problems of sufficient severity to induce mobilizations of experts with a variety of often conflicting explanations and solutions?

The bottom-most explanation, as it seems to me, is that the United States is still a very new country, barely launched in terms of the age of the countries of Europe in which it has its cultural roots. This new country, extended over a half continent of great natural beauty and hitherto untapped vast resources—a literal gold mine of natural greatness—was gradually cobbled into a half-continent society, by hook, crook, civil war, great application of labor and almost total lack of coherent foresight. Like Topsy, it just grew. And this is the way most countries rise, have their day in the sun and eventually decline.

Nations and constitutions are not made, contrary to fabulists, by small groups of wise men who meet and agree upon a covenant that will forever guide them. Men do meet, however, and draw up covenants which, however, become subject to slow alteration under the test of practice.

Enduring constitutions, in other words, are never made by single assemblies of representative men but, if they are achieved at all, are made by the historical action of generations. A body of men can, by means of a document, start the process, as was the case with Magna Carta in England and the Constitution of 1787 in the United States. But the document they produce is never the veritable constitution of the nation which, in the course of time, shapes its own constitution in political struggle through trial and error.

As long as there is serious controversy over what is constitutional and what not, as was for many centuries the case in England, the nation has not achieved its constitution. Only when controversy dies down and there is general agreement about what is constitutional and what not can one say that a nation has at last achieved the constitution best suited to its position. The United States, manifestly, with controversy still raging over what the Constitution means and intends and what not, is still in the stage of forming its Constitution, and not by the processes set forth in the document itself.

The operative Constitution of the United States, in fact, as every expert agrees, does not consist merely of the document of 1787 and its amendments. There is far more to it—special unstipulated usages and conventions, qualifying and enlarging decisions of the Supreme Court and the implications of a broad spectrum of free-ranging executive and congressional actions. Many of these actions, far from being accepted, are merely tolerated by the public or roundly criticized.

Thus the nation itself has a long-range but sluggish input into constitutional evolution by reason of what it will and will not willingly accept.

Under this dispensation—until further changes are made—the one-man executive, as was once the case with the English king, has the greatest freedom of action, after which come the powerful courts. Congress, constitutionally divided and sub-divided and even more minutely sub-divided in practice owing to the cultural and other disparities of a variegated national constituency, has the least freedom of action.

Something that ought to be said at this point however is that the Constitution is the product of a far higher level of thought than the national average thought level of the population as a whole. And while its boosters have projected an extravagant estimate of the Constitution, the political performance and aspirations of the population on the average has been far short of the values implied by the Constitution.

So, although the Constitution may not be all that it is cracked up to be, neither is the population as a whole. The Constitution, despite its cracks and fissures, is more high-minded on the whole than "the people".

What do the people want? Pollsters determine this by sample surveys, which always show divisions, mostly rather evenly balanced pro and con. The courts however have an easier method of finding answers. They merely look into the Constitution. There one finds, subject to judicial interpretation and extrapolation, precisely what the people as an entity want. The crowd listening in the courtroom does not consist of "the people", nor do even all the inhabitants in the surrounding city. But here, outlined in the document, one finds, always, what a majority of the people, in formal assembly, always want, subject to special judicial insight and elaboration that supplies what is lacking.

Yet no individual in any instance can state with finality what the Constitution stipulates. If one points to a Supreme Court decision that is as much as a week old, it is a decision that may already be fading, subject to further fine-tuning.

As it turns out, only the government can say what the will of the people is, first through the courts but also through the President and even through Congress. Whatever the government action is, in fact, turns out to be the will of the people under constitutional theology. If any individual disagrees, it can only mean that he is in disagreement with the people, a serious matter under the rule of democracy although democracy is not recognized in the Constitution.

Yet, whether they knew it or not, the framers were probably wise in restoring the discarded British government of 1776 in a disguised form, now to be improved with whatever capability the people were able to muster. What has been accomplished so far has been some loosening of the original constitutional fetters, but otherwise little change. The very loosening of constitutional restraints accomplished along the route of interpretation and reinterpretation however would seem to pave the way toward the time when constitutional improvement will be wrought on a greater scale.

The Constitution, then, as it stands, is by no means the system the United States is ultimately fated to embrace. For there is a great deal of room for improvement—a great deal . . .

Ten

A
RENEWED
CALL FOR A
SECOND CONVENTION

As this book is being completed there is a movement of desperation throughout the country for convoking a constitutional convention. Its stated purpose would be to obtain a constitutional amendment to require Congress to approve only balanced budgets. The intent of this provision would be to put brakes on the wide-open appropriating and borrowing power. For over-appropriating and over-borrowing and under-taxing is what has produced the inflation that since 1960 has severely eroded the people's assets—cash in bank deposits, holdings of fixed-income securities including government bonds, long-term leaseholds, pensions and annuities, life insurance policies, wages and salaries, etc.

Under the goad of the National Taxpayers Union, a private citizens' group, the legislatures of 28 states out of the constitutionally required 34 have to date petitioned for a convention to achieve the desired end. Congress itself has declined to submit such an amendment to the state legislatures. Calling such a convention is a procedure in accord with a provision of the thrice-sacred Constitution (Article V). Whether the pro-amendment forces will succeed in the tortuous process of obtaining approval of the necessary 34 states—a purposely difficult process devised by the framers to balk the thrice-sacred people—remains to be seen.

What is most striking about this movement, which all precedent decrees will come to little or nothing, is the panic it has engendered in leading national politicians of both parties, from President Carter down. "The radical and unprecedented action of convening a constitutional convention might do serious, irrevocable damage to the Constitution," the President wrote to Vern Riffe, speaker of the Ohio House of Representatives.

Here indeed is an outlandish notion—first, that any action prescribed in the rigid Constitution could be "radical"; second, that members of a large number of state legislatures could propose anything "radical"; finally, that procedures for grass-roots action set forth clearly in the time-hallowed, ineffably sacred Constitution could do serious irrevocable damage to the Constitution itself. Certainly if the framers had installed such a dangerous provision they would themselves have been far less than the paragons they are usually hailed as having been by politicians and constitutional devotees.

The scene began to take on the aspect of a black comedy as Vice President Walter Mondale, Senator Edward Muskie of Maine, Senator Edward Kennedy of Massachusetts and other ascendant Democrats echoed President Carter.

Republicans, forever commending themselves as great budget-balancers (although they are not), were completely in accord with Democrats in late 1978 and early 1979 in visualizing a constitutional convention as a looming disaster of the first water. House Minority Leader John Rhodes of Arizona stigmatized the end sought by convention proponents as unworkable. Senator Barry Goldwater of Arizona felt that if a convention was convoked, "We may wind up with a Constitution so far different from that we have lived under for 200 years that the Republic might not be able to continue." His assumption here was that members of a new convention were likely to be malicious mischief-makers and that the Constitution as it stood was so nearly perfect that it could not be improved.

Republicans and Democrats alike, far and wide, assailed the proposal as certain to lead to destruction, thereby showing far less faith in "the people" than the original framers whom Jeffersonian historians have berated as having shown too little faith. A White House "task force" hastily assembled by President Carter to defeat further state endorsements of the convention call described the prospect as a "nightmare" and a potential source of "serious dangers to our economic, social and political system." The group assumed apparently that these systems were beyond reproach but they are precisely what large groups of people are increasingly decrying. "Perhaps," an Iowa state legislator warned, "just perhaps you're inviting an entire rewrite of the Constitution that has existed since 1787."

As nobody has suggested such a general rewriting it would seem that many politicians believe people harbor a secret yearning to dismantle the Constitution line by line. Why they should wish to do so with a system the media uniformly assures the world is perfect is not evident. To be sure, the media may be mistaken.

Much speculation was let loose in the press that a special convention, once it got into motion, would at least produce amendments abolishing free speech and press, forbidding abortion and in general dismantling all the purely verbal and often ineffective guarantees of civil and legal rights. "The people", in convention assembled, were obviously not trusted by the politicians. They were the enemy, strangely objecting to being fleeced by fully constitutional processes.

In calling for an amendment that would require a balanced budget each year the movers for a convention were in fact striking not at the extant system of government but at a lucrative racket the politicians have been staging for themselves and their immediate clients: the providers of public services and holders of government contracts. The debate, as at all times, whatever the manifest issue, was about money —who collects and dispenses it, who must give it up or over-pay. As the Corporate States needs a lot of funding there is much money at stake.

Under the Constitution—as many people are becoming tardily aware —it is elected federal officials who make the determinations of what is to be done and who must pay for it and in what ways. And that the officials hold transcendent jobs is made clear by the millions upon millions contributed by many citizens to install and keep happy Congressmen and Presidents. The private parties who put up this electoral money evidently feel it is helpful in tilting decision-making their way.

The main decision Congress and the President makes that is of steady effect on the citizenry concerns appropriations—that is, how much is to be spent up to and beyond a half-trillion dollars and what for. The proceeds are supposed to come from taxes but here, in response to citizen sensitivity, the government tends to understate the cost. Because the government has taken to spending more than it takes in, the result is inflation—a steady rise in the prices of goods and services.

The difference between what it spends and what it takes in the government makes up by deviously operating the money-printing machine, so that the quantity of money in circulation exceeds the quantity of available goods and services. Prices therefore tend to rise and money and money-values held by citizens decline in purchasing power. Holders of assets thereupon find themselves being steadily nudged toward the government welfare lines, there to join other government dependents.

All that the government has been doing in these respects is strictly constitutional. For the Constitution empowers it, first, to lay taxes without limit (Article I, Section 8, Paragraph 1). It is empowered in the very next paragraph to borrow money on the credit of the United States—

that is, the taxpayers—also without limit. At the time the Constitution was up for debate in 1787-88 many writers objected vociferously to these provisions but were not heeded by the majority.

As to inflation, Paragraph 5 empowers the government, through Congress and the President, not only to coin money but to "regulate the value thereof". In other words, under the Constitution a dollar is worth whatever Congress and the President determine it to be by their fiscal decisions, and for nearly three decades officials, Republican and Democratic alike, have decreed that it be worth less.

The process by which the printing press is brought into play is somewhat veiled, like much in the Constitution, so that the public does not quite know what is taking place. Armed with appropriations by Congress, approved by the President, the Treasury must come up with the money. If tax receipts are not sufficient to yield a Treasury balance, the Treasury simply has printed short-term notes and bonds and sends these over to the Federal Reserve Bank, the nation's central bank.

In receipt of these securities the Federal Reserve simply credits the Treasury with a deposit for the total amount. The Treasury draws checks against these deposits. And these checks are new money.

Or the Treasury may simply offer the securities for sale in the open market, receiving therefore the checks of buyers. In recent years government "paper" has been less attractive to buyers so that interest rates have had to be scaled up to more than 10 per cent, a measure of the doubt in the market about the value of the offerings.

But when the market will not accept the new securities, for whatever reason, there is always the Federal Reserve to resort to. The Federal Reserve either keeps the securities in its vaults or forces them upon member banks. If it does the latter, it leaves less of their deposits available for non-governmental loans, draining liquid funds out of the banking system—deflationary. If it merely holds them—government I.O.U.s against future tax collections—it adds to existing money supply, fueling inflation. Money is printed by the government to cash all checks as they return for collection to the Federal Reserve.

There are two stages in the printing process—first the printing of Treasury bills, notes and bonds and, finally, the printing of money to pay off the net overflow of checks.

The process however begins in Congress.

It could be, as the Cassandras lament, that a constitutional convention would take the bit in its teeth and go beyond enacting a budget-balancing amendment. If it did, it would be doing no more than did the sanctified Federal Convention of 1787, which was empowered solely to propose amendments to the Articles of Confederation.

But the fears of convention opponents are palpably synthetic. They just don't want the budget-balancing amendment. For whatever a new convention came up with—and it could propose a variety of constitutional improvements, as these pages have made clear—it would need to submit its work to the legislatures or conventions of at least 38 states. And as all (except one state) have two-house legislatures, in effect this entails that 75 or 76 legislative bodies would need to approve. The chances of getting any great new constitutional departure approved by this many bodies is almost nil.

Again, assuming that an amendment providing for a balanced yearly budget were approved, the situation would be about where it was to begin with. For the government would still have the sole power to interpret the Constitution. And there are many ways, known to accountants, to present the same figures with a view to showing a budget unbalanced under one method to be balanced under another.

And if a budget were found to be unbalanced by non-government people, and the government refused to shape it to their approval, what would they be able to do about it? They could not sue and have the Supreme Court issue a mandamus to the Executive to do his duty (*Marbury v. Madison*).

As these pages have shown plentifully, if they have shown anything, the government runs the Constitution, not the Constitution or "the people" the government. And this consequence is inevitable under any form of government.

As I have already pointed out, the nearest any people can come to having any say about the government—leaving to one side special-interest groups who are able to persuade by arcane methods—is under a system such as the British have. And in Britain the people may determine only what general policy shall prevail in a government, not the specific steps taken to implement that policy. But the British may, through the opposition party, raise formal and pointed questions about those steps, which they do in a regular weekly parliamentary procedure.

In order to do this the British must have, as they do, parties able to enforce their policies upon party members in the House of Commons. Americans, lacking such effective parties, have absolutely no control over the actions of any of the three branches of government. And even if they had such parties, and one was in a clear majority, it could not affect constitutional procedures owing to the two-thirds and three-fourths rules for constitutional changes. The British may alter their Constitution at any time by a majority in Parliament.

The United States is, comparatively, in a constitutional straitjacket with the office-holders—or rather a minority of office-holders—at all times able to block constitutional changes.

All Americans may do is to exercise the franchise at mechanically exact intervals, whether or not they feel any need of an election. They go to the polls, or stay away if they wish, like prisoners in lockstep. And the men they elect are able to go their own way until the next election. At that time, if the electorate is so disposed, they may be ousted.

But the outgoing office-holder will be replaced by one in an equally independent formal position. The electorate has no more constitutional control over him than it had of his predecessor. As history has shown, replacing one man with another in offices where the man, once installed, is completely independent with respect to his actions, usually produces very little result.

Added to the many reasons that could be cited for why Americans have been unable to develop effective political parties that have control over their members in office, then, is the fact that there is little motivation under the Constitution for having political parties because a mere majority is not sufficient to produce timely changes in the Constitution. A political party able to lay down principles the government would be obliged to follow would need to win such a preponderant number of offices as to defy all probabilities. It would need to control two-thirds of Congress and three-fourths of the state legislatures.

To get out of the constitutional vise the government therefore has taken to bending the Constitution, a game that can go pretty far as has been shown by post-World War II Presidents—and Congress.

SELECTED BIBLIOGRAPHY

Abraham, Henry J. *Justices and Presidents*. Penguin Books, N.Y., 1975.

Acton, Lord. *Essays in the Liberal Interpretation of History*. University of Chicago Press, 1967.

Adams, Charles Francis, ed. *The Works of John Adams*. Little Brown & Co., Boston, 1850–56.

Adams, Henry. *History of the United States during the Administrations of Jefferson and Madison*. Abridged edn., Prentice-Hall, Englewood Cliffs, N.J., 1963.

Adams, John. *Diary and Autobiography*. Edited by L. H. Butterfield, Harvard University Press, 1961.

Adams, John and John Q. *The Selected Writings of John and John Quincy Adams*. Alfred A. Knopf, N.Y., 1946.

Adams, Randolph G. *Political Ideas of the American Revolution*. Barnes and Noble, N.Y., 1958.

Alden, John Richard. *The American Revolution, 1775–1783*. Harper & Row, N.Y., 1954.

Association of the Bar of the City of New York, Special Committee on Congressional Ethics. *Congress and the Public Trust*. Atheneum, N.Y., 1970.

Bagehot, Walter. *The English Constitution*. D. Appleton & Co., N.Y., 1877.

Bailey, Thomas. *Presidential Greatness*. Appleton-Century Co., N.Y., 1966.

Bailyn, Bernard. *The Ideological Origins of the American Revolution*. Harvard University Press, 1967.

Baker, Leonard. *John Marshall: A Life in Law*. Macmillan Publishing Co., N.Y., 1974.

Barth, Alan. *Prophets with Honor*. Alfred A. Knopf, N.Y., 1974.

Beard, Charles A. *An Economic Interpretation of the Constitution of the United States*. Macmillan Co., N.Y., 1913.

Beer, Samuel H., et al. *Patterns of Government: The Major Political Systems of Europe*. Random House, N.Y., 1958.

Belmont, Perry. *An American Democrat*. Columbia University Press, 1940.

Berger, Raoul. *Executive Privilege: A Constitutional Myth.* Harvard University Press, 1974.

———— *Government by Judiciary.* Harvard University Press, 1977.

———— *Impeachment: The Constitutional Problems.* Harvard University Press, 1973.

Blackstone, William. *Commentaries on the Laws of England.* Edited by J. W. Ehrlich,, 2 vols., Capricorn Books, N.Y., 1959.

Boardman, R. S. *Roger Sherman, Signer and Statesman.* University of Pennsylvania Press, 1938.

Boorstein, Daniel J. *The Americans: The Democratic Experience.* Random House, N.Y., 1973.

Boudin, Louis. *Government by Judiciary.* Ginn & Co., Boston, 1911.

Bowen, Catherine Drinker. *Miracle in Philadelphia.* Little Brown & Co., Boston, 1964.

Boyd, Julian P. *The Papers of Thomas Jefferson.* Princeton University Press, 1955.

Brant, Irving. *James Madison.* 6 vols., Bobbs-Merrill Co., N.Y., 1941–61.

Brooks, Robert C. *Corruption in American Politics and Life.* Dodd, Mead & Co., N.Y., 1910.

Brown, Robert E. *Charles Beard and the Constitution.* Princeton University Press, 1956.

Bryce, James. *The American Commonwealth.* 2 vols., Macmillan Co., N.Y., 1893.

Burns, James MacGregor. *Congress on Trial.* Harper & Bros., N.Y., 1949.

———— *Uncommon Sense.* Harper & Row, N.Y., 1972.

Butzner, Jane. *Constitutional Chaff.* Columbia University Press, 1941.

Channing, Edward. *A History of the United States.* 5 vols., Macmillan Co., N.Y., 1907–27.

Clark, Walter. *Government by Judges.* Address delivered at Cooper Union, N.Y., January 27, 1914. Senate Document No. 610. 63rd Congress, 2nd Session. Government Printing Office, Washington, D.C., 1914.

Cochran, Hamilton. *Noted American Duels and Hostile Encounters.* Chilton Books, Philadelphia, 1963.

Code of Federal Regulations: The President. Government Printing Office, Washington, D.C., 1976.

Cohen, Morris Raphael. *Law and the Social Order.* Harcourt Brace & Co., N.Y., 1933.

———— *Reason and Law.* Free Press, Glencoe, Ill., 1950.

Commager, Henry Steele, ed. *Documents in American History.* Appleton-Century-Crofts, N.Y., 1962.

Constitution of the United States: Analysis and Interpretation, The. Annotation of cases to June 29, 1972. Congressional Research Service, Library of Congress. Government Printing Office, Washington, D.C., 1973.

Corwin, Edward S. *The Constitution and What It Means Today.* 13th edn., Princeton University Press, 1975.

———— *Supplement* to above (by Harold W. Chase and Craig R. Ducat), Princeton University Press, 1978.

———— *Court over Constitution*. Princeton University Press, 1950.

———— *The Doctrine of Judicial Review*. Princeton University Press, 1914.

———— *The President: Office and Powers*. New York University Press, 1948.

———— *The Twilight of the Supreme Court*. Yale University Press, 1934.

Cox, Archibald. *The Role of the Supreme Court in American Government*. Oxford University Press, N.Y., 1977.

Craven, Avery. *The Coming of the Civil War*. University of Chicago Press, 1971.

Craven, Wesley Frank. *The Legend of the Founding Fathers*. New York University Press, 1956.

Crosskey, William W. *Politics and the Constitution in the History of the United States*. 2 vols., University of Chicago Press, 1950.

Cunliffe, Marcus. *American Presidents and the Presidency*. American Heritage Press, N.Y., 1968.

Current, Richard N. *Daniel Webster and the Rise of National Conservatism*. Little Brown & Co., Boston, 1955.

Davis, John P. *Corporations: A Study of the Original Development of Great Business Combinations and Their Relations to the Authority of the State* (1897). Capricorn Books, N.Y., 1961.

Department of State. *Documentary History of the Constitution*. Washington, D.C., 1894–1905.

Dickinson, H. T. *Bolingbroke*. Constable & Co., London, 1970.

Dictionary of American Biography. Charles Scribner's Sons, N.Y., 1964.

Dolbeare, Kenneth M., and Edelman, Murray J. *American Politics*. D. C. Heath & Co., Lexington, Mass., 1974.

Dorson, Norman, and Gillers, Stephen. *None of Your Business: Government Secrecy in America*. Viking Press, N.Y., 1974.

Dumbauld, Edward. The *Constitution of the United States*. University of Oklahoma Press, Norman, Okla., 1964.

Dunne, Gerald T. *Hugo Black and the Judicial Revolution*. Simon & Schuster, N.Y., 1977.

Elliot, Jonathan. *Debates in State Conventions on the Adoption of the Federal Constitution*. 4 vols., Washington, D.C., 1836.

Encyclopedia Americana. Americana Corporation, N.Y., 1971.

Encyclopedia of American History. Harper & Row, N.Y., 1970.

Ewing, Cortez Arthur Milton. *The Judges of the Supreme Court, 1789–1937*. University of Minnesota Press, 1938.

Farrand, Max. *The Framing of the Constitution of the United States*. Revised edn., Yale University Press, 1965.

Farrand, Max, ed. *The Records of the Federal Convention of 1787*. Revised edn., 4 vols., Yale University Press, 1966.

Fehrenbacker, Don E. *The Dred Scott Case: Its Significance in American Law and Politics*. Oxford University Press, N.Y., 1978.

Feuer, Lewis S. *Ideology and the Ideologists*. Harper & Row, N.Y., 1975.

Finer, Herman. *The Presidency: Crisis and Regeneration*. University of Chicago Press, 1960.

Fischer, David Hackett. *The Revolution of American Conservatism: The Federalist Party in the Era of Jeffersonian Democracy*. Harper & Row, N.Y., 1965.

Fiske, John B. *The Critical Period in American History*. Macmillan Co., London, 1894.

Flexner, James Thomas. *George Washington*. 4 vols., Little Brown & Co., Boston, 1965–72.

Ford, Paul Leicester, ed. *Essays on the Constitution, 1787–1788*. Burt Franklin, N.Y., 1970.

——————— *Pamphlets on the Constitution of the United States, 1787–1788*. Brooklyn, N.Y., 1888.

Frank, Jerome. *Law and the Modern Mind*. Brentano's, N.Y., 1930.

Fraser, Leon. *English Opinion of the American Constitution*. Columbia University Press, 1915.

Friedman, Laurence M. *A History of American Law*. Simon & Schuster, N.Y., 1973.

Friedman, Leon, and Israel, Fred L. *The Justices of the United States Supreme Court, 1789–1969*. 4 vols., Chelsea House, N.Y., 1969.

Galloway, G. B. *History of the House of Representatives*. Crowell, N.Y., 1962.

Gavin, James M. *On to Berlin*. Viking Press, N.Y., 1978.

Haines, Charles Grove. *The American Doctrine of Judicial Supremacy*. University of California Press, 1932.

Halperin, Morton H., et al. *The Lawless State*. Penguin Books, N.Y., 1976.

Hamilton, Alexander, et al. *The Federalist Papers*. Edited and collated with the Constitution by Clinton Rossiter, New American Library, N.Y., 1961.

——————— *The Basic Ideas of Alexander Hamilton*. Edited by Richard B. Morris, Pocket Library, N.Y., 1957.

Haraszti, Zoltán. *John Adams and the Prophets of Progress*, Harvard University Press, 1952.

Harrington, James (1611–1677). *The Political Writings of James Harrington*. Selected and edited by Charles Blitzer, Bobbs-Merrill Co., N.Y., 1955.

Hatch, Louis C. *A History of the Vice-Presidency of the United States*. American Historical Society, N.Y., 1934.

Hawke, David F. *The Colonial Experience*. Bobbs-Merrill Co., N.Y., 1966.

——————— *Paine*. Harper & Row, N.Y., 1974.

——————— *A Transaction of Free Men*. Charles Schribner's Sons, N.Y., 1964.

——————— *U.S. Colonial History*. Bobbs-Merrill Co., N.Y., 1966.

Heidenheimer, Arnold J., ed. *Political Corruption*. Holt, Rinehart & Winston, N.Y., 1970.

Heitman, Francis B. *Historical Register of Officers of the Continental Army during the War of the Revolution.* Genealogical Publishing Co., Baltimore, 1967.

Hildreth, Richard. *History of the United States.* 6 vols., Harper & Bros., N.Y., 1849–52.

Hill, Christopher. *The World Turned Upside Down: Radical Ideas during the English Revolution.* Viking Press, N.Y., 1972.

Hockett, Homer Carey. *The Constitutional History of the United States.* 2 vols., Macmillan Co., N.Y., 1939.

Hofstadter, Richard. *America at 1750: A Social Portrait.* Alfred A. Knopf, N.Y., 1971.

Horton, Paul B., and Leslie, Gerald R. *The Sociology of Social Problems.* Appleton-Century-Crofts, N.Y., 1955.

Horwill, Herbert W. *The Usages of the American Constitution.* Oxford University Press, N.Y., 1925.

Hume, David. *Philosophical Works.* 4 vols., Little Brown & Co., Boston, 1854.

———— *Political Essays.* Bobbs-Merrill Co., N.Y., 1953.

Hunt, Gaillard, ed. *The Writings of James Madison.* 9 vols., G. P. Putnam's Sons, N.Y., 1900–10.

Hutchison, David. *The Foundations of the Constitution* (1928). University Books, Secaucus, N.J., 1975.

Irving, Clive. *Pox Britannica: The Unmaking of the British.* Saturday Review Press, N.Y., 1974.

Jackson, Donald Dale, *Judges.* Atheneum, N.Y., 1974.

Jackson, Robert H. *The Struggle for Judicial Supremacy.* Random House, N.Y., 1941.

Jacobson, David L., ed. *The English Libertarian Heritage.* Bobbs-Merrill Co., N.Y., 1965.

Jefferson, Thomas. *The Writings of Thomas Jefferson.* Edited by Andrew A. Lipscomb and Albert Ellery Bergh, Thomas Jefferson Memorial Association, Washington, D.C., 1904–5.

Jennings, Ivor. *The British Constitution.* Cambridge University Press, 1966.

Jensen, Merrill. *The Articles of Confederation.* University of Wisconsin Press, 1966.

———— *The Making of the American Constitution.* D. Van Nostrand Co., N.Y., 1964.

———— *The New Nation.* Alfred A. Knopf, N.Y., 1950.

Jensen, Merrill, ed. *Documentary History of the Ratification of the Constitution.* Vols. 1 & 2, State Historical Society of Wisconsin, 1976.

———— *Tracts of the American Revolution, 1763–1776.* Bobbs-Merrill Co., N.Y., 1967.

Jones, Peter d'Alroy. *The Consumer Society: A History of American Capitalism.* Penguin Books, Harmondsworth, England, 1965.

Josephson, Matthew. *The Politicos.* Harcourt Brace & World, N.Y., 1938.

———— *The President Makers.* Harcourt Brace & World, N.Y., 1940.

———— *The Robber Barons.* Harcourt Brace & Co., 1934.

Kane, Hartnett T. *Gentlemen, Swords and Pistols*. William Morrow Co., N.Y., 1951.

Kelly, Alfred H., and Harbison, Winfred A. *The American Constitution*. W. W. Norton & Co., 1970.

Kenyon, Cecelia M., ed. *The Antifederalists*. Bobbs-Merrill Co., Indianapolis, 1976.

Key, V. O. *Politics, Parties and Pressure Groups*. 4th ed., Crowell, N.Y., 1958.

King, C. R. *Life and Correspondence of Rufus King*. G. P. Putnam's Sons, N.Y., 1894–1900.

Kolko, Gabriel. *The Triumph of Conservatism: A Reinterpretation of American History, 1900–1916*. Macmillan Co., N.Y., 1963.

———— *Wealth and Power in America*. Frederick A. Praeger, N.Y., 1962.

Kramnick, Isaac. *Bolingbroke and His Circle: The Politics of Nostalgia in the Age of Walpole*. Harvard University Press, 1968.

Lane, Robert E. *Political Ideology: Why the American Common Man Believes What He Does*. Free Press, N.Y., 1962.

———— *Political Life; Why and How People Get Involved in Politics*. Free Press, N.Y., 1959.

Lasky, Victor. *It Didn't Start with Watergate*. Dial Press, N.Y., 1977.

Lee, Richard Henry. *Letters from the Federal Farmer to the Republican* (1788). Quadrangle Books, Chicago, 1962.

Levy, Leonard W. *American Constitutional Law, Historical Essays*. Harper & Row, N.Y., 1966.

———— *Essays on the Making of the Constitution*. Oxford University Press, London, 1969.

———— *Jefferson and Civil Liberties*. Harvard University Press, 1963.

Lieberman, Jethro K. *How the Government Breaks the Law*. Stein & Day, N.Y., and Penguin Books, N.Y., 1973.

Lipset, Seymour Martin. *Political Man: The Special Bases of Politics*. Doubleday & Co., N.Y., 1960.

Lukas, J. Anthony. *Nightmare: The Underside of the Nixon Years*. Viking Press, N.Y., 1973.

Lynd, Staughton. *Intellectual Origins of American Radicalism*. Pantheon Books, N.Y., 1968.

McCaleb, Walter F. *The Aaron Burr Conspiracy*. Dodd, Mead & Co., N.Y., 1903.

McCloskey, Robert G. *The American Supreme Court*. University of Chicago Press, 1960.

McDonald, Forrest. *E Pluribus Unum: The Formation of the American Republic, 1776–1790*. Houghton Mifflin Co., Boston, 1965.

———— *We the People: The Economic Origins of the Constitution*. University of Chicago Press, 1958.

McIlwaine, C. H. *The American Revolution*. Cornell University Press, 1923.

———— *Constitutionalism, Ancient and Modern*. Cornell University Press, 1940.

McLaughlin, A. C. *Constitutional History of the United States.* Irvington, N.Y., 1935.

McMaster, John Bach. *The Political Depravity of the Founding Fathers.* Farrar, Straus & Co., N.Y., 1964.

Main, Jackson Turner. *The Anti-Federalists: Critics of the Constitution, 1781–1788.* University of North Carolina Press, 1961.

———— *Social Structure of Revolutionary America.* Princeton University Press, 1965.

———— *The Sovereign States, 1775–1783.* Franklin Watts, N.Y., 1973.

Mason, Alpheus. *American Constitutional Law.* Prentice-Hall, N.Y., 1954.

Massachusetts. *Debates and Proceedings in the Convention of the Commonwealth of 1788.* William White, Boston, 1856.

Mattox, Absalom H. *A History of the Cincinnati Society . . .* With names, army record, and rank of members . . . P. G. Thomson, Cincinnati, 1880.

May, Henry F. *The Enlightenment in America.* Oxford University Press, N.Y., 1976.

Mellon, Matthew T. *Early American Views on Negro Slavery* (1934). Bergman Publishers, N.Y., 1969.

Meyers, Marvin, ed. *The Mind of the Founder: Sources of the Political Thought of James Madison.* Bobbs-Merrill Co., N.Y., 1973.

Miller, Arthur Selwyn. *The Supreme Court and American Capitalism.* Free Press, N.Y., 1968.

Miller, John C. *Alexander Hamilton and the Growth of the New Nation.* Harper & Row, N.Y., 1959.

———— *Alexander Hamilton, A Portrait in Paradox.* Harper & Bros., N.Y., 1959.

———— *The Federalist Era, 1789–1801.* Harper & Row, N.Y., 1960.

Montesquieu, Baron de (Charles Louis de Secondat). *The Spirit of the Laws* (1748). Hafner Press, N.Y., 1949.

Morgan, Edmund S. *The Birth of the Republic, 1763–1789.* University of Chicago Press, 1956.

Morris, Richard B. *The American Revolution Reconsidered.* Harper & Row, N.Y., 1967.

———— *Seven Who Shaped Our Destiny.* Harper & Row, N.Y., 1973.

Morris, Robert. *Account of Robert Morris' Property.* Personally signed, n.d. George Bancroft Collection, New York Public Library. Inventory of holdings submitted in judicial bankruptcy proceedings. Shows that Morris land operations extended to Georgia, Florida, Louisiana and the Gulf Coastal region as well as Ohio Valley, etc.

Murphy, Walter F. *Congress and the Court.* University of Chicago Press, 1962.

Myers, Gustavus. *History of the Supreme Court.* Reprint, Burt Franklin, N.Y., 1968.

Nader, Ralph, Study Group. *The Monopoly Makers.* Grossman Publishers, N.Y., 1973.

Nevins, Allan. *The American States during and after the Revolution, 1779–1789*. Macmillan Co., N.Y., 1924.

Nicholson, Max. *The System: The Misgovernment of Modern Britain*. Hodder and Stoughton, London, 1967.

Oberholtzer, Ellis Paxson. *Robert Morris, Patriot and Financier*. Macmillan Co., N.Y., 1903.

O'Leary, Cornelius. *Elimination of Corrupt Practices in British Elections, 1868–1911*. Clarendon Press, Oxford, 1962.

Oliver, Peter. *Notes on Education in the United States in 1800*. New York Public Library, N.Y., 1944.

Paine, Thomas. *Common Sense*. Bobbs-Merrill Co., N.Y., 1953.

Parks, Henry Bamford. *The American Experience*. Alfred A. Knopf, N.Y., 1959.

Parton, James. *The Life and Times of Aaron Burr*. Mason Brothers, N.Y., 1958.

Pattinson, D. H. *The Reception of the American Constitution in Britain*. Ph.D. thesis, University of Birmingham, U.K., 1941.

Pearson, Drew, and Allen, Robert S. *The Nine Old Men*. Doubleday Doran & Co., N.Y., 1936.

Polsby, Nelson W. *Emerging Coalitions in American Politics*. Institute for Contemporary Studies, 1978.

Poore, Benjamin Perley. *The Federal and State Constitutions, Colonial Charters and Other Organic Laws of the United States*. Compiled by order of Congress, Government Printing Office, Washington, D.C., 1871.

Powell, Thomas Reed. *Vagaries and Varieties in Constitutional Interpretation*. Columbia University Press, N.Y., 1956.

Pritchett, C. H. *American Constitutional Issues*. McGraw-Hill, N.Y., 1962.

Projector, D. S., and Weiss, G. S. *Survey of Financial Characteristics of Consumers*. Board of Governors of the Federal Reserve System, Washington, D.C., 1966.

Randall, J. G. *Constitutional Problems under Lincoln*. D. Appleton & Co., N.Y., 1926.

Richey, Russell E., and Jones, Donald G. *American Civil Religion*. Harper & Row, N.Y., 1974.

Robbins, Caroline. *The Eighteenth-Century Commonwealthman*. By arrangement with Harvard University Press, Atheneum, N.Y., 1968.

Robbins, Caroline, ed. *Two English Republican Tracts*. Cambridge University Press, 1969.

Rodell, Fred. *Fifty-five Men*. Telegraph Press, Harrisburg, Pa., 1936.

———— *Nine Men: A Political History of the Supreme Court from 1790 to 1955*. Random House, N.Y., 1955.

Rossiter, Clinton. *Conservatism in America*. Alfred A. Knopf, N.Y., 1955.

———— *The First American Revolution*. Harcourt Brace & World, N.Y., 1956.

———— *Parties and Politics in America*. Cornell University Press, 1960.

———— *The Political Thought of the American Revolution*. Harcourt Brace & World, N.Y., 1953.

———— *1787: The Grand Convention*. Macmillan Co., N.Y., 1966.

Schachner, Nathan. *The Founding Fathers*. Putnam, N.Y., 1954.

Schlesinger, Arthur M. *Prelude to Independence: The Newspaper War on Britain, 1764–1776.* Alfred A. Knopf, N.Y., 1957.

Schlesinger, Arthur M., Jr. *The Imperial Presidency.* Houghton Mifflin Co., Boston, 1973.

Schmeckebier, Laurence F., and Eastin, Roy B. *Government Publications and Their Use.* Brookings Institution, Washington, D.C., 1969.

Schmidhauser, John R. *The Supreme Court: Its Politics, Personalities, and Procedures.* Holt Rinehart & Winston, N.Y., 1960.

Schubert, Glendon. *The Judicial Mind.* Northwestern University Press, 1965.

———— *Judicial Policymaking.* Scott, Foresman Co., Chicago, 1965.

Schuyler, Robert Livingston. *The Constitution of the United States.* Macmillan Co., N.Y., 1923.

Schwartz, Bernard. *From Confederation to Nation.* Johns Hopkins University Press, 1973.

Seitz, Don C. *Famous American Duels.* Thomas Y. Crowell, N.Y., 1929.

Senate Library. *Presidential Vetoes.* Government Printing Office, Washington, D.C., 1978.

Shaw, Peter. *The Character of John Adams.* University of North Carolina Press, 1976.

Simms, Henry H. *Life of John Taylor.* William Byrd Press, Richmond, Va., 1932.

Smelser, Marshall. *The Democratic Republic, 1801–1815.* Harper & Row, N.Y., 1968.

Smith, J. Allen. *The Spirit of American Government* (1907). Harvard University Press, 1965.

Sparks, Jared. *Life of Gouverneur Morris.* Gray & Bowen, Boston, 1832.

Stein, David. *Judging the Judges.* Exposition Press, Hicksville, N.Y., 1974.

Stevens, William Oliver. *Pistols at Ten Paces: The Code of Honor in America.* Houghton Mifflin Co., Boston, 1940.

Story, Joseph. *Commentaries on the Constitution of the United States* (1833). 3 vols., Da Capo Press, N.Y., 1970.

Swindler, William E. *Court and Constitution in the 20th Century: The Old Legality, 1889–1932.* Bobbs-Merrill Co., N.Y., 1969.

———— *Court and Constitution in the 20th Century: The New Legality, 1932–1968.* Bobbs-Merrill Co., N.Y., 1970.

———— *Court and Constitution in the 20th Century: The Modern Interpretation.* Bobbs-Merrill Co., 1974.

Swisher, Carl Brent. *American Constitutional Development.* Houghton Mifflin Co., Boston, 1954.

———— *The Growth of Constitutional Power in the United States.* University of Chicago Press, 1963.

———— *Historic Decisions of the Supreme Court.* D. Van Nostrand Co., N. Y., 1969.

Symmes, John Cleve. *The Correspondence of John Cleve Symmes.* Edited by Beverley W. Bond Jr. Macmillan Co., N.Y., 1926.

Tocqueville, Alexis de. *Democracy in America* (1835). Introduction by John Stuart Mill, 2 vols., Schocken Books, N.Y., 1964.

Thomas, William Sturgis. *The Society of the Cincinnati: Original, Hereditary and Honorary Members*. Tobias A. Wright, N.Y., 1929.

Thompson, Faith. *The First Century of Magna Carta*. University of Minnesota Press, 1925.

Thorpe, F. N. *Constitutional History of the United States, 1865–1895*. 3 vols., Da Capo Press, N.Y., 1970.

Twiss, Benjamin R. *Lawyers and the Constitution: How Laissez-Faire Came to the Supreme Court*. Princeton University Press, 1942.

Van Deuson, Glynden G. *The Jacksonian Era, 1828–1848*. Harper & Row, N.Y., 1959.

Ver Steeg, Clarence L. *Robert Morris, Revolutionary Financier*. University of Pennsylvania Press, 1954.

Warren, Charles. *The Supreme Court in United States History*. 2 vols., Little Brown & Co., Boston, 1922, 1926.

Washington, George. *Writings of George Washington*. 39 vols., Government Printing Office, Washington, D.C., 1931–44.

White, G. Edward. *The American Judicial Tradition*. Oxford University Press, N.Y., 1976.

Williamson, Chilton, *American Suffrage, 1760–1860*. Princeton University Press, 1960.

Willoughby, Westel W. *Constitutional Law of the United States*. 3 vols., Baker, Voorhis & Co., 1929.

Wood, Gordon S. *The Creation of the American Republic, 1776–1787*. University of North Carolina Press, Chapel Hill, N.C., 1969.

Wormuth, Francis D. *The Vietnam War: The President Versus the Constitution*. Center for the Study of Democratic Institutions, Fund for the Republic, Santa Barbara, Cal., 1968.

Wright, Benjamin F. *The Growth of American Constitutional Law*. Phoenix Books, University of Chicago Press, 1967.

Young, Donald. *American Roulette: The History and Dilemma of the Vice Presidency*. Viking Press, N.Y., 1974.

NOTES

CHAPTER ONE

[1] See Thomas Reed Powell, *Vagaries and Varieties in Constitutional Interpretation,* Columbia University Press, 1956, passim. The literature on the twistings and turnings of the Court is very large.

[2] Merrill Jensen, *The Making of the American Constitution,* D. Van Nostrand Co., 1964, p. 140.

[3] Forrest McDonald, *We the People,* Phoenix Books, University of Chicago Press, 1963, p. 14.

[4] Joseph Story, *Commentaries on the Constitution of the United States,* Da Capo Press, N.Y., 1970, vol. 1, pp. 295-300.

[5] John Herman Randall, *The Career of Philosophy,* Columbia University Press, 1962, vol. 1, p. 634.

[6] David Hume, *A Treatise of Human Nature,* Everyman's Library, E. P. Dutton & Co., N.Y., vol. 2, p. 95.

[7] *The Encyclopedia Americana* (1971), "The United States: Sectional Conflict and Preservation of the Union, 1815-1877," vol. 27, Sec. 17, p. 576.

[8] Herman Finer, *The Presidency: Crisis and Regeneration,* University of Chicago Press, 1960, pp. 9-10, 60.

[9] Ibid, pp. 5-7.

[10] Paul B. Horton and Gerald R. Leslie, *The Sociology of Social Problems,* Appleton-Century-Crofts, N.Y., 1955. "Social problems" has been made into a special branch of American sociology, similar to pathology in medicine.

[11] Herbert W. Horwill, *The Usages of the American Constitution,* Oxford University Press, Oxford, 1925, p. 22.

[12] Ibid., pp. 8-9.

[13] Edward S. Corwin, *Court Over Constitution,* Princeton University Press, 1938, pp. 86-7.

[14] *New York Post,* final ed., November 26, 1971, 4:1-2.

[15] *New York Post,* September 13, 1972, 13:1.

[16] Amitai Etzioni, "America's Alienated Majority", *New Leader,* November 4, 1968.

[17] Louis Harris, "Building Public Confidence in Financial Institutions in the Seventies", *Financial Analysts Journal*, March-April 1973, p. 24 et seq.

[18] Alexis de Tocqueville, *Democracy in America*, Alfred A. Knopf, N.Y., 1945, vol. 1, p. 226.

[19] James Bryce, *The American Commonwealth*, Macmillan & Co., London, 1888, vol. 2, pp. 524-5.

[20] Ibid., p. 517.

CHAPTER TWO

[1] Jackson Turner Main, *The Anti-Federalists*, University of North Carolina Press, 1961, reprinted by Quadrangle Books, Chicago, 1964, p. 249.

[2] Ibid.

[3] Charles A. Beard, *An Economic Interpretation of the Constitution of the United States*, Macmillan Co., N.Y., 1914, p. 218.

[4] Henry Adams, *History of the United States during the Administrations of Jefferson and Madison*, abridged ed., Prentice-Hall, Englewood Cliffs, N.J., 1963, p. 139.

[5] Main, op. cit., pp. 249-55.

[6] Forrest McDonald, *We the People: The Economic Origins of the Constitution*, University of Chicago Press, 1958, passim.

[7] Main, op. cit., pp. 4-5; Richard Hofstadter, *America at 1750: A Social Portrait*, Alfred A. Knopf, N.Y., 1971, pp. 26, 30-5, 60, 134, 143-4.

[8] Main, op. cit., pp. 4-5.

[9] Hofstadter, op. cit., pp. 26-7.

[10] Caroline Robbins, *The Eighteenth-Century Commonwealthman*, Atheneum, N.Y., 1968, passim.

[11] Bernard Bailyn, *The Ideological Origins of the American Revolution*, Harvard University Press, 1967, passim.

[12] Christopher Hill, *The World Turned Upside Down*, Viking Press, N.Y., 1972, passim.

[13] Burgh, *Disquisitions*, vol. 1, p. 83.

[14] Robbins, op. cit., p. 116.

[15] Ibid., p. 122.

[16] Frederick E. Croxton and Dudley J. Cowden, *Applied General Statistics*, Prentice-Hall, N.Y., 1944, p. 273. Chapter 3 discusses the frequency curve in detail and the Croxton-Cowden book may be used for other relevant mathematical aspects. However, any treatise of a similar nature will supply the same kind of technical information.

[17] Seymour Martin Lipset, *Political Man*, Doubleday Anchor Book, 1963, p. 185; V. O. Key, *Politics, Parties and Pressure Groups*, 4th ed., Crowell, N.Y., 1958, p. 625.

[18] David Hume, "On the Immortality of the Soul," in *Of the Standard of Taste and Other Essays*, Library of Liberal Arts, Bobbs-Merrill, Indianapolis, 1965, p. 164.

[19] Zoltán Haraszti, *John Adams and the Prophets of Progress*, Harvard University Press, 1952, Grosset and Dunlap Universal Library, 1964, pp. 35-6.

CHAPTER THREE

[1] Edward S. Corwin, *Court Over Constitution*, Princeton University Press, 1938, pp. 216-17.

[2] Homer Carey Hockett, *The Constitutional History of the United States*, Macmillan Co., N.Y., 1939, vol. 1, p. 256.

[3] *The Records of the Federal Convention of 1787*, ed. by Max Farrand, Yale University Press, 1911, vol. 3, p. 242. These records, composed mainly of Madison's detailed notes on the Philadelphia constitutional convention but also of others' briefer observations, are hereafter referred to simply as "Farrand."

[4] Madison's Notes, Farrand, vol. 2, pp. 645-6.

[5] Letter to Robert Walsh, February 5, 1811. Jared Sparks, *Life of Gouverneur Morris*, 1832, vol. 3, pp. 260-5; Farrand, vol. 3, p. 418.

[6] Letter to Gouverneur Morris, February 27, 1802, in Hamilton's *Works*, ed. by Henry Cabot Lodge, N.Y., 1885-6, vol. 8, pp. 591-2.

[7] Department of State, *Documentary History of the Constitution*, Washington, D.C., 1894-1905, vol. 55, p. 584; Farrand, vol. 3, p. 297.

[8] Letter of November 2, 1788, to C. L. Turberville, in Gaillard Hunt, *The Writings of James Madison*, vol. 5, pp. 298, 300; Farrand, vol. 3, p. 354.

[9] Letter of October 8, 1788, to Philip Mazzei, in Hunt, op. cit., vol. 5, p. 267; Farrand, vol. 3, p. 353.

[10] *Documentary History of the Constitution*, vol. 4, pp. 273-6; Hunt, op. cit., vol. 4, pp. 389-91; Farrand, vol. 3, p. 77. The italicized words were in code in the original.

[11] *Documentary History of the Constitution*, Department of State (1894-1905), vol. 4, pp. 334-6; Farrand, vol. 3, pp. 134-5.

[12] Hunt, *Fragments of Revolutionary History*, Brooklyn, 1892, p. 156; Farrand, vol. 3, p. 82.

[13] Letter dated September 28, 1787. *American Historical Review*, vol. 3, pp. 313-14; Farrand, vol. 3, p. 100.

[14] Letter to Weedon Butler, October 8, 1787, British Museum, Additional MSS., 16602; Farrand, vol. 3, pp. 102-3.

[15] *Pennsylvania Magazine of History and Biography*, vol. 2, pp. 191-2; Farrand, vol. 3, pp. 242-3.

[16] Letter to Robert Walsh, February 5, 1811; Sparks, op. cit., vol. 3, pp. 260-5; Farrand, vol. 3, p. 418.

[17] Letter dated February 24, 1815; Sparks, op. cit., vol. 3, pp. 338-9; Farrand, vol. 3, pp. 421-2.

[18] Sparks, op. cit., vol. 3, p. 312.

[19] First published in *Magazine of American History*, vol. 7, pp. 352-3, from MS. owned by William Few Chrystie. Although the MS. bears no date as a whole, the last date mentioned in it is October 1816, and by reason of other internal evidence historians believe it written largely in that year; Farrand, vol. 3, p. 423.

[20] C. R. King, *Life and Correspondence of Rufus King*, vol. 1, p. 359; Farrand, vol. 3, p. 355.

[21] *Documentary History of the Constitution*, vol. 5, pp. 168-9; Farrand, vol. 3, p. 355.

[22] December 11, 1787, Farrand, vol. 3, p. 166.

[23] Ibid., pp. 142, 161.

[24] Ibid., p. 143.

[25] Ibid., pp. 161-2.

[26] Farrand, vol. 2, p. 588.

[27] *The Correspondence of John Cleve Symmes*, ed. by Beverley W. Bond Jr., Macmillan Co., N.Y., 1926, pp. 206-7.

[29] McHenry's Notes, Farrand, September 17, 1787, vol. 3, pp. 649-50.

[29] *Documentary History of the Constitution,* vol. 4, p. 320; Farrand, vol. 3, pp. 103-4.

[30] *Documentary History of the Constitution,* vol. 4, p. 807; Farrand, vol. 3, p. 339.

[31] *The Works of John Adams,* ed. by Charles Francis Adams, 1850-6, vol. 8, p. 467.

[32] Ibid., p. 464.

[33] Ibid., vol. 6, pp. 430-2.

[34] Letter, February 5, 1805, ibid., vol. 9, p. 590.

[35] Ibid., p. 602.

[36] Letter, April 24, 1824.

[37] *The Papers of Thomas Jefferson,* ed. by Julian P. Boyd, Princeton University Press, 1955, vol. 12, pp. 438-42.

[38] Henry H. Simms, *Life of John Taylor,* William Byrd Press, Richmond, Va., 1932, p. 100.

[39] Ibid.

[40] *The Writings of Thomas Jefferson,* ed. by Andrew A. Lipscomb and Albert Ellery Bergh, Thomas Jefferson Memorial Association, Washington, D.C., 1904-5, vol. 15, pp. 40-2.

[41] Jefferson to Giles, April 20, 1807, in Lipscomb and Bergh, eds., *The Writings of Thomas Jefferson,* 1904-5, vol. 11, p. 191.

[42] James Parton, *The Life and Times of Aaron Burr,* Mason Brothers, N.Y., 1857, p. 171.

[43] Ibid.

[44] Ibid., pp. 171-2.

[45] Perry Belmont, *An American Democrat,* Columbia University Press, 1940, p. 477.

[46] Farrand, vol. 2, pp. 641-3.

[47] Madison's Notes, Farrand, vol. 2, p. 643.

[48] Ibid., pp. 644-6.

[49] Ibid., p. 646.

[50] Ibid., pp. 646-7.

[51] Jonathan Elliot, *Debates in State Conventions on the Adoption of the Federal Constitution,* vol. 4, pp. 277-86; Farrand, vol. 3, pp. 253-5.

[52] Elliot, ibid., pp. 315-16; Farrand, vol. 3, p. 256.

[53] Farrand, vol. 2, p. 350.

[54] *Encyclopedia of American History,* Harper & Row, N.Y., 1970, p. 543.

[55] Ibid.

[56] *Letters and Other Writings of James Madison,* vol. 3, pp. 442-3; Farrand, vol. 3, p. 464.

CHAPTER FOUR

[1] That the gathering was more like a political caucus than a convention is a point developed by John P. Roche, "The Founding Fathers: A Reform Caucus in Action," *American Political Science Review,* vol. 55 (1961), p. 799.

[2] The United States today has more than 3,000 counties and in colloquial parlance the individuals always found in and around government at the county center— elected officials, appointees, lawyers, contractors, promoters, place-hunters, propagandists, fixers, lobbyists—are referred to as members of "the court-house gang". The main body of this motley group is always present, whatever party is nominally in the ascendant. In the state and national capitals there are similar groups—all quite natural but out of harmony with the myth of government by "the people."

[3] Forrest McDonald, *We the People,* Phoenix Books, University of Chicago Press, 1963, p. 54.

[4] Melanchthon Smith, *An Address to the People of the State of New York, by a Plebian* (1788), in Paul Leicester Ford, ed., *Pamphlets on the Constitution of the United States, 1787-1788,* Brooklyn, N.Y., 1888.

[5] Clinton Rossiter, *1787: The Grand Convention,* Mentor Books, New American Library, N.Y., 1966, pp. 127-8.

[6] Farrand, vol. 3, p. 76.

[7] McDonald, op. cit., pp. 38-110.

[8] McDonald, op. cit., p. 106.

[9] An excellent account of the constitutional debate and power struggle between radicals and conservatives is to be found in Merrill Jensen's *The Articles of Confederation,* more especially chapter 7, "The Problem of Sovereignty," University of Wisconsin Press, 1940, 6th printing, 1966. The conservatives scored a big gain by name-juggling, styling themselves Federalists although they were the very opposite, an early example of Orwellian New-Speak long antedating the pseudo-Marxist anti-people "People's Republics". See also Jensen's *The New Nation,* Alfred A. Knopf, N.Y., 1950, and Vintage Books, N.Y., 1965.

[10] James Harrington, *The Commonwealth of Oceana,* Library of Liberal Arts, Harrington's *Political Writings,* Bobbs-Merrill Co., Indianapolis, 1955, p. 44. Rather than cite a primary edition I cite a reprint that is more readily accessible to the general reader.

[11] Rossiter, op. cit., p. 125.

[12] Farrand, vol. 1, p. 35; vol. 3, pp. 557, 563, 588; as to Wyeth, Rossiter, op. cit., p. 141.

[13] Peter Oliver, *Notes on Education in the United States in 1800,* New York Public Library, N.Y., 1944, pp. 9-10.

[14] Ibid., pp. 12-13.

[15] Ibid., p. 17.

[16] The military rankings of all are to be found in Francis B. Heitman, *Historical Register of Officers of the Continental Army during the War of the Revolution,* Genealogical Publishing Co., Baltimore, 1967.

[17] William Sturgis Thomas, *The Society of the Cincinnati: Original, Hereditary and Honorary Members,* Tobias A. Wright, N.Y., 1929. The names are listed alphabetically in this source, passim.

[18] James Thomas Flexner, *George Washington and the New Nation,* Little Brown & Co., N.Y., 1970, pp. 220-1.

[19] Don C. Seitz, *Famous American Duels,* Thomas Y. Crowell, N.Y., 1929, p. 17.

[20] William Oliver Stevens, *Pistols at Ten Paces: The Code of Honor in America,* Houghton Mifflin Co., Boston, 1940, p. 7.

[21] Ibid., p. 31.

[22] Ibid., pp. 14-21.

[23] Ibid., p. 20.

[24] Ibid., p. 42; Seitz, op. cit., p. 106.

[25] Ibid., p. 161.

[26] Ibid., p. 25.

CHAPTER FIVE

[1] Catherine Drinker Bowen, *Miracle in Philadelphia,* Little Brown & Co., Boston, 1964, p. 199.

[2] Gordon S. Wood, *The Creation of the American Republic, 1776-1787*, University of North Carolina Press, Chapel Hill, N.C., 1969, pp. 3-4.

[3] Zoltán Haraszti, *John Adams and the Prophets of Progress*, by arrangement with Harvard University Press, Grosset & Dunlap, 1964, p. 31. "John Adams was the greatest political thinker whom America has yet produced," said political scientist Harold Laski. Quoted, ibid., p. 46.

[4] John Adams, *Diary and Autobiography*, Harvard University Press, 1961, vol. 3, pp. 331-3.

[5] Haraszti, op. cit., p. 31.

[6] John P. Davis, *Corporations*, Capricorn Books, N.Y., 1961, pp. 157-208.

[7] David Hutchison, *The Foundations of the Constitution*, University Books, Secaucus, N.J., 1975, passim. This book consists wholly of source tracings in massive detail.

[8] Drafts of the committee of detail may be found in Farrand, vol. 2, pp. 129-75, and the final draft at pp. 177-92.

[9] For a survey of characteristics of the state constitutions see Jackson Turner Main, *The Sovereign States, 1775-1783*, Franklin Watts, N.Y., 1973, pp. 180-221. See also Allan Nevins, *The American States during and after the Revolution, 1779-1789*, Augustus M. Kelley, N.Y., 1969, pp. 117-205.

[10] John B. Fiske, *The Critical Period in American History* (1888), p. 286.

[11] Max Farrand, *The Framing of the Constitution of the United States*, Yale University Press, rev. edn. 1965, p. 201.

[12] Ibid., pp. 80, 91-112, 113-14, 122, 134-5, 141, 146, 149-52, 166ff., 177, 183, 201-3.

[13] For a penetrating discussion of what was compromised and what not at the convention see Robert Livingston Schuyler, *The Constitution of the United States*, Macmillan Co., N.Y., 1923, reprinted 1952, pp. 85-127.

[14] Farrand, *Records*, vol. 2, p. 364.

[15] Ibid., vol. 2, p. 169.

[16] Ibid., vol. 1, pp. 48, 50.

[17] Ibid., vol. 1, p. 133.

[18] Ibid., vol. 1, pp. 512-14.

[19] Ibid., vol. 1, p. 49.

[20] Ibid., vol. 1, p. 51.

[21] Ibid., vol. 1, p. 288.

[22] Ibid., vol. 1, p. 299.

[23] Ibid., vol. 1, p. 289.

[24] Ibid., vol. 1, p. 285.

[25] Ibid., vol. 2, p. 52.

[26] John C. Miller, *Alexander Hamilton, Portrait in Paradox*, Harper and Bros., N.Y., 1959, p. 51.

[27] Ibid., p. 197. See also pp. 155, 180, 185-8, 197-9.

[28] Farrand, vol. 1, p. 533.

[29] Ibid., vol. 1, p. 534.

[30] David Hume, *Of the Standard of Taste and Other Essays*, Library of Liberal Arts, Bobbs-Merrill Co., N.Y., 1965, pp. 108-9; *An Inquiry Concerning Human Understanding*, same publisher, 1955, p. 33; *An Enquiry Concerning the Principles of Morals*, Open Court Publishing Company, La Salle, Ill., 1947, p. 74. According to Hume in his essay "The Stoic", "every man, however dissolute and negligent, proceeds in the pursuit of happiness with as unerring a motion as that which the

celestial bodies observe, when, conducted by the hand of the Almighty, they roll along the ethereal plains." In other words, if any man, anywhere, under any governmental system, tried to avoid pursuing happiness, he could no more do it than he could defy the law of gravitation. Hume's essays were widely read in the latter half of the eighteenth century.

[31] David F. Hawke, *A Transaction of Free Men*, Charles Scribner's Sons, N.Y., 1964, p. 149.

[32] Ibid., p. 147.

[33] Farrand, vol. 1, pp. 430-1.

[34] Ibid., vol. 1, pp. 422-3.

[35] Ibid.

[36] *The Selected Writings of John and John Quincy Adams*, Alfred A. Knopf, N.Y., 1946, p. 325.

[37] R. S. Boardman, *Roger Sherman, Signer and Statesman*, University of Pennsylvania Press, 1938, pp. 267-8.

[38] A good brief account of the ratification process is given in Forrest McDonald, *E Pluribus Unum: The Formation of the American Republic, 1776-1790*, reprinted as *The Formation of the American Republic, 1776-1790*, Penguin Books, Baltimore, 1965, pp. 209-36.

[39] Forrest McDonald, *We the People*, p. 164.

[40] The debates in Pennsylvania and all extant material bearing on the ratification convention are reported in *The Documentary History of the Ratification of the Constitution, Ratification of the Constitution by the States: Pennsylvania*, vol. 2, State Historical Society of Wisconsin, 1976, 779 pages. Additional volumes are in preparation.

[41] McDonald, *The Formation*, p. 129.

[42] Ibid., p. 213.

[43] Farrand, *Records*, vol. 1, pp. 513-14.

[44] Ibid., vol. 2, p. 640.

[45] McDonald, *The Formation*, pp. 233-4.

[46] See the elaborate analysis in McDonald, *We the People*, pp. 255-357.

[47] Ibid., pp. 163-254.

[48] See *The Antifederalists*, ed. by Cecelia M. Kenyon, Bobbs-Merrill Co., Indianapolis, 1966; Jackson Turner Main, *The Anti-Federalists: Critics of the Constitution, 1781-1788*, University of North Carolina Press, 1961, and Quadrangle Books, Chicago, 1964. In the latter work see especially the essay on the literature of anti-Federalism. Earlier and less complete publications of anti-Federalist views were edited by Paul Leicester Ford and published under the titles of *Essays on the Constitution of the United States* (1892) and *Pamphlets on the Constitution of the United States, 1787-1788* (1888). Both publications contain contributions by Federalists and anti-Federalists, the latter including Elbridge Gerry, George Clinton, Robert Yates, Samuel Chase, Luther Martin, Spencer Roane, James Winthrop, Melanchthon Smith, Richard Henry Lee and George Mason. See also *The Anti-Federalist Papers*, Morton Borden (ed.), Michigan State University Press, 1965.

[49] George Washington, *Writings*, vol. 29, pp. 525-6.

CHAPTER SIX

[1] Sir Ivor Jennings, *The British Constitution*, Cambridge University Press, 1966, p. 106.

[2] Ibid., p. 110.

³ Ibid., p. 98.

⁴ Ibid., p. 77.

⁵ Ibid., p. 195.

⁶ On the Supreme Court as a policy-making body see Arthur Selwyn Miller, "Some Pervasive Myths about the United States Supreme Court", *St. Louis University Law Journal*, vol. 10 (1965), and the same author's *The Supreme Court and American Capitalism*, Free Press, N.Y., 1968, p. 4 and passim. The general literature on this aspect of the Court is quite large.

⁷ Jennings, op. cit., pp. 196-7.

⁸ Ibid., pp. 74-5.

⁹ James Bryce, *The American Commonwealth*, vol. 1, ch. 15.

¹⁰ J. Allen Smith, *The Spirit of American Government*, p. 196.

CHAPTER SEVEN

¹ *Ex parte McCardle*, 7 Wall. 506. The case is discussed extensively in Charles Warren, *The Supreme Court in United States History*, Little Brown & Co., Boston, 1926, vol. 2, pp. 464-88.

² The Yates "Letters of Brutus" appeared in the *New York Journal and Weekly Register* in the latter weeks of 1787 and during January, February and March 1788. Numbers 11, 12 and 15 are reproduced in Corwin, *Court over Constitution*, pp. 231-62.

³ *The Public Statutes at Large of the United States of America, 1789-1845*. Charles C. Little and James Brown, Boston, 1850, vol. 1, p. 81.

⁴ Warren, op. cit., vol. 1, pp. 242-3.

⁵ Charles Grove Haines, *The American Doctrine of Judicial Supremacy*, University of California Press, 1932, pp. 89-121.

⁶ Ibid., p. 45.

⁷ Ibid., p. 49.

⁸ Ibid., p. 45.

⁹ Ibid., pp. 56-7.

¹⁰ Ibid., p. 33.

¹¹ Ibid., p. 34. Edward Jenks in an article titled "The Myth of Magna Carta" in *The Independent Review*, 4:260, pointed out that Coke invented the legend of Magna Carta, the legend that in this document English liberty was born and consecrated. Much research has disclosed this as simply not so. For a succinct and scholarly treatment of Magna Carta and its role in British history see Anne Pallister, *Magna Carta: The Heritage of Liberty*, Oxford University Press, London, 1971. As Pallister points out, only four clauses of thirty-seven paragraphs of the Magna Carta of 1237, which alone was discontinuously operative over any considerable length of time, survive in the British Constitution today. "Yet the validity of three of them is somewhat dubious," the author pointedly remarks (p. 101). The original Magna Carta of 1215, about which American politicians from time to time bawl to the heavens in mock piety, was a dead letter soon after issued and was not known to scholars until the seventeenth century. Magna Carta, as anyone can determine by reading a translation, far from a liberating document, was a yoke for centuries on the British common people who attained freedom only with its gradual liquidation. The entire Magna Carta story, as commonly told, is a tissue of myth.

¹² Allan Nevins, *The American States during and after the Revolution, 1779-1789*, Macmillan Co., N.Y., 1924, pp. 168-9.

¹³ Farrand, vol. 2, pp. 298-300.

[14] Edward S. Corwin, *Court Over Constitution*, Peter Smith, Gloucester, 1957 (reprint), p. 204.

[15] Ibid., p. 192.

[16] Ibid., pp. 201-2.

[17] The shabby intellectual performance of the Court in *Pollock* is given precise analysis by Corwin, ibid., pp. 177-209.

[18] *The Constitution of the United States of America: Annotations of Cases Decided by the Supreme Court of the United States to December 24, 1970*, Senate Document No. 92-82, revised, 92nd Congress, 2nd Session, Government Printing Office, Washington, D.C., 1973, pp. 1597-1619. This basic book, which amounts in effect to the actual Constitution of the United States as expounded to date, is hereafter referred to as *Annotations*.

[19] For details of this period see Matthew Josephson, *The Robber Barons*, Harcourt, Brace & Co., N.Y., 1934; *The Politicos*, Harcourt, Brace & World, N.Y., 1938; and *The President Makers*, Harcourt, Brace & World, N.Y., 1940.

[20] *Annotations*, pp. 1789-1797.

[21] Edward S. Corwin, *The Twilight of the Supeme Court*, Archon Books, Hamden, Conn., 1974, p. 114. First published by Yale University Press, 1934.

[22] Ibid., p. 117.

[23] Morris Raphael Cohen, *Law and the Social Order*, Harcourt, Brace & Co., N.Y., 1933, pp. 152-3. The material of the four preceding paragraphs is here reported.

[24] David Hume, "Of Commerce", *Political Essays*, Library of Liberal Arts, Bobbs-Merrill Co., N.Y., 1953, pp. 130-41.

[25] Peter d'Alroy Jones, *The Consumer Society: A History of American Capitalism*, Penguin Books, Harmondsworth, England, 1965, p. 99. Cited by Miller, infra.

[26] Arthur Selwyn Miller, *The Supreme Court and American Capitalism*, Free Press, N.Y., 1968, pp. 42-3. This easily readable book traces in specific detail the constitutional interlock between government and corporations in the United States. It contains only one major flaw: the credence given to the theory that non-owning managers control corporations.

[27] For a highly readable account see William F. Swindler, *Court and Constitution in the 20th Century: The Old Legality, 1889-1932;* and *Court and Constitution in the 20th Century: The Modern Interpretation*, Bobbs-Merrill Co., N.Y., 1969, 1974, passim.

[28] A large number of these cases are given and discussed in William F. Swindler, *Court and Constitution in the 20th Century: A Modern Interpretation*. Bobbs-Merrill Co., N.Y., 1974, pp. 172-221.

[29] Benjamin F. Wright, *The Growth of American Constitutional Law*, Phoenix Books, University of Chicago Press, 1967, pp. 180-1. Originally published by Holt, Rinehart and Winston, N.Y., 1942. Without the usually long and tedious analyses of most writings about the Court, this book in brief compass shows the exact thrust of its decisions.

[30] Ibid., pp. 148, 154.

[31] Ibid., p. 154.

[32] Ibid.

[33] Ibid., pp. 154-5.

[34] Ibid., p. 108.

[35] Miller, op. cit., pp. 73-4.

[36] Ibid., p. 163.

[37] Ibid., p. 8.

[38] *Psychology Today: An Introduction,* a group survey published under the aegis of thirty-eight doctoral consultants based in leading universities, CRM Books, Del Mar, California, 1970, p. 430.

[39] *Survey of Financial Characteristics of Consumers,* Board of Governors of the Federal Reserve System, Washington, D.C., 1966, p. 6.

[40] Ibid., p. 96.

[41] James D. Smith and Stephen D. Franklin, 'The Concentration of Personal Wealth, 1922-1969", *The American Economic Review,* vol. 64, no. 2, May 1974, p. 162.

CHAPTER EIGHT

[1] Richard M. Pious, *The American Presidency,* Basic Books, N.Y., 1979, pp. 36-46, 47-84 and passim.

[2] Text in *Congressional Record,* vol. 112, no. 43 (March 11, 1966), pp. 5274-9. It is given searching critical discussion by Francis D. Wormuth in *The Vietnam War: The President Versus the Constitution,* Center for the Study of Democratic Institutions, Fund for the Republic, Santa Barbara, Cal., 1968.

[3] Victor Lasky, *It Didn't Start with Watergate,* Dial Press, N.Y., 1977, passim.

[4] Jethro K. Lieberman, *How the Government Breaks the Law,* Stein & Day, N.Y., 1973, republished by Penguin Books, N.Y., 1973.

[5] John Adams, *Diary and Autobiography,* ed. by L. H. Butterfield, Harvard University Press, 1961, vol. 3, p. 219.

[6] *Presidential Vetoes,* Senate Library, Government Printing Office, Washington, D.C., 1978, p. ix.

[7] *Code of Federal Regulations: The President,* Government Printing Office, Washington, D.C., 1976, p. 1069.

[8] *New York Times,* December 24, 1978, 18:1.

[9] Edward S. Corwin, *The Constitution and What It Means Today,* Princeton University Press, 13th edn., 1973, pp. 130-1.

[10] U. S. Judiciary Committee (Senate), Hearings, etc., 85th Congress, 1st Session, 1957, Government Printing Office, Washington, D.C., p. 58.

[11] McDougal and Lans, "Treaties and Executive Agreements", *Yale Law Journal,* vol. 54, pp. 181, 205.

[12] Ibid., pp. 137-8.

[13] *U.S. v. Belmont,* 301 U.S. 324, 1937. There is also the already cited case of *U.S. v. Pink.*

[14] Corwin, op. cit., p. 138.

[15] Ibid., p. 179.

[16] The episode is fully treated in Walter F. Murphy, *Congress and the Court,* University of Chicago Press, 1962, pp. 154-223.

[17] *U.S. v. Curtiss-Wright Corporation,* 299 U.S., 304, 316-19, 1936; *U.S. v. Belmont,* 301 U.S., 324, 1937; and *U.S. v. Pink,* 315 U.S., 203, 1942.

[18] Laurence F. Schmeckebier and Roy B. Eastin, *Government Publications and Their Uses.* Brookings Institution, Washington, D.C., 1969, pp. 363-5. The nature of executive agreements is discussed; a bibliography is appended.

[19] Nelson W. Polsby, *Emerging Coalitions in American Politics,* Institute for Contemporary Studies, 1978, passim.

[20] Article I, Section 3, Sub-section 7; Section 6, 1 and 2; Section 9, Sub-section 8; Article II, Section 1, Sub-section 6; and Article III, Section 1.

[21] Donald Dale Jackson, *Judges,* Atheneum, N.Y., 1974, pp. 139-40.

[22] *The Works of John Adams,* ed. by Charles Francis Adams, Charles C. Little and James Brown, Boston, 1859, vol. 6, p. 408.

[23] Thomas Bailey, *Presidential Greatness,* Appleton-Century Co., N.Y., 1966, pp. 23-34. Pros and cons about presidential standings broadly discussed.

[24] Lincoln's actions are discussed and analyzed in J. G. Randall, *Constitutional Problems under Lincoln,* D. Appleton and Co., N.Y., 1926.

[25] *Ex parte Merryman,* 17 Fed. Cas. 144 (No. 9487) (C.C.D.Md., 1861).

[26] For details of the havoc see William F. Swindler, *Court and Constitution in the 20th Century: The New Legality, 1932-1968,* Bobbs-Merrill Co., N.Y., 1970, pp. 2-100.

[27] *Duncan v. Kahanamoku* and *White v. Steer,* 327 U.S. 304.

[28] *Youngstown Sheet & Tube Co. v. Sawyer,* 343 U.S. 579 (1952).

[29] Corwin, op. cit., p. 151. The delegation of legislative power to the President was upheld by the Supreme Court in *Yakus v. U.S.,* 321 U.S. 414 (1944).

[30] *Youngstown Sheet & Tube Co.,* 343 U.S. 579, 615-26.

[31] *U.S. v. Peewee Coal Co., Inc.,* 341 U.S. 114 (1951).

[32] Corwin, op. cit., p. 157.

[33] *Santiago v. Nogueras,* 214 U.S. 260 (1909); *Op. Atty. Gen.* 13 (1898); *Tucker v. Alexandroff,* 183 U.S. 424, 435 (1902). and *Madsen v. Kinsella.* 343 U.S. 341 (1952).

[34] Corwin, op. cit., p. 159.

CHAPTER NINE

[1] Herman Finer, *The Presidency: Crisis and Regeneration,* University of Chicago Press, 1960, 1974 edn., p. 42.

[2] Ibid., p. 43.

[3] Ibid., p. 84.

[4] Many of the cases are cited and the pros and cons briefly discussed in Swindler, *Court and Constitution in the 20th Century: The Modern Interpretation,* pp. 172-87.

[5] Ibid., p. 174.

[6] *New York Times,* January 9, 1979, A14:2-4.

[7] Finer, op. cit., p. 306.

[8] Ibid., p. 310.

[9] Louis C. Hatch, *A History of the Vice-Presidency of the United States,* American Historical Society, N.Y., 1934, ch. 8, and Donald Young, *American Roulette: The History and Dilemma of the Vice Presidency,* Viking Press, N.Y., 1974. The latter estimates the total vote at "about" 200 and the former states that until 1929 the vice-presidential vote was cast 191 times.

[10] Ibid., p. 302.

[11] Ibid., pp. 329-41.

[12] Ibid., p. 304.

[13] Arthur S. Link, "Woodrow Wilson", *Encyclopedia Americana,* 1970, vol. 29, p. 11.

[14] September, 1970 (vol. 57, pp. 324-51).

[15] For a full ventilation of the situation read General Gavin's revealing book: James M. Gavin, *On to Berlin,* Viking Press, N.Y., 1978.

[16] All information about his condition is taken here from Jim Bishop's *FDR's Last Year,* William Morrow & Co., N.Y., 1974, a remarkably thorough account based on an abundance of official, documentary and living sources.

[17] Ibid., pp. 5-6.

Index of Persons

Index of Statutes and Constitutional Cases